AXIS POWER

COULD NAZI GERMANY AND IMPERIAL JAPAN HAVE WON WORLD WAR TWO ?

DR. WILLIAM ROGER TOWNSHEND

Amazon CreateSpace

2012

Dedicated in Memory of

Mum and Dad, their RAF service in WWII, and for everything
And
Steve Handley, friend and historian

Dr. William Roger Townshend

Axis Power: Could Nazi Germany and Imperial Japan have won World War Two? / by Dr. William Roger Townshend

Amazon CreateSpace 2012

ISBN – 13: 978 – 1477610732
ISBN – 10: 1477610731

Acknowledgements

Production, Cover and technical support by James Lynn Page

Advice and encouragement from Miklos Gombos, Nigel and Gina Carter, and Katie McCall

Contents

List of Tables

INTRODUCTION:

WAR, POWER AND STRATEGY

'You might not be interested in war, war is interested in you'

Clausewitz

Was the escape of the BEF at Dunkirk a miraculous victory against incredible odds, or was it a 'close run thing'? What about the Battle of Britain and the German invasion of Russia, or the Battle of Midway? Just as important, if the Axis powers had won any of these battles or campaigns, would it have led to them winning World War Two? For these and other presumed to be 'decisive' battles and campaigns of World War Two; *Axis Power* looks at what did happen, what, with plausible Axis strategy changes, could have happened, and at the consequences for the wider war of both.

But first a few thoughts on why World War Two was important. *Axis Power* is about war, power and strategy. It is about the largest struggle ever for world domination and whether the Axis powers, principally Nazi Germany and Imperial Japan, could have won World War Two. What Clausewitz might have wanted us to do next is to think for a moment on the statement: 'war is interested in you'. If you are not interested in war already, this gives all of us a very good reason to be so, and to consider the importance of war, strategy, and especially of World War Two. War is destructive, cruel, devastating and frightening, but it matters, a very great deal. It has major consequences for individuals, leaders, states and nations, and for determining history itself. The larger the war, the larger the consequences, and the largest wars of all, world wars or 'hegemonic wars'; have massive consequences for the entire world, often for decades following the conclusion of the conflict.

A hegemonic war is one where all of the most powerful nations are involved. As the name suggests, it is a war of hegemony, for world domination. The future of the international system, and thus of the world is at stake. A different outcome means a different system of power, ideology, politics, values, economics and so forth. Fortunately such wars do not occur very often, only four in the last two hundred years: The Napoleonic War 1800-1815, World War One 1914-1918, World War Two 1939-1945, and the Cold War 1946-1991. Today we live in a world where the systems of power, politics, economics, values and ideology, are directly dependent on the outcome and even course of those last two hegemonic conflicts.

There are reasons for the focus on the WW2 Axis. First as we know, the Allies did in fact win so considerations of alternatives for the Allies amounts to variations on a theme, primarily of timing. Secondly, the effect of an Axis victory would have been so much greater on the post-war world, strategically, politically, economically and ideologically. We need only think for a moment, how different our world might be, had the Axis won. Our question is could the Axis powers have won World War Two? Or was Allied victory inevitable?

It is one of the first, and largest, questions that come to mind for anyone with an interest in World War Two. There is no consensus about the answer. During the early years of the war the Allies certainly didn't believe that victory was inevitable or automatic. Nonetheless Allied leaders, partly to maintain morale during a period when they were losing, expressed confidence that they would win, in the end. In the early decades after 1945, it was a common theme among commentators that the Allies had a very close escape. The Axis powers, it seems, had victory in their grasp on a number of occasions; Dunkirk, the Battle of Britain, in the Mediterranean, even against Russia during 1941 and 1942. They only lost it seemed, due to making apparently obvious mistakes, with Hitler himself getting most of the blame for these. Even the Americans were shaken by Pearl Harbor and were lucky to win at Midway. Only the Soviet Union, for what can now be seen as blatant Cold War propaganda and ideological reasons, claimed that victory over the Axis powers was inevitable. Mind you, come to think of it, they thought, or claimed, the same thing about Communism in the world after 1945!

Later, as more facts on the balance of military power and economics became available, the pendulum of opinion swung to the other extreme. Allied victory was deemed inevitable, the primary reason being that they had overwhelming resources. The only Axis mistake was starting a war they couldn't win in the first place. This 'economic determinist' view is not unchallenged however. The Axis powers, especially Germany, are also, often grudgingly, acknowledged to have been very professional and efficient at waging war, more so than the Allies. This went a long way to offsetting Allied numerical and economic superiority. Yet for the Axis powers, not far enough, they still lost in the end. So where, within this wide range of views, does the balance of probability lie?[1] The war itself was essentially a struggle for power, for world domination. Power and strategy were the two most important factors determining the course and outcome of World War Two. The Allies generally had more power. The Axis however, might have been able to offset this by better and alternative strategy. Power and strategy are the essential themes.

Power, means the mobilization of resources, especially military and economic resources, for the purpose of achieving the national interest. In 1939 there was a multi-polar international power system, dominated by between six and eight 'great powers': Britain, France, Germany, Soviet Russia, Japan and the USA. These countries were not all of equal power, and Italy and China were also on the margins of great power status. There were also at least three ideological paradigms: Liberal democracy-capitalism, Soviet communism and Axis totalitarianism. Within the Axis alliance there were some differences between the European dictatorships of Germany and Italy and the more collectivist ideology of Imperial Japan. Alliance relations between the European Axis powers and Japan were also uncertain in the early stages of the war. What brought the three Axis great powers together was their objective of overturning the existing international, territorial, military, economic and political order. It was an order that the Axis considered to be dominated by the democratic-capitalist powers.

There were divisions between these powers as well, even though all of them had a democratic system of government and a capitalist economic system. Britain and France each had large colonial empires, and were defending the territorial and economic status quo from which they benefited. Their victory in the First World War, and the Versailles settlement that followed, confirmed that status quo in Europe, the wider world, and in international economics. In contrast the USA was anti-colonial, and not just for altruistic reasons. The European colonial empires, although largely underdeveloped, covered a third of the global land area. The rival American capitalism had global economic ambitions, and wanted access to these, and other potential markets and resources, such as China, even Europe and Russia. Finally, Soviet Russia was a revisionist power as well, having lost territory after 1918. Soviet Russia opposed all forms of capitalism, and considered the Axis dictatorship and Allied democratic ideologies, to be merely different variants of it.

It would be a big mistake therefore, to consider World War Two as a purely ideological conflict. All of the great powers were also strongly nationalist. Stalin's Russia acted much like its tsarist predecessor in foreign and security affairs, and had to appeal to Russian patriotism as much as communism during the dark days of 1941 and 1942. Alliances, as we will see, were based more on national interests, of which national security is always the most important, followed by economics. Prior to 1941 there was no certainty even about the Axis and Allied alliance combinations. Russia could have joined either side or remained neutral. America was neutral for over two years until Pearl Harbor, and only then was the European War and the Sino-Japanese War merged into a single truly global conflict. It would therefore be more accurate to consider World War Two as a struggle for power and security, primarily between the great powers. The assertion and expansion of political ideologies, was dependent on the attainment of military and economic security, not the other way around.

With only Britain and France upholding the status quo the future of the international power system, even world domination, was at stake. By the end of the war in 1945 only two great powers, the USA and USSR, remained, now termed 'superpowers', because of both their increased power and reduction in number to two. Not only had Germany, Italy and Japan been defeated, but Britain and France were so weakened that they were incapable of meeting the enhanced criteria of 'superpower'. The Cold War that followed was dependent on the USA and USSR emerging as the dominant superpowers as a result of World War Two. The post-Cold War world that emerged after 1992 appears, at least for a while, to have only one dominant power, the USA, now upgraded again to the ultimate ranking of 'hyperpower'. Chinese power was much overrated by the Americans in both World War Two and the Cold War, and only now, in the post-Cold War world, has it grown to great power status.

Much of what we now take for granted in world politics, international organizations, democratic government, economics and global markets, even Western liberal cultural norms and values; is dependent on the distribution of world power and especially on American 'hyperpower'. Whether one supports, opposes, or is neutral about such matters, it often seems like an automatic progression, even a natural order that the world is now how it is. In fact this is almost certainly not the case. The world of today is directly dependent on the Cold War world and its outcome. That in turn only emerged due to the outcome of World War Two. It is in World War Two that the USA, and all that goes with it, assumes its ascent to world power and global leadership. We must therefore consider again Clausewitz's challenging claim, 'war is interested in you'. World War Two was massively important for it shaped, even determined, much of how the world is today. The central questions we need to consider are therefore: was history fairly inevitable? Or were different courses or outcomes of World War Two possible? If they were, then how likely were they?

Strategy is the other central theme of the book. It is not just a narrative of what happened in a number of well known and commonly presumed to be 'decisive' campaigns of World War Two. By 'strategy' we mean, 'the art of employing all available resources for the purpose of achieving a successful outcome in a conflict between armed forces, states, or alliances'.[2] Strategy, as defined above, has two major sub-variants which are central for our purposes: 'operational or military strategy' and 'grand strategy'. Military or operational strategy is about the deployment and use of armed forces for the purpose of winning campaigns and battles. The course and outcome of World War Two was above all determined by military conflicts, within which are included naval and air, as well as ground conflicts, and combinations thereof. Grand strategy includes all aspects of military and operational strategy, plus the use of all other resources to achieve a successful outcome for the state. These other resources are primarily economic production, politics and diplomacy. Technology, logistics, intelligence assessments, ideology, propaganda, and morale are also important factors at the appropriate level of strategy.

Each chapter deals with an individual battle, campaign or event, and all chapters have the same general organization and aim. Each combines three themes: a narrative overview of events; an analysis of alternative strategies in order to determine if the campaign was 'a close run thing'; and an assessment of the consequences of the actual and alternative outcomes for the war overall.

All chapters include a strategic survey and a narrative overview of what happened. Yet the aim is to do more than that, and in particular ask 'why' and 'if', each of the campaigns were 'decisive', and how they relate to the war as a whole. First, within the narrative we concentrate on the strategy of both sides, and examine the course and outcome of the campaign. We ask how likely the actual course and outcome was? Was it almost inevitable that one side or another would win, or was it as Wellington said about the Battle of Waterloo, 'a close run thing'? It may even be that the actual outcome was unexpected, given the balance of forces involved, or the presumptions and calculations of the commanders and commentators of the time. The French 1940 and Midway campaigns are cases in point. Narrow or unexpected outcomes might really have moved the course of history.

Secondly, in order to answer these questions, we examine alternative Axis strategies, options and possibilities. The alternatives that are investigated are entirely about decisions and options available at the time. With the exception of the German mobilization strategy, there are no changes to the availability of forces, or technology, or the role of chance. The opportunity cost of the various strategic options also becomes a factor to consider here. For example, some believe that the Germans had a good chance of capturing Moscow in the autumn of 1941, rather than divert their forces southward to encircle the large Russian forces around Kiev, which was the actual strategy they chose. On the other hand, advancing directly against Moscow, might have given the Russians opportunities at Kiev. It becomes a matter of strategic choices or options, in this case Kiev or Moscow, but possibly or probably not both.

Thirdly, we consider the consequences of the campaign outcome for the war as a whole, asking how decisive it was. Was it decisive to the outcome of the war? In other words, could a campaign that the Allies won, have been won by the Axis powers? If so, how likely was it? And would that have led to an Axis overall victory in the war? If not, the campaign might still be decisive for what happened next, or for the course of the war, pushing it in a particular direction, but not changing the ultimate outcome. In particular we also analyze the consequences of any alternative strategies or outcomes that we have identified. In short, what would likely have happened next if the Axis had won the battle or campaign under investigation?

The fall of France in 1940 was a massive and unexpected German victory that set the strategic parameters for much of what followed. It created the conditions for a realistic possibility of overall Axis victory. The early chapters consider the possibility and consequences of British defeat in 1940-41 at Dunkirk, The Battle of Britain and in the Mediterranean. Instead, British survival and Russian and American involvement, neither of which was inevitable, moves the focus to the actual turning point campaigns of Barbarossa-Moscow, Stalingrad-Caucasus, Pearl Harbor and Midway. Many of these battles and campaigns are iconic, even mythical, in the national consciousness and identity of the relevant victor nations. There is no problem with this, other than, like the retelling of a tale from ones youth, being alert to exaggeration sometimes creeping into the story over the years. Conversely the traditional story is often incomplete. The context and relationship of a campaign to the war as a whole can easily be neglected. It doesn't deserve to be, and the aim of balance and accuracy of context enhances the story. The real and actual achievements of the veterans of these battles, certainly don't need to be boosted by myth, and are enhanced by an assessment of the wider context.

We cover only those campaigns or battles considered most important and decisive for the course and outcome of the war. The focus is military, strategic in its wider sense as previously defined, and analyzing if the Axis could have won. It is inherent in the subject also, that the emphasis is on the period 1939 to 1942 inclusive, when the possibility of Axis victory was highest. There is a weighting also towards the European War. Despite the authors own interest in naval warfare, this is because of the assessment that Germany came closer to victory than Japan did. Nevertheless the two wars were intertwined, impacting in particular on American policy and strategy. Without American involvement in both the European and Pacific Wars, the Allies probably couldn't have won in either.

Some historians adopt a deterministic approach and believe that the general course and outcome of World War Two was inevitable. The main argument for this is economic. The odds favored the Allies because they had greater resources. The chapter on 'overwhelming force' deals with this, and considers the framework of the overall balance of power at the time. Alternative economic strategies for the Germans, and economic warfare, specifically the Battle of the Atlantic are included here.

11

The aim is not to give a comprehensive or chronological narrative of the entire war; there are plenty of good general works on that already. Nor do we cover the social, or moral, or a myriad of other individual non-strategic topics. This is a book about world power, high diplomacy and strategy, and whether the Axis powers could have won various decisive battles, campaigns and the war. It is not, no matter how horrendous they were, about the internal dictatorships, policies or ideologies of Nazi Germany, Fascist Italy, Imperial Japan or Soviet Russia. Again we leave that to specialists in those particular sub-areas of World War Two. Where these matters do, sometimes, impact on power, strategy and campaign outcomes, they are woven into the story. In particular, the dictatorship ideologies of Germany and Russia impacted the diplomatic and strategic relations, and actions, between these two powers.

Finally, the reader needs to be alerted to some definitional considerations. The terms: Russia, Soviet Russia, Soviet Union and USSR are used interchangeably, meaning the state, its government and armed forces. Where sometimes a distinction is required between this, and Russian, Ukrainian and other ethnic national groups, territories, nationalisms, or peoples, we note it directly. Britain is convenient shorthand for the more accurate but readably cumbersome 'British Commonwealth-Empire'. The fuller term is used where the independent Commonwealth or Dominions, of Canada, Australia, New Zealand and South Africa, and/or the colonial empire, primarily India, had a significant or sometimes predominant role. The North African and Far Eastern campaigns are the main cases in point.

Size is not everything in war, but it is the first basis of analysis. The assessment of the balance of forces for campaigns and battles, inevitably involves a lot of war statistics. Their primary purpose is to give comparisons between the resources available to each side. The most important and simple rule with regard to war statistics, is always to compare like with like. Sometimes statistics on war, in different books, appear to be contradictory. The other important rule, when this happens, is simply to consider carefully the caveats and what the statistics apply to. For example a given force, be it ground, naval or air, will have both an overall strength and a combat strength. Overall strength will always be larger than the combat strength because it will also include supply, service, transport, administrative and other forces, i.e. non-combat forces, but which are still part of the armed forces.[3]

In this book, ground combat forces, means the total number of troops and heavy weapons where cited, in divisions and their share of combat support, such as heavy artillery, at corps, army and army group level. Ground force divisions were also the basic 'counting' unit in World War Two. The size of divisions varied between type, nationality, and whether or not they were at full strength. A good rule of thumb however, including its share of higher formation combat units, is about 20,000 combat troops per division. Russian divisions, from 1942, were smaller, about 10,000 in the division itself, slightly more if we include its share of combat support. We therefore use a broad definition for 'combat forces', which is appropriate for the large strategic sized campaigns and battles which are our subject matter. Other accounts, more tactically focused, might not be compatible with this, sometimes including only infantry actually in direct contact with the enemy, a narrow definition.

The difference between overall and combat strength was especially large in the British and American forces, due to their larger number and proportion of non-combat troops. This is sometimes referred to as the 'divisional slice', and was often as high as 50,000 i.e. typically averaging about 15,000 in the division itself, about 5,000 as its share of combat support from higher formations, and say 30,000 non-combat forces in higher formations and in the theatre as a whole.

In increasing order of size, divisions, corps, armies, and army groups, will be the main types of ground force formation that we will meet. The division was the largest unit that had a standardized organization. Above this, the corps would contain a variable number of divisions, from two up to a number easily controlled by a single commander, say five, sometimes more. The same principle then applies to armies and army groups. Each of the higher formations would also contain specialized sub-units, both combat and non-combat. The Japanese, and from late 1941 the Russians, skipped the corps level of organization. Consequently their armies were somewhat smaller than their Western counterparts. Russia used the term 'Fronts' instead of army groups. Russian 'Fronts' had names rather than numbers, which would change as their location changed. They also included a tactical air component called air armies. 'Front' (capitalized), therefore means the largest of Russian military formations, equivalent to an army group; while 'front', means a continuous line of battle, such as 'eastern or western front', where opposing forces meet.

At sea we are primarily concerned with major combat vessels. In descending order of power and size this means: aircraft carriers, capital ships (battleships and battlecruisers), cruisers, destroyers, escorts and submarines. Standard United States Navy (USN) abbreviations are sometimes used for the various types and sub- categories of ships, a list of which can be found in the appendices. In the air, combat aircraft means fighters and bombers of various types. Total combat aircraft strength is used as the basic calculation where possible. Again, for any given force, this will be higher than other definitions, such as 'operational', 'serviceable', 'front line', or 'first line', in other accounts. Aircraft production is another important theme. Total aircraft production, includes trainers and transports as well as combat types. Typically two thirds to three quarters were combat types, but the proportion varied by nation, time and circumstances.

Another caveat to watch for with regard to war statistics is the geographic area or front to which they apply. The length of a campaign is another consideration. The aggregate total number of troops employed over a lengthy campaign, will be larger than the forces initial size, or its size at any one time. This is because over a period of time, a given force will take casualties, but also replacements to maintain its strength, and sometimes reinforcements. Casualties and losses, unless further clarified, mean the total of killed, wounded and prisoners. In the Russian chapters especially, the term 'irrecoverable' loss appears. This means killed, missing and prisoners i.e. irrecoverably lost to the army concerned for the duration of the war. Some of the wounded in contrast, would, after a time delay, serve again in some capacity or other. None of this need be taxing if we apply the two basic rules; compare like with like, and take care as to the caveats.

Many historians would say that the 'what if's?' are an indulgence, and that the 'what did happen' is more important and sometimes difficult to understand as it is. Well, both are important, and most people find the 'what if's?' interesting and a natural question to ask. We will let you into a little secret. Even historians, perhaps secretly, wonder about the 'what if's?' of history, and in this case of World War Two. So let us indulge, and by looking at the alternative strategies available in different campaigns or battles, we should gain more insight into the actual events themselves as well.

Notes to Introduction

1. For two contrasting views see; John Ellis, Brute Force: Allied Strategy and Tactics in the Second World War, Andre Deutsch Ltd, London, 1990; and Richard Overy, Why the Allies Won, Jonathan Cape, London, 1995. As his title suggests, Ellis believes that Allied victory was virtually inevitable due to overwhelming resources, and despite generally poor strategy and tactics. Overy believes that the Axis powers were very close to winning in 1942. Moreover, that Allied victory was mainly due to factors other than overwhelming military and economic resources.
2. Our definition of 'strategy' is based on that given in; R.E. Dupuy and T.N. Dupuy, The Collins Encyclopedia of Military History: From 3,500 BC to the Present, 4th Edition, BCA, London, 1993, p 1,313.
3. We have footnoted many of the statistics, mostly to secondary sources that are more accessible to the general reader. Mostly they are non controversial. Where the author has doubts the relevant comment is made in an extended footnote. For those wanting further reading, the invaluable start-

ing point is; John Ellis, <u>The World War II Databook</u>, BCA and Aurum Press Ltd, London, 1993. In general, when a source is from a particular national point of view, always be alert to exaggeration of the enemy forces and casualties, and diminution of ones own. This is particularly the case with Soviet sources during the Cold War period 1945-1990, and accounts derived thereof. Apply the 'like with like' and 'care to caveats' rules to correct this, and try to cross reference. Post-communism, G.F. Krivosheyev, <u>Soviet Casualties and Combat Losses in the Twentieth Century</u>, trans. Lionel Leventhal Ltd, Greenhill Books, London, 1997, is a notable exception and corrective for Russia. We acknowledge it as a primary statistical source for many accounts of the eastern front since, including Chris Bellamy, <u>Absolute War: Soviet Russia in the Second World War</u>, Macmillan, London, 2007, which we have relied on.

CHAPTER 1

FRANCE AND DUNKIRK

'Wars are not won by evacuations'[1]

Churchill

Opening Moves: The Polish and Norwegian Campaigns

World War Two in Europe began on September 1st 1939 with the German invasion of Poland. France, Britain and her Commonwealth-Empire declared war on Germany on September 3rd, making it a full scale European war, but not yet a full global conflict. The Polish campaign lasted one month, with Warsaw being captured on September 28th, and Polish military resistance ending on October 5th. In scale it was a considerable campaign, medium sized by World War Two standards. It cannot be classed as a decisive campaign on its own for the basic reason that it was very one sided. Nevertheless it is instructive to consider the factors that determined the outcome. The balance of forces; Germany's 'blitzkrieg' strategy and the Nazi-Soviet Pact would all have continuing consequences into the more important France-Dunkirk campaign that followed.

The first factor to consider in determining why any campaign or battle was won and lost is always the balance of forces. Germany initially mobilized 4.2 million troops in her armed forces in September 1939, including 3.7 million ground forces, of which the 2.5 million combat forces were organized in 103 divisions.[2] Of these 1.5 million organized in 52 divisions, including all of her mobile forces consisting of 6 panzer, 4 light, and 4 motorized infantry divisions, were deployed against Poland. Germany had 3,200 tanks, of which 2,100 were on the Polish front. The Luftwaffe consisted of 2,900 combat aircraft, of which 1,100 were deployed against Poland. In contrast Poland was outnumbered in all categories. Poland only managed to mobilize 1.2 million out of a theoretical 2.4 million trained men because the campaign was over so quickly. By traditional military calculations, given the advantage of being on the defensive, these troop odds were not too bad, and by First World War standards Poland might have been able to hold, and force a stalemate. Poland's greatest weakness was in the most important categories of tanks and aircraft. Mobilized Polish tank strength was about 700, but only 200 of these were technically equal to even German light tanks. Combat air strength was 700 of which 400 were serviceable. Germany also had a strong qualitative advantage. German forces were better trained, led, and organized, and her military equipment was generally superior in most categories.

As important, German military doctrine emphasized the new concept of 'blitzkrieg', or lightening war. For the 'blitzkrieg' strategy, all of the German tanks were deployed with the mobile panzer and light divisions; where as Poland's tanks were distributed in small numbers within her 40 infantry and cavalry divisions. This enabled the Germans to concentrate their power, using the mobile ground forces cooperating with the Luftwaffe for breakthrough offensives, followed by fast moving and deep armored exploitations. In this way the 'blitzkrieg' strategy would enable them to envelope and isolate the opposing army from its command, control and logistical infrastructure.

Geography also favored the Germans, who attacked Poland on three sides, from East Prussia in the north, Germany proper in the west, and from recently occupied Czechoslovakia in the south. The plan was for a double strategic envelopment, eventually converging on Warsaw and Brest-Litovsk respectively, isolating all of the Polish forces in the west of their country into several pockets. If these multiple German advantages were not enough, Poland contributed to her own defeat by a major error in her own strategic deployment. The Poles spread their slow moving infantry armies out along their very long 1,750 mile frontier with German controlled territory. The combined result was an unexpectedly rapid German conquest of Poland, with low losses of 13,000 killed and 27,000 wounded. Poland's losses of 66,000 killed and 134,000 wounded were five times as many. There were 700,000 prisoners captured by the Germans and 200,000 went into Russian captivity. Only 80-100,000 Poles escaped into neutral Romania, these later forming the basis for Polish forces in exile. Even without making mistakes, there wasn't much Poland could have done to change the military outcome.

Nor was any realistic assistance available from the Western Allies. It took two weeks to mobilize, and three weeks to complete the deployment of the conscript army of France, using First World War methods. France mobilized 86 divisions in continental France, of which by September 20th, 72 were in the north-east theatre, including 57 on the German frontier behind the Maginot Line. By this time Poland was already collapsing, and there was nothing substantial the French could have done to dislodge the 45 or so German infantry divisions in the west, backed by the partially completed Siegfried Line fortifications. Apart from this the French had prepared for a defensive war, and although they had as many tanks as the Germans in total, they had no equivalent doctrine to the 'blitzkrieg'. Any French offensive would be slow using First World War methods, based on artillery and infantry, with tanks in support rather than spearheading the attack. As for Britain, the first two divisions, of an eventual 13 of the BEF, didn't complete their deployment to France until October, after Poland had surrendered.

One final significant factor that was important for subsequent events in the west, leading to the French debacle, was the diplomatic situation. On August 23rd 1939, foreign ministers Ribbentrop and Molotov signed the Nazi-Soviet Pact, which divided Eastern Europe into two spheres of influence. A secret protocol of the Pact partitioned Poland between Germany and Russia. Russia invaded Poland on September 17th to take control of its allocated share. The one great power that could have realistically altered the outcome of the campaign was thus allied to Germany, although neutral towards the Western Allies. Significantly for the 1939-1940 campaigns, the strategic and diplomatic situation was quite different to that of 1914, when France and Britain had halted the German invasion of France at the decisive Battle of the Marne, creating a stalemate that lasted until 1918. Many commentators at the time thought that the early stages of the Second World War would be similar to that of the First, with the presumed superior overall economic and military resources of Britain and France eventually deciding the outcome in their favor. These calculations were incorrect, for unlike 1914-1917, there was no Russian ally to form an eastern front in 1939-1940. This would allow Germany to use almost her full strength against the West in 1940, which, while it wouldn't give a clear numerical superiority, was certainly more favorable to it than when the Schlieffen Plan was defeated in 1914. The strategy of taking on their opponent's one at a time was essential for the Axis if they were to gain an overall victory.

The period from October 1939 to April 1940 was known as the 'phony war'. On land and in the air there was very little activity. At sea, Germany was under a naval blockade from the superior Allied fleets, and countered with the U-boat campaign, which became the start of the Battle of the Atlantic. This situation favored the Western Allies whose plan was to avoid a direct clash of the main armies on the western front, and a possible repeat of First World War trench warfare and the associated heavy losses. Instead they aimed to defeat Germany by economic pressure, especially the blockade, and attack her indirectly to supplement this. Plans were made, some of them rather unrealistic, to bomb the sources of German oil supplies at Baku in Russia, and Ploesti in neutral Romania.

In the north both Britain and Germany had plans, which were carried out independently and almost simultaneously, to intervene in Norway. Norway was strategically important as a key transport route for German imports of iron ore from neighboring Sweden. Swedish iron ore was vital at this time for German steel production, heavy industry, and thus war production of all kinds. Britain planned to mine the Norwegian shipping lanes, Germany aimed to conquer Norway. The German invasion of Norway and the occupation of Denmark began on April 9th 1940, and the pre-planned British operations a day later. Only small land forces were involved, consisting of

6 German, 6 Norwegian, and the equivalent in brigades of about two British and French divisions. As with all ground operations at this time the Germans had superior quality, leadership and organization. There were virtually no armored forces involved on either side, and the key to success was naval and air power.

German air superiority was able to prevent British naval forces from interdicting the German invasion. The Germans rapidly seized key ports in south and central Norway including Oslo, and forced the British to evacuate their intervention force from the Trondheim area in central Norway. Only at Narvik in the extreme north, out of German air range for a time, were the Allies able to secure a base. However in the long term, Narvik would be vulnerable and operations here were soon overshadowed by the disaster unfolding in France during May and June 1940. Narvik was evacuated by June 9th 1940, leaving Germany in control of Norway and Denmark.

Of significance for the future, the Norwegian campaign marked the first serious interaction of naval and air power. The results were inconclusive at this stage of the war. A German cruiser and smaller ships on both sides had been sunk by aircraft. Capital ships though, had only suffered light damage, although naval operations had been inhibited by the threat of enemy air power. The balance of strength between naval and air power would be important when considering a possible German campaign against Britain. Both sides suffered moderate naval losses in the Norwegian campaign, and these impacted on the smaller German fleet most. Again this would be important later.

Operation Fall Gelb: The French Campaign to Dunkirk

May 10th 1940 was one of the most decisive days of the Second World War, for two reasons. Firstly, the German invasion of France and the Low Countries finally started. This offensive, codenamed 'Fall Gelb' (Case Yellow), would result in the conquest of France within six weeks and thus of the war taking a completely new, and to contemporaries, unexpected direction. Almost nobody on the Allied side, and even many Germans, expected France, which had held out for four years in 1914-1918, to collapse so quickly. Secondly, whilst French resistance weakened, British resistance strengthened, with the replacement of Chamberlain by Churchill as Prime Minister on that same day.

The French 1940 campaign will be examined, focusing mainly on events and strategy leading up to the Dunkirk and subsequent evacuations. The Allies believed at the time that they had been defeated by overwhelming numbers, which we now know wasn't the case. The real reason was superior strategy by the Germans, combined with some errors and a slowness to react by the Allies. Since the outbreak of war the German armed forces had expanded in overall size from 4.2 million to 5.6 million by May 1940. The number of divisions grew from 103 to 153 including 10 panzer and 6 motorized infantry divisions. Of these totals, 135 divisions including all of the mobile forces and OKW reserves were available for the offensive in the west. Only 10 infantry divisions were garrisoning Poland due to the diplomatic security provided by the Nazi-Soviet Pact, and there were 8 divisions in Norway and Denmark. The attack force in the west amounted to about 2.75 million combat troops. The total tank force had expanded more modestly since the Polish campaign, from 3,200 to 3,400, of which 2,574 were allocated to the 10 panzer divisions with the remainder in reserve and for training. Only 627 of the tanks deployed for the western offensive were of the more powerful Panzer III and IV medium types. The Luftwaffe's combat aircraft strength was about 3,700 of which 2,750 were in the west. The Germans also had 500 transport aircraft, one airborne and one air landing divisions; forces to which the Allies had no equivalents.

In many comparisons, the Allies were the numerical equals of the Germans. With 3 million men mobilized overall, including the Army of 2.7 million in 110 divisions, France provided by far the vast bulk of the Allied forces. In the north-east of France there were 94 French divisions including 6 armored, termed DCR and DLM, [3] and 7 motorized infantry. Britain had 13 divisions in France of which 9 motorized infantry were with the BEF. If we include the 22 Belgian and 10 Dutch divisions, then the total Allied combat ground force, in the north-east theatre, was about equal to the attacking Germans. Manpower strength was somewhat greater at 3.75 million, although this total would include non-combat forces, including all of the 650,000 Belgian, the 400,000 Dutch armed forces, and the total 400,000 British strength in France.

Overall Allied tank strength was also larger at 3,600, of which 3,000 were French and 600 British. Of these, about 800 Allied tanks: 100 British Matildas, 300 French Char-Bs and 400 Somua 35s, were medium types. Both sides therefore had predominantly light tanks and overall technical quality was about equal. Unlike the Germans only about half of the French tanks were deployed in their armored divisions, with the rest being distributed among the infantry. The Allies therefore had a slight overall armor superiority, but it wasn't concentrated for either attack or counter attack at decisive points. Only in the air did the Germans have a moderate numerical superiority. The French had about 1,200 combat aircraft, and 300 of Britain's 1,500 combat aircraft were initially deployed in France. The Belgians had about 180 and the Dutch less than 100 combat aircraft. By the standards of the time this massive Allied ground force operating on the strategic defensive, should have had a good chance of halting the invader. In scale the

1940 French campaign, of which the Dunkirk battle and evacuation was a component, would be the equal second largest campaign of World War Two, and fourth largest in history.[4] It would be a massive and decisive campaign.

In terms of strategy, the Allies were out thought and out maneuvered. The Allies anticipated that the German plan would be a repeat of the Schlieffen Plan of 1914. That plan consisted of a wide strategic envelopment of the Allied left flank, violating the neutrality of Belgium, and in the 1939 version of Holland as well, and avoiding the fortifications of the Maginot Line to the south. For a time in 1939 this was indeed the preferred German war plan. The allies were ready for it and had a counter strategy called 'Plan D or Dyle'. Unlike 1914 when the Allies left flank was initially partly open and vulnerable, the plan was to deploy strong forces, the Allied 1st Army Group consisting of the BEF and three French armies, the 1st, 7th, and 9th on the Belgian border at the outset. If and when Germany invaded Belgium, the Allies would advance to meet them on a line from Antwerp to the river Dyle, just forward of Brussels. It was hoped that a stalemated front could be formed in central Belgium and along the river Meuse, linking with the Maginot Line. Such a position would protect the industrial region of north-east France and about half of Belgium. This was the strategy implemented by the Allies on May 10th 1940 in response to the German offensive. Unfortunately for them the German plan had changed, due to a combination of circumstances and reassessment. Some of the German planners, including the new 'panzer generals' such as Manstein and Guderian, with support from Hitler, favored an alternative plan. In January 1940 an aircraft carrying a copy of the original plan crashed in neutral Belgium, and it was feared it was compromised to the Allies.

The new German plan 'Fall Gelb', designed by Manstein, that was actually used still involved an invasion of Belgium and Holland, but with weaker forces than originally envisaged. It used a total of 29 divisions including 3 panzer, organized in the two armies of Army Group B, commanded by Bock. The Allies implemented their 'Plan D' to counter this German attack on this northern part of the front. Unfortunately the main weight of the German offensive was now in the center, using their Army Group A, commanded by Rundstedt. Army Group A consisted of 45 divisions, including 7 panzer and 6 motorized divisions, organized in Panzer Group Kleist and the 4th, 12th and 16th armies. These were backed on this decisive sector by the full strength of the Luftwaffe in the west. Moving through the almost undefended and difficult forest and hilly terrain of the Ardennes, the armored fist of Army Group A struck the French 2nd and 9th armies that were holding the hinge of the Allied front on the river Meuse between Dinant and Sedan. It took the Panzer Group Kleist three days to traverse the Ardennes, which the Allies had considered to be impassable to large forces, especially tanks.

The Germans had achieved a decisive concentration of combat power, especially of armor and tactical air forces, at a decisive part of the front. They didn't wait for the infantry divisions or heavy artillery to fully deploy. Instead, and supported by the Luftwaffe, used as 'flying artillery', they immediately attacked and broke through the French defenses on the Meuse in three places on May 13-14th. The low quality infantry divisions of the French 9th Army and part of the 2nd Army quickly disintegrated as organized military units. Brave but futile sorties, by the outnumbered and outclassed Allied tactical air forces, failed to destroy the German bridgeheads across the Meuse. Uncoordinated counter attacks by three French armored divisions, acting individually, against the three panzer corps of Group Kleist also failed. By the 16th of May the panzers had advanced 50 miles beyond the Meuse into an empty space, on a front that was also about 50 miles wide.

By this time the Allied northern group of armies, 1st Army Group, including the BEF and the French 1st and 7th Armies, about 35 divisions in total, had completed their move into Belgium. Unfortunately they had entered a trap. There was near panic among Gamelin's French high command at the speed of the German breakthrough and exploitation advance. The French were also uncertain of the objective of the German panzer group, fearing an immediate advance on Paris. In fact the panzers advanced directly westwards, aiming for the English Channel at the mouth of the river Somme near Abbeville, which they reached on May 20th. The German panzer group had advanced an unprecedented 150 miles in six days. The Allied armies on the western front had been cut in two. About 1.3 million troops including the BEF, French 1st and part of the 7th Armies, as well as the Belgium armed forces were cut off in the northern pocket. The 400,000 strong Dutch forces had already surrendered on May 14th, defeated rapidly, by a combination of a conventional ground invasion, airborne assaults against the Rhine bridges, and the bombing of cities, notably Rotterdam and The Hague. We should not allow confusion between a distaste of the German political dictatorship of Nazism, and objective military analysis, to obscure the fact that the 'Manstein Plan' was one of the great stratagems of military history. In chess terms the Allies had thought one move ahead, but the Germans anticipated that, and were two moves ahead. However, they narrowly failed to achieve an immediate checkmate.

From the Abbeville-Amiens area the Panzer Group Kleist turned right and advanced northward, isolating British brigade sized garrisons at Boulogne on the 22nd of May and Calais on the 23rd. By this time the German panzer spearheads were only 10 miles from Dunkirk, the last port of escape for the trapped Allied 1ˢᵗ Army Group. The southern flank of the German 'panzer corridor', along the rivers Somme and Aisne was shielded by 6 motorized infantry divisions, reinforced rapidly by the three infantry armies of Rundstedt's Army Group A. The German high command also transferred two of the three panzer divisions from their northern Army Group B, plus the 2ⁿᵈ and 9ᵗʰ Armies from OKW reserve, to reinforce the successful breakthrough, a sound strategic move.

They then made one of the most celebrated mistakes in military history. On May 24ᵗʰ the panzer group halted for two days, with only a weak French infantry division and a brigade sized British force defending the front near Dunkirk. The Germans had far superior forces, three panzer divisions and the equivalent of two motorized divisions in the immediate area, and ready to advance and take Dunkirk the next day.

Up to this point the Allies had always been a step behind the fast moving Germans. The Germans had the initiative and the Allies were left, sometimes slowly, reacting to events. The Allies were uncertain how to respond. Initially even Churchill was against withdrawing from Belgium, arguing in conversation with French Premier Reynaud, that the German offensive would have to halt after five or six days to resupply, just as had happened with the Ludendorff offensives of 1918. The next Allied plan was to pull the trapped 1ˢᵗ Army Group back south-westward and counter attack against the panzer corridor. On May 21ˢᵗ the BEF launched such an attack at Arras. However, with only two divisions and the only British tank brigade, it failed due to insufficient strength and a claimed lack of support from the French 1ˢᵗ Army. Still, the Arras attack did briefly slow the advance of Rommel's 7ᵗʰ Panzer Division, and caused concern at OKH and OKW that the panzer spearhead might be severed from the supporting infantry armies. Finally on the 25ᵗʰ of May, after the fortuitous panzer halt, Gort commanding the BEF took the definite decision to retreat to the sea, at Dunkirk. The British Government endorsed this decision a day later, and on the 27ᵗʰ ordered the evacuation, operation 'Dynamo', to begin. The British Admiralty, anticipating such an eventuality, had already begun advanced preparations and the collection of shipping some days before.

These changes of strategy caused friction between the British and French. The British felt that the French were giving insufficient support, such as at Arras and the failure to launch a substantial relief offensive from the south. The French blamed the British for their unilateral decision to retreat to Dunkirk. In the event, that decision was taken only just in time, for the bulk of the BEF was still around Lille, 60 miles from Dunkirk when the German armor halted for two days between May 24ᵗʰ and the 26ᵗʰ. On the 28ᵗʰ the BEF and the French 1ˢᵗ Army were further imperiled when Belgium surrendered, opening a gap in the front to their left, facing east. This gap was also only closed just in time, and the Belgian's received blame from their allies for their decision. By narrow margins the remains of Allied 1st Army Group, less two French corps cut off at Lille, managed to form a defensible perimeter at Dunkirk.

Around 860 vessels of all sizes, of which about 500 were the famed 'little ships' took part in the evacuation. There was a heavy loss from this force, 243 ships were recorded sunk, including 6 British and 3 French destroyers, and 179 small craft.[5] During the nine day operation, between May 27th and June 4th 1940, 338,000 men were evacuated, of which 225,000 were from the BEF and 113,000 were French. A majority, 240,000, came out from Dunkirk harbor, showing the importance of proper port facilities for such an operation. The other 98,000 were evacuated directly from the beaches by the 'little ships'. In contrast, most of the military equipment of the BEF, including all its 600 tanks, 2,300 field, anti-tank and anti-aircraft artillery pieces, 82,000 vehicles, and even many lighter items such as 90,000 rifles were lost. It would take months to replace the material losses and to regroup the evacuated troops into organized and properly equipped military units. The 600 tanks for example, amounted to five months production at 1940 rates. Over 90,000 French troops became casualties or prisoners in the immediate battles around Dunkirk, of which 50,000 were lost around Lille as noted above, and 40,000 were the rearguard captured at Dunkirk itself.

The RAF played an important role at Dunkirk. In the earlier part of the campaign they were outnumbered and outclassed. At Dunkirk itself the balance was more even. During the nine day evacuation phase the British lost 106 aircraft compared to 156 German in this sector. The evacuation and battle zone was well within the range of the 600-700 strong RAF Fighter Command in Britain itself. They were supported by a better command and control organization than existed in France. Conversely the Luftwaffe was nearer the limits of its range, especially for fighters, since they hadn't yet redeployed to advanced air bases or built new ones.

The BEF was saved and total disaster averted. Nevertheless, Churchill was correct when he said to Parliament on June 4th, 'We must be careful not to assign to this deliverance the attributes of a victory. Wars are not won by evacuations.'[6] The evacuation at Dunkirk merely prevented an even greater defeat. As it was the first stage of the Battle of France from May 10th to June 4th was a major Allied disaster. Over 1.4 million French, British, Belgian and Dutch troops were either casualties or prisoners. A total of 65 divisions, half the starting strength, had been wiped out of the Allied order of battle. French tank strength was reduced to about 1,200 from the original 3,000, and most of the 600 strong British tank forces had been lost. German losses in this stage of the campaign were only 18,000 killed and 43,000 wounded.

The Fall of France

When the Germans began the second stage of their offensive, codenamed operation 'Red', on June 5th 1940, the numerical balance had changed radically, it was now heavily in their favor. The Germans now had 143 divisions available on the western front including OKW reserves. The panzer and mobile forces were still at full strength with 10 panzer and 6 motorized divisions. The Allies, primarily France, had only 71 divisions to cover the front that was now over 400 miles long, from the estuary of the Somme at Abbeville, to Luxembourg, and then, protected by the Maginot Line, extending along the Franco-German border to Switzerland. The Allies included three French and one incomplete British armored division in their order of battle, as well as two Polish and one British infantry divisions. In total this amounted to about 1,500,000 combat troops, but they were outnumbered almost two to one overall and in the crucial category of armor.

In the air, the situation remained about the same as on May 10th when the campaign had started. Allied air strength had been maintained, due to an increase in both British and French aircraft production. The French Air Force actually ended the Battle of France slightly stronger than when it began. Even so the Allies remained outnumbered in the air overall, and the French on their own by more than two to one. Except for 10 squadrons of fighters sent before Dunkirk, Britain withheld from reinforcing its air force in France, preferring to preserve its strength for the Battle of Britain.

With an overall numerical superiority of two to one, it was easier for the Germans to achieve the rule of thumb, three to one combat odds, to secure a successful breakthrough on a specific sector. Their army was more combat effective by a factor of about 1.3 to 1 than the Allies. By combat effectiveness we mean the professional quality of an army organized into its combat units. This includes factors such as training, unit leadership, experience, morale, manpower quality, combined arms coordination and unit organization.[7] The quality of the German armies enhanced their numerical superiority and they were able to concentrate their panzer force to achieve greater than 3 to 1 combat odds at their chosen points of attack. The defending French fought rather better than previously. However, the disaster of the first stage of the campaign meant that the balance of forces, both in strength and effectiveness, was too adverse.

Two major panzer breakthroughs were made, by Bock's Army Group B near Amiens between June 5th and 7th, and by Rundstedt's Army Group A around Reims between June 9th and 12th. From these breakthroughs the

German mobile forces rapidly exploited in several directions; westwards towards the Atlantic, south-west to the Loire, south towards Lyon and the Rhone valley and south-east to the border with Switzerland. Paris fell on June 14th, and the French armies including those still defending the Maginot Line, became isolated and disintegrated. It was the largest victory yet by the new German 'blitzkrieg' strategy. On June 25th with over half its territory occupied, France surrendered. Overall French losses since May 10th were 120,000 killed, 250,000 wounded and about 2 million prisoners. Comparative German losses, at 43,000 killed and 112,000 wounded, were light considering the scale of the campaign. Britain lost 11,000 killed, 14,000 wounded and 41,000 prisoners in the French campaign as a whole.[8]

What is less well known is that a new, albeit smaller, BEF fought in the second stage of the Battle of France, after Dunkirk. There was also a further series of evacuations during this phase, codenamed operation 'Aerial'. A total of five British divisions, 1st armored, 3rd, 51st, 52nd and 1st Canadian, took part in the campaign after Dunkirk, although three of these were hasty reinforcements and equally hastily evacuated, seeing little or no action. There were also a large number of supply, administrative, and lines of communication troops from the original BEF that remained in France after Dunkirk. In total about 150,000 British troops were involved in this phase of the campaign.

As the second Allied disaster unfolded these forces had all to be evacuated. Operation 'Aerial' took place between June 15th and 25th. It consisted of several operations, using the Royal Navy and mostly larger transport vessels rather than the 'little ships' used at Dunkirk. The distances involved were longer, and the main embarkation ports were Cherbourg, St Malo, Brest, St Nazaire, Nantes, La Pallice, and finally Bordeaux and Bayonne. In all the considerable total of 192,000 men, of which 144,000 were British or Canadian, 18,000 French and 30,000 Poles and Czechs were evacuated.[9] There were two major failures for the British during this phase. At St Valery en Caux, near Dieppe, the 51st Highland Division was cut off on June 11th, and 8,000 troops were captured before they could be evacuated. The other low point was when over 3,000 troops were killed when the liner *Lancastria* was sunk by aircraft at St Nazaire on June 17th.

Overall, the fall of France was a massive and decisive victory for the Germans, completely altering the course of the war from what contemporaries expected. For this reason alone it was one of the decisive campaigns of World War Two. It was a major German victory in its own right, brought about, primarily, by Manstein's Ardennes offensive, one of the great stratagems of military history. The Allied strategy of creating a defensive stalemate on land, while wearing Germany down economically, was in ruins. France, which possessed the principal army of the Allies, had been knocked out of the war in a six week campaign. Not even a future fully mobilized British Empire could compensate for the loss of French land power. The loss of France and the subsequent German control of most of Europe's natural, economic and industrial resources also meant the collapse of the Allied blockade strategy.

With France defeated and Britain isolated, the Axis powers now had a realistic chance of an overall victory in the war as well. However, the eventual outcome was still far from certain. It meant that if the Allies were going to win the war, that the conflict would have to be prolonged, become global in scope, require the full power of America and Russia on the Allies side, and would likely end both Europe's and Britain's previous leading role in the world. None of this was inevitable or obvious to contemporaries in July 1940. In the immediate term Britain had narrowly escaped an even worse disaster. The successful use of British sea power, with operations 'Dynamo' and 'Aerial', had evacuated about 375,000 British and 160,000 Allied troops. This compares with total British losses of 66,000 during the French campaign, and of course, well over two million French and one million Belgians and Dutch. The outcome could have been much worse for Britain. In order to evaluate the importance of 'Dunkirk' we need to ask how likely was a worse outcome? Moreover, would it have meant a British defeat and German victory in the war overall?

Dunkirk: An Allied Worse Case Scenario

By considering hypothetical, but plausible, variants on actual outcomes, we can help explain the decisiveness or otherwise of battles and campaigns within the context of the war as a whole, as well as determining whether an Axis victory was possible. With regard to the Dunkirk evacuation, rather than the Battle of France overall, there is strong consensus among historians that the Germans should have been able to prevent the evacuation, and thus complete their victory in the first phase of the French campaign. The primary reason why this didn't occur was the halting of the German Panzer Group Kleist between May 24th and 26th. They were only 10 miles from Dunkirk, facing minimal opposition, while the bulk of the BEF was still 60 miles away. At that moment most of the BEF and the trapped French and Belgian forces were facing south and east, while the main threat was to their rear and coming from the west. Gort, as we have seen, didn't make his final and independent decision to retreat to Dunkirk until May 25th. If the Germans had continued to advance, as the local panzer corps commanders such as Guderian wanted, the bulk of Allied 1st Army Group would have been cut off from Dunkirk and captured. Moreover the port itself, rather than the open beaches, were more important for the evacuation, even assuming, which is unlikely, that in this scenario many Allied troops could have reached the sea at all. When Churchill ordered operation 'Dynamo' to begin on May 26th, after the panzer halt, the expectation was that only 45,000 men rather than the actual 338,000 could be saved. Had the panzer group not halted, the total evacuated would likely have been even less than that.

A secondary reason that has been put forward by Churchill himself, which facilitated the miracle of Dunkirk, was the time gained by the British defense of hastily reinforced Boulogne and Calais.[10] In fact Boulogne fell on the 23rd of May, before the panzer halt, and Calais on the 26th. Churchill doesn't claim that the resistance of these two ports played any part in the halt order. Rather that, even with the halt order, the Germans would still have captured Dunkirk if it were not for the defense of isolated Calais. In conclusion here, we can say for definite that if it wasn't for the halt of Panzer Group Kleist from May 24th to 26th, virtually all of the Allied 1st Army Group, and the 338,000 men saved at Dunkirk, would have been lost. There were no Allied strategic options available at that point of time, which could have prevented such a result, had the Germans continued to advance. The battle would have been similar, although larger, than what actually happened at Lille, where two isolated French corps fought on surrounded until their ammunition became exhausted after three days.

What is controversial, are the reasons why the Germans halted before Dunkirk, and who gave the order and was to blame. The commonest target for blame for the halt order was Hitler himself and his OKW senior generals, Keitel and Jodl. In fact Rundstedt, commanding Army Group A, seems to have initiated the order, although Hitler and the OKW certainly agreed with it. Yet the German commanders were divided. The OKH, led by Brauchitsch and Halder, who were the more professional general staff, but intermediate in the command structure between Hitler's OKW and the Army Group A, saw no reason to halt. The panzer corps commanders at the front including Guderian also favored an immediate advance. The halt was only temporary, but major in its consequence, and the advance was resumed on the 26th of May, but led this time by infantry forces.

The panzer divisions were being preserved for the second stage of the campaign. Concern to preserve the strength of the panzer divisions was one of several reasons suggested for the halt. It was unfounded since there were still 1.500 tanks immediately operational, over 50% of full strength, and most of the rest were only temporarily out of action, due mainly to normal mechanical attrition rather than enemy action. Hitler was receiving reports on the panzer divisions apparently declining tank strength. He didn't realise that if needed, it would only take 3-4 days of rest and maintenance to restore full strength. In fact 753 panzers were permanently lost during the French campaign, including 485 during the first stage. Campaign replacements came from the 800 tanks in the panzer reserve and production during May and June, about 270 tanks at the 1940 rate. Margins weren't great, but manageable. Wet Flanders terrain unsuitable for tanks was another false reason for the halt. The corps and divisional commanders on the spot didn't consider this a problem, and they were already past the Aa canal, the last anti-tank defense line before Dunkirk, which the Allies had insufficient forces to defend anyway.

Rundstedt especially, feared that the mobile forces would become too far separated from the follow up infantry armies. Indeed he had temporarily halted Panzer Group Kleist twice before, on May 17th and 21st, for similar reasons. In fact the infantry armies moved faster than anticipated on all these occasions, often into undefended space to secure the flanks of the panzers, especially against the French forces to the south of the Somme and Aisne. The Allies were far to slow to organize any successful counter attacks that might sever the panzer spearhead at any time during the campaign. Goering also played a part, assuring Hitler that the Luftwaffe could prevent the evacuation without the need for a ground attack against Dunkirk. It couldn't.

None of these factors were valid, as all the German decision makers quickly realized by the 26th, but too late to prevent the British from securing a defensible perimeter at Dunkirk. This does show the uncertainties of the time that influenced decisions and this for the side that was winning at that point of the battle. How much worse things were for the Allies, who were losing and under immense pressure, helping to explain many of their mistakes and slowness to react. Finally, there is a political aspect to higher strategy. One of the more unlikely reasons suggested for the panzer halt, was that Hitler let the BEF escape to preserve Britain's honor and to get her to agree to a peace treaty. Hitler might have had a love-hate view of Britain, and saw the preservation of a British Empire outside Europe as a source of stability, and as a future ally to an Axis dominated Europe. Even so, a strategy that strengthens an opponent is illogical as a means of making them negotiate. Few people today give much credence to this as a cause of the halt order. It is one of those inexplicable myths of war.

Political factors were far more important in Allied strategy, due to friction, exacerbated by defeats, between the British and French. Britain faced the dilemma throughout the French and Dunkirk campaigns, of balancing the preservation of her own forces, principally the BEF and the RAF, against sending reinforcements to maintain France in the war. At some point a state has to look more exclusively to its own defense when it seems that an important ally is irretrievably lost. The problem is accurately determining the situation, a dilemma the USA would soon face in the war with regard to Britain, just as Britain did with France in May-June 1940.

Consequences of Dunkirk: Actual and Potential

The successful evacuation at Dunkirk, coming at the end of a disastrous three week campaign for the Allies couldn't prevent the fall of France. That was the first, largest, and most immediate consequence for the next stage of the war. The forces saved, minus all of their heavy, and much of their light equipment, were insufficient to alter the outcome of the second stage of the French campaign. Only one of the BEF divisions from Dunkirk, the 3rd Infantry, was able to be re-equipped and serve briefly in the second stage, although most of the 113,000 French evacuated did return to France.

The second major consequence is usually presumed to be that the escape of the BEF allowed Britain to rally, continue the war, and ultimately with the help of the USA and Russia, defeat the Axis five years later. If so, then Dunkirk certainly is one of the most decisive battles of history. Yet this is presumption, and leaps the story ahead too far. The more relevant question is whether a British defeat at Dunkirk would have meant an immediate Axis victory? Alternatively, would the consequences be the lesser, but still significant ones of a change in the course of the war, or else a delay in a still ultimate victory for the Allies?

The worse case scenario for Britain would have been the capture and loss of the 225,000 men, mainly combat forces, from the 9 infantry and 3 territorial divisions that escaped at Dunkirk, plus 4,000 men from Boulogne. To these might be added the 144,000 men evacuated in operation 'Aerial' which were mostly service troops, but did include 5 divisions. The total number of troops evacuated needs to be placed into the context of Britain's overall strength, military situation, and hence its capacity to continue the war. The British armed forces, excluding the Commonwealth and Empire, in June 1940 had 2,223,000 personnel, of which 1,656,000 were army, 276,000 navy and 291,000 air force personnel.[11] This force was also expanding fast. One year later, in June 1941, Britain had 3,291,000 personnel, of which 2,221,000 were army, 405,000 navy and 665,000 air force personnel. The average rate of expansion in the year following Dunkirk and the fall of France is therefore about 90,000 per month, of which nearly 50,000 were ground forces. In fact recruitment would have been slightly higher, since the modest losses in the upcoming Greek and early North African campaigns also needed to be replaced at this time.

The absolute maximum possible extra loss of 375,000 men in France, would have taken 4 months to replace, or 7-8 months if we take into account that they were mainly ground forces. To replace the loss at the faster rate would have meant a decision to divert the available recruits and training capacity towards the army. This would have slowed the expansion of the navy, and especially the RAF, at least as far as manpower was concerned. This calculation is the worse case one. Operation 'Aerial' was difficult and there were, as we have seen, a couple of significant setbacks. However, the margins were not as tight as they were at Dunkirk, where truth really was stranger than fiction. The Germans could definitely have prevented the evacuation of the 225,000 men saved at Dunkirk. All they needed do was allow Guderian to continue his advance without halting, and thus cutting the BEF off from the sea. The Allies couldn't have stopped him. In contrast, the Germans were in no such advanced position to prevent operation 'Aerial' from saving the remaining 144,000 British troops in France. The 375,000 men in total evacuated from France, were about 23% of the total strength of the army in June 1940. This is a significant total and proportion, but assuming there were no immediate demands on the army, such as a German invasion of Britain, they were replaceable in 4 to 8 months depending on resource priorities between the three armed services.

Nevertheless, we also need to consider that the Dunkirk force especially, contained a higher proportion of Britain's ground combat force. In July 1940 there were 28 divisions defending Britain, including 2 armored divisions, one Canadian and one ANZAC division, plus 2 British divisions in Egypt and the Middle East. The British totals include 14 of the 16 divisions that were evacuated from France and then quickly reformed, but not fully rearmed. In terms of combat divisions the evacuated forces represent almost 50% of Britain's total, rather than the 23% of the army as a whole. Moreover the Dunkirk BEF divisions were the best in terms of quality and training. The evacuated troops would provide the cadres and training base, which would facilitate the future expansion of the army. A total disaster at Dunkirk would thus have reduced Britain's army strength by up to a quarter, and its combat force by about half, and slowed expansion by an average of 6 months. The situation might not have been quite as bad as that because the forces which were rescued still needed to be re-equipped. The process of replacing the lost equipment took that long anyway. Britain was very weak in tanks, artillery, and anti-tank and anti-aircraft guns in July, and even in September 1940. The 28 divisions in Britain were at full strength in troops and rifles, but not in heavier equipment.[12]

The absence of the best trained and most experienced half of the combat forces in the second half of 1940 could have hurt Britain badly, especially if it had to deal with an invasion. This is a very important caveat. The loss of the BEF on its own at Dunkirk might not have been decisive for Britain's survival. In combination with a German invasion it certainly would have been, but that is jumping ahead of the story a little. Psychologically, the capture of the BEF at Dunkirk and the knowledge that they wouldn't have to defeat them again in Britain itself, would have boosted German determination to invade. It would also have changed their calculations. German intelligence overestimated the size of Britain's home army at 40 divisions compared to the actual 28. A reduction of 12 trained BEF divisions lost at Dunkirk, even if hastily replaced by newly raised untrained ones, represents a significant proportion. The Germans would have calculated it as a one third reduction, rather than the actual half, but still appearing to make the ground war stage of 'Sealion' more feasible.

Finally, following Mussolini's declaration of war on June 10th 1940, we don't think that the loss of the BEF, assuming no 'Sealion', would have had much immediate impact on the new theatre of war in the Mediterranean. There would still have been enough forces to conduct the historical campaigns in North Africa, Greece, and Iraq-Syria. The numbers involved in those campaigns were small at this point in the war, and there were considerable contributions from Australia, India, and South Africa. As far as ground forces were concerned then, margins would have been much tighter regarding home defense, but absent an invasion, a vital caveat; a failed Dunkirk evacuation on its own wouldn't, in military terms, have prevented Britain from continuing the war.

The strongest British defenses for the upcoming Battle of Britain would be the RAF and the Royal Navy. The navy lost 6 destroyers sunk and 19 damaged out of 39 engaged at Dunkirk and a total of 150 worldwide. No larger warships were lost. Ironically if the BEF's campaign had been worse than the historical one, largely preventing evacuation, then naval losses would have been less. Either way, the navy's power is only very slightly reduced by the Dunkirk campaign. Of course the Allies lose the French fleet, and the Axis added the Italian fleet to their strength at this time. However, that is a result of the French campaign overall, not the specific battle and evacuation of Dunkirk. Unless France itself could have been saved, the loss of its fleet and the addition of the Italian fleet to the Axis would have happened anyway. Dunkirk itself had very little impact on the balance of naval power compared to what it would otherwise be.

The crucial decision regarding the RAF was that Churchill accepted the advice of Dowding, the head of Fighter Command, to retain a minimum of 25 fighter squadrons, about half of the total strength, for the defense of Britain. A greater RAF commitment, especially of the crucial fighter squadrons, would be very unlikely to have altered the course of the second stage of the French campaign. The two to one overall balance of forces in the Germans favor, on the ground as well as in the air, enhanced by superior German combat effectiveness and the advantage of the operational initiative as well, was too much. It would have been a futile sacrifice by Britain, at best delaying the fall of France by a short time. If Britain had committed too much of its air strength to the battles of France and Dunkirk, it would be exposed to unfavorable odds and circumstances. This was due to the inferior command and control system, including a lack of radar, in France compared to Britain. It would have risked, in Dowding's view, the defeat of the RAF in the Battle of Britain. As it was about 400 British fighters were lost in France, and it was early July before the strength was rebuilt to 650, the same as at the start of the French campaign in May.

In conclusion therefore we can say that Dunkirk wasn't decisive for the navy's capacity to defend Britain and continue the war, even using worse case scenarios. The RAF was also just above the minimal level needed, although a heavier commitment to France would have put Britain itself at much greater risk. In that sense the decision to maintain the minimum 25 fighter squadron defense of Britain itself was a decisive and correct strategy for Britain. Overall considering all three services, there are good reasons to conclude that even a worse than historic outcome for Britain at Dunkirk, wouldn't have prevented it from continuing the war. Dunkirk was therefore not quite as decisive, in the strictly military context, as is commonly presumed.

One possible German strategic option that has been suggested, both contemporary and post de facto, was an immediate, probably improvised invasion of Britain following Dunkirk, or even before completing the second stage 'Case Red' of the French campaign. On May 21st 1940, the day after Panzer Group Kleist had reached the English Channel at Abbeville, and cut the Allied armies in France in two, there was a meeting between Hitler and Raeder, head of the German Navy. This might have been a possible missed opportunity to at least begin contingency planning for an early invasion of Britain. In fact no decision, even to begin planning was made at this time, which would have been necessary for any invasion in July, immediately following the French campaign. Raeder was relieved because he had no confidence in the navy's ability to carry out an invasion. Hitler seemed to believe that Britain's military situation was hopeless enough already that it would accept peace terms without an invasion. There was also a plan in July 1940, devised by the Luftwaffe's Field Marshall Kesselring. This was for an improvised airborne invasion against British airfields, swiftly reinforced with air landing forces (i.e. units brought into captured airfields by transport aircraft). They would then seize a port and reinforce by sea.

These early versions and variants of operation 'Sealion' were designed to take advantage of Britain's weakness immediately after Dunkirk. It is true that British ground forces were badly distributed during June-July 1940, being deployed for an invasion against the east coast rather than the southern one. Still, as we have seen there were considerable, if poorly equipped ground forces in Britain, and a full strength navy and adequate air force which would have to be defeated first. An airborne invasion on its own would have been far too weak. Germany had only one airborne/parachute, and one air landing division in 1940. Any early or improvised invasion would be incompatible with everything we know about amphibious invasions during World War Two. Such invasions were the most difficult and complex large scale operations of war. The 1944 Allied invasion of France for example, took six months of planning from decision to execution. Finally, it is inconceivable that Germany would have attempted an invasion of Britain before completing the conquest of France. To German contemporaries, France was seen as a major military power, as strong as in 1914-1918, with the best army in Europe. The rapid German victory in the second stage of the French campaign wasn't considered the military inevitability that it does today, with all the facts and calm analysis at our disposal. We do not therefore consider that any immediate, improvised, or airborne only, invasion of Britain, even had the BEF been lost at Dunkirk, would have succeeded.

One final factor in considering how decisive the Dunkirk evacuation was is the psychological one, and the question of British morale. Unfortunately it is an intangible factor in war, and thus more difficult to answer than the sometimes quantifiable military and strategic considerations. Despite the unreliability of press information and censorship, it was obvious in general terms to the British public, that a disaster was unfolding in France. There was immense relief at the 'miracle of Dunkirk' and the escape of the BEF. Hence Churchill's guarded warning that it wasn't a victory, but a lesser defeat. Had the BEF been captured it would have been the greatest defeat in British military history, far larger than the surrender of Singapore or Tobruk in 1942. Such a loss would have been as impossible to disguise as the actual close run escape. It was the 'miracle of Dunkirk' itself, combined with Churchill's inspirational leadership, which strengthened British resolve at this point. The loss of the BEF might have reduced the British will to continue the war, and created pressure to make peace. On the other hand, using the public's response to the Battle of Britain and the 'blitz' bombing campaign as a guide, it might have strengthened British morale. We cannot be sure, but on balance it seems unlikely that public morale would have completely broken even in a worse case Dunkirk scenario. After all, no British home territory had been lost or its cities seriously bombed at that point of the war. Still, an otherwise important positive psychological factor for Britain would have been missing for the next stage of the war.

A related factor to consider is political, and the morale and attitude of the ruling elite in a worse case scenario. Churchill had only just become Prime Minister on May 10th, the very day the invasion of France began. He was far from secure politically at this time. The Foreign Secretary Lord Halifax, not Churchill, was presumed by most contemporaries to be the likely successor to Chamberlain as P.M. Chamberlain fell from office because he got the blame for the ineptitude of the Norwegian campaign. In fact Churchill, who was First Lord of the Admiralty, was more responsible for that naval centered campaign and its shortcomings. Instead he escaped censure at the time and the Norway campaign was quickly overshadowed by the larger French campaign and the Battle of Britain. Dunkirk was the first major battle with Churchill as P.M. The evacuation meant that he became associated with success as well as determination. This was in sharp contrast to previous events, including what was by then seen as the disastrous pre-war diplomacy of appeasement and search for peace. After Dunkirk Churchill's political position and the policy of victory at all costs, was practically unchallengeable.

As it was there were secret discussions by Britain's War Cabinet for three days from May 25th to 28th, on the question of whether to begin negotiations or continue the war.[13] Italy was suggested as a possible mediator. That idea was rejected by Italy which soon declared war on Britain and France on June 10th. A negotiated peace was rejected by the British Cabinet due to the likely poor terms they could expect at that point. Consideration was also given to the likely affect that starting negotiations would have on national and military morale, as well as the attitude of the USA to the war and support for Britain. The probable results were considered to be negative in both these areas. Once peace negotiations began, and it would be difficult to keep it secret, morale and support for any change back to continuing the war, should that be needed, would diminish. As for the USA, there was no chance under any circumstance that it was going to enter the war in mid-1940. Roosevelt was facing a presidential election in November 1940, and he had little public support for American intervention in a European war. Roosevelt did aim to support the Allies in ways short of war, and this would be less likely if there was doubt that Britain was determined to continue the fight. Overall, and since Britain was still undefeated militarily, it was agreed that she had nothing to lose by continuing.

However, the timing of these discussions is significant, occurring simultaneous with the German halt order and its immediate consequences. Had 'Dynamo' failed and the BEF been lost, Churchill's position would have been much more uncertain. Churchill would have got the blame, and even the Norway campaign might have been re-examined and come back to haunt him. There would have been increased pressure within Britain's political establishment for a reconsideration of a compromise peace option. How uncertain Churchill's position would have been, and how much pressure for peace, is impossible to calculate. It would have been worse than the historical situation.

In conclusion we can say that with regard to the military and strategic considerations, that although important, the Dunkirk evacuation wasn't quite as decisive a battle as is commonly presumed. The Dunkirk battle itself, given the situation after the Germans had broken through to the English Channel, could easily have gone the other way. All the Germans needed to do, was to continue on, instead of temporarily halting, and the BEF would have been cut off from the sea and destroyed. We don't think though, that such a worse defeat at Dunkirk, on its own, would have knocked Britain out of the war and led to an immediate and overall German victory following the Battle of France, but prior to the Battle of Britain. As for the subsequent course of the war, some British actions such as the build up of the RAF and later the bombing campaign, plus some naval activity, might have been delayed due to lesser resources, and allocation changes to replace any army losses at Dunkirk. Depending on decisions about resource priorities, other immediately pending campaigns in North Africa and the Mediterranean could still have gone ahead as they did historically.

In contrast the combination of a BEF disaster at Dunkirk and an invasion of Britain that reached the ground war stage, is an entirely different matter, and a far more dangerous scenario for Britain. The other main qualification is the unknown morale and especially political consequences of any BEF disaster. There was therefore a minority possibility of a compromise peace following a Dunkirk worse case scenario. However in a material sense, there was no reason why Britain couldn't continue the war. The rapid and unexpected German conquest of France in May-June 1940 was one of the decisive campaigns and stratagems of history, creating major new and favorable circumstances for a possible Axis overall victory. They had won the Battle of France decisively, but the Battle of Britain would still have to be fought.

Notes to Chapter 1

1. Winston S. Churchill, <u>The Second World War, Volume 2</u>, p 103, Penguin Books, London, 1985.
2. For these and following German strength and divisional statistics see, M Cooper, <u>The German Army 1933-1945: Its Political and Military Failure</u>, Macdonald and Jane's, London, 1978.
3. Ellis J, <u>Brute Force</u>, 1990, p 5 fn. The French had three heavy armored divisions (DCR), or ***Division Cuirassees Reserve***, and three ***Light Mechanized Divisions*** (DLM). The term DLM is a misnomer; they each contained 240 tanks, including 80 of the Somua 35 medium tanks, fully the equal of the German Panzer III and IV mediums. Two more DLM's were formed during the course of the campaign, but only after the original three

had been lost in the debacle of the first stage. A fourth DCR was also formed later, commanded by De Gaulle.

4. The WW2 eastern front campaign 1941-45 was, by a wide margin, the largest land war ever, with 29 million Russians and 10 million Axis troops involved from first to last. (In aggregate, not all at one time of course). The WW2 western front in 1940 involved almost 7 million men (3 million Germans, 3.75 million Allies), as did the 1944-45 western campaign (5 million Allies, including a high proportion of service troops, and 2 million Germans). In WW1, primarily because of its longer timescale, the western front 1914-18 (25 million in aggregate: 9 million Germans, 16 million Allies) was larger than in WW2. The underrated WW1 eastern front 1914-17, with about 20 million troops involved (c12 million Russians, maybe more, 8 million Central Powers) almost matched it in scale. The only other historical campaign of comparable size, was the Sino-Japanese War from 1937 to 1945. Accurate numbers are less certain, but approximately 2 million Japanese and 5 million Chinese troops were involved at the front in aggregate.

5. Churchill, <u>WW2 Vol 2</u>, table on p 89-90. There may, as he acknowledges, have been more 'little ships' than those officially listed.

6. Ibid, p 103.

7. T.N. Dupuy, <u>Understanding War</u>, Leo Cooper, London, 1992, p 87-88, and chapters 8, 9, and 10 generally. See also J.F. Dunnigan, <u>The Russian Front: Germany's War in the East 1941-45</u>, Arms and Armor Press, London, 1978, p 83. Dupuy calculates German combat effectiveness superiority over the British and French in 1940 at 1.2 to 1, Dunnigan at 1.35 to 1.

8. John Ellis, <u>The World War II Databook</u>, BCA, London, 1993, p 255.

9. Donald Macintyre, <u>The Naval War Against Hitler</u>, B.T. Batsford Ltd, London, 1977, p 46.

10. Churchill, <u>WW2 Vol 2,</u> p 70-73.

11. For this and following British armed forces statistics, see John Terraine, <u>The Smoke and the Fire</u>, BCA, London, 1981, table on p 219.

12. Churchill, <u>WW2 Vol 2</u>, tables and graphics on p 239 and p 243.

13. See, Ian Kershaw, <u>Fateful Choices: Ten Decisions that Changed the World 1940-1941</u>, Penguin Group, London, 2007, p 28-47.

CHAPTER 2

THE BATTLE OF BRITAIN

'Hitler knows that he will have to break us in this Island or lose the war...
But if we fail, then the whole world, including the United States...will
sink into a new Dark Age'[1]

Churchill

Strategic Situation and Balance of Forces

With the fall of France the strategic parameters of World War Two altered
drastically from those of pre-June 1940. There would be no chance from
then on that it would in general, follow a course similar to that of 1914-
1918. With France and its large army of over 100 divisions defeated, there
would be no western front or large scale land warfare in continental Western Europe for the foreseeable future. In this theatre the focus would be on
air and sea warfare and a possible German invasion of Britain. The entry
of Italy into the war on June 10th 1940 extended its geographic scope to the
Mediterranean, North Africa, East Africa and potentially the Middle East.
Although still a European war rather than a world war at this point, it was
also clear that in the longer run if Britain was to prevail, it would need allies. There were only two viable great power allies available, the USA and
Soviet Russia. For the time being Britain and its Commonwealth-Empire
were on there own facing the German-Italian Axis.

Initially Hitler, rather unrealistically, hoped that an isolated Britain would
make peace. It was a month later on July 16th, before Hitler issued his 'Directive 16' for the planning of operation 'Sealion' to begin. There was no
specific date set for the invasion, other than that the expedition should be
ready for mid-August. This was an unrealistic time scale. The Army had
made no advanced preparations for such an eventuality. No studies had
been done, and more importantly there were no specialized units trained
for amphibious operations. The Navy had done some previous planning,
but had no practical preparations in place. They considered that it was impossible to collect the large amount of shipping needed in such a short
time. The shipping requirement was for 155 large transport vessels and
over 3,000 smaller craft, mainly converted barges, tugs and motor boats.
There were no specialized landing craft of the types that the Allies would
use later in the war, and no time to build them.

The Army and Navy also had different priorities and for a while planning
went ahead independently by each service. The Army wanted a broad front
invasion between Folkestone and Brighton, and even a supplementary and
separate attack in the south-west of England at Lyme Bay. The Navy

wanted a much narrower invasion front, which would be easier to protect during the crossing phase. However, they were even doubtful about their ability to do that. As a result of these problems the invasion date was put back to mid-September, almost the latest it could be in 1940 due to the finite limitations of weather and tides from October onwards. What everyone agreed on, was that air superiority was essential and would have to be in place prior to the transport and landing phases. Goering was optimistic that the Luftwaffe could achieve this. Even if it did, the Luftwaffe would still have to counter Britain's naval superiority in the invasion zone.

Both the Luftwaffe and the RAF had taken considerable losses during the Battle of France and neither was fully ready for a new campaign until mid-July. Dowding's RAF Fighter Command had lost 400 fighters in France, out of an initial strength of about 650, excluding reserves. However, after Churchill had appointed Lord Beaverbrook as Minister for Aircraft Production, these losses were quickly replaced. Fighter production now had priority, and grew from an average of just under 200 per month from January to April, to 325 in May, 446 in June, and then stabilizing at about that level for the rest of the year.[2] Fighter Command was back to full strength with 644 serviceable single engined fighters on July 6th. The Luftwaffe had lost 1,469 combat aircraft destroyed and damaged during the French campaign.[3] The Luftwaffe total includes damaged aircraft, and bombers, so is not directly comparable to the British fighter losses. Still, at over 50% of the total initial combat strength in the French campaign, it is considerable and helps explain the slow build up to the Battle of Britain.

In June 1940 the Luftwaffe had an all front operational strength of 3,327 combat aircraft.[4] In July, 2,715 of these aircraft were deployed in three air fleets for operations against Britain, Luftflotten 2 and 3 in France, and the smaller Luftflotten 5 in Norway. This total included 893 single engine Me109 fighters, 246 Me110 twin engine heavy fighters, 316 dive bombers and ground attack aircraft, and 1,260 twin engine medium bombers, mainly He111s, Ju88s, and Do17s. In comparison on July 6th 1940, RAF Fighter Command throughout Britain had 644 serviceable single engine fighters, plus 373 immediately available reserves and 181 other reserves, a total of 1,198.[5] About one third of the RAF fighters were Spitfires and two thirds Hurricanes. In addition there were about 100 inferior Blenheim and Defiant fighters available. Although not involved directly in the battle, RAF Bomber Command had 560 operational combat aircraft available on July 11th, plus 285 reserves available within 2 days, and another 128 within 4 days, a total of 973.[6] Bomber Command was involved in attacks on the German invasion fleet gathering at ports in France and the Low Countries, as well as against German cities in the later stages of the battle.

The Germans therefore had an initial numerical superiority, but it wasn't as large as is generally assumed. If we compare the German operational total in the west of all types of combat aircraft, i.e. 2,715, with the serviceable strength of RAF Fighter Command, i.e. 644 plus 100 obsolete types, then we can arrive at the commonly used ratio of almost 4:1 in the Germans favor. This is a very superficial analysis. Comparing operational and serviceable strength is not quite a like with like statistic. Serviceable strength is always less than full operational strength. In this case of the Luftwaffe's 2,715 operational combat aircraft in theatre, only 1,980 were immediately serviceable, compared to about 740 serviceable RAF fighters, a ratio of about 2.5 to 1. We prefer to use the higher figures, encompassing as much of the total strengths for air forces whenever possible. It is also known that the RAF had a higher number of reserves, almost doubling total fighter strength to 1,198, and bomber strength to 973. Again this is not strictly a like with like comparison with Luftwaffe operational strength, the ratio against British fighters only would again be 2.5 to 1, but it does tell us that the RAF was better prepared for a long attritional battle with heavy losses. Finally, the above comparisons are a snapshot of the initial situation in July. Aircraft losses in all theatres of World War Two were always heavy over any given period compared to full strength at a specific point in time. This 'turnover', if that is not too abstract a term to use for losses, was much higher in the air war than it was on land or at sea.

This high turnover rate meant that aircraft production becomes a very important factor in air warfare over an extended period, such as the four months of the Battle of Britain, and indeed in all theatres throughout the war. In aircraft production, contrary to the popular view today and the intelligence estimates at the time, Britain had a significant advantage, even in 1940. Total aircraft production including combat and non-combat types such as transports and training planes in 1940 was: Britain 15,049, Germany 10,826.[7] That is a very significant overall advantage of 3:2 in Britain's favor. This is the overall total and Britain had to cover the Mediterranean theatre as well out of this production. However, even if we include Italian production for 1940, which is 2,943, it is still the case that Britain built slightly more aircraft than both Axis powers combined. Britain's advantage in combat aircraft production, i.e. fighters, bombers and ground attack aircraft, is somewhat less. Combat aircraft production in 1940 was: Britain 7,771, Germany 6,201, and Italy 1,795; Axis total 7,996. The British and combined Axis combat totals are about equal, with Britain retaining a slight advantage over Germany alone.

There is a similar situation with regard to fighter production alone in 1940, which was: Britain 4,283, Germany 2,746, and Italy 1,155; Axis total 3,901. The important comparison is the British 3:2 advantage in total fighter production over Germany. Even this understates the British superiority, because the German total includes the inferior Me110 twin engine heavy fighters, where as almost all British production was single engined Hurricanes and Spitfires. Finally, we can narrow down to the production of single engine fighters alone, during the actual period of the battle from July to October 1940 inclusive, which is: Britain 1,908, Germany 755.[8] If we were to include the Me110s then the German total would be about 1,000, which still gives Britain a 2:1 fighter production advantage during the actual battle. Even though Britain was relatively short of trained pilots to fly all these aircraft, its higher aircraft production, in all levels of comparison, was a major advantage.

Aircraft performance and quality as well as the circumstances of the battle are also important factors to consider. Most air combat losses were caused by the single engine fighters, the German Me109s, and the British Spitfires and Hurricanes. German bombers proved incapable of defending themselves without fighter escort. The Me109 and the Spitfire were evenly matched, while the Hurricane was only slightly inferior. Both types of British fighter were armed with 8 machine guns, which were considered by most German and some British pilots, to be outmatched by the Me109s two machine guns and two much more powerful 20mm cannons. The Me109 and the Spitfire each had top speeds of about 350 miles per hour, and both were slightly faster than the Hurricane. For fighter combat or 'dog fighting' as it was known, the Me109s higher rate of climb gave it an advantage, but this was reversed when it came to turning and maneuvering where both British types had the edge.

A more serious 'strategic' handicap for the Me109 was its short range of 412 miles. In practice the combat radius was short of the theoretical 200 miles because of the need to conserve fuel for use in combat. The Me109 couldn't escort bombers much further north than a line, London to Bristol. The Germans didn't have operational drop tank technology at this time in the war. Both sides also had aircraft types that would fail the test of combat, and were either withdrawn from the battle due to heavy losses and incapacity to perform their role, or had their operations restricted. These included the British Defiant fighter, and the German Me110 heavy fighter and Ju87 'Stuka' dive bomber.

With regard to pilots the Germans had a slight advantage. German pilots were moderately better trained than British ones in 1939-40. On average, German pilots received 260 flying hours of training, including 100 in combat types, compared to 200 and 65 respectively for British pilots.[9] The Germans also had more combat experience, many were veterans from campaigns in the Spanish Civil War, Poland and France. With this experience they had superior combat tactics, which were in place at the start of the battle, well ahead of the British. Both sides were at full strength in pi-

41

lots and air crew at the start. The German training system, despite the losses in France, was turning out more pilots than there were aircraft. For Britain, the reverse was the case, and pilots rather than planes were a limiting factor on the RAF Fighter Command maintaining its strength. In July the RAF's operational training units turned out about 180 fighter pilots, rising to 260 per month in August and thereafter.[10] The fighter pilot training rate was therefore only about half the fighter aircraft production rate. British replacement pilots were also short of training, especially on the combat types, and they became more vulnerable in combat as the battle of attrition proceeded.

On the other hand the Germans suffered the higher losses overall, including 521 Me109 pilots between July and September inclusive, compared to Fighter Command's 381.[11] They also made administrative mistakes such as flying multiple sorties per day, not resting their fighter pilots properly and transferring some to replace bomber crew losses. In contrast Britain reinforced its Fighter Command pilots with transfers from other air services, such as the Fleet Air Arm and Bomber Command. Britain also used Commonwealth pilots and exiles from the air forces of occupied countries such as Poland and Czechoslovakia. These measures meant that Fighter Command pilot strength actually increased from 1,259 on July 6th at the start of the battle, to 1,735 at the end, on October 26th. Even during the period of heavy losses in August and September it remained stable around 1,400.[12] Finally the higher German losses were more irrecoverable, since pilots and crews shot down but not killed over Britain became prisoners. In contrast about half of the British pilots shot down over their own territory would later return to the battle. Fighter Command lost 414 pilots killed compared to 915 fighters lost in air combat from July to October inclusive.

The British had one other well known advantage due to the battle being fought over friendly territory. The British coastal radar system gave early warning of attack. Radar warning was part of the world's first integrated air defense system, including command and control of the intercepting fighters based on sector air stations. When working properly this system would prevent the RAF being caught on the ground, thus countering a successful German tactic that had been used in Poland and France. Even so, it was often touch and go with the front line 11 Group due to the short flying times to their airfields in south-east England from France. Moreover the radar chain and the sector command stations, which amazingly were located above ground, were both vulnerable to attack. The Germans even had good reconnaissance on their locations. However, they failed to recognize their full significance or take advantage of these vulnerabilities, a crucial mistake.

Intelligence was poor on both sides. Britain over estimated German combat air strength at up to 5,000, and aircraft production at 1,800 per month of which 1,400 were supposedly combat types.[13] As we have seen, actual German combat strength was about 2,700-3,300, and average monthly production in 1940 was less than 900, including about 500 combat aircraft. The Germans fairly accurately estimated RAF Fighter Command strength at 600-700 fighters at the start of the battle. Thereafter though, the Luftwaffe's intelligence department underestimated British fighter production at a level of 180-300 per month, instead of the actual 450-500. Both sides overestimated the losses that they were inflicting, based on pilots claims. The Germans exaggerated more than the British. This was all the more serious for them when combined with the underestimate of British production. The result was that as the battle continued they underestimated British fighter strength which eventually hurt German morale. The Germans thought that they were closer to victory than they actually were. Both commanders and front line crews couldn't understand how Fighter Command could maintain full strength, which it did at 650-750 serviceable fighters throughout the battle.

Overall therefore, the balance of air power was much more even than is commonly presumed. German numerical superiority is overestimated in many accounts. Moreover the circumstances of the battle favored Britain. Britain's relative weakness in pilots has to be balanced against the advantages of being on the defensive and fighting the battle over British territory. These British advantages include: radar and the air defense system, German fighter range limitations, the capacity to recover some of the pilot losses, and higher aircraft production.

The Course of the Battle: July-October 1940

The battle itself is usually considered to break down into several phases, based on the change of targeting priorities by the Luftwaffe. Phase one is the preliminary build up lasting from July 10th to August 7th. Both sides were still recovering from the campaign in France. The German targets were British coastal ports and shipping, especially in the English Channel. Britain was forced to restrict shipping convoys here, first to night time operations and later to halt completely. The Navy also withdrew the 5 destroyers based at vulnerable Dover to Portsmouth. German fighter combat tactics proved superior at this time, but Britain responded by starting to adopt the German techniques. Air combat losses in the four and a half weeks from July 10th to August 10th inclusive were 84 British and 227 German.[14]

In phase two from August 8th to the 23rd the battle greatly intensifies. On August 1st Hitler issued his 'Directive 17' which dealt with the air phase of operation 'Sealion'. The first priority was to destroy the RAF in as brief a time as possible. He had told Admiral Raeder the day before that it would have to be largely achieved in eight days; otherwise the invasion would have to be postponed until the spring of 1941. There were to be attacks directed in the first instance against formations in flight, their ground facilities, and their supply centers, then against the British aircraft industry. When this was completed the Luftwaffe was to turn against British ports especially London to cut the countries supply lines from North America and the wider world. Ports on the south coast were to be spared because the Germans anticipated that they would be needed later to supply their invasion forces. Attacks against cities were to be reserved for reprisals only. The tactical targets in this phase were the British radar stations and forward fighter airfields. In modern NATO terminology these operations would be termed 'counter air', meaning attritioning or countering an enemy air force and its infrastructure, on the ground if possible.

After extended preliminaries and delays the offensive proper began on August 13th, code named *Adlertag* or 'Eagle Day'. Goering thought he could destroy the RAF in four days of good weather. The weather was poor on the 14th reducing the number of Luftwaffe sorties to one third of its maximum. Despite this the five days from August 13th to 17th inclusive were the most intensive of the battle. Attacks against the Fighter Command airfields of 11 Group in south-east England began to inflict damage to the command and control system. Fighter Command's pilots also begin to suffer extreme fatigue at this point, which would reduce their efficiency in the next stage of the battle. However, attacks against the chain of radar stations were not sustained and the Germans failed to disable the network. The German Ju87 'Stuka' dive bombers suffered heavy losses and were withdrawn from the battle at the end of this phase. Attacks by Luftflotten 5 from Norway, with bombers operating outside the range of fighter escorts, also suffered badly and were discontinued. Air combat losses in the two weeks from August 11th to 24th were 193 British and 406 German.

Phase three from August 24th to September 6th was the period that was relatively the most favorable for the Luftwaffe in the entire battle. The Germans increased the ratio of fighters to bombers in their raids to about two to one in this period. Typically they would be using most of their fighters but only half of their bombers at any one time. Their tactic was to bring the RAF to battle in the air against unfavorable odds, whilst continuing attacks against airfields and sector stations. This seemed to work, causing Fighter Command to lose pilots faster than they could be replaced. The surviving British fighter pilots became desperately tired and the poorly trained replacements suffered heavy losses. At the same time the bases of 11 Group, in the front line of battle, as well as some sector control centers began to be knocked out of action more permanently.

Conversely just as the Germans seemed to have found a combination of successful tactics, the British command was in some disarray. Their were tactical disputes between Air Marshall Park commanding 11 Group, who advocated a flexible forward defense using fast reacting individual squadrons, and Air Marshall Leigh-Mallory's 'big wing' tactic. The latter involved assembling larger defensive formations of 35-50 aircraft from his 12 Group in the British midlands. This took time and they were often only able to engage the Luftwaffe after it had bombed its targets. Dowding himself might even have been considering withdrawing Fighter Command northward, out of range of the Me109s, but conceding air superiority to the Germans in the south-east.

The one bright spot for Britain in this phase was that a sequence of events began which would contribute to the Germans changing their tactics. On August 24th German bombers had attacked London by mistake which prompted a reprisal by RAF Bomber Command against Berlin. As a result the Germans would soon change their strategy to attack cities, which had previously been banned by 'Directive 17'. The air combat losses in the two week period from August 25th to September 7th were 285 British and 380 German. The loss ratio still favored the British but by much less than before. Moreover, the German losses were divided between fighters and bombers where as the British loss was from Fighter Command alone. Fighter losses on their own strongly favored the Germans at this point, which accounts for them gaining the upper hand and for Fighter Command's exhaustion.

Phase four from September 7th to 30th is the turning point of the Battle of Britain. The Germans partly abandon the priority objectives of 'Directive 17', i.e. attacking the RAF directly, and the successful operations that they had conducted in the previous two weeks. They had been close to victory, at least over the south of England where the invasion was planned to take place. However, due to the unreliable intelligence they didn't realise it at the time. Instead the Germans started the new strategy of attacking cities directly, partly as reprisals for the British bombing of Berlin. The attacks on London began on September 7th and lasted for 76 consecutive days. Initially the British were caught out by the change of tactics and failed to intercept the early direct attacks. London suffered heavily, and later when raids were intercepted, it was recognized that they couldn't be stopped completely. It proved to be true that at least some bombers would always get through, especially with night attacks. Yet the Germans didn't have the strength to simultaneously conduct 'terror attacks' on London, and continue the grinding pressure on Fighter Command that had been previously winning the battle for them. With its airfields and sector stations relatively free from direct attack, Fighter Command began to recover. The shift to attacks on London also meant that the Luftwaffe came into range of Fighter

Command's 12 Group, whose 'big wing' tactics became more effective in the changed circumstances.

Although September 15th, celebrated as 'Battle of Britain Day', is often considered to be the peak of the battle this is not really the case. It is better seen as the Germans last great effort to gain air superiority so that 'Sealion' could take place. It failed because the circumstances of the battle again favored the British. With the RAF not being attacked directly, it could better control the intensity of operations and the rates of loss or attrition that it could endure. The intensity of combat operations and losses actually fell during this period compared to the previous phases of 'counter air' operations against the RAF. Air combat losses in the three week period from September 8th to 28th were 191 British and 340 German. Losses on both sides were slightly less than in the two weeks of phase three and the ratio returns to almost 2:1 in Britain's favor. As a result of the failure to destroy the RAF and achieve air superiority, Hitler ordered 'Sealion' to be provisionally postponed on September 17th. The invasion date had already been put back again, to September 24th, and the 27th was the very last practical date for it in 1940, due to tide requirements and poor weather conditions thereafter. Attacks by the British Bomber Command against the invasion fleet also contributed to the demise of 'Sealion'. However, the German losses were manageable at about 10%, including 21 out of 170 large transport ships, and 214 of 1,918 invasion barges sunk or damaged. On 12th October Hitler definitely postponed 'Sealion' until the spring of 1941.

Phase five lasting from October 1st to 31st is the aftermath of the battle. With 'Sealion' postponed the Luftwaffe attempted to maintain pressure on Britain by continuing to bomb cities. Heavy losses in daylight though, meant that there was a shift of emphasis to night attacks. Night bombing was less accurate but losses were lower. Neither Britain nor Germany had any significant night fighter capability at this time, and the only, and not very effective defense, was anti-aircraft artillery. The intensity of operations and levels of combat loss decreased further as both sides attempted to recover. This phase marks the transition from the Battle of Britain proper, to the 'Blitz', consisting of predominantly night bombing attacks against cities, lasting until May 16th 1941. Air combat losses for the four and a half weeks from September 29th to October 31st are 162 British and 380 German. Britain therefore maintains its advantage in the air battle despite the fact that it cannot actually protect its cities from attack.

During the entire four month period of the Battle of Britain from July 10th to October 31st, the total air combat losses are 915 for Britain's Fighter Command and 1,733 for the Luftwaffe, divided about evenly between fighters and bombers. The overall strain on both air forces was even higher than this due to accidents, aircraft destroyed on the ground, damaged and written off aircraft and British bomber combat losses of 307 aircraft. The air combat loss ratio over an extended period of the battle of attrition is thus 2:1 in favor of Britain. The RAF Fighter Command was just about able to sustain this level and ratio of attrition, the Luftwaffe couldn't. This is the central fact that accounts for the British victory.

Was the Battle of Britain a Close Run Thing?

Churchill's remarks about the 'few', there were just under 3,000 of them overall including replacement pilots, are largely correct; they shot down twice as many German aircraft as they lost, and that forced the Luftwaffe to concede defeat. The 'few' were or course supported by many more RAF ground personnel not directly involved in combat but still at some risk. As we have seen though, this is not the whole story. Other parts of the 'legend' of the Battle of Britain are less accurate than they might be, and give an incomplete view of the overall war situation in the British theatre of operations during the second half of 1940.

The overall odds or balance of forces over the four months of the air campaign, both numerically and taking into account all the circumstances, was more even, and not weighted heavily in the Germans favor. That doesn't mean that a British victory was inevitable or that the Germans couldn't win. Fighter Command still had to fight, the 'few' still had to be brave and skilful, but from a more even, rather than adverse position than is commonly presumed. They would have risen to the challenge under any circumstances. However, the wider circumstances, the strategy, decisions and mistakes of both sides also matter, and affected the outcome. Changes in these factors could also, perhaps, have altered the result or the course of events and thus later the decisive consequences of the Battle of Britain. It is therefore necessary to examine the air strategy options, and mistakes of both sides, to see if that would have made any difference. Moreover we also have to consider the wider naval and ground war context, recalling that the air phase of the Battle of Britain was a prelude to a possible invasion. Only then can the battle be placed in its proper strategic and historical context and its 'decisive' consequences considered.

The Germans definitely made at least one major strategic mistake that reduced their chances and might have cost them victory. That mistake was the shifting of the Luftwaffe's attacks to cities, especially London, and away from Fighter Command's airbases and control centers. This change occurred around September 6th-7th, just when their previous 'counter air' strategy was making progress and the air combat loss ratio was near to equality, having previously been 2:1 in Fighter Command's favor. Two basic causes contributed to the change in German targeting strategy. The first is that poor Luftwaffe intelligence meant that they were unaware that the battle was shifting in their favor. There had been so many 'false dawns' of victory previously, due to under estimating the RAF's resilience and recovery capacity, combined with over estimating its losses. Despite increased losses, Fighter Command's operational strength was still maintained at around 700. This was due to the superior number of British reserves, backed by higher aircraft production. Yet the fighter reserves were dwindling. British pilot fatigue combined with less well trained replacements was affecting Fighter Command's effectiveness. With loss rates approaching one to one and the German losses being divided between fighters and bombers, it just needed time for this attrition to work through to Fighter Command's front line strength. The Germans just didn't give enough time for their successful 'counter air' strategy to work through. Instead, and thinking that it had failed, they decided to change tactics. The other reason for the change, the desire for retaliation bombing attacks against cities, merely reinforced this. The next important German mistake was their failure to persist in attacks against the British radar stations. Again this would have helped the 'counter air' battle, by disrupting British early warning capacity and resulted in higher aircraft losses on the ground.

There is a common theme here, shared by all sides in the pre-war and early war period. This is that air war strategists over estimated the offensive and the idea that victory in the air could be achieved by one big blow in a short space of time. It couldn't. Most evidence shows that strategies like 'counter air', or later in the war 'strategic bombing', had to be applied consistently over a longer period than was previously thought if they were to achieve results. The same applies to air targeting policy. Even though we are using some hindsight to draw this conclusion, it is still the case that the maintenance of and persistence with a primary objective is a cardinal principle of strategy. The Luftwaffe's failure to maintain its priority focus on the destruction of the RAF, and to persist with the necessary 'counter air' targeting strategy, was an avoidable mistake. A final German tactical error was that Goering overrode his more professional fighter commanders and forced them to operate in close escort to bombers, instead of giving them tactical flexibility. Again this breaks the well known principle that leaders should delegate to the appropriate level of command and decision making. If the Germans had persisted with their successful strategies, most but not all analysts consider that they could have defeated Fighter Command and achieved at least temporary air superiority in the south-east of England. However, that on its own doesn't mean that they would have won the Battle of Britain. The clarifications, 'temporary' air superiority, and in the south-east, but not necessarily other areas of England, are important.

In contrast and despite some controversial debates, Britain made fewer mistakes than Germany and no major strategic errors at all. The dispute between Air Marshall's Park and Leigh-Mallory over operational tactics didn't hurt Fighter Command that much. In fact each tactic was used at the right time and in the appropriate circumstances. In the earlier phases of the battle, Park's flexible tactics were the best there was to counter the Luftwaffe's 'counter air' raids against Fighter Command and its infrastructure. After September 7th, once the bombing of London had started, there were fewer but larger Luftwaffe raids. Leigh-Mallory's 'big wing' tactics were an appropriate response. Given that the battles were by then in range of his 12 Group, they were also more practical than before. Fighter Command did sometimes fail to identify the Luftwaffe's targets, notably on September 7th when they switched to target London. That was only a minority occurrence though and not unusual in war. No armed force gets the entire myriad of small tactical decisions correct, there are simply too many of them.

The other major criticism Dowding received, was over his decision to maintain a large force of up to 20 squadrons protecting the north of Britain, which was only attacked once. Still, it is sound strategy to maintain a strategic reserve for emergencies. The reserves in the north of Britain were used to rotate squadrons, allowing some respite for the tired and depleted forces of 11 Group in the front line of battle. This further enhanced Fighter Command's ability to sustain the attritional battle. The Germans had no equivalent system. Making no major strategic command mistakes contributed to achieving victory for Britain.

This is not all. Unlike Germany, Britain still had one major air strategy option in reserve that it never used. It didn't have to, having won the battle without it. If Fighter Command had been defeated due to unacceptable losses in 11 Group's area in the south-east of England, it could still have withdrawn to the English midlands. That would have placed it out of range of the Me109 fighters that were causing most British air combat losses. The Germans couldn't have attacked the RAF directly much further north than the London-Bristol line, without exposing their unescorted bombers to unacceptable losses, while achieving little. Fighter Command would have had time to recover in this scenario. Safe from direct attack, it could also have controlled the intensity of combat and thus indirectly even the rates of loss it was prepared to endure. There would have been a cost to this strategy though. It would have conceded, at least temporarily, air superiority to the Luftwaffe over the invasion target area. Moreover, an unopposed Luftwaffe would also be recovering its strength, and be able to disrupt Fighter Command's control systems, including the radar chain in the south-east. This would have resulted in a huge gap in the coastal radar warning line. British aircraft production might also have been affected to some extent. The Spitfire factory at Southampton, and others around London, was well within Luftwaffe range.

The British intention, had they been forced into this 'pull back' strategy by persistent Luftwaffe 'counter air' operations, would have been to return to the air battle if and when the invasion started. Both Fighter and Bomber Commands would have been fully engaged in such a battle. However, with the radar warning, command and control system probably out of action, the circumstances of such a battle would have been more equal, rather than favoring Britain as they had previously. If that were all, then in such a scenario, an air Battle of Britain would have favored the Germans at that point. Yet we have to consider the wider context. To force Britain to make peace, the Germans would need to have invaded and conquered it in a ground war. The RAF was only Britain's first line of defense, in the event it alone was enough. Were they needed, the Navy and the Army would form the second and third lines.

In sequence, the British Royal Navy would have formed the second line had the RAF faltered. In terms of relative power it was Britain's strongest armed force. At the start of the war in 1939, Britain and the USA had the equal largest navies in the world. The British fleet was massive. Its major combat vessels consisted of 12 battleships, 3 battlecruisers, 7 aircraft carriers, 15 heavy and 47 light cruisers, 159 destroyers, excluding escort vessels, and 38 submarines. Except for submarines, the German navy was vastly outclassed in all categories. On the outbreak of war it comprised only 2 battleships, 3 pocket battleships, 2 heavy and 6 light cruisers, 23 destroyers and 57 submarines. The pocket battleships approximated in power to large heavy cruisers rather than battleships or battlecruisers. Even though the German ships were nearly all newly built within the previous ten years, and were mostly individually superior to their British counterparts, this doesn't make up for their vast numerical inferiority.

As ever these comparisons need to be placed within the context of the circumstances of the battle, but again this hardly improves the German position. The entry of Italy and exit of France from the war meant that Britain had to maintain a strong fleet in the eastern Mediterranean and the Red Sea. In June 1940 this comprised 4 battleships, 1 aircraft carrier, 11 cruisers, 25 destroyers and 6 submarines, overall about 20% of its global strength. There were other forces, notably up to about 25 cruisers, but no capital ships, scattered around the trade routes of the British Commonwealth-Empire and thus unavailable to defend Britain itself. Naval losses between September 1939 and July 1940, including the Norwegian campaign and at Dunkirk, had been manageable, notably the battleship **Royal Oak**, the carriers **Glorious** and **Courageous**, one cruiser and about 15 destroyers. The destroyer losses and one aircraft carrier had been replaced by new construction. German losses in the Norwegian campaign, from their smaller fleet, were relatively much more serious, with 3 cruisers and 10 destroyers sunk. Both German battleships, the **Scharnhorst** and

Gneisenau had also been damaged in Norway, and were still under repair throughout the period when 'Sealion' was planned to take place. The Norwegian campaign, although a defeat for the Allies, could have had significant implications for the Battle of Britain in 1940, had the latter proceeded to the naval phase.

The Kriegsmarine thus had only 1 heavy and 2 light cruisers, 4 destroyers and 19 torpedo boats immediately available to protect any invasion fleet in August-September 1940, a pitifully inadequate force for such a crucial operation. In comparison the Royal Navy had 5-7 battleships and battlecruisers, 2-3 aircraft carriers, 9-13 cruisers, and 51-57 destroyers, available in home waters in June-September 1940 to contest any invasion. This overwhelming force could even have been modestly reinforced, although not immediately, by the 1-3 capital ships, 1 aircraft carrier, 1-2 cruisers and about 10 destroyers, that were typically deployed in Force H at Gibraltar. Gibraltar would still have been safe from any Italian attack at this time, and would only have been at risk if Franco's Spain had allowed the Axis powers the use of its territory. There was also an average of 25-30 destroyers on Atlantic convoy duty that could have been drawn upon. The risks to Britain in this theatre would have been greater since the Battle of the Atlantic was in a favorable phase to the U-boats; the 'first happy time'. The Germans would also have tried to use minefields in the narrow waters around the Dover Strait and submarines to redress the balance. In addition they had a large superiority of heavy artillery covering the Dover Straits, including 13 'super heavy' guns of 11-15 inch calibre.[15] All this would have helped the Germans, but probably not enough. They would have been heavily dependent on the Luftwaffe to counter the British surface fleet superiority.

Had 'Sealion' been attempted there would have been a series of huge naval-air battles as the British fleet attempted to intercept it, and to prevent German resupply and reinforcement attempts should an initial beachhead have been achieved. The traditional view is that air power would have had the edge over surface sea power in such a contest. This needs further consideration. It is true that the aircraft carrier replaces the battleship as the most powerful type of capital ship during World War Two. Moreover in general, surface fleets without air cover suffered badly when exposed to land based air attack. However, the increased dominance of air power over traditional surface sea power wasn't very far advanced in 1940. The 'changeover' probably occurs slightly later. The aircraft plays a decisive roll in the battles of: Taranto in November 1940, Cape Matapan in March 1941, the *Bismarck* chase in May 1941, and the destruction of Force Z and Pearl Harbor in December 1941. Two of these battles though, Taranto and Pearl Harbor, were air attacks on a stationary fleet in port. Both the Cape Matapan and the *Bismarck* battles also required a battleship surface action to conclude them. Only the sinking of the battleships *Prince of Wales* and *Repulse* by Japanese land based naval air force medium bombers, is a conclusive example of the destruction of a fleet at sea by air power alone.

Yet, unlike Japan's naval air force in 1941-42, the German Luftwaffe didn't have specialized anti-ship aircraft or the necessary training and tactics fully in place in 1940. The Luftwaffe's large medium bomber force wasn't very accurate or effective against ships at sea. The Ju88, modified to be armed with torpedoes, was an exception, but it was 1942 in operations against the Russian convoys before the Germans actually used this capability. The primary German anti-shipping aircraft in 1940 was the Ju87 'Stuka' dive bomber, of which 482 were available in June-September 1940. The 'Stuka' force in 1940 was considerable, but not overwhelming, and they were vulnerable without strong fighter protection.

The Norwegian, Dunkirk and Crete campaigns being close in timing, and juxtaposing the Luftwaffe against British surface fleets, provide the closest practical evidence to the likely outcome of a contested 'Sealion'. In the Norway campaign in April-May 1940, the Allies lost 1 cruiser and 4 destroyers sunk by air attack. Another 5 cruisers and 2 destroyers were damaged. At Dunkirk 9 destroyers, including three French, were sunk and 19 damaged. In the evacuation of Crete from May 20th to June 1st 1941, the British lost 3 cruisers and 6 destroyers sunk, and 2 battleships, 1 aircraft carrier, 5 cruisers and 8 destroyers damaged. The Luftwaffe wasn't able to prevent the Royal Navy from carrying out its missions in any of these battles, despite the heavy losses that it inflicted. Still, cruisers with only moderate armor, and destroyers protected by almost no armor at all, were clearly vulnerable to air attack. The poorly armored pre-war aircraft carrier fleet was similarly vulnerable. Heavily armored battleships were probably still relatively safe at this point in the war, they could be damaged, but it was difficult to sink them by bombing alone.

Even so the British Admiralty had planned to keep its valuable capital ships north of the Wash, outside of German fighter range, in any invasion battles, unless the Germans risked their own battleships. Britain's Home Fleet battleship force, based at Scapa Flow in northern Scotland, was 30 hours steaming away from the Dover Straits and both sides calculated that it probably wouldn't be able to intercept the initial invasion anyway. That task would be undertaken, if an accurate and timely intelligence warning was available, by the more vulnerable lighter forces. Unless the invasion could have been accurately anticipated and the British achieved a night interception in the English Channel, the German first wave would have successfully landed. That on its own wouldn't have decided the outcome, since the invasion would still have to be supplied and reinforced.

There would have been continuing air-sea battles in the invasion zone over the subsequent days or weeks. The remaining strength of the RAF would have been committed to give the fleet fighter cover and bomb the German beachhead. Given the very effective German anti-aircraft or 'flak' defenses, evidenced in the French campaign, British bomber attacks would likely have been suicidal. Fighter Command though, would have been able to give some limited protection to the fleet. In general, night naval battles would have favored the British, because neither the Germans nor any other power had an effective night time air attack capability against ships. Any daylight naval-air battles would have been more balanced, or favored the Luftwaffe.

Whether the British Admiralty would have risked their capital ships in an attempt to tip the balance remains uncertain. On the one hand Britain's 300 year naval tradition suggests that it would have risked everything, at what would have been a pivotal historical moment. Conversely, the British fleet was also the most valuable of political, as well as military assets. Had the war situation deteriorated for Britain, requiring peace negotiations, then the fleet would have been a defeated British Government's strongest bargaining asset to achieve reasonable terms. The fate of the British fleet was also of paramount concern to the USA, since it was so crucial to the global balance of naval power, and impacted the USA's own military security. With it, the Americans would have naval superiority over the combined Axis powers, including Japan. Without it, there would be a period of slight inferiority, until the 'two ocean navy' shipbuilding program bore fruit in 1943. Britain could therefore have used the fleet as diplomatic leverage with the Americans, in order to retain their support, or attempt to get them to enter the war. Churchill himself was well aware of all this and he even hinted at these possible implications in his secret correspondence with President Roosevelt.[16] In the interim the Americans would of course still have the geographic advantages of the Atlantic and Pacific, and of defending land based air power in North America. The decision over how far to risk, or preserve, the British battle fleet, would have taken place at the highest political level, by Churchill himself.

Overall, Britain's second line of defense, the Royal Navy was at least as strong, and probably stronger, than the first line of RAF Fighter Command that narrowly won the actual battle. If the RAF had lost, which it could have since the margins were slight and the Germans made avoidable mistakes, then on balance the probability is that the British fleet, supported by the remains of the RAF, could still have defeated any German invasion attempt in 1940. However, British naval losses would have been heavy, especially among the cruiser and destroyer force, and the valuable battle fleet might have been put at risk. It is more likely that British success would have occurred during the naval-air battles to prevent German resupply to any beachhead, rather than interception of the initial invasion itself. This is a similar conclusion to that drawn by the RMA Sandhurst in 1973, when they conducted a map exercise to determine the outcome of 'Sealion' if both sides had implemented their 1940 plans. Even so, we are still dealing with probabilities, not certainties. To complete the analysis we should examine the third line of defense in 1940, Britain's home army.

The army formed the third and relatively weakest line of Britain's defense against invasion in 1940. The army had plenty of manpower with strength of 1,656,000 in June 1940, and it was expanding at about 50,000 per month over the next year. Overseas garrisons including 50,000 in the Middle East and 75,000 elsewhere were minimal. Army manpower in Britain was thus over 1.5 million once the BEF had been evacuated from France. They were all armed, helped by supplies from the USA sent in July, including half a million rifles and 900 75mm field artillery guns. The problem was that most were non-combat troops; a matter that Churchill rightly complained about in many wartime memos to Britain's less than efficient administrators.[17]

In July the combat force consisted of 2 armored and 26 infantry divisions, including one each from Canada and Australia, plus 8 independent brigades. Of these only about half, principally 12-14 of the ex-BEF divisions plus the Commonwealth forces, were fully trained. In June this force had only 180 tanks, 786 field guns and 167 anti-tank guns, about half its establishment in tanks and field guns and only 15% of the anti-tank gun requirement.[18] By September the 2nd Canadian Division was added, and tank strength had increased to 348 medium and 514 lights, and anti-tank guns to 500. Artillery production, at only 220 guns between May and September, was a low priority. If the 900 guns of First World War vintage received from the USA are included, then the British home army was moderately well equipped by then in heavy weapons, anti-tank guns still being an important exception.

This army of about 30 division equivalents, was therefore only about half fully trained and equipped in June-July, and more or less equipped but still with the same training deficiencies in September. Nor was it ideally deployed. The deployment emphasis on the east coast, which was appropriate before the fall of France, persisted until August. In September there were only 9 infantry divisions and 2 armored brigades defending the entire south coast from Cornwall to Kent, a frontage of over 300 miles. These could be reinforced by a strategic reserve of 2 armored and 4 infantry divisions. Finally, in terms of 'combat effectiveness', evidence from other theatres and post-war studies shows that the British and indeed all of the Allies, were on average less efficient than the Germans, assuming numerical equality.

The German army would require only a small fraction of its total strength of 165 divisions to conquer Britain. The limiting factor was sea transport. The final version of the 'Sealion' plan was for an invasion force of 27 divisions, about the same size as the defending British army.[19] Like the defenders, the invasion force couldn't reach the battle zone all at once. The invasion target zone was the 60 miles of Kent and Sussex coast between Ramsgate and Brighton. The first wave of the invasion was to consist of 9 infantry divisions, of the 9th and 16th Armies, about 170,000 troops to be landed over 4 days. Only the first echelon of 6,700 men of each division, 60,000 in all, could be landed on the first day. In addition, assuming they had air superiority, the Luftwaffe's 500 Ju52 transport aircraft could parachute the small 7th Airborne Division of about 10,000 men in one day. The 22nd Air Landing Division, 12,000 strong, would follow up once airfields had been seized. There were no panzer divisions in the first wave, but at least 310 tanks were allocated to its 9 infantry divisions. The second wave of reinforcements was planned to consist of 6 panzer and 3 motorized divisions, which would therefore include about 1,500 tanks. Nine more infantry divisions in a third wave would follow later. Assuming that the Germans could have landed their first echelon, which seems probable, and followed up with the rest of the first to third waves, which was less likely due to possible intervention by the Royal Navy, how might the ground war have developed?

After establishing a wide bridgehead, the plan was to begin the main advance inland after about a week. The initial objective of this advance was a line from Portsmouth to the Thames estuary at Rochester. As the second wave of mobile divisions became operational, the Germans would have started a classic breakthrough and exploitation 'blitzkrieg' to the west of London, aiming to encircle the capital and reach the line Gloucester-Ipswich before advancing northward.

In scale 'Sealion' with a planned 70,000 men to be landed on the first day, would have been less than half the size of 'Overlord' the Allied invasion of Normandy in 1944, when 177,000 men including airborne forces, were landed on D-Day. However, that would probably have been enough to secure a beachhead, since the British coast defense was also weak, the equivalent of only three infantry divisions in the immediate invasion zone. One possible German weakness was that Rundstedt's two armies, the 9th around Brighton and the 16th in the Folkestone-Ramsgate area, would initially have been separated into two beachheads. The landing front of 'Sealion' was planned to be wider than the 50 miles of 'Overlord', yet deploying only half the initial force. Still, the British were probably too weak to exploit such a temporary vulnerability. Also, and using the French and North

African campaigns as evidence, they would likely have reacted slowly as well.

The initial landing would have been followed by a build up phase, as both sides attempted to reinforce as fast as possible. If the coastal defense had been breached, the British plan was to fall back to an inland defense called the GHQ line. The GHQ line protected London and extended westward to the Severn estuary. If both sides had implemented their pre-planned strategies, it is likely that the decisive land battle would have been fought to the west of London, as the Germans attempted to break through the GHQ line and then exploit northwards, and encircle the capital with their mobile panzer forces. If the Germans had even reached the GHQ line, which implies that all of England south of London to Bristol, including the south coast supply ports, would already have been lost, Britain's chances wouldn't have been good. The GHQ line wasn't fortified like the Maginot or Siegfried Lines. The two armies would have been about numerically equal by then, both having brought their reinforcements to the front. The German panzer forces though, would have had superior numbers, better tanks, training, experience, organization and combat effectiveness. It would have likely been a repeat of what had just happened in France, and what would happen in the North African campaign once Rommel's Afrika Korps became operational in March 1941. In short, the Germans had all the advantages in any ground war, and these would only increase over time.

Britain's best chance, in retrospect, would have been to attempt to counter attack immediately with whatever small armored reserve was available. The aim would have been to isolate the German beachheads if possible, and to restrict the Germans into a small territory, to deny them room to re-inforce and stop them using their superior mobile warfare strategies. Churchill would likely have encouraged such a strategy rather than defend-ing at the GHQ line. Even this might not have worked, unless the Royal Navy had succeeded in cutting the Germans sea supply lines, within days probably of the invasion, to prevent them increasing their ground strength.

Overall the Battle of Britain was a fairly close run contest. On balance Bri-tain had the overall advantage, although not a conclusive one. After all Britain did win the air battle, just, and they still had the 'pull back' air strategy in reserve. However, avoidable German command mistakes did contribute significantly to their defeat. If the battle had gone to the naval-air phase, Britain probably had still the advantage, although it likely wouldn't have prevented an initial landing. Only with any ground war phase, would the advantage have been heavily in Germany's favor.

Decisive Consequences of Victory or Defeat

Churchill stated to Parliament on June 18th 1940 'Hitler knows that he must break us in this island or lose the war'.[20] British survival and continuation of the fight in 1940, was certainly a necessary pre-condition for the eventual Allied victory. The Battle of Britain that ensured that survival, is therefore one of the decisive battles of history. Yet it doesn't automatically follow, and wasn't clear at the time, that the survival of Britain on its own meant an inevitable Allied victory. Other future major events would still have to take place before Allied victory was assured. The entry into the war of both the USA and Russia would be required. Russia would have to win its own great battles of survival, and it would be 1942 before other decisive turning point campaigns would take place.

Nevertheless the British victory in the Battle of Britain is a decisive turning point in its own right. It meant, more so than Dunkirk, a change in the course of the war. Until the Battle of Britain there had been an uninterrupted series of Axis victories and Allied defeats. The defeat of France was massive and unexpected, moving the war in a new, pro-Axis direction. British survival partly corrected this and at least postponed an immediate end to the war. Both sides had thus to reassess the overall political and strategic situation. Britain was safe from invasion until at least the spring of 1941, after which, from about May onwards weather conditions would allow the Germans a renewed attempt at 'Sealion', if they so choose. Churchill's leadership was made absolutely secure and the political objective became victory at all costs. Britain now had some time and a safety margin to develop new political and military strategies.

There were two active theatres of military operations following the Battle of Britain: Britain itself and the Mediterranean theatre. Around Britain, the Atlantic supply line had to be secured. The Battle of the Atlantic was in the pro-German phase of the U-boat's 'first happy time'. Even so, British losses in the Atlantic were not heavy enough to force Britain from the war, and the battle would shift back to Britain's advantage in the summer of 1941. Indeed, British military production for all three services continued to grow during 1941. The RAF was given resource priority, and Churchill wasn't content to remain on the defensive. Bomber Command, although not very effective at this time, was the main instrument of direct counter attack. At the same time, as soon as Britain itself seemed safe from invasion, the Mediterranean and Middle East theatre was reinforced. Again the British took to the offensive wherever and as soon as they could. There were early, if limited, British victories at sea, such as at Taranto and Cape Matapan, and on land over the Italians in Egypt-Libya and in Italian controlled Ethiopia. None of this of course could immediately threaten Germany's solid control of most of Europe. However, it does show that the war had reached a period of, albeit temporary, strategic stalemate, where neither side could achieve an immediate decisive victory.

Britain was also expanding its primary diplomatic strategy, which was to acquire extra practical support from the USA and their entry into the war if possible. The British victory and survival enhanced its strategic value for the USA's own security. In May-June 1940, as France was collapsing and Britain's survival seemed in doubt, the USA passed the 'two ocean navy' bill, which was to begin a massive construction program to double the size of its fleet. Clearly the Americans at that point feared they might be on their own against the Axis in the near future, and needed to look to their own security first.

This policy then shifts to increased support for Britain. In July, as previously noted, the USA striped its army reserve weapon stocks to an irreducible minimum, to supply Britain with 500,000 rifles, 900 artillery pieces and other equipment. In September 1940 they started the transfer of 50 destroyers to Britain in return for the use of British bases in the West Indies. This is followed by the secret 'ABC' strategy meetings between the two powers in January 1941. Then in March 1941, with Britain unable to buy American weapons due to financial difficulties, the 'Lend Lease' bill is passed, supplying them, in practice, for free. Finally, from June 1941 the USA starts to protect Allied convoys, and then gradually extends the limit of its security zone in the western Atlantic. The USA sends marines to garrison Iceland in July. By the autumn of 1941 the USN is almost in a state of undeclared war against the Axis. British survival in 1940 therefore resulted in an increasing American policy of maximum support to Britain, but short of war. The outcome of the Battle of Britain therefore had major consequences for the neutral great powers as well as the contemporary belligerents.

Germany had three broad strategic options open to it to try and defeat Britain after the fall of France. The most direct of these, the invasion of Britain, had been blocked and postponed until the spring of 1941. That left two other strategies, both of which were indirect and time consuming. First, they could intensify the blockade of Britain by sea and air. The U-boat offensive in the Battle of the Atlantic had already been increased following the capture of French naval bases on the Atlantic coast. This brought the U-boats closer to the British convoy routes, thus increasing their time on patrol and therefore their effectiveness. To supplement this, the Germans shifted their air offensive to night bombing attacks against cities, thus attempting to attack the British economy directly. The second strategic option was to take the offensive in the Mediterranean, targeting

British territories in that area such as Gibraltar, Malta and Egypt. This would require a redeployment of part of the Luftwaffe from the 'Blitz' against Britain, but could otherwise be carried out simultaneously with the blockade strategy.

In addition there were political concerns for the Axis leadership that had been intensified by their failure to carry out 'Sealion'. The objective of preventing American entry into the war to help Britain was unchanged by the German defeat in the Battle of Britain. Peace or victory over Britain, by any method, would likely have prevented America entering the war on its own. Hitler considered that the USA was likely to enter the war in 1942, so the issue had to be settled in 1941.

This wasn't all. As important for Germany was the complicated political and strategic relationship with Stalin's Russia. Although Nazi Germany and Soviet Russia had agreed a neutrality pact in 1939, they remained strategic and ideological rivals. Hitler and the Nazis were long term ideological enemies of the communists. Moreover they, and the German military leaders, considered Russia a growing strategic military threat that needed to be dealt with. Russia was also seen as a vast source of raw materials and living space for an expanding Germany. In the more immediate term, Hitler also believed that Britain's refusal to make peace was explained by plans for an alliance between Britain and Russia.

Even though Britain remained in the war, it could do little in the near term to harm Germany. Specifically, since there was no western ground front, Germany wouldn't be risking the unsound strategy of a two front war by attacking Russia in 1941, before Britain was defeated. That assumed that victory over Russia would be achieved quickly, before the end of 1941. There therefore seemed, in Hitler's view at least, to be an opportunity in 1940-1941 to both eliminate the perceived Soviet Russian threat, and re-move a potential British great power ally at the same time. The genesis for the German decision to invade Russia is thus a very complicated combination of long and short term factors. British survival in the autumn of 1940 does seem to be a contributing short term factor to the German decision to invade Russia. That decision certainly was a decisive one, which would transform the course of the war, and probably its outcome as well.

For Stalin's Russia the most decisive event of 1940 was the collapse of France rather than the Battle of Britain. Stalin's strategic calculation in 1939, when he made the Nazi-Soviet Pact with Germany, was that the war in the west would be a long mutually exhausting struggle, which would weaken both sides. Russian security would be enhanced by such an out-come and it would become the diplomatic arbiter of Europe. The fall of France destroyed this strategy. Britain's survival was nevertheless significant. Stalin still considered that Germany wouldn't attack Russia before Britain was defeated. Russian diplomatic policy was to continue and even intensify their cooperation with Germany in this situation. They didn't want to antagonize the Axis and made no attempt to secretly ally with a Britain, which they mistrusted as much as the Axis powers. Nevertheless they still hoped that Britain would remain in the war, thus buying Russia as much time as possible before any clash with the Axis. The Russians had also prepared military contingency plans for an offensive against Germany, giving them a possible although dangerous alternative strategic option. The survival of Britain in 1940 therefore altered the course of the war and changed to varying extents the strategic, political and diplomatic calculations of all the great powers, both belligerent and neutral.

A comparative analysis of the probable strategic situation following a possible German victory in the Battle of Britain, also demonstrates the decisive importance of the battle. If 'Sealion' had reached the ground war stage and our previous 'alternative scenario' had occurred, then the war is likely to have ended sometime in late 1940. That would have been highly probable, but perhaps not quite a complete certainty under those circumstances. Unlike a defeated France, Churchill's Britain at least intended to try and continue the war from Canada and the rest of the British Commonwealth-Empire. The task would have been immensely more difficult than the actual situation and probably impossible. With Britain itself occupied, the rest of the Commonwealth-Empire, even over five years, would only have been able to mobilize less than 50% of the manpower and an average of about 20% of the military industrial production of the actual combined total.[21] Any exiled British government would have been almost totally dependent on the USA, which it must be stressed was still neutral. The political class would again have become divided and forced to reconsider some kind of peace treaty. In Britain itself a new government, not necessarily a fascist one, would have had to negotiate terms to try and protect the welfare of a people under occupation, similar to the situation in Vichy France. As noted, control of the fleet would have been a vital factor in negotiations with either or both of Germany and the USA. Finally, Britain would likely have lost territories in the Mediterranean from Gibraltar to the Middle East, either by conquest or diplomacy.

The strategic and political context for US policy would also have been transformed. All sides were of course aware of the importance of the British fleet in the balance of world naval power in 1940. Globally, the USN plus an intact British 1940 fleet were larger than the combined Axis fleets of Germany, Italy and Japan. The USN on its own would have been slightly inferior to the combined Axis powers until the start of 1943, assuming no losses in the interim. In the unlikely event that the British 1940 fleet fell under German control, due to diplomacy, then the situation would have been much more dangerous for the USA. Readers may make their own calculations of this, and other combinations, using table 1.

Table 1: Naval Power on Entry into War: 1939-1941
(Dec 1941 for USA & Japan, 1939-40 for others.)

	CV,CVL	BB	CA	CL	DD	SS
France	1	5	7	12	70	77
Britain	7	15	15	47	159	38
USA	7	17	18	19	171	112
USA+Britain	14	32	33	66	330	150
Germany		4	5	6	23	57
Italy		6	7	12	61	98
Japan	10	11	18	17	113	63
Axis Total	10	21	30	35	197	218

With Britain occupied and more or less out of the war, the Americans would have been much more likely to have remained neutral. They would have protected Canada and Australia, and tried to preserve the rest of Britain's empire from Axis control. Conversely, major offensive military operations against an Axis controlled Europe, without Britain as a base, would have been almost impossible given geography, and the technical and logistical limitations of the 1940s. Not even the largest World War Two strategic bomber, the American B29, which didn't enter service until 1944, had the range to carry out trans-Atlantic operations. The massive American 'two ocean fleet', which at maximum speed of construction only comes into service in 1943-1945, would still have given them enough naval-air power to protect the western hemisphere.[22] However, it would likely not have been sufficient, even supported by the remains of the British 1940 fleet, to project superior land and air power against an Axis Europe that would be allied to Japan by that time. If Britain left the war in 1940, the Axis would even have had access to the resources of an allied or defeated Russia by 1943.

There would have been two 'island hopping' invasion routes available to the Americans. The northern route would be the climatically difficult one of Canada, Greenland, Iceland; and then targeting Axis controlled Britain or Norway. The southern route would have fewer bases and be even longer, either direct to the Azores, or via Brazil, Dakar, the Canaries; and then targeting Portugal, Spain or Morocco. Either way a fully mobilized Axis Europe, with land based air superiority, plus logistical and geographical advantages, would probably have been able to defend successfully against such invasions. Of course the Americans could still have developed the atomic bomb. However, nobody knew if it would work in 1940-41, so we cannot consider that it would have been a dominant factor in a decision over war or peace at that time. Given such near impossible military obstacles, and in 1941 the unknown, but hardly beneficial attitude of Japan or even Soviet Russia, continued US neutrality was likely. Without the USA, any exiled British Government would have made peace.

That leaves the situation of Germany and Russia to be considered in a post-conquest Britain scenario. Germany would have been in a dominant position in 1941. All the remaining neutral states in Europe would have moved diplomatically closer to the Axis, some like the Balkan countries and Spain, even Vichy France, would probably have joined outright. Most importantly, Germany would have had complete freedom of action with regard to Soviet Russia. Most likely would have been an earlier than historical 'Barbarossa'. As we will see, the historical 'Barbarossa' only failed by a narrow margin. Unencumbered by the need for a preliminary diversion to secure the Balkans against non-existent British intervention, and modestly reinforced by the ground and especially air forces, that were historically deployed in Western Europe and the Mediterranean, its chances of success would have increased.

Alternatively the Axis could have maintained their treaty with Russia, and even encouraged it to join the Axis. There was actual support for such a policy within the German Foreign Ministry. Russia, assuming it wasn't attacked, would have willingly enhanced its actual pro-Axis policy and even joined the alliance. It would have had little choice. Either way, once Japan joined in 1941, the Axis would have had a good chance of controlling most of Eurasia, and thus forcing a global superpower stalemate with the USA. The USA would have led the Americas and the remains of the British Empire.

We can therefore only partly agree with Churchill's opening quote. The British victory in 1940 saved Britain, but it didn't, on its own mean, that Germany would lose the war. If Germany had won the Battle of Britain, then most of Eurasia, but not the USA or the Americas, would have fallen to an Axis dark age.

However it is analyzed, the Battle of Britain is one of the most decisive battles of World War Two, and indeed of history. It changed the course of the war from its post fall of France pro-Axis direction. It didn't win the war for the Allies, but by keeping Britain in it allowed for the necessary conditions, namely the entry of the USA and Russia, to occur, which would eventually bring about that result. The battle itself could have gone either way, but on balance, contrary to the common view, the overall circumstances moderately favored Britain. The British victory was probable although far from certain. If the minority possibility of a German victory had occurred, it would probably have ended the war in an Axis victory before the USA and possibly Russia had entered it. Such an Axis victory wouldn't have meant complete conquest of the Allies, as actually happened in reverse in 1945. Instead there would have been a global stalemate and an 'alternative cold war' over the following decades, between the USA and a Eurasian alliance of the Axis powers. The stakes were high indeed in 1940, and probably not just for Britain.

Notes to Chapter 2

1. Churchill, Vol 2, p 198.
2. ibid. Vol 2, p 640.
3. Ellis, Brute Force, p 31.
4. Ellis, WW2 Databook, table 27, p 237. Total derived from addition of sub-totals of combat types.
5. ibid. p 232.
6. Churchill, Vol 2, tables on p 641-642.
7. Ellis, WW2 Databook, table 92, p 278, and for what follows on aircraft production. Table 93, p 278-79, gives a breakdown into combat types.
8. Ellis, Brute Force, table 26.
9. ibid. p 205.
10. Liddell Hart, History of the Second World War, Pan Books, London, 1973, p 99.
11. Ellis, Brute Force, p 27 fn.
12. ibid. table 27. Although, Hart, Hist of 2WW, p 99, disagrees, and says that fighter pilot strength drops to a low of 840.
13. Churchill, Vol 3, p 36. Also see Appendix D, p 694-96, for discussion of the issues. Also Hart, Hist 2WW, p 100-102.
14. Churchill, Vol 2, table on p 299. For this and what follows on losses during each phase of the battle.
15. Eddy Bauer (original text). Peter Young (Ed), The History of World War II, Orbis Publishing Ltd, London, 1983, Vol 3 (of 30), p 243.
16. Churchill, Vol 2, p 51. In a letter to Roosevelt, on May 20th 1940, he notes, 'If members of the present [British] Administration were finished and others came in to parley amid the ruins, you must not be blind to the fact that the sole remaining bargaining counter with Germany would be the Fleet …'. Table 1 gives the details of the global naval balance of power in 1940.
17. Churchill, Vol 2, Appendix A, p 619-621, gives the situation in December 1940. In conclusion (point 10, p 621), Churchill writes, '…we still have over 2,000,000 men-i.e., nearly 60,000 men mobilized for each of 34 divisions. [Including two Commonwealth divisions in Britain, and three British divisions in the Middle East] Before I can ask the Cabinet to

assent to any further call-up…it is necessary that …at least a million are combed out of the fluff and flummery behind the fighting troops, and made to serve effective military purposes.' They never were combed out. Churchill doesn't give the War Office's reply, perhaps because there wasn't a viable counter argument. The incident is illuminating in a number of respects. It shows how inefficient and wasteful the British, and later the Americans, were in their allocation of military manpower. Also, in that they had this luxury, how relatively secure the two Western Allied maritime powers were, even Britain in 1940, compared to all other combatants. Had Britain been invaded, it is an interesting question as to whether this manpower policy would have changed. Would more, hastily trained and equipped, combat divisions have been formed? Or would huge masses of supply and administration troops have simply surrendered?

18. Ellis, <u>Brute Force</u>, p 14. For this and what follows on British ground forces preparations.

19. Bauer, <u>WW2 Vol 3</u>, p 241-243. For this and what follows on 'Sealion'.

20. Churchill, <u>Vol 2</u>, p 198.

21. The Commonwealth-Empire mobilized 5.5 million men over 1939-45, compared to 5.9 million from Britain, i.e. almost 50% of the 11.4 million wartime total. Canadian tank production, 1939-45, was 5,678 compared to 27,896 for Britain, 17% of the combined total. Aircraft production (all types) was: Britain 131,549, Canada 16,341 (11%), other Commonwealth-Empire 3,081 (2%), total 150,971. Escort Vessels: Britain 413, Canada 191 (31%), Australia 12 (2%). There was no Commonwealth capability to build naval vessels larger than cruisers. Merchant shipping: Britain 6.4 million tons, Commonwealth, mainly Canada, 2.7 million tons (30%). Source: Ellis, <u>WW2 Databook</u>, table 9, p 227-228, table 87, p 277, table 92, p 279, tables 95-96, p 280. The combined Commonwealth-Empire, without Britain, wasn't insignificant, and given the advantages of geography, was probably capable of defending itself. However, it would have been totally incapable of liberating a German occupied Britain.

22. See table 8, chapter 7 for US and Japanese Naval construction.

CHAPTER 3

THE MEDITERRANEAN 1940-1943

'Rommel, Rommel, Rommel! Whatever matters but beating him?'[1]

Churchill

'If the enemy had chosen they could have spared and ferried, at an accepted cost, the forces necessary to make our position [in North Africa] untenable'[2]

Churchill

Strategic Overview and Balance of Forces

These two statements by Churchill, sum up a profound reason why the Allies, principally Britain and its Commonwealth-Empire, won the war in the Mediterranean theatre, and why the Axis lost. For Britain, the theatre was a strategic priority from 1940 to 1943. For the Axis it wasn't. They also hint that things could have been very different.

The Mediterranean theatre was of strategic importance for several reasons. As with the Battle of Britain, the interdependence between control of land, sea and air was a central feature. This linkage was especially important between sea control in the Mediterranean itself and the land campaign in North Africa. When Mussolini's declaration of war on Britain and France on June 10th 1940 extended the scope of the war to this theatre, control of the Mediterranean was divided. Britain controlled the west from Gibraltar, and the east from Egypt. Gibraltar and the Suez Canal, along with Aden at the entrance to the Red Sea, all controlling strategic choke points, were known as three of the 'keys that locked the world'. Britain retained control of all three throughout the war, and the Allies benefited greatly from the freedom of strategic action it gave them, and from the corresponding restrictions upon the Axis. Control of the central Mediterranean was contested between Britain and the Axis. British control of Malta didn't give it quite the same 'lock' as Gibraltar and Suez did. Malta could be neutralized as a military base due to Italian control of Sicily and Libya on either side.

The North African campaign was interdependent with the need to control the Mediterranean, but more so for the Axis than the Allies. Axis armies in Libya depended on seaborne supplies and reinforcements moving a distance of 200 to 500 miles on a north-south axis across the central basin of the Mediterranean from Italy. The British supply line was a much longer 2,000 mile route along the west-east axis between Gibraltar and Egypt, with Malta mid-way between them. As an alternative, Britain also had the much longer Cape route around Africa to Egypt and the Middle East. This route typically added over a month to the journey compared to the passage through the Mediterranean. Most, but not all, British shipping connecting with the Middle and Far East, India and Australasia, actually avoided the Mediterranean until 1943. In the Middle East, if the Allies were to have lost Egypt and its sea supply line to Suez, they had an alternative route here as well, into the Persian Gulf at Basra, and later at Abadan in Persia (Iran), occupied in 1941 by a joint Anglo-Soviet invasion. Britain was fairly secure in the Middle East itself, controlling the pre-war territories of Iraq, Jordan and Palestine. There would be internal unrest in Iraq in 1941 and there was also a potential threat from Vichy French controlled Syria. Any Axis attack into the Middle East would probably have to come through Egypt first. Axis invasions from the north via the Russian Caucasus, or through Turkey, were more distant possibilities, which nevertheless still had to be guarded against.

The great prize in the Middle East apart from its geographic position was oil. However, Middle Eastern oil was far less important in the 1940s than it was to become in the post-war world. Average annual oil production in millions of tons in 1939-1945 was: Iraq 5, Persia (Iran) 10, Saudi Arabia 1, Bahrain 3 and Egypt 1.5. Production had not even started in Kuwait and some of the Gulf States that are important today. The Middle East overall only provided about 7% of the average total world production of about 300 million tons per annum at this time. Even so, Middle Eastern oil was the main local source of supply for the British Empire and its forces in the region itself, as well as for Africa, India and the Far East. Oil for Great Britain itself and most of the rest of the Allied global war effort, except for Russia, came from the USA which produced an average of 200 million tons per year, over 60% of the world total. Oil for the European Axis came primarily from Romania and German synthetic production, each of which produced an average of 5-6 million tons p.a.[3] Japan once it entered the war, and oil was a primary determinant in its decision to do so, would be dependent on the 7 million tons produced by the Dutch East Indies (Indonesia). Oil was a vital economic and strategic commodity during World War Two, just as it is today. However, the geography of its production and transport was very different. The Axis powers could only meet their minimum oil needs with difficulty for most of the war. Axis control of the Middle Eastern and the adjacent Russian Caucasus oilfields, which produced 75% of Russia's 30 million ton pre-war output, was a major strategic objective for them. Even were they to capture them, the Axis would still have had the problem of transport to their industrial centers from these rather distant oilfields.

Next, there was actual and potential military activity in other adjacent territories. Italy had a large, mainly colonial army in its east African territories of Ethiopia, Eritrea and Somalia. These could potentially threaten the important Allied sea route through the Red Sea near Aden, as well as British controlled Sudan and Kenya. However, these Italian forces were also isolated from Italy and Libya, and would become increasingly vulnerable to attack over time. There were also three important medium power neutral states in the region that were potentially useful for either side: Spain, Vichy France and Turkey. Spain and Vichy France were pro-Axis, and their entry into the war or Axis military access to their territory could threaten Allied control of vital Gibraltar. Turkey was a potential diplomatic or even military target for both sides. It was a persistent aim of Churchill to bring Turkey into the war on the Allied side. An Allied Turkey could threaten Axis control of the Balkans including Romanian oil, and allow for a new supply route to Russia once it had entered the war. Conversely an Axis conquest or alliance with Turkey would open a second front for Britain in the Middle East, as well as threaten Russian control of the Caucasus and its oilfields.

There were therefore several important strategic, economic, and diplomatic objectives at stake in the Mediterranean theatre. However, Italy was the only great power participant in the war that was located here, and it was the weakest of them at that. It was a matter of dispute, for both sides, how important the region was within the context of the war as a whole. This is reflected in the relative priorities that the different powers gave to Mediterranean strategy. For Italy it was obviously central for Mussolini's great power imperial ambitions, and ultimately for survival. For Germany the theatre was largely a secondary one. Their main aim was to prevent their Italian ally from being defeated and they neglected some important strategic opportunities here. For Britain, and Churchill in particular, the Mediterranean was a major, even a primary priority, both defensively to protect the Empire, and offensively to try and knock Italy out of the war. The Americans largely disagreed with the British priorities. For them the Mediterranean theatre was tertiary to both Western Europe and the Pacific. Disagreement and the need for cooperation between the members of each alliance is thus one more factor to keep in mind when we consider the events and strategies, both actual and potential, in the Mediterranean theatre.

Although Italy was the weakest of the great powers overall it did posses a first class fleet. The Italian navy was the fourth largest in the world in 1940, about equal in size to that of France, which deleting the ships sunk by the British attack at Oran on July 2nd 1940, had just left the war. The Italian fleet, all concentrated in the central Mediterranean, consisted of 6 new or recently modernized battleships with 2 more under construction, 7 heavy and 12 light cruisers, 59 destroyers (excluding the smaller torpedo boats) and 98 submarines.[4] Most of the ships were more modern than their British counterparts, and technically their equals, except for having an inferior armor protection system. There were also weaknesses. Most importantly, the Italians had no aircraft carriers. This need not have been a problem since the fleet's operational theatre was mostly within the range of land based aircraft. Unfortunately cooperation between the Italian navy and air force was poor. Other problems included a lack of radar, inferior ASW technology and techniques, and a limited stock of fuel oil, which in time would restrict operations.

Britain's Mediterranean fleet was divided between Gibraltar and Alexandria in Egypt. Strength varied over time, but the fleet at Alexandria in 1940-41 was maintained at a typical strength of about 3-4 battleships, 1 aircraft carrier, 6-10 cruisers and about 20 destroyers. Force H at Gibraltar had a greater variability in its strength as it could be quickly reinforced from the Home Fleet in Britain itself, depending on the situation in home waters and the Atlantic. Typically Force H would contain 1 aircraft carrier and 1-3 capital ships plus a modest cruiser and destroyer escort.[5] At Malta Britain generally relied on submarines, rather than surface forces, due to its proximity to superior Axis land based air power. Despite having a slightly smaller fleet that was divided due to geography, British commanders were far more offensively minded. They gained a morale ascendancy over their Italian counterparts by vigorously contesting Italian control of the central basin of the Mediterranean by fleet patrols, and sending convoys to maintain Malta as an offensive base against the Axis sea supply line to their armies in North Africa. The Italians, partly for political reasons, aimed to preserve their premier asset and tended to avoid battle. Their naval strategy was that of maintaining 'A fleet in being'.

In the air the Italians had an initial overwhelming overall operational strength of 759 fighters and 1,064 bombers in June 1940.[6] These however, had to cover all the various sub-fronts in the Mediterranean and the aircraft were generally inferior in quality to Allied ones. Over the course of the Mediterranean War, Italian aircraft production proved inadequate to maintain this strong initial strength, which gradually declined to 1,200 combat aircraft in 1943. In comparison the British initially had less than 400 combat aircraft in Egypt and the Middle East. Conversely as the war proceeded British air power increased due to higher production and the strategic priority given to this theatre.

On land the Italians again had a very large initial numerical superiority. On mobilization the Italian army in 1940 had 2 million men, organized into 73 divisions, mostly infantry. They had 236,000 troops and 339 tanks in 14 divisions in Libya, and 90,000 Italian and 100,000 colonial troops in Italian East Africa. In comparison there were about 90,000 British and Commonwealth-Empire forces in the entire Middle East theatre, of which 36,000 were in Egypt.[7] Again however, the British were superior in factors such as training, organization and combat efficiency. British tanks and armored warfare doctrines were also superior to those of the Italians, although inferior to the Germans. Finally the region was a top priority for British and Empire ground and air force reinforcements. Churchill started reinforcing the Middle East even before victory in the Battle of Britain was achieved.

The North African Campaign and Strategy 1940-1943

The North African campaign was the central focus of activity within the Mediterranean theatre for both sides for most of this period. When the strategy of either side occasionally deviated from this it tended to be to its disadvantage. The central land campaign in Libya and Egypt can be divided into five phases based on the see-saw changes of initiative and fortune between the two sides. In the first phase, despite the apparent, and primarily numerical, advantages that Italy appeared to enjoy in 1940, it was Britain that generally had the initiative. In September 1940 five of the 14 Italian divisions in Libya advanced slowly into Egypt. They soon halted after only 60 miles at Sidi-Barrani and resumed a defensive posture. They didn't seriously challenge the more mobile 2 division British 'Western Desert Force', later to become the 8th Army, defending at Mersa-Matruh 75 miles further back.

On December 9th British General Wavell, with 31,000 troops and 275 tanks in the 7th Armored and 4th Indian divisions, began the offensive named after him.[8] In a series of battles at Sidi-Barrani, Bardia, Tobruk, and Beda-Fomm, Wavell's Western Desert Force sequentially destroyed four separate Italian forces, each of which were about equal in size to his own, but inferior in armored strength. In just two months, by February 7th 1941, the British had advanced 500 miles and captured all of Cyrenaica, the eastern half of Libya. The Italian 10th Army of 9 infantry divisions was almost totally destroyed losing 130,000 men, mostly prisoners, and 380 tanks. Total British losses were less than 2,000 killed and wounded. The campaign demonstrated once again the superiority of mobile warfare and armored divisions over larger infantry based armies. The Italians were totally out maneuvered at the operational level in Libya.

They also failed in higher strategy as well by failing to maintain their focus on North Africa. In October 1940, Mussolini opened a second campaign by declaring war on Greece. An Italian army of 10 divisions with 162,000 men advanced from Albania, but was defeated and then driven back by a Greek army of almost equal size.[9] It was a fatal distraction and a strain on the limited Italian shipping capacity, which moved more supplies and replacements to the Albanian-Greece front than to the North African one in late 1940. The Italian defeats on land were supplemented by a major naval disaster, when a British carrier based air attack sank three of Italy's six battleships at Taranto on November 11th 1940. The first phase of the Mediterranean campaign was thus a successful one for Britain on land and at sea.

It ended though with a strategic error. Instead of preparing for a renewed advance in Libya before the Axis could regroup there, Churchill and Wavell decided to intervene in Greece. The Italians still had 5 divisions in Libya that had previously been guarding the Tunisian border against France. The Germans were also about to send reinforcements, so it wouldn't have been a certainty that the British could have advanced to Tripoli and cleared the Axis from North Africa at this point. However, the balance of forces and circumstances was better for the Allies in North Africa than in the Balkans. Instead a new BEF, of 57,000 men and 100 tanks in two ANZAC infantry divisions and one armored brigade, was sent to reinforce Greece during March 1941.

In the second phase of the campaign from March to June 1941 the advantage swings to the Axis. Germany intervenes simultaneously to support its failing Italian ally in three areas. Firstly in the Balkans, German diplomacy secured alliances with Hungary, Romania and Bulgaria. When a new government in Yugoslavia refused to join the Axis alliance, the Germans invaded both Yugoslavia and Greece. This was to forestall any possible British intervention, such as had occurred at Salonika in 1915-18, and to secure their strategic right flank for the upcoming invasion of Russia. Secondly, the Luftwaffe reinforced the Italians in Sicily in order to neutralize Malta as an offensive base. Thirdly, the movement of the Afrika Korps to Libya, under General Rommel, began on February 15th 1941.

Rommel attacked on March 24th before the transport of the entire Afrika Korps to Libya was complete. The Axis had a slight initial superiority of one panzer and two Italian divisions (including one armored), compared to two British divisions (one armored). Again however, it was superior German combat and operational techniques combined with Rommel's leadership, rather than numbers, which won the battle for the Axis. In less than three weeks up to April 12th 1941, the Axis recaptured all of Cyrenaica up to the Egyptian border, except for Tobruk which was besieged. The British were thus almost back where they had started in North Africa when Italy entered the war. Meanwhile in the central basin of the Mediterranean the Axis now had about 400 combat aircraft, half of which were German, enough to neutralize Malta from January until May 1941. In May 1941 the Afrika Korps reached a size of about 40,000 troops and 260 tanks in two panzer divisions and one light division. The British navy and dwindling

RAF strength at Malta were unable to prevent this Axis deployment across the Mediterranean to Libya.

In the Balkan campaign larger forces were involved. A German army group of 32 divisions, of which only 24 were actually used, plus 14 Italian divisions, opposed 28 Yugoslav, 20 Greek and 3 British divisions. The forces again seemed evenly matched, on paper. However, with support from 430 combat aircraft and 600 tanks against only 100 British tanks, the Germans had overwhelming superiority in the instruments of 'blitzkrieg'. The offensive opened on April 6th 1941 and Yugoslavia was rapidly conquered in 12 days and Greece in 21 days. Yugoslav casualties were about 100,000 killed and wounded, plus 344,000 prisoners. Greece suffered 70,000 casualties and 270,000 captured. British casualties were 12,000, but once again the Royal Navy came to the army's rescue, completing the evacuation of 51,000 men from Greece by April 27th, but without their heavy equipment. The Italians had lost 102,000 men in their failed invasion from Albania over the previous five months. In comparison German losses in the 21 day campaign were only 5,000, which again demonstrated the overwhelming speed of operations and the combat efficiency of their army over opponents of equal or slightly greater size. The campaign also showed that difficult terrain, in this case the mountains of the Balkans, was no obstacle to the 'blitzkrieg' either.

The situation was different though when they had to cross a sea controlled by the Royal Navy, as the battle for Crete showed. On March 28th 1941 the Italians suffered yet another naval defeat, when 3 cruisers and 2 destroyers were sunk and the new battleship *Vittorio Veneto* was damaged at the Battle of Cape Matapan. With the Italian fleet temporarily weakened and the Luftwaffe possessing overwhelming air superiority with 570 combat aircraft and 500 transport planes, the Axis powers decided that an airborne led attack against Crete was preferable to a predominantly seaborne invasion. The Allies had a garrison of 28,000 British Commonwealth and 14,000 Greek troops on the island. Although they had almost no air strength, only 25 tanks and were short of artillery, the Allies did have forewarning of the invasion from the 'Ultra' code breaking system. Even so they still lost the battle, against the smaller 22,000 elite but lightly equipped German airborne and air landing forces. The margin was narrow however, and the German losses of 6,000 from this small specialized force, plus another 5,000 in an ill judged attempt to reinforce the attack by sea, were heavy in comparison to the Balkan campaign proper. Once again the British navy went into harms way, but this time was only able to evacuate 16,000 of the garrison, ending the Battle of Crete on May 31st. Naval losses were heavy with 3 cruisers and 6 destroyers sunk, and 2 battleships, 1 carrier, 5 cruisers and 8 destroyers damaged. The heavy losses to the German airborne force, however, persuaded Hitler, who was obviously unaware of the special role of 'Ultra' in the battle, to halt such operations in the future. This was a major strategic error by Germany.

The first half of 1941 also saw operations in three sub-theatres, Iraq, Syria and Ethiopia. In contrast to the Allied disasters in Libya and the Balkans, it was the Axis who were entirely eliminated from these three countries. Britain had to divert 102,000 troops in 5 divisions for five months in order to clear the Italians from Ethiopia. The result was that the great majority of the nearly 200,000 strong, but isolated, Italian army in Ethiopia surrendered by the end of May 1941.[10] An Iraqi revolt was defeated in that same month before it could receive any aid from the Axis, and the 35,000 pro-Axis Vichy French force in Syria was defeated by 20,000 British between June 8th and July 12th 1941. These campaigns removed any threat of an Axis pincer movement against the Middle East, at least for the time being. The Axis also failed to follow up their victories in the Balkans and North Africa. The British feared that they might attempt airborne led invasions of Cyprus, Syria, Malta or Suez, none of which occurred. Instead in June 1941 the Germans invaded Russia, and the British were therefore able to regain the initiative in the Mediterranean.

In phase three of the North African campaign, which lasts from June to December 1941, the balance of forces shifts back in favor of the Allies. This phase includes the famous eight month siege of Tobruk between April and December 1941. Rommel couldn't advance into Egypt while the 36,000 strong garrison at Tobruk, 60 miles to the west, posed a threat to his supply lines. Nor was he able to capture the fortress with a set piece attack, a form of warfare that favored the defending British, whist simultaneously holding the Libyan-Egyptian frontier. Two such attempts in April and May both failed. The British kept Tobruk supplied by sea and built up their forces on the frontier in preparation for a counter offensive. The first British offensive in June 1941, codenamed 'Battleaxe' involving small and equal forces of about 2 to 3 divisions, 200 tanks and 200 aircraft each, was a complete failure. Wavell was relieved of command and replaced by Auchinleck.

More importantly the British were able to build up the 8th Army faster than the German-Italian 'Panzer Group Afrika' in the second half of 1941. The transfer of the Luftwaffe's Fliegerkorps VIII to Russia after the Balkan campaign ended left only Fliegerkorps X, to cover both Malta and North Africa. This allowed the British to more easily supply and reinforce Malta and Tobruk. RAF strength, built up to 10 squadrons, submarines, and surface 'Force K' consisting of 2-3 cruisers and 2-4 destroyers, all based at Malta, were able to seriously disrupt the Axis supply route to Libya during this period. More generally the Afrika Korps received few reinforcements anyway due to the strategic priority of 'Barbarossa'. In contrast Churchill renewed his focus on Egypt, and the British Middle East Command was also free by this time from any threat from Ethiopia, Iraq or Syria, and thus able to redeploy accordingly.

By November 18th 1941 when the much larger operation 'Crusader' offensive began, the British had a slight manpower advantage of 118,000 against 113,000 Axis, of which less than 50,000 were the more efficient Germans.[11] Moreover 6 of the 9 Axis divisions were Italian ones, each of which cannot be compared in combat power to the 7 British and Commonwealth divisions. The Allies had a larger material superiority with 700 tanks plus 500 in reserve, against 250 German and 146 Italian ones with only 50 in reserve.[12] In the air the RAF had 700 serviceable combat aircraft compared to 120 German and 200 Italian.[13] The battle could still have gone either way, but in the end the superior material and logistics of the Allies, especially the commitment of the tank reserve to replace attrition losses in the three week long battle, overcame the continuing German advantage in combat effectiveness. The result was that besieged Tobruk was relieved, and by December 28th the front had moved 500 miles westward to El-Agheila on the Cyrenaica-Tripolitania border once again. The Axis suffered 33,000 casualties including 13,000 German, compared to 18,000 for the Allies during operation 'Crusader'.[14]

Once again the side that had maintained its strategic focus on the North African front had emerged victorious. Moreover Allied material superiority and the strategic priority Churchill placed on the Mediterranean and Middle Eastern theatres as a whole was making itself felt. The total British and Commonwealth armed forces strength throughout the Middle East, including it must be said a large non-combat force and garrisons, increases significantly from 280,000 in January 1941, to 530,000 in June, and to 635,000 in February 1942.[15] The Mediterranean was the only active land war theatre for the British Commonwealth-Empire from July 1940 to December 1941, and it had significant and increasing defense in depth within the region overall.

Even so, at the turn of 1941-1942 the pendulum swings again for phase four of the campaign. The overall reason is similar to before, a shift of higher strategic focus, this time by both sides. To be fair the change in Allied strategic priorities was outside their control. On December 7th 1941 Japan entered the war, and an entire new theatre of operations for the British Commonwealth-Empire in the Far East became active. Reinforcements from Britain, moving by the Cape route, were diverted from the Middle East to the Far East. Moreover India and Australia, both of which had been concentrating their war efforts on the Middle East theatre, were now threatened directly by Japan's intervention. Two experienced Australian divisions, out of an ANZAC total of four in the Middle East, were redeployed to Australia. Henceforth the Far East would be the strategic priority for India, Australia and New Zealand. Only 4 of the 17 Indian divisions that saw combat in the war after Japan's intervention served in the Mediterranean theatre, compared to 13 in Burma and Malaya.

British sea power also reaches a nadir at the end of 1941, due to the loss of 6 of the 22 valuable capital ships and aircraft carriers with which it had started the war. This once again limits its control in the Mediterranean, and especially the maintenance of Malta as an offensive base. In November 1941 the carrier *Ark Royal* was sunk by a U-boat near Gibraltar, and the next month the Mediterranean Fleet lost the battleships *Barham,* sunk at sea, and the *Valiant* and *Queen Elizabeth* sunk in Alexandria harbor by Italian midget submarines. The last two were put out of action for many months until they could be salvaged. Since no capital ships were immediately available as replacements due to the requirements of the Home Fleet, and now the Eastern Fleet, which had just lost the battleships *Prince of Wales* and *Repulse*, the East Mediterranean Fleet was temporarily reduced to 3 cruisers and a few destroyers. Bold action by the Italian navy at this point, which didn't occur, could have given them almost complete sea control of the Mediterranean.

The Axis response to Rommel's first defeat and especially the threat to his army's sea supply line was to send serious German reinforcements to the region. However, the Axis grand strategic priority in 1942 was still Russia, not the Mediterranean. Fliegerkorps II was transferred to Sicily from Russia, which combined with the existing Fliegerkorps X would form a complete air fleet: Luftflotte 2, under Field Marshall Kesselring. This reinforcement doubled average German combat air strength to 550-650, plus up to 800 of the less effective Italian machines. The Germans also transferred an initial force of 10, and later 25 U-boats to the theatre, which achieved better results against Allied shipping than the entire Italian submarine fleet. The air reinforcements in particular allowed Malta to be neutralized once more. Indeed, between January and April 1942, the island goes through its most intense phase of siege and air bombardment. It is only very gradually after June 1942 that Malta starts to recover, due to air reinforcements flown from carriers and some epic convoy battles, culminating in operation 'Pedestal' in August.

The shift in the air and naval balance in favor of the Axis allows Rommel to be reinforced and start to replace the losses suffered in 'Crusader'. Characteristically Rommel launches the first stage of his second offensive on January 21st 1942, before his build up is complete and only three weeks after Cyrenaica had been lost. By February 4th 1942 the dispersed 8th Army is pushed back 300 miles to the 'Gazala line', just forward of Tobruk. A four month stalemate then ensues while both sides build up their strength and prepare to take the offensive. Rommel's force, now upgraded to 'Panzer Army Afrika', strikes first, launching the second stage of his 1942 offensive on May 26th.

Both armies were slightly larger than for the 'Crusader' battle and this time would be almost equal in strength in the air, as well as in ground forces. On paper the Panzer Army Afrika appears to be slightly inferior, with a strength of 113,000 troops including 50,000 Germans, 560 tanks of which 330 were German and 230 Italian, plus 77 in reserve, and 530 combat aircraft.[16] As before the 3 German divisions (of which 2 were panzer), were much more combat efficient than the 6 Italian (1 armored), or the opposing 6 larger British divisions (2 armored) and 4 independent brigades (2 armored). The comparative overall strength of 8th Army was 125,000 troops, 850 tanks plus 450 reserves, and 600 combat aircraft, all of even quality.

Rommel used a classic mobile attack around the 8th Army's open desert flank, and then defeated repeated counter attacks by its armored reserve using superior combined arms combat tactics, (tanks, anti-tank, infantry, artillery and air power). Tobruk was taken on June 21st 1942 and the Axis were then able to advance 300 miles, capturing almost half of Egypt, before being halted at El-Alamein on July 1st 1942. This was Rommel's greatest victory in the desert war, and it caused the 8th Army 75,000 casualties, including 33,000 captured at Tobruk, compared to Axis losses of 40,000.[17] Yet again, under Rommel's superior generalship, the German army had demonstrated its higher combat effectiveness against an opponent of somewhat superior strength. The Axis were now only 70 miles from Alexandria, but had fallen just short of a total victory in the North African campaign. Two perennial problems prevented that from happening. First was logistics, the gradual revival of Malta which the Axis had declined to invade in preference to the exploitation advance into Egypt. The sea supply problem was now exacerbated by the very long, 1,300 mile, land supply route along the coast from Tripoli to El-Alamein. Secondly, the British, increasingly backed by American military industrial production, were once again reinforcing the front faster and in greater numbers than the Axis. The stage was set for the final swing of the North African see-saw.

The fifth phase of the campaign begins with the first of the three battles of El-Alamein. The last of these is the most famous and the battle often referred to by that name. First Alamein begins on July 2nd and continues intermittently for most of that month. Only small forces were involved and both armies were exhausted after the rapid 300 mile movement from the Gazala-Tobruk battlefield. The Axis army was the more exhausted of the two, and it is this combined with supply shortages, especially fuel, that accounts for their defeat and halt. Casualties were 13,000 Allied and 7,000

Axis, but the Axis could less afford the loss, with much of their army still moving up from Libya and not yet at the front. The geography of the Alamein front was also unique in the North African campaign. Uniquely there was no desert flank due to the impassable terrain of the Qattara Depression, 40 miles south of the coast. The position couldn't be outflanked and was, along with the Nile or the Suez Canal, the best natural defensive position in the North African theatre.

Meanwhile as both armies recover during August, Churchill makes another command change, appointing Alexander as C-in-C Middle East, and Montgomery to command 8th Army itself. Second Alamein, also known as the Battle of Alam-Halfa, lasts from August 31st to September 7th 1942, and is Rommel's final attempt to break through before British strength becomes too great. The numerical balance with for example, 700 British tanks plus 250 in reserve, compared to 500 Axis tanks evenly divided between German and Italian, favors the Allies, but no more so than at Gazala-Tobruk or 'Crusader'.[18] The difference this time was the circumstances of the battle. The Axis, like in 'Crusader' but unlike Gazala-Tobruk, were short of supply, especially fuel. The restricted terrain, as noted, favored the defense, and it made Rommel's operational plan predictable. The Axis still attempted a mobile flanking attack, but attacked through, rather than around, the weaker southern part of the British front. However, Montgomery was ready for this, and countered with the classic strategy of 'refusal of flank'. He had organized a flank guard reserve defensive line along the Alam-Halfa ridge, at a 90 degree angle to the main front, which Rommel's attacking panzer force was unable to penetrate. Rommel realized within three days that he couldn't win, and withdrew to avoid heavy attritional losses.

The strategic initiative in the campaign now passed irretrievably to the British side. Montgomery resisted pressure from Churchill to launch a premature offensive, until he had built up for 7 weeks to gain an overwhelming superiority. At Third Alamein the divisional comparison of 4 German (including 2 panzer) and 8 Italian (2 armored), for a total of 12 Axis against 10 British Commonwealth (3 armored) divisions, gives an incomplete analysis. The Allied formations were larger and had better logistical support, and some Axis units were under strength. The total Allied troop strength was 230,000, against 104,000 Axis, of which 50,000 were German and 54,000 Italian.[19] Allied material superiority was even greater, with 1,029 tanks plus 1,200 reserves, against 521 of which 242 were German and 279 Italian, with only 22 in reserve. In artillery for which the battle is famed, 906 Allied field and medium guns were opposed by only 460 Axis ones, and the ammunition expenditure during the battle according to some accounts was as high as 10:1. In the air, Allied superiority was greater than ever, with 1,500 combat aircraft of which 1,200 were serviceable, compared to 350 serviceable Axis planes. The air sortie ratio was also a similar 4:1 in the Allies favor. The British thus had a greater overall numerical advantage than ever before, with ratios ranging between two and four to one, and even greater at the point of attack. The Axis did have the advantage of being entrenched in a defensive position protected by a strong minefield and the German half of their army retained its combat effectiveness advantage. However, this wasn't enough to outweigh the now crushing numerical imbalance in all categories, and the Allied logistical advantage.

The battle opened on October 23rd and consisted of a well planned and methodical set piece offensive on the northern coastal sector of the line. It was basically a battle of attrition, that ended 12 days later in a British victory when Axis material and logistical resources became exhausted. Allied losses were heavy with 13,500 killed and wounded and 432 tanks destroyed. However, Axis losses were irreplaceable with 25,000 killed and wounded, 30,000 prisoners and 450 tanks. This was the largest and most decisive battle in the campaign. The Axis loss was so large, both absolutely and proportionate to the size of both armies, that they had to abandon Egypt and Libya, and retreat 1,400 miles to the Tunisian border, reached on February 1st 1943. The pendulum had swung for the last time in North Africa. There would be no Axis comeback from Alamein.

The Allied victory at Alamein on November 4th 1942 was complemented by a complete change in their favor of the strategic situation in the Western Mediterranean as well. On November 8th 1942, only 4 days after Alamein, the Allies, initially mostly American ground units protected by predominantly British naval forces, launched operation 'Torch', the invasion of Vichy French North Africa. Landings were made at Casablanca on the Atlantic coast of Morocco, and inside the Mediterranean at Oran and Algiers in Algeria. After a brief resistance the French changed sides and joined the Allies. Hitler responded by eliminating the Vichy regime in France itself and rushing German reinforcements by air and sea to Tunisia. This action could only delay the inevitable Axis defeat in Africa. Yet the delay was rather longer than the Allies expected. It was six months after Alamein and 'Torch', on May 13th 1943, before the Axis forces in Tunisia surrendered. The renamed 'Army Group Afrika' was finally defeated by a rather methodical Allied pincer offensive by 8th Army from the east, and the ex-'Torch' 1st Army from the west.

The Axis had suddenly made their greatest effort in North Africa right at the end. In the Tunisian campaign the Axis Army Group Afrika, consisting of the reinforcing 5th Panzer Army and the remains of Rommel's Panzer Army Afrika, reached a size of almost 250,000 men, of which 130,000 were German and the rest Italians.[20] There were 8 German divisions (including 4 panzer), and 7 Italian (1 armored) by then, all under strength of course and poorly supplied. However, the Axis had been able to ship 500 replacement German tanks to Tunisia, mostly in November and December 1942.[21]

The German force it should be noted was therefore twice the size of Rommel's Afrika Korps earlier in 1942, when a campaign victory seemed to be within reach. Moreover the Tunisian build up occurred under even more adverse logistical conditions than before, due to a gathering Allied sea and air superiority around the Axis supply route across the Sicilian narrows. The effort is a pointer to what could have been possible earlier, had Axis strategic priorities in the Mediterranean been different. In the event it was all too late and of no avail, against the two armies of the Allied 18th Army Group which in March 1943 comprised 500,000 men and 1,800 tanks, in 20 full strength divisions.[22] In the air the Allies had 2,500 combat aircraft compared to 500 German and 450 Italian. By the end of 1942 the British had finally achieved permanent naval superiority as well, thus preventing any 'Axis Dunkirk', for their army group trapped in Tunisia. It was the largest victory on land for the Western Allies up to that point in the war.

The North African campaign is therefore not a simple matter of Axis rise and fall. The different phases of the 'see-saw' show that both sides had opportunities and possible chances for overall victory in the theatre earlier than was historically the case. There were three general reasons that account for the eventual Allied victory in the campaign. First, the Allies maintained a grand and operational strategic focus and priority on the region better than the Axis did. Both sides made strategy errors as we have seen. However, overall, the Mediterranean was a priority for Britain, where as for Germany it was generally subordinate to the Russian campaign. Secondly, the British seemed to understand the interdependence of the naval and land campaigns better, and their actions reflected this. The Axis failure to even attempt to capture Malta was a major strategic error by them in this context. Thirdly, in the end superior Allied production, combined with the decisions to prioritize its deployment to the Mediterranean theatre, eventually gave them overwhelming superiority on land, at sea and in the air. Rommel's superior leadership and the continuing German quality edge on land was insufficient to counter these Allied advantages indefinitely, and the Italian's proved to be less efficient than their opponents. It could, however, have been very different.

Axis Strategic Opportunities in the Mediterranean

The key to success in the Mediterranean for the Axis, was for the Germans to make the region a strategic priority, and then to maintain that priority with the objective of comprehensively weakening Britain and its Empire. The best opportunity for this was in 1940-41, prior to the involvement of Russia and the USA in the war. There was also a secondary opportunity during 1942. Admiral Raeder and the OKM were the main proponents of a German Mediterranean strategy in 1940-41, as an alternative to invading Russia. Raeder's plan was to seize control of both exits to the Mediterranean at Gibraltar and Suez. This would close the Mediterranean to British shipping, thus severing the so called 'lifeline of the empire' to India and the Far East. Once Gibraltar was seized the advance might continue down the Atlantic coast of Africa, optimistically even to Dakar at the continent's western tip. With the cooperation of Spain and Portugal, air and submarine bases would be established in the Canaries, Azores and Cape Verde islands. This would then facilitate operations for the ongoing Battle of the Atlantic against Britain and help deter the USA from entering the war. Similarly the capture of Suez would be exploited by advances into Palestine and Syria. This would bring the Axis up to Turkey's southern border, thus pressurizing it to move into the Axis diplomatic orbit. The Axis forces, in the Levant by then, would also be in a position to advance towards the oilfields of Iraq and even Persia.

There was also support for such a strategy from the German Foreign Ministry which would prepare the necessary diplomatic groundwork. The Nazi-Soviet Pact was still in place at this time, and the Tripartite Pact between Germany, Italy and Japan had just been signed in September 1940. These agreements were planned to be the precursors to a more grandiose Europe-Asian alliance, between the three Axis great powers and Russia. Within this overall grand alliance, there would be a smaller but important Mediterranean component consisting of Italy, Spain and Vichy France. Goering, as well as some strategists within the OKW, had similar plans, but with one very important difference. These leaders, who were politically much closer to Hitler than either the Navy or Foreign Ministry, saw the Mediterranean strategy as an interim one, prior to 'Barbarossa' the invasion of Russia, not a complete alternative to it. One practical difference would be the limited time for Mediterranean operations, given that 'Barbarossa' was planned to start in May or June 1941. The other problem would be limited resources, and of course, the conflict of priorities and eventually the subordination of any Mediterranean strategy to 'Barbarossa'.

As we have seen a much slimmed down, primarily defensive strategy, that was limited to the objective of preventing Italy's collapse, and late to start and subordinate to 'Barbarossa', was the historical option. That strategy lost the Mediterranean War for the Axis and 'Barbarossa', without defeating Britain first, might have lost the war as a whole for them. Once the Battle of Britain had been lost and 'Sealion' postponed, a comprehensive Mediterranean strategy, combined with continued pressure in the Atlantic, probably a slimmed down 'Blitz' and defiantly no 'Barbarossa', was possibly the best strategy for the Axis in 1940-41. The questions that remain are how practical would it have been? How far would it have got? Finally, what would have been the likely consequences?

Gibraltar was vital because of its strategic position. The Germans had a detailed military plan to capture it, operation 'Felix'. The plan was to open the Spanish frontier to German forces on January 10th 1941 and to launch the attack on Gibraltar on February 8th.[23] The problem was that Franco's Spain wasn't prepared to enter the war on the Axis side at this time. Spain demanded, deliberately excessive, supplies of armaments and raw materials that Germany couldn't meet, and territorial compensation from Vichy France of Morocco and Oran, as well as Gibraltar itself. The real issue however, was that Spain feared Britain, and wasn't convinced that Axis victory was a certainty, due to Italy's lack of military progress and then defeats in the second half of 1940. Axis control of Suez was one of Franco's conditions for Spain's entry into the war.

Germany and Italy could have been far more persistent and effective in their diplomacy with Spain, and combined this with invasions against Egypt and Malta, thus easing Spanish concerns. The Axis only required the use of Spanish territory and air bases in order to attack Gibraltar, which could have been granted without Spain entering the war itself. The risk for Spain would then have been a possible declaration of war by Britain. Alternatively the Axis could have negotiated, from a position of strength, with an occupied France, for the transit through and the use of bases in French North Africa. This French option, without Spain, would have made the military operation itself more difficult, but Gibraltar was well within air range of French Morocco, which would at least have allowed them to make Gibraltar useless as a British naval and air base. Finally, since Spain and Vichy France were rivals, even the implied threat of favor to one or the other, would have given the Germans diplomatic leverage in order to acquire the necessary bases.

In North Africa the decision to deploy the Afrika Korps was made with Fuhrer 'Directive 22' on January 11th 1941. The first troops arrived at Tripoli on February 15th and Rommel's first offensive, with only the 21st Panzer Division present, began on March 24th 1941. It took three months to deploy the entire Afrika Korps of two panzer and one light divisions, completing in May 1941. The decision could have been made at any time after the fall of France in June 1940, advancing this timetable by up to six months. Rommel, characteristically, could then have begun his first offensive in September 1940, providing the armored spearhead to the initial Italian advance at that time. At the very latest the decision should have been made in October 1940, once the outcome of the Battle of Britain was known. Such a timetable would have had several advantages. The Italian disaster due to Wavell's offensive, which started in December 1940, when 130,000 men and 9 divisions were lost, would have been avoided. With the Afrika Korps involved early, and the Italian 10th Army still operational, the Axis would have had overwhelming superiority, in numbers, German combat effectiveness, and leadership. With only 2 or 3 British divisions, including only one armored and weak air power at this time, Egypt would have fallen. Not even the defensive advantages of the Alamein position would have been enough to balance such multiple Axis advantages.

Returning to the Gibraltar situation, an early Axis success in Egypt would have influenced Franco to cooperate as required. Once the Axis had access to Spanish bases there can be little doubt that 'Felix' would have succeeded as well.[24] The forces assigned and available for 'Felix' included the Luftwaffe's Fliegerkorps VIII, consisting of about 350 combat aircraft, of which about 240 were the Ju 87 'Stuka' dive bombers, especially useful against ships. There was a specialized 'siege train' of 50 heavy batteries of artillery, including super heavy (i.e. battleship size) weapons, such as railway guns, and huge mortars specially designed for use against fortifications. These weapons were actually used successfully in 1942 to capture the Russian naval fortress of Sevastopol in the Crimea. The final assault on Gibraltar itself would have used a division of elite mountain troops and other specialized units. It would have been an epic battle in Britain's military history, but given the odds and circumstances, could only have had one outcome. Gibraltar, its modest garrison of about 10,000 men, isolated from naval and air support, would have fallen. Had Britain made a naval relief attempt, it would only have exposed valuable ships to German air power in adverse circumstances. British air support, except for any vulnerable aircraft carriers, would have been zero. Gibraltar's airfield was easily within range of any Axis artillery in Spain and would have been inoperable. Finally, the planned German 'Felix' expedition contained 2 panzer and 3 motorized divisions, one each of which would have deployed into Spanish Morocco, ready to advance if necessary down the Atlantic coast of French North Africa. The rest of this mobile force was a contingency one, to seize Lisbon in case Portugal, an old ally of Britain, swayed from neutrality.

With both exits to the Mediterranean secured by early 1941, Malta would have been untenable as well. As it was, Malta was neutralized by Fliegerkorps X between January and April 1941, which permitted the transfer of the Afrika Korps to Libya with few losses. There is no reason why this air operation couldn't have been brought forward by 2-3 months, immediately after the Battle of Britain. Malta could then have been invaded as well. Malta's garrison was weak, only 5,000 men when Italy entered the war and 10,000 men and 50 combat aircraft at the end of 1940. If the Axis had sequenced their invasion after the Gibraltar and Egypt operations, it would have been isolated as well. With Italian naval superiority from Gibraltar to Suez, there could have been no serious British help for Greece either. British controlled Cyprus would also have shared the fate of Malta, further facilitating a second stage offensive from Egypt into the Middle East proper. The Axis Balkan campaign could still have proceeded unchanged, and simultaneous, with these other Mediterranean operations. Or alternatively Hitler might have restrained Mussolini from the Greek adventure altogether, had he had prior warning, which historically he didn't.

Either way, the fate of Greece, in grand strategic terms, would have made no difference to the rest of the plan, except that absent British intervention in Crete, the airborne forces would have been available for other more promising targets such as Malta, Cyprus or Suez. Finally, the Luftwaffe with a total of 3,500 combat aircraft on all fronts by the turn of 1940-41, would have had ample strength for the extra Mediterranean operations. About one extra Luftflotten, up to 1,000 extra combat aircraft, would have been required, including the Fliegerkorps VIII for Gibraltar, and say one extra fliegerkorps for Rommel. The extra fliegerkorps would mean that the actual deployment of Fliegerkorps X wouldn't have been divided between two targets: Malta and Egypt. Overall, a comprehensive Mediterranean strategy after the Battle of Britain, would have required about half of the Luftwaffe. The other half would have remained in Western Europe, to keep pressure on the British economy, and to support the Kriegsmarine in the Battle of the Atlantic.

There was a second, though lesser, strategic opportunity for the Axis to dominate the Mediterranean in 1942. The main difference was that the Axis was at war with Russia by this time and the eastern front had resource priority. Even so, as we have seen, they did transfer Fliegerkorps II from the Russian front to the Mediterranean in early 1942, doubling German air strength in the Sicily area to about 600 combat aircraft. This force was able to neutralize Malta as a threat to Rommel's supply lines from January to May 1942 inclusive. Resources were tighter in 1942 than in 1940-41, and more so in air forces than ground forces. With only 3-4 divisions (including 2 panzer) in the Afrika Korps, out of an all front total of about 230 (25 panzer), Rommel was still able to launch his second and strongest offensive that year. Reinforcements could have been made available, as they were after Alamein for the Tunisian campaign. These would have doubled the size of the Afrika Korps in early 1942 instead. The problem was logistics, and Malta.

Supply was a recurring problem and a potential limiting factor on increasing the size of Rommel's forces. At the start of the campaign in October 1940, an investigative mission by German General Thoma concluded that, in addition to the Italians, 4 panzer divisions was the maximum German force that could be maintained in North Africa and also the minimum for success. The Italian force was at its peak in 1940 with 14 divisions and 236,000 men. As we have seen, Wavell's initial offensive quickly destroyed most of these and they never fully recovered. In 1942 the Italians averaged 8 small divisions: 2 armoured, 1 motorized, and 5 infantry; only 54,000 troops, plus 92,000 largely non-combat forces scattered all the way back to Tripoli. The Italian divisions in North Africa were only half the size of their German counterparts and required only 100 tons of supply per day for combat operations, compared to 300 tons for German panzer and 200 tons for infantry divisions.[25]

Until Tunisia, Rommel's Afrika Korps didn't even reach Thoma's maximum. From May 1941 it contained 3 divisions (15th and 21st Panzer and 90th Light), reinforced by the 164th Infantry just prior to Alamein in August 1942, only 50,000 troops in all. The Luftwaffe had 12,000 men and between 350 and 530 combat aircraft through 1942. A generous 500 tons for the air forces, gives a total daily supply requirement for the combined German-Italian forces in 1941-42 of 2,500 tons, and 3,000 tons for Thoma's maximum. In addition to this, it has been estimated that 30-50% of the fuel was wasted in transit between Tripoli and the front. The daily fuel requirement was 400-500 tons; 38% of the supply of the mechanized divisions.[26] Even at the higher estimate, when the supply line was at its longest between Tripoli and Alamein, this adds 500 tons (100 tons per panzer division), giving a requirement for the actual Alamein force of 3,000 tons per day, and 3,500 tons for Thoma's maximum capability.

What was the Axis supply capacity for the North African campaign? On average, over the entire campaign between June 1940 and May 1943, 203,000 tons per quarter, or 2,200 tons per day were landed. The maximum ever dispatched, prior to shipping losses, was 300,000 tons, or 3,300 tons per day; and the minimum landed, after losses, was 150,000 tons, or 1,600 tons per day.[27] Comparing this with the 3,000 tons per day maximum requirement shows that the logistic situation was tight, and pertinently, the variation between acute shortages such as during the 'Crusader' and Alamein battles, but also modest surplus, such as for Rommel's 1941 and 1942 offensives. Allied interdiction, especially from Malta accounts for much of the variation.

However, Axis capacities were actually greater than this. Only a portion of the shipping available was used to supply North Africa. Most wastefully, over 1940-43, 7,055 ships sailed in convoys to Greece, to which a land route was available, compared to 4,030 ships to Africa. Libyan port capacity was also more than sufficient. Tripoli, the main supply port, handled the maximum 3,300 tons per day ever received. Its actual capacity was greater still. In February 1943, under Allied control, and only a month after its capture and Axis demolitions, it handled up to 6,300 tons per day.[28] In addition Benghazi, control of which varied, had a capacity of 2,700 tons; reduced by Allied bombing to 700-800 tons. Similarly, Allied interdiction reduced Tobruk from its 1-2,000 ton capacity to 600 tons. Therefore, even after reduction due to Allied bombing and interdiction, Axis daily port capacity was at least 3,300 tons for Tripoli alone, 4,000 tons including Benghazi, and 4,600 tons while Tobruk was controlled as well. The absolute maximum for all three would be 10-11,000 tons per day, 6,300 tons for Tripoli alone.

Finally, more trucks were needed for the land supply route beyond Tripoli; the estimates vary between 3,500 and 8,000.[29] This isn't trivial, but it wasn't a huge number either. There were 10,000 trucks in Panzerarmee already. About 120,000 trucks were used for the French 1940 campaign and twice that for 'Barbarossa'. German production was over 50,000 and Italian about 17,000 per year. Overall numbers, of trucks, tanks, divisions or whatever weren't the problem. Even an enhanced Axis North African campaign, was relatively small compared to the war overall, or to 'Barbarossa', or even passive garrisons in France and elsewhere. Only small reductions and transfers, whatever the category, from these larger theatres would be needed to double Rommel's force.

The capability to supply a double strength Afrika Korps, 6-8 panzer or motorized divisions, plus the existing Italian force was there. Three extra panzer and one motorised division would need 1,100 tons per day, plus at most 400 tons of extra fuel to cover road transit wastage. When combined with the existing 3,000 tons per day maximum need, the total is 4,500 tons at most. Reallocating shipping from the Greek route alone could have doubled and nearly trebled the average 2,200 tons per day received. Libyan port capacity, even Tripoli alone, was enough. Invading Malta and increasing the Luftwaffe as previously discussed would have seriously reduced Allied interdiction, further increasing Axis supply margins. If Egypt was captured, a repaired Alexandria, a port larger than Tripoli, and the RN forced from the Mediterranean, would have solved all problems. It was a matter of decision not capability.

The Axis had prepared two operational plans relevant for a 1942 Mediterranean strategy, 'Hercules' and 'Orient'. Operation 'Hercules' was a plan for the invasion of Malta, which was prepared in April 1942 with the required forces largely in place.[30] There was a huge air armada of 1,500 combat aircraft, of which 650 were German, and 850 Italian, plus 300 German transport planes. One German and two Italian airborne divisions and 5 Italian seaborne invasion divisions would have been involved, i.e. about 80,000 combat troops, and the Italian fleet still had naval superiority in the central Mediterranean at this time. Given that the Malta garrison consisted of only 30-35,000 men of all services, 4 infantry brigades, almost no air force, and was short of supply due to the intensive air bombardment between February and May 1942, then the Axis invasion would have had a very good chance of succeeding.

The reason it wasn't carried out was that after the Battle of Gazala-Tobruk (May 26th-June 21st 1942), Rommel, authorized by Hitler, immediately advanced towards Suez instead. There wasn't enough air power to carry out both the Malta and Suez invasions at the same time. They could only be done sequentially, which was the original plan. The rather opportunistic change of plan was a mistake. The originally planned sequence: Tobruk – Malta – Suez, would have given the Axis better results. Malta should have been invaded first, and then taking advantage of the improved logistical situation, extra ground forces, plus much of the air power from Sicily, sent to reinforce Rommel for an advance on Suez. With Malta secured, adequate logistics and the reinforced Afrika Korps and its air power doubled in size, the Axis would have had superiority at Alamein until about November 1942 and equality thereafter. As we have seen from the historical battles, a German force that was adequately supplied, with its combat effectiveness advantage, and Rommel, tended to win even against double their own numbers or near equality if the Italians are included. With equal or superior numbers of Germans alone, they would have had an excellent chance of advancing as far as Suez.

Operation 'Orient' was a strategic plan prepared in July 1941, for the Axis invasion of the Middle East in late 1941 or 1942.[31] This plan assumed that Russia would have been defeated by the end of 1941, which wasn't the case. Nevertheless it is worth considering as the basis of a possible Axis Middle East strategy modified for the circumstances of 1941 or 1942. 'Orient' was to consist of a three pronged offensive. First, from the Caucasus, a panzer corps would drive southward through Persia. Second, from Bulgaria, if Turkey were acquiescent, an army of 10 divisions, 5 of them armored or motorized, would traverse Anatolia into Syria and Iraq. If Turkey resisted double that strength would be required. Thirdly, with the Allies stretched on the northern fronts, the Axis army in North Africa would advance on Cairo. The Axis were fully aware, as Raeder pointed out to Hitler in February 1942 and elsewhere, that the ultimate objectives and keys to British power in the Middle East, were the supply ports of Suez and Basra.

Churchill himself considered that if they had so chosen, the Axis could have spared the necessary forces to make Britain's position untenable.[32] However 'Orient' or a variant of it, would have been a more difficult operation than 'Felix', 'Hercules', or an advance to Suez. The German 1942 offensive in Russia was directed against the Caucasus and appeared to renew the threat of a pincer attack against the Middle East. The 'Orient' assumption that the Caucasus part of the operation would be successful, or that Russia would collapse overall, is too large and problematic to deal with here in the context of Middle Eastern strategy alone. Even if this precondition was in place, and it applies only to 1942, and not 1940-41, the Persian part of the offensive alone would have had to cover 600 miles to the Persian Gulf at Abadan and Basra. The Zagros Mountains and logistical problems would have put the panzer corps at a disadvantage.

An advance through Turkey would have similar problems of distance and logistics. Moreover the diplomatic task of getting Turkey to allow the transit of Axis forces, would have been much harder than with Spain or Vichy France in relation to Gibraltar. Turkey was strongly neutral and not pro-Axis. It wouldn't have yielded diplomatically unless Russia had collapsed, or an Axis advance from Egypt via Palestine and Syria had reached its southern border, placing Turkey in an impossible situation. If the Axis had got as far as Syria via the southern route, they wouldn't need Turkish territory anyway to advance on Basra. An Axis invasion of Turkey wouldn't have been an easy option either. The resources of 20 divisions, half of them mobile, plus a superior air component, would only have been available while Russia was neutral or had been defeated. The Turkey variant was part of Goering's plan in 1940-41, before 'Barbarossa'. Turkey was no push over militarily. In 1939 it had a peacetime army of 195,000 in 20 divisions, expanding on mobilization to 1 million men and 50 divisions, albeit infantry based and not well equipped. World War One had shown what tough fighters the Turks were. With the defensible water lines of the Bosporus and Dardanelles, a large territory with difficult mountainous terrain, poor logistics, and long distances to the Iraqi border, it might have been difficult and time consuming for even the Axis 'blitzkrieg' to conquer it. But not impossible, the German 'blitzkrieg', using a similar sized force over difficult terrain, but a smaller territory, had conquered Yugoslavia and Greece in three weeks.

Thus both northern pincers of any 'Orient' plan were more difficult than it first appears. In 1941 any Caucasus-Persian operation was impossible while Russia was neutral. Stalin would never have agreed to Axis forces transiting his territory. The transit by diplomacy variant of the Turkish option in 1941 was almost impossible as well. Britain, and Russia which wanted the Turkish straits for itself, would have backed Turkish diplomatic resistance. An Axis military option against Turkey in 1941, absent 'Barbarossa', would have worked, eventually, but it would have been difficult. In 1942 with Russia in the war and undefeated, both the northern military pincers of 'Orient' would have been near impossible, and strict Turkish neutrality would have prevented the transit option. The northern pincers of 'Orient' were thus more of a threat than a reality for the British Middle East, certainly once Russia was in the war and still fighting. Even so the British still had to, and historically did, guard against this threat. The British forces in the Middle East were always split and dispersed; they couldn't just send everything to the North African front.

That leaves the southern offensive from Suez to Basra to consider. Logistics and distance would have been problems and limiting factors for both sides. It is 900 miles as the crow flies from Suez to Basra, across an inhospitable inland desert. The more realistic route of Suez, Palestine, Syria, Baghdad and Basra, is about 1,100 miles. Which ever side was closer to their sea supply bases; Basra and the Persian Gulf for Britain; Suez, Alexandria, and then the Palestine-Lebanon ports for the Axis; would have had a logistical advantage. Rommel himself stated to Halder, C-of-S of OKH, in the spring of 1942, that he would need two extra panzer corps for any new offensive beyond Suez. In total this would mean a double strength Afrika Korps of up to 8 mobile divisions, of which 4 or more would be panzer divisions. The Italians would add about the same number of divisions, over half of which were infantry, their actual 1942 pre-Alamein army. This gives an Axis force for the Egyptian pincer of 'Orient' in 1941 or 1942, of about the same size as 'Army Group Afrika' reached with the maximum effort in Tunisia in early 1943. The total troop strength would have been about 200-250,000, half of them German, with around 600 German and 250 Italian tanks. The air component would have been larger for a 1941 offensive (no 'Barbarossa'). It could have still been one or two Fliegerkorps strong, about 300-650 combat aircraft in 1942, with the activation and timing of a 1942 'Felix' (Gibraltar) being the variable factor.

In early 1941 Britain and the Commonwealth-Empire had only 6 divisions including one armored in all of the Middle East, and 3 divisions in Kenya, 280,000 men in all, including scattered garrisons and non-combat forces. Even without considering that Italian East Africa was still unconquered and that there was unrest in Iraq and a pro-Axis Vichy French Syria, the balance of combat forces would have been heavily against Britain. The Axis could probably have reached Basra in 1941, thus eliminating the British Empire in the Middle East. The later they attempted 'Orient' however, then the greater would be the British build up, with a shift in the likely outcome. By early 1942 Britain had 635,000 men and 16 divisions in the Mediterranean theatre overall. Even assuming an even heavier defeat than historically was the case, at Gazala-Tobruk, and then the loss of Egypt and the Suez sea supply route, which would have weakened this force, the balance would have been more even. Palestine and Lebanon would probably have been lost, but as the logistic balance changed due to lengthening Axis, and shortening Allied land supply lines, a stalemate might have been reached somewhere in Syria or Iraq. Britain could still have held on in late 1942, but only just.

Overall then, Britain would have had great difficulty in defending against such a comprehensive Axis, and especially German, Mediterranean strategy, particularly in 1940-41, and even in 1942. The Germans had easily enough ground and air forces to implement such a strategy in 1940-41, and with shorter distances, could have deployed the extra forces to the Mediterranean faster than Britain. In 1942 even with Russia in the war, the capture of Malta, Egypt and Gibraltar would still have been possible. In contrast Britain had almost no extra resources too send. The Mediterranean theatre was the strategic priority for Britain anyway after 'Sealion's' postponement. Their actual historical deployment in the theatre overall, was the maximum that the British Commonwealth-Empire could have achieved. The likely results outlined above couldn't be prevented by any British counter strategy. The actual strategy, apart from the mistaken intervention in Greece, was the best Britain had, and it wouldn't have been enough. Britain could only, perhaps, have held on and responded on the extreme periphery of the theatre.

In the Atlantic, Britain did have contingency plans and a small expeditionary force of 5,000 troops ready to seize the Spanish Canary Islands. There is no doubt that Churchill would have responded in this way had Spain entered the war, or even allowed the Axis to attack Gibraltar from its territory. Whether the lesser, Axis 'transit option', would have meant a full state of war between Britain and Spain is not certain. There were similar British plans to counter Axis attempts to gain bases or control of the Portuguese Azores and Cape Verde Islands. Britain would have had the advantage in these operations, because of the maritime environment. Only the Canaries would have been within range of Axis air power, and even that would have required an extended advance along the African Atlantic coast, through French Morocco, which would have brought political complications.

In the Middle East the Axis could have advanced as far as Suez in either 1940-41, or 1942. In 1941 they had a good chance or reaching Basra as well, and a complete victory in the theatre. The British would have been pushed back as far as the Sudan, supplied via the Red Sea. The only bright spot for the Allies in these Axis Mediterranean scenarios is that Italian East Africa might still have fallen on the historical schedule. At these points, as the Axis reached the limits of their logistical capacity, and the strategic and economic value of further targets diminished, a point of balance would have eventually been reached. However, it would have been a point of balance, far more favorable to the Axis than the historical situation.

Consequences for the Wider War

Continuing the alternative Axis strategies considered above first. Such a comprehensive Axis strategy would have secured Italy from defeat while Britain alone was in the war, and perhaps indefinitely or until or if Germany was defeated. The historical German objective for its Mediterranean intervention, i.e. saving Italy, would therefore have succeeded better than was actually the case. With the Mediterranean and North Africa from Gibraltar to Suez under Axis control, it would have been much more difficult for the Allies even in 1943-45. Operation 'Torch' would have been near impossible, or at least a very slow advance starting in far away Morocco. In the Middle East it would have been a very long way back from Suez or Basra. Italy would have been as secure defensively, as it was possible to be.

Britain would certainly have been heavily damaged in many ways by such an Axis strategy, much more so than historically. The vital strategic choke points of Gibraltar, Malta, and Suez would have been lost. The Axis would have control of the small Sinai oilfield, and perhaps the larger ones at Kirkuk in Iraq, and even Persian Abadan. There is no doubt that Britain would have fought to the end, against the odds, in this important theatre, with many national interests at stake. Its armed forces losses would almost certainly have been heavier than historically, and extra naval losses especially, would have affected the next stage of the war. The psychological effect on morale at all levels, of a series of defeats, even disasters, in the Mediterranean would also have hurt Britain. Another psychological result would have been to encourage unrest in Britain's colonies, from Egypt to India, further stretching its military resources. Churchill himself was the foremost advocate of a strong British Mediterranean strategy, so defeats here might even have weakened his political position, although hardly fatally. The 'lifeline of the empire' through the Mediterranean would have been lost, but the much longer 'lifeline' round South Africa would have remained intact. This sea line of communication (SLOC) to South Africa would however, have become more vulnerable to Axis attack in the Atlantic near Gibraltar. Axis, including Italian, submarines, air forces and surface raiders, could have reinforced the Battle of the Atlantic in that area.

However, even these multiple losses and set backs in the Mediterranean, on their own, would probably not have forced a British surrender. This is because Britain's industrial and armaments production capacity and the Atlantic lifeline to North America would still have been largely intact. Britain could have continued the war. Still, assuming the Axis had conquered the Mediterranean in the six months of the winter of 1940 and the spring of 1941, they would have enhanced strategic flexibility for the next stage of the war. With a continuing 'Britain first' policy, a renewed attempt at 'Sealion', starting sometime between May and September 1941 inclusive, would have been the optimum strategy.

The considerations for such a 'Second Battle of Britain' would have been similar to our analysis of 1940, but with some new factors. Britain would have had the period since the Battle of Britain in 1940 to improve its defenses, balanced against the likely heavy losses suffered in Mediterranean operations. However, with control of Gibraltar and an extra eight months to plan and prepare, increase their air forces and build proper landing craft, the Axis would also have been stronger than in 1940. The Italian fleet could potentially have been redeployed via a captured Gibraltar, to the French Atlantic ports, under Luftwaffe protection. The crucial balance in naval forces would still have favored Britain against the combined, near full strength, German and Italian fleets, but not as much as before. In May 1941 the Axis would have had up to 4 German and 5 Italian battleships in total, compared to 16 British capital ships, with similar ratios in cruisers and destroyers. This is assuming there were no adverse and extra British naval losses in an interim Mediterranean campaign. We think there would have been, and the naval situation in 1941 wouldn't have been as favorable to Britain as historically. Evan a two to one ratio would have been a major change from the massive British naval advantage in September 1940,[33] and the Axis would still have had superior air power. Under these circumstances a 1941 'Sealion' would have had a higher chance of success than in 1940, perhaps greater than even. Such an operation, facilitated by the previous Mediterranean strategy, would have been the decisive one, with the outcome of the war at stake.

Any Axis Mediterranean strategy starting directly after the Battle of Britain in 1940 would have been completed well before the entry of the USA into the war in December 1941. Roosevelt was committed to support Britain by increasing measures, short of war, from about August 1940. There is no reason to think that the heavy British defeats envisaged in an Axis Mediterranean strategy would either speed, or slow, the American policy. Roosevelt proceeded with his policy as fast as was politically possible in his judgment. We must recall that even the damage and loss of USN destroyers in the undeclared involvement in the Battle of the Atlantic, before Pearl Harbor, didn't lead to a US declaration of war on Germany and Italy. In the end it was the European Axis that declared war on the USA, making Roosevelt's domestic political task easier.

A more likely change involving the USA would have been in strategy after it entered the war, assuming Britain survived that long. In the actual war the US military especially were only reluctant converts to involvement in the Mediterranean theatre. Operation 'Torch' in 1942 was a result of several factors: British prominence in Allied strategy that year; the relatively easier practicability of 'Torch' compared to any early invasion of France; opportunism, since North Africa was the only active land front at the time; and finally Roosevelt's political aim of getting the US into action in Europe that year. Roosevelt wanted to target Germany first; where as the American public's priority was vengeance against Japan for Pearl Harbor. Had the British position in the Mediterranean been demolished, even as late as 1942, all of the above arguments for a 'Torch' strategy, bar Roosevelt's political one, would have been negated. Still, this is a consideration for Allied strategy in 1943-45, not Axis strategy in 1940-42. It is sufficient to say that even for the USA, the Mediterranean option would have been much more difficult, even impossible, with Gibraltar and Suez lost.

Axis victory in the Mediterranean would have influenced the stance of the minor neutral states in their favor. Vichy France's change of sides, from Axis to Allied in November 1942, would have been delayed or prevented. Again this would have made 'Torch' more difficult and less likely and indeed the two events were interdependent. Spain, already pro-Axis, and influenced by even interim Axis success such as at Suez or Malta would have moved even closer to the Axis. It was very reluctant to declare war though and still might not have done so. A neutral Spain, giving the Axis transit to Gibraltar, and a trade conduit to South America, would actually have been better for them than its formal entry into the war. Even the strongly neutral stance of Turkey would have been pressured by increasing Axis success in the eastern Mediterranean. The most dangerous consequence of this would have been for Russia, and the emergence of a new threat to the Caucasus and its vital oilfields.

The Axis military strategic and diplomatic position towards Russia would eventually have been enhanced by success in the Mediterranean and especially the Middle East. The Axis would have had enhanced flexibility for either of their two basic grand strategic options. The first of these was to attempt to bring Russia into the Axis alliance proper, the German Foreign Ministry option previously outlined. The alternative strategy was the invasion or Russia, 'Barbarossa'. A defeated or weaker than historical Britain would have placed an even larger military burden on Russia than was actually the case. Even the implied threat of 'Barbarossa' under these circumstances would have pushed Russia towards the Axis diplomatically, or as a minimum kept it within the Nazi-Soviet Pact of 1939. The closing of the

Mediterranean would also have undermined the strategic value for Russia of the traditional objective of control over the Bosporus and the Dardanelles. Strategically, if the Axis had captured Iraq, or gained access to Turkish territory, then the 'Barbarossa' option would have threatened Russia on two fronts. A second, medium sized front could have been opened, posing a direct and immediate threat to Russia's Caucasian oilfields.

There could have been some benefits in the shorter term for Russia however. In general any increased Axis strategic focus on the Mediterranean, meant a lesser immediate focus against Russia. A 1940-41 Axis Mediterranean option, while Russia was neutral, would likely have been part of a 'Britain first' strategy. Whether Britain had been defeated by a follow up 1941 'Sealion' or not, it would at least have delayed the threat of 'Barbarossa' until 1942. Russia would have gained valuable time to prepare for war. If Britain had collapsed of course, any 1942 'Barbarossa', if and when it did occur, would eventually have been worse for Russia fighting alone. Theoretically the Axis might have aimed for a historical 1941 'Barbarossa' even after a temporary diversion against Gibraltar, Malta and Suez. That would have been risky in terms of the timetable. As it was, some historians consider the Balkan campaign delayed 'Barbarossa' by up to six vital weeks anyway. If anything had gone wrong, the Axis might have found the Mediterranean campaign achieving a momentum of its own, and dragging on into middle 1941, delaying or weakening 'Barbarossa'.

The affect of a 1942 Axis Mediterranean option, with Russia already in the war, is easier to calculate. It would have benefited Russia, but not by much. There were 19 panzer and 16 motorized divisions in Russia and 3 panzer divisions in France in mid-1942. Thus some of the extra reinforcements for Rommel, over and above the historical ones, would have come from the eastern front, and some from France. This would have only slightly weakened the German 1942 offensive against Russia. The size of the likely extra redeployment, about 4 mobile divisions (2-3 panzer), was limited by the logistic capacity of North Africa. This size of force would have likely made the vital difference for Rommel's small army, but was small by eastern front standards.

A comprehensive Axis Mediterranean strategy in 1940-41, as outlined here, would certainly have altered the course of World War Two. In that sense the theatre can be considered a decisive one. However, the important qualification to this assessment is that, on its own, such a strategic option wouldn't have forced Britain to surrender, and therefore immediately altered the outcome of the war. The strategy, if successful, which we think would have been very probable as discussed, would however, have created favorable conditions for the next stage of the war for the Axis. It could have been followed by a renewed attempt at operation 'Sealion' in spring or summer 1941, with more favorable odds for the Axis than in 1940. The USA and Russia were both still neutral at that point, so if successful, a 1941 'Sealion' would have ended the war at that time. Unless that is, the Axis then renewed it by launching 'Barbarossa' against an isolated Russia in 1942. They didn't have to do that; they could have simply continued the Nazi-Soviet Pact of 1939 instead.

A 1942 Mediterranean option by the Axis, with Russia and the USA already in the war, would still have been possible, but more difficult. This strategic option, still capturing Malta, Egypt and possibly Gibraltar, would also have significantly altered the course of the war. Italy would have been strongly protected from the historical British-USA Mediterranean counter offensives of 1943-45. However, the Axis 1942 option, wouldn't have led to an immediate overall Axis victory either. An extension of the war or a strategic stalemate in 1943-44, is the best that they might have achieved. A follow up 'Sealion' was impossible in 1943 once the USA was in the action. In any case, the Russian campaign meant that the Axis wouldn't be able to spare forces for 'Sealion', no matter what happened in the Mediterranean. Russia's position in 1942-43 would have been about the same as the historical one. On the one hand a few extra German forces in North Africa would have, very slightly, reduced their eastern front army. On the other hand the Axis might have reached the Middle East from Egypt, and threatened the Caucasus from there. Even if the Axis had got this far, the survival of Russia would still have been determined more by the much vaster battles, or else strategy changes, on the eastern front itself. Again the verdict is that a 1942 Axis Mediterranean strategy, would have improved their overall position compared to the historical situation. However on its own, it wouldn't have won the war for the Axis.

Let us return now to the historical campaign and draw some final conclusions. For Britain, the Mediterranean was the only theatre where there were active land fronts with any chance of success while fighting alone. It is not true to say that there were no British victories on land before the (3rd) Battle of Alamein. Wavell's offensive, 'Crusader', the conquest of Italian East Africa, Vichy Syria and the Iraqi revolt; are the cases in point. However, Alamein is the only battle in this theatre that can be ranked as a 'decisive' battle of World War Two. It was a 'turning point' battle that marks the maximum extent of Axis territorial expansion in the region. It initiated the Axis decline, saved the Suez Canal, and heralded 'Torch' only four days later. Alamein was the start of the long road back for the Western Allies. It was also psychologically important, boosting the morale of a war weary Britain, and added to Axis woes, coinciding with the much larger defeat at Stalingrad. The Mediterranean campaigns of the Western Allies, primarily Britain, didn't alter the course of the rest of the war in 1940-

42; they were about the only strategy that they could pursue before 1943. However, just as with the potential for Axis strategy in the region, the decisive nature of the historical campaigns has to be clarified. Allied victory in the Mediterranean led to the defeat of Italy in 1943. It didn't win the war overall, against Germany, and probably wasn't the most decisive component of overall victory either. But that is another story, for Allied strategy in 1943 and beyond. Let us turn now, to possibly the most decisive campaign of the war in Europe, 'Barbarossa'.

Notes to Chapter 3

1. Bauer, WW2 Vol 8, p 757.
2. Churchill, Vol 3, p 491.
3. On oil production, see Ellis, WW2 Databook, tables 76,81,82,83, and 84, p 274-276.
4. Dupuy, Encyclopedia of Military History, p 1152. Totals include ships completed in 1940.
5. Churchill, Vol 2, see map on p 389, for position in June 1940.
6. Ellis, WW2 Databook, footnote to table 30, p 239.
7. Hart, Hist of 2WW, p 116-117. Bauer, WW2 Vol 3, p 264.
8. Dupuy, Encyclopedia of Military History, p 1168 and 1172-73. For this and what follows on the Wavell offensive.
9. ibid, p 1168.
10. Hart, Hist of 2WW, p 128-129.
11. John Keegan (Ed), The Times Atlas of the Second World War, Guild Publishing, London, 1989, p 80.
12. Ellis, Brute Force, p 263.
13. Hart, Hist of 2WW, p 191.
14. ibid. p 207.
15. Churchill, Vol 3, p 698 gives January 1941 position. Vol 3, p 707 for June 1941. Hart, Hist of 2WW, p 280 gives figure for February 1942.
16. Hart, Hist of 2WW, p 281 gives comparisons. Ellis, Brute Force, p 263 gives tank strengths.
17. Dupuy, Encyclopedia of Military History, p 1186.
18. Ellis, Brute Force, table on p 263 for comparisons of tank strengths in various North African battles.
19. For these and following Alamein statistics, see Bauer, WW2 Vol 10 p 924, Hart. Hist of 2WW, p 310-311, and Ellis, Brute Force, p 263. There is slight variation between sources. The lowest calculation, presumably combat forces only, is 195,000 Allied and 80,000 Axis.
20. Hart, Hist of 2WW p 451 gives a comparison of Axis Army Group Afrika strength from various sources including Churchill, Eisenhower and Alexander. Hart himself suggests 170-180,000 which is rather lower than most of the other estimates around the 240-250,000 level. Even so it

doesn't alter the fact that the late Axis effort in early 1943 doubled its strength compared to pre-Alamein.

21. Ellis, <u>Brute Force</u>, p 304 fn.

22. Hart, <u>Hist of 2WW</u> p 431 fn. The Allies had a 2:1 troop superiority, and far more in equipment holdings and supplies by the end of the Tunisian campaign.

23. Bauer, <u>WW2 Vol 4</u>, pp 311-312 for details on operation 'Felix'.

24. ibid. p 311-312.

25. Ellis, <u>Brute Force</u>, pp 50, 251, 258.

26. ibid. p257. Dunnigan J.F. <u>How to Make War</u>, Arms and Armour, London, 1982, p310, gives 38% of German supply is fuel. Author's calculations from this confirms Ellis' 400 tons of fuel per day minimum for the front.

27. Ellis, <u>Brute Force</u>, p251 and table 45.

28. Churchill, <u>Vol 4</u>, pp 658-660, gives 6,000 tons for Tripoli and Benghazi combined, and 6,300 tons for Tripoli in February 1943, enough for Montgomery's 160,000 troops, which was larger than Panzerarmee, totally motorised, and supply wasteful. Ellis, <u>Brute Force</u>, p 258 on Benghazi.

29. Ellis, <u>Brute Force</u>, pp 259-60.

30. Bauer. <u>Vol 8</u>, p 764-68.

31. Churchill, <u>Vol 3</u>, p 490-491.

32. ibid. p 491. See opening quote to this chapter.

33. See Chapter 2 for details of Axis naval weakness in 1940. The German fleet was, temporarily, depleted due to losses and damage in the Norwegian campaign. The Italian fleet was confined to the Mediterranean due to British control of Gibraltar and Suez. Table 1, Chapter 2, shows the size of the British, German and French fleets at the outbreak of war, and in 1940 for Italy. In August 1940 the Germans added the *Bismarck* to their fleet, and the *Tirpitz* in February 1941, giving a total of 4 battleships, plus the two pocket battleships *Sheer* and *Deutschland* which approximated to heavy cruisers in power. At Taranto in November 1940, the Italian battleship *Cavour* was sunk permanently, but the *Littorio* and *Duilio* were raised and repaired by April and May 1941 respectively, leaving Italy 5 battleships by then. Britain started the war with 15 battleships, losing the *Royal Oak* in 1939, but completing the *King George V* and the *Prince of Wales* for a global total of 16 by May 1941. Two carriers had been lost and three completed since the outbreak of war, giving strength of 8 in May 1941.

CHAPTER 4

BARBAROSSA – MOSCOW 1941

'When Barbarossa begins the world will hold its breath'

Adolf Hitler

'You have only to kick in the door and the whole rotten structure will come crashing down'[1]

Adolf Hitler

Genesis: July 1940-June 1941.

The largest land area in the world, the longest and the deepest battle front ever, the largest army in the world, more tanks than all the rest of the world's armies combined; the greatest artillery in the world, the largest air force in the world, and the coldest climate in the world. So why did Germany break the first rule of strategy, and invade Russia?

There is no single answer. Only a combination of reasons can give an explanation for the most momentous decision of World War Two. Even then the explanation might not be satisfactory. It doesn't necessarily mean the decision was the correct one, or the only possible decision in the circumstances to achieve the objective of winning the war for the Axis. Some of the reasons for the German invasion of Russia are, at best, on the very edge of the concept of grand strategy.

These are the ideological causes, primarily Hitler and the Nazi's long term political objective to destroy what they considered to be the polar opposite ideology of Soviet Communism. On its own however, this is far from sufficient. Even if Hitler and the Nazi's were determined, no matter what, to attack Soviet Russia, it doesn't explain the timing, or the fact that they were able to restrain themselves until 1941, having done business with Stalin with the non-aggression treaty of 1939. Next is 'Lebensraum', the idea that the growing German population needed to expand its territorial control in order to survive and compete with other nations. The only possible adjacent area of expansion was considered to be the more sparsely populated countries to the east of Germany, rather than the industrial states to the west such as Britain and France.

This is closely linked to the need for control of large raw material reserves, as the basis for a future superpower status, and competition at the very top rank of world power, such as with the USA. Again, Russia with its vast resources fitted the theory. This is partly ideological and partly geopolitical. In particular the geopolitical theories of Mackinder and Haushofer, which broadly stated that control of Eastern Europe and Eurasia (i.e. Russia), meant control of the 'heartland' of the 'continental world island' (Europe, Russia, Asia, and sometimes Africa is included). This would give them control of the greatest resources in the world, which would be the basis for world power. Geopolitics with its inclusion of power and resources, brings us within the bounds of grand strategy, but is still rather long term.

To complete the explanation we must consider the more immediate political and strategic situation after the fall of France, set against the background of the more ideological factors just outlined. The most immediate of these strategic factors was that the attempt to conquer Britain by a direct attack, operation 'Sealion', had just been defeated in September 1940. Germany was forced to seek a more indirect alternative to bring the war to a victorious conclusion. At the same time they were puzzled by Britain's decision to continue from what many Germans, and others, considered to be a hopeless military situation. The answer, they concluded, was that Britain was hoping for or already planning a secret alliance with the USA or Soviet Russia, or both. It was estimated that the USA would be ready to enter the war on Britain's side in 1942.[2] There wasn't much the Axis could do to stop that, other than not to provoke the Americans and attempt to conclude the war beforehand.

Russia was different, already well armed, and despite the 1939 treaty with Germany, it could potentially join the war at any time. Even if it didn't do so immediately, the threat would remain and grow more dangerous if and when the Americans came into the war in 1942. In the meantime Germany was seen as increasingly dependent on Russian raw materials, especially oil, that were being supplied under the terms of the 1939 treaty. If the war dragged on, then Germany would be open to blackmail from Russia, and Stalin might become the diplomatic 'arbiter of Europe', even without a declaration of war. The Germans were alarmed by Russian actions even during and after the French campaign. In mid-June 1940 Russia annexed outright the three Baltic States, which had been made protectorates in October 1939, within its sphere of influence according to the Nazi-Soviet Pact. This was followed between June 28th and July 3rd 1940 with the annexing of Bessarabia and Northern Bukovina from Romania. Bukovina was outside the terms of the Nazi-Soviet Pact, and this move brought Russia very close to the oilfields of Romania which were vital for Germany.

The Russian action did however push Romania into alliance with the Axis. Over the following months, there was a period of diplomatic and security competition in the Balkans between the Axis powers, primarily Germany, and Russia. Foreign Minister Molotov's visit to Berlin in November 1940 failed to resolve these issues, and henceforth both sides saw each other as an increasing threat. Hungary, Romania and Bulgaria became Axis allies, while Yugoslavia after a military coup on March 27th 1941, attempted to ally with Soviet Russia. The German invasion of Yugoslavia and Greece in April 1941, as we have seen, finally secured the Balkan flank for the Axis powers.

When 'Barbarossa' began the Axis powers claimed that they were merely defending themselves against a Soviet threat. For 45 years during the Cold War, this was dismissed by both the Soviet communists and the Western powers as the propaganda of a discredited and defeated enemy dictatorship. It is now known, since the collapse of Soviet Russia in 1989-91, that the situation was far more ambiguous. There was indeed serious strategic and political planning by Soviet Russia to take the offensive against the European Axis powers. There are known to have been at least four offensive operational strategic plans, completed in July 1940 and on September 18th 1940, March 11th 1941, and May 15th 1941.[3] Historians and strategists cannot agree though on the implications of this. It could be that this was merely prudent contingency planning within the context of the Soviet offensive military doctrine of the time. However, it could also mean that a pre-emptive operational offensive, or even a preventive war, was being prepared by the Soviet Union. A pre-emptive offensive is when you are certain you are about to be attacked, and you attack first in order to gain a military advantage. A preventive war is more political and long term, designed to counter a threat that you are certain is coming, but only eventually. There is also dispute about the timing of a possible Soviet offensive or declaration of war, varying from July 6th 1941, only two weeks after 'Barbarossa', to as late as 1942.[4]

Not only were there war plans, but Russia had begun preliminary mobilization at the outbreak of war in September 1939, and this was accelerated from February 1941 onwards. Russia's armed forces expanded from 1,943,000 men in September 1939 to 4,629,000 in June 1941.[5] The armed forces were also deployed operationally in a manner consistent with the aforementioned military plans. That is to say, they were deploying for offensive operations, not defensive ones, and many formations were in forward positions. The Germans suspected all this in general terms only during 1940. By March and April 1941 they had proper intelligence about the Soviet offensive oriented deployment, but only in the western most of the Russian military districts and the buffer zones acquired under the 1939 Nazi-Soviet Pact. All these reasons, especially in combination, contributed to the Axis threat perception from Soviet Russia.

Hitler, the OKW, and the leaders of the army and air force at the OKH and OKL respectively, considered that the 'Russian problem', as they termed it, would have to be dealt with in 1941, in a short 'blitzkrieg' campaign, prior to any American intervention in 1942. If successful, Germany and the European Axis powers, with the resources of a conquered Russia under their control, would be ready to face the future Anglo-American alliance on more equal terms. The destruction of Soviet Russia as an independent great power would also remove a potential threat to Japan in East Asia. Japan, allied with the European Axis by the Tripartite Treaty in September 1940 and with its back free from Russia, could then expand in the Pacific and draw part of the American war effort away from Europe and the Atlantic. This was grand strategy on the largest scale, with high risks, and world domination at stake. Incredible as it seems, 'Barbarossa' the most gigantic and costly land war in history, wasn't planned as a strategic objective just in itself. It was designed to be an 'interim solution', prior to a renewed attempt to conquer Britain and to stalemate the USA in 1942.[6]

Serious planning for 'Barbarossa' began at two German leadership conferences on July 21st and 31st 1940, i.e. before the outcome of the Battle of Britain was known. At the second of these conferences, Hitler announced his intention to attack Soviet Russia in the spring of 1941. Military planning by the armed forces and army high commands, OKW and OKH respectively, then commenced and continued until 'Fuhrer Directive 21, Case Barbarossa' was completed on December 18th 1940. The overall strategic objective was 'to crush Russia in one rapid campaign even before the conclusion of the war with England'.[7] The provisional starting date was May 15th 1941, and the 'short campaign' was expected to last five months, prior to the Russian winter i.e. ending by October 15th 1941. During the planning period however, it remained unclear what overall German grand strategic priorities were. Various Mediterranean plans, such as for the Gibraltar, North African and Balkan operations, and Raeder's wider scheme, were ongoing, simultaneous with preparations for 'Barbarossa'. Historians and strategists even disagree on whether December 18th or sometime later, was the final irrevocable decision date to proceed. The decision was Hitler's, but he was broadly supported by the OKH, Goering and the OKL, and most of the OKW. The OKM (navy) and the Foreign Ministry preferred the wider Mediterranean options.

There was also disagreement about the operational strategy for 'Barbarossa', in particular over the sequencing and priorities between objectives, including Moscow, Leningrad, Kiev and the Ukraine. In the end a compromise was reached on operational objectives, but the problems would return, perhaps fatally, once the campaign was under way. Hitler and his military commanders did agree on the first stage objective, which was to destroy the Russian armies by encirclement battles west of the Dnieper-Dvina line. Then the disputes arose and the following compromises were made for stage two. Army Group Center, the strongest of three army groups, would halt and half its forces would swing north to support Army Group North attacking Leningrad. The other half of Army Group Center would remain in readiness to move south into Ukraine. Army Group South would then occupy Ukraine. When Leningrad and Ukraine had been secured, the advance on Moscow would resume.[8] The final objective was the line of the Volga, from Astrakhan on the Caspian Sea to Gorky, and then northwards to Archangel on the Arctic Ocean. The OKH wanted Moscow to be the primary territorial objective. This was in line with the central strategic principle that there should be one priority objective chosen, that must be maintained, and if taken will win the war outright. The problem was that in Russia's special case, because of its size, it wasn't certain that the fall of Moscow, or anywhere else, would end the war. It hadn't worked for Napoleon in 1812 after all.

The Balance of Forces: Could Russia be Defeated?

Napoleon, despite capturing and briefly controlling Moscow, failed spectacularly in his 1812 Russian campaign. He lost almost his entire strongest army group and failure in Russia was the single most important factor in the collapse of his empire in 1814-15. With the benefit of hindsight, Napoleon's defeat is often used in comparison with Hitler's, and the two events combined are used as evidence to claim that it was, or is, impossible to defeat Russia. It is certainly strong evidence; however it is not completely conclusive. Russia has been defeated in war, at least in a limited way, and the Russian state has also collapsed. In 1854-55 Russia was defeated in the Crimean War by a British, French and Turkish alliance. In 1904-05 it lost the Russo-Japanese War. In both these cases the defeats were followed by unfavorable peace treaties for Russia. Yet these were limited wars, and defeat wasn't a matter of survival for either side.

World War One is a much more significant case; because of its timing only 25 years previous to 'Barbarossa'; Russia's primary adversary, which was Germany; and its scale, which was 'total war' like World War Two. Russia was defeated by Germany, albeit allied to Austria Hungary and Turkey. The Russian state collapsed in revolution in late 1917, under the strain of total war and defeat. At the Treaty of Brest-Litovsk in March 1918, Russia lost Ukraine, White Russia (Belarus), The Baltic States, Finland and the Trans-Caucasus. These lost territories had a total population of 56 million out of the Russian Empire's 171 million in 1914, and economic, industrial and resource losses were of a similar proportion. Also significant was that Germany achieved this victory while fighting a two front war. At the peak in October 1917, Germany deployed 99 divisions against Russia (plus 40 Austro-Hungarian and about 12 Turkish in the Caucasus), compared to 141 divisions on the western front against Britain and France. These were pertinent comparisons for the German military and political leaders in 1940-41, most of who had served in World War One, and some of them on the eastern front. Having defeated France in 1940, a formidable opponent for them in 1914-18; defeating Russia in a one front land war in 1941, wasn't considered the impossible military task that it seems today. The Axis leaders also believed, perhaps too readily, that the Soviet political system would collapse under the strain of war. We should however remind ourselves, with hindsight admittedly, that the Soviet political system was indeed vulnerable, as its collapse in 1989-91 showed.

Russia certainly had massive strengths, but it wasn't completely invincible as is often believed. Acquiring an accurate intelligence assessment of Russian power has also been a major problem historically. There has been a tendency, even by the professionals, to heavily overestimate or underestimate Russian power. Napoleon underestimated Russia. In the Crimean and Russo-Japanese wars, Russian power was overrated, as it was in World War One. In World War Two, Russian power was underestimated by both the Axis and the Western Allies. Finally, during the Cold War, Russia was, perhaps deliberately, overrated once more. Almost no analysts predicted the rapid collapse of the Soviet bloc in 1989-91; it was a major intelligence failure. With these caveats and difficulties in mind, let us now consider the military power available to both sides in June 1941.

The already mobilized German armed forces, the Wehrmacht, had a size of 7,234,000 personnel in June 1941. Of these 5,150,000 were ground forces in the army and Waffen SS: of which 3,950,000 were combat forces and 1,200,000 were in the replacement army. The ground combat forces were organized into 208 divisions, of which 21 were panzer, and 14 motorized. There were 5,262 tanks and 390 mobile assault guns, of which 3,332 tanks and 250 assault guns were deployed with the 19 panzer divisions on the eastern front.[9] The rest of the armor, except for about 250 tanks with the Afrika Korps, was in reserve for replacements, or used for training. Half of the tanks deployed in the east were the more powerful Panzer III and IV medium tanks, and the remainder light tanks. Total Luftwaffe operational combat aircraft strength was 3,451, of which 2,713 were on the eastern front.[10]

A total of 148 of the 208 divisions were deployed on the eastern front, including the OKH strategic reserve. Of the remainder there were 38 divisions in Western Europe, mostly in France; 12 divisions in Denmark and Norway, of which 5 in the Arctic would support the Finns against Russia; 7 divisions in the Balkans and 3 divisions, including 2 panzer with Rommel in North Africa. Thus about 75% of the ground and air force combat forces were deployed offensively on the eastern front for 'Barbarossa'. The other 25%, along with most of the navy, were containing Britain, in the henceforth secondary theatres of the Mediterranean and Western

Europe. The 'Barbarossa' invasion force was the largest ever, but only slightly larger than the concentration against France in 1940, and it was deployed on a 1,000 mile front from the Baltic to the Black Sea, twice the length of the western front in 1940. The deployment of forces between the three army groups on June 22nd 1941 was as follows.[11]

Army Group North:
16th and 18th Armies, 4th Panzer Group, with 29 divisions including 3 panzer and 3 motorized. Luftflotte 1 with 540 combat aircraft.

Army Group Center:
4th and 9th Armies, 2nd and 3rd Panzer Groups, with 50 divisions including 9 panzer and 6 motorized. Luftflotte 2 with 1,252 combat aircraft.

Army Group South:
6th, 11th and 17th Armies, 1st Panzer Group, with 41 divisions including 5 panzer and 3 motorized. Luftflotte 4 with 772 combat aircraft.

OKH reserves:
2nd Army, 28 divisions including 2 panzer and 2 motorized. C-in-C Luftwaffe with 51 combat aircraft.

Allied Forces:
Finland Front
The Finnish Army of 18 divisions, plus 5 German divisions in North Norway.
Luftflotte 5 with 98 combat aircraft.

Army Group South: Romanian Front
3rd and 4th Romanian Armies, with 14 division equivalents. 1 Hungarian and 3 Slovak divisions. 3 Italian divisions (from 7th August).

The total combat strength of the German eastern front army was about 3,150,000 plus about 530,000 from the Axis allied forces.[12] The German forces were at a peak of morale and combat efficiency, and their previous battles, and subsequent analysis, showed that they were superior in combat power and effectiveness to any army of equal size. It has been calculated that the German army, in and throughout both world wars, had a combat effectiveness superiority over the Western Allies of between 1.2 and 1.35 to 1. This means that every 100 Germans, when organized into combat units, was equivalent in their military capabilities in any given task, to 120 or 135 British, French or Americans. The German combat effectiveness advantage over Soviet Russia was 3.1 to 1 in 1941, 2.58 to 1 in 1943 and still 2 to 1 in 1944.[13] Of the Axis allies, the Finnish army which had held out in the Winter War of 1939-40 for four months, against a Russian army group that reached three times its own size, was nearly on a efficiency par with the Germans. The Romanian, and later the Hungarian and Italian divisions that served on the eastern front, were estimated by the OKH to have a combat power only half that of German divisions.[14]

From the statistical and order of battle outline above, the following should also be noted. The main striking force of the German army was the four panzer groups, operating in cooperation with the Luftwaffe. These would be renamed 'panzer armies' from October 1941, a more accurate designation, for each was more powerful than the infantry based all arms armies. However, there were only 19 panzer and 14 motorized infantry divisions, compared to 120 infantry divisions deployed for 'Barbarossa'. This proportion wouldn't change much for the rest of the war because German industry was insufficient to create a fully mechanized army, nor was there enough fuel for such a force either. Using the 'blitzkrieg' strategy, the mobile forces would create breakthroughs and spectacular exploitation movements and encirclements. However, the slower but more numerous infantry based formations, or more accurately 'all arms' units, were still needed to take and hold ground, and to complete the defeat of encircled and isolated enemy forces. Army Group Center with half of the mobile forces and air power, was both the strongest army group, and the axis of main effort for 'Barbarossa', targeted ultimately on Moscow. Finally it should be observed that even though an exceptional 75% concentration of effort was achieved on the eastern front, 'Barbarossa' could have been, albeit modestly, stronger still, if Britain had been forced from the war beforehand. That might have made a difference if the margins were tight.

'Barbarossa', not 'Overlord', was the largest invasion in history. However, the defending Russian forces were even larger. By the expedient of not demobilizing the time expired annual conscription classes from 1939 to 1941, the Russian armed forces had quietly expanded to 4,629,000 by June 1941. This was still only partial mobilization however. Within ten days of the start of 'Barbarossa' another 5 million reserves were mobilized, although not all were organized and deployed into units within that timescale of course.[15] The total number of trained men available including the June 1941 armed forces, and the previously trained reserve conscription classes from 1925 to 1938, was between 11 and 12 million. Equipment existed on a vast scale. The 24,000 Russian tanks outnumbered those of the combined armies of the rest of the world. The Red Air Force, with at least 15,000 combat aircraft overall, was the largest in the world. The best estimate, using post-1990 information, of the number of army divisions in June 1941, *prior* to full mobilization, is 303 including 61 armored, 31 motorized, and 198 infantry divisions.[16] About 25% of these 303 divisions were still in the process of mobilization and were under strength. The 1st Strategic Echelon that was immediately facing the Axis invasion, mostly west of the Dnieper-Dvina line and including forces facing Finland, consisted of about 3 million men, 12,000 tanks and 6,000 combat aircraft.[17] These were organized in 170 divisions, and deployed from north to south as shown below.[18]

1st Strategic Echelon

Northern Front (Leningrad M.D.)
7th, 14th and 23rd Armies with 21 divisions. 18 air regiments with c 700 combat aircraft.

North Western Front (Baltic M.D.)
8th and 11th Armies, III and XII Mechanized Corps with 25 divisions including 4 tank and 2 motorized. 13 air regiments with c 500 combat aircraft.

Western Front (Western M.D. [White Russia])
3rd, 4th, 10th and 13th Armies, VI, XI, XIV, XVII and XX Mechanized Corps with 44 divisions including 12 tank and 6 motorized. 21 air regiments with c 800 combat aircraft.

South West Front (Kiev M.D.)
5th, 6th, 12th and 26th Armies, IV, VIII, IX, XV, XVI, XIX, XXII, XXIV Mechanized Corps with 58 divisions including 16 tank and 8 motorized. 91 air regiments in the South West and South Fronts in total with c 4,000 combat aircraft.

South Front (Odessa M.D.)
9th and 18th Armies, II and XVIII Mechanized Corps with 22 divisions including 4 tank and 3 motorized. Unknown number of air regiments, included in the total of 91 above.

The 'Fronts' were the largest Russian combined service, army and air force wartime combat organizations, the equivalent of a western army group and were based on the peacetime military districts (M.D.). Air regiments contained 36 to 48 combat aircraft each, and these tactical air forces were organized in wartime into 'Air Armies' of varying size under the control of the Fronts.

Behind these forces of the 1st Strategic Echelon, which were deployed for the offensive, was the 2nd Strategic Echelon, assigned to the Stavka or Soviet Supreme Military Command. These 2nd Strategic Echelon forces were deployed behind the Dnieper and in May 1941 consisted of 47 divisions in the 22nd, 20th, 21st, 16th and 19th Armies, deployed on a north-south axis. This force was in the process of mobilization and expansion to about 80 divisions, and 28 divisions of it were in motion to reinforce the 1st Strategic Echelon when the war began. The Stavka also contained 21 air regiments, and there were another 53 air regiments elsewhere in European Russia including the air defense forces. The total air power in European Russia was 217 air regiments with 9,100 combat aircraft, with another 115 air regiments with 4,800 combat aircraft in the process of formation. It seems that on the outbreak of war that there were therefore 170 divisions in the 1st Strategic Echelon, up to 80 divisions in the 2nd Strategic Echelon, and about 50 divisions in the rest of Soviet Russia including 30 in the Far East facing Japanese controlled Manchuria.

It is clear from the above that the partially mobilized Russians were about equal in initial combat troop strength at the front to the already mobilized Axis, but that they had a massive numerical superiority in equipment. Russia was caught by the German attack in the middle of an ongoing mobilization, which if completed would have given it a large overall manpower and combat manpower superiority as well. The 303 division army, already 75% mobilized, and contrasted with the Germans 208 division army, was only an interim size. Full mobilization would have brought all the 303 divisions to full strength, which many were not in June 1941, and continued to expand the total force. Each division after deployment retained a cadre of officers in its base or mobilization camp. With these and newly mobilized reserves, from the 11 to 12 million trained men available, a new unit, the 'second formation' or 'invisible division' is then formed. It takes time of course for the new division to shake down and become a coherent military formation. It is also equipped from older mothballed and stored weaponry, which in 1941 was only enough to form infantry divisions, rather than tank or motorized ones. Of course the 'invisible divisions' were inferior in combat power to the existing ones, but they were there, or rather would appear unexpectedly over the course of the 1941 campaign, potentially doubling the size of the Russian army.

The other major consideration, derived from the Russian order of battle tabulation, is that they were deploying for a strategic offensive or a preemptive attack. The main Russian offensive was planned to be from the Kiev Military District, using their most powerful force, the South West Front, which was to advance into southern Poland and then swing to the right towards the 1939 German-Polish frontier. In contrast to the German concentration in the center, the Russians considered this southern front to be the most important. Unfortunately for Russia, the offensive operational deployment of the 1st Strategic Echelon, which hadn't properly completed its mobilization, made it vulnerable in the defensive battle that it would be forced to fight. Large offensive orientated forces of the Western and South Western Fronts were deployed in the Bialystok and Lvov salients respectively, which were vulnerable to attack. The Russian partial mobilization and offensive operational deployment, was therefore a major weakness for the Russians that partially offset their numerical superiority.

The other main weakness was in terms of quality. Most of the equipment was obsolete and the troops were unfamiliar with the small amounts of new weapons, such as the 967 T34 medium and 508 KV heavy tanks. These were technically superior to the best German tanks in 1941, but they constituted only a small part of the total Russian tank force. Training, organization, leadership and general efficiency were all greatly inferior to that of the Germans. Only 27% of the huge tank force was fully serviceable at any one time. The army had been purged by Stalin in 1937-38, with the loss of 25,000 officers and the debacle of the Winter War against Finland in 1939-40 had shown the world that it had not yet recovered.

They were also in the middle of a major reorganization, in particular the formation in 1940-41 of 30 large mechanized corps, each consisting of two tank and one motorized divisions. Each mechanized corps had an establishment strength of 36,000 troops and 1,030 tanks. There was barely enough armor available for all these, and on average they had only received 50% of their full complement of tanks when the war started. There were masses of artillery, but the 'mechanized' corps had only one third of their official allocation of motor transport. The 61 recently formed Russian tank and 31 motorized divisions, except for the few T34 and KV tanks available, were inferior in every other way, such as training, organization and mobility, to the 19 panzer and 14 motorized divisions of the Germans. Russian supply services including ammunition and fuel, as well as radio communication at strategic and tactical level, were also very inadequate.

The army reorganization, as well as mobilization, and the offensive deployment, were all still incomplete when 'Barbarossa' started. The Russians were attacked at just the wrong time, before they were ready and in vulnerable positions, by the vastly more experienced and combat ready Wehrmacht.

The Barbarossa Campaign: June-December 1941

June 22nd 1941 was another of those rare and decisive dates in history. The German led invasion of Soviet Russia altered the previous course of World War Two, and one way or another the campaign would be the single most important factor in determining its outcome in Europe. Much larger than the previous western campaigns we have covered; it will be treated as one campaign during 1941, but divided into phases, based on timing, geography, and operational strategic objectives. This is for analytical purposes and clarity. In practice the 'phases', like the relationship between individual battles and the campaign, were more seamless.

Phase one is alternatively referred to as the 'frontier battles', and is the German attempt to destroy the Red Army west of the Dnieper-Dvina line, up to a depth of between 200 and 300 miles. This was to be accomplished by a series of armored breakthroughs, exploitation movements and operational encirclements of the Russian armies. The ground offensives were supported by an initial 'counter air' offensive across the entire front by the Luftwaffe's three air fleets. Despite being outnumbered by over two to one in the forward areas alone, the Luftwaffe destroyed about 4,600 Russian aircraft in the first three days of Barbarossa. Unlike Britain in 1940, the Russians lacked radar and an effective air defense system. Consequently two thirds of their aircraft losses occurred on the ground. By July 12th the Red Air Force had lost 6,857 combat aircraft compared to Luftwaffe losses of only 550.[19] This meant that the Luftwaffe had achieved air superiority very early on and was to maintain it for the rest of the 1941 campaign and well into 1942. It was henceforth an important German advantage, allowing them to give fairly unhindered tactical air support to their ground forces, and to disrupt Russian ground counter attacks for most of this period. The Luftwaffe was stretched though by the extent of the Russian space that it had to cover. Moreover, it had problems redeploying behind the advance to new airfields for its relatively short ranged tactical air forces.

The most powerful German striking force was Bock's Army Group Center, containing two panzer groups, Hoth's 3rd on its left, and Guderian's 2nd on its right, each supported by an infantry army. This was deployed on a 280 mile sector of the front, between East Prussia and the Ukrainian border south of Brest-Litovsk. These faced the Soviet Western Front in White Russia. As we can see by comparing the orders of battle previously outlined, the two sides appeared to be evenly matched. However, the Russian formations were still mobilizing and were under strength when the invasion began. The much more combat effective German Army Group Center totaled 1,180,000 troops, 1,770 tanks, and 1,252 combat aircraft.[20] The Russian Western Front was deployed in an exposed salient around Bialystok. It numbered a relatively weak 647,000 troops, but an estimated 5,000 tanks and 800 aircraft.

The two panzer groups each supported by an infantry army attacked with strong localized combat superiority on both flanks of Western Front. Despite disorganized, but sometimes unexpectedly stubborn resistance, such as at Brest-Litovsk, they broke through and achieved a double encirclement of Western Front. The outermost pincer movement converged and captured the Front HQ at Minsk on June 28th. By July 10th Western Front was almost destroyed, in just 18 days, suffering 418,000 killed, wounded and mostly prisoner casualties. Material losses, including 4,800 tanks and 9,400 guns, were massive and almost total. The Russians did however attempt at least three, albeit brief, uncoordinated and badly organized counter attacks, with their six mechanized corps during these battles. They all failed, one attack losing 800 of 2,000 tanks committed, despite the Germans surprise at the quality of the few T34 and KV tanks involved. These encirclement battles of Bialystok and Minsk would be the template for future battles of this type. After completing the destruction of the Western Front in White Russia, Army Group Center advanced towards the 'land bridge', a 50 mile wide corridor between the rivers Dvina and Dnieper near Smolensk, on the road to Moscow. Here they had a new surprise, four and then six new Russian armies, from the 2nd Strategic Echelon and Stavka reserves, were blocking their path. Army Group Center had nevertheless advanced between 280 and 370 miles on this sector in only 18 days.

German progress in the north was almost as spectacular. Leeb's German Army Group North in East Prussia with 641,000 troops, 570 tanks and 540 combat aircraft, was superior in combat power to its opponent the Russian North Western Front.[21] North Western Front, defending the Baltic States on a 200 mile front, had an estimated 400,000 troops, 1,300 tanks and 500 combat aircraft.[22] With approximate overall numerical equality and all the previously noted German 'quality' or combat effectiveness advantages of training, organization, experience and leadership, there could be only one outcome. On the Baltic coast the German 18th Army advanced through Lithuania and captured Riga on July 2nd. Inland from this the 4th Panzer Group, supported by 16th Army, advanced even faster, breaching the Dvina line at Dvinsk on June 26th, after previously defeating a Russian mechanized corps counter attack that included 100 of the heavy KV tanks. On July 8th the 4th Panzer Group captured Pskov, at the southern tip of Lake Piepus, and one of its panzer corps then advanced northward, reaching the river Luga only 80 miles from Leningrad on July 13th. By this time, only three weeks into the campaign and assisted by anti-Soviet revolts, Lithuania, Latvia and about half of Estonia had fallen. The Russian North Western Front avoided mass encirclement by a rapid retreat of 250 to 280 miles, but still suffered 90,000 casualties and 1,000 tanks destroyed. German progress slowed though once they entered Russia proper, and the Soviets still held northern Estonia at the end of the 'frontier battle phase'.

To the south of the Pripyet Marshes, which formed a natural division of the eastern front into two zones, was Rundstedt's Army Group South. They faced the strong South Western and Southern Fronts and made relatively slower progress. The very long front here was itself divided into two by the eastern end of the Carpathian Mountains. In the northern sector, Kleist's 1st Panzer Group and the 6th and 17th Armies, had 797,000 men and 750 tanks, supported by Luftflotte 4's 772 combat aircraft.[23] These faced the South West Front, defending the huge 500 mile salient of Lvov, with

870,000 men in 4 armies and an estimated 5,000 tanks and 3,000 aircraft. Rundstedt's Army Group, led by Kleist's panzer group, advanced in a south-easterly direction towards Kiev, and then towards the great bend of the river Dnieper at Dnepropetrovsk. They wouldn't reach those objectives in this early phase, being delayed by a series of counter attacks by South West Front's mechanized corps (it had 8 of them) near Rovno. Nor were there any massive encirclements at this stage.

In Romania along the 300 mile southern sector of the front, there was only the German 11th Army of 175,000 men, plus the weaker Romanian 3rd and 4th Armies, but crucially no panzer or mobile forces. They were opposed by Southern Front's 320,000 men, and an estimated 1,300 tanks and 1,000 aircraft. The Axis were able to capture Bessarabia, the province that Russia had gained in the 1939 Pact, but without armor they couldn't form a southern pincer to trap South West Front's exposed salient around Lvov, in the extreme west of Ukraine. Even so, the more evenly balanced border battles in Ukraine, still cost the Russians 173,000 casualties, a massive 4,400 tanks and 1,200 combat aircraft, and a German advance of 180 to 200 miles by July 6th.[24]

Phase one of 'Barbarossa', the attempt to destroy the Russian army west of the Dvina-Dnieper line, which lasted less than 3 weeks, was a clear and massive Axis victory, but not yet a decisive one. The Russians had suffered a total of 680,000 casualties (killed, wounded, prisoners) compared to 92,000 Germans, in just three weeks, up to July 12th. The Axis had advanced between 180 and 370 miles in 18 days, depending on the sector. The Russian material losses were even more significant. These amounted to about 10,200 tanks and 6,800 combat aircraft, which was almost half the overall strength of 24,000 tanks and 15,000 aircraft throughout the Soviet Union in June 1941. Artillery and other types of equipment losses were of a similar proportion. The heavy equipment losses within the 1st Strategic Echelon on its own, which actually fought the frontier battles, were close to total. Nor could this heavy equipment, lost in just three weeks, be replaced quickly. Tank production for the entire year of 1941 was 6,590, and aircraft production was 15,735, including 12,377 combat types.[25] In terms of divisional formations the Germans, fairly accurately, assessed on July 8th that 89 out of 164 encountered had been destroyed, including 20 out of 29 [there were actually 36] tank divisions. The 1st Strategic Echelon's Western Front had been destroyed in the center of the line. On both flanks however, North Western Front, and South Western and Southern Fronts survived, although severely damaged. These flank army groups would be the, very controversial, objectives of phase two of 'Barbarossa'.

First though, Army Group Center would have to fight a new battle at Smolensk, against the 2nd Strategic Echelon and newly organized Stavka reserves that Zhukov had deployed there, blocking the route to Moscow. The Russians could replace their manpower losses out of the 5 million recently mobilized conscripts. German intelligence was aware of the Russian 1st Strategic Echelon, although not of the massive scale of heavy equipment. However, they vastly underestimated the extent of Russian reserves behind the Dnieper, and Russian mobilization and military production resources. The Germans had won the 'frontier battles' convincingly, but they had miscalculated that this would win the war for them.

The Battle of Smolensk began on July 10th, as 2nd and 3rd Panzer Groups from Army Group Center advanced to secure the 'land bridge', and to gain bridgeheads across the Dvina around Vitebsk on their left, and over the Dnieper on their right. Smolensk fell on July 15th, and new encirclements were created where the Russians lost 310,000 men, 2,500 tanks and 3,000 guns between July 18th and August 5th. However the intense fighting here, including the Timoshenko counter offensive, slowed and then contributed to the halting of the advance of Army Group Center. Logistical problems, due to the rapid 440 mile advance in 7 weeks over difficult country, had also contributed to a temporary halt of the two panzer groups by the start of August.

Meanwhile Army Group North's 4th Panzer Group was halted on July 24th at the river Luga to allow the infantry armies to catch up. It missed a possible opportunity to utilise a temporarily open road to Leningrad. By the time the advance resumed on August 8th, Russian reinforcements were blocking the gap. In the Ukraine, Army Group South had finally managed to encircle and capture 100,000 Russians along with 317 tanks and 858 guns at Uman, about 100 miles south of Kiev between August 2nd and 8th, a modest victory by 'Barbarossa' standards. They had now linked up with the Axis forces from Romania and were approaching Kiev. However, the Russian South Western and Southern Fronts, minus the massive equipment losses of the first phase, were still largely intact, although battered.

By the second week of August the stage was set for phase two of 'Barbarossa'. The strategic dispute between Hitler and the OKH's Brauchitsch and Halder, over the phase two operational objectives, now resurfaced. Hitler prevailed, with a series of directives between July 19th and August 12th, which broadly followed the original plan. This was a decisive time, and a major mistake, which might have cost him the campaign and the war. At this point Army Group Center, the strongest army group, had advanced further than the other two, forming a large salient around the Smolensk 'land bridge' area. The operational strategy was now to secure the flanking objectives of Leningrad and the Ukraine first, before resuming the advance on Moscow in the center. Army Group Center went over to the defensive, and was to remain so for two months until the start of October. Since 'Barbarossa' began they had advanced 440 miles in 7 weeks, and were only 200 miles from Moscow. Half of Hoth's 3rd Panzer Group was diverted from the center to help Army Group North, and Guderian's 2nd Panzer Group turned south, away from Moscow. Army Group North's advance on Leningrad resumed on August 8th. Novgorod fell on August 15th and Tallinn on August 28th, completing the conquest of Estonia. By 8th September they had advanced 100 miles in a month, a slower rate than before, to reach Lake Ladoga. This cut Leningrad's 452,000 troops and 3 million civilians off from the rest of Russia. However, they didn't attempt to take the city due to yet another change of strategy. Instead, the greatest siege in history had begun, it would last 900 days and almost one million would die.

On August 25th Guderian's 2nd Panzer Group, supported by 2nd Army, began its advance from Army Group Center's sector of the front. They advanced in a *southward* direction, forming the northern pincer of a gigantic encirclement of the Russian South West Front that was defending Kiev and the Ukraine. Army Group South's 1st Panzer Group led the advance from a bridgehead in the Dnieper bend at Kremenchug on September 11th, to form the southern pincer. Stalin had been alerted by his commanders of the danger. He refused to give up Kiev and Ukraine and allow a withdrawal from the obvious trap. The pincers closed 150 miles east of Kiev on September 16th. Kiev fell on the 19th and the largest battle so far ended on September 26th. It was a catastrophe for the Russian South West Front and elements of the neighboring Southern Front and newly formed Central Front. Their losses were about 700,000 including 665,000 prisoners, as well as 884 tanks and 3,714 guns. An entire Front, equivalent to an army group, and the strongest one at that, containing four armies, had been wiped out. Around 150,000 men escaped to the east, from which was later formed a new South West Front.[26] The conclusion of the Battle of Kiev marked the end of phase two of 'Barbarossa'. Kiev was a massive German victory, but it still wasn't decisive enough to end the war. It would be trumped by the largest battle of all: Moscow.

The third and final phase of 'Barbarossa' was the offensive against Moscow, codenamed 'Typhoon'. Operations on the flanks were secondary to 'Typhoon', but they didn't cease altogether. In the north there was stalemate. The siege of Leningrad was tightening, but the Germans had insufficient strength to seriously attack it, due to a transfer of forces back to Army Group Center for 'Typhoon'. In the Ukraine after the Battle of Kiev, Army Group South advanced eastwards against weakened opposition, its 6th Army capturing Kharkov on October 25th after a 5 day battle. Another 100,000 Russians were isolated and forced to surrender near the Sea of

Azov between October 10th and 18th. The front line finally stabilized at Rostov due to the autumn mud at the end of October. The Germans briefly held this important city, the 'gateway to the Caucasus' between November 21st and 30th, before a Russian counter offensive drove them out. On the Black Sea coast, the Russian garrison of Odessa, which had been under siege, was evacuated by sea between October 2nd and 16th. In the Crimea the Russians had a strong natural defensive position at the northern Perekop isthmus, and were able to hold against German attacks for a month between September 24th and October 28th. They then fell back to the fortress naval city of Sevastopol for another epic siege.

The start of 'Typhoon' had been further delayed from September 15th to October 2nd while the previous strategy of flank offensives against Leningrad and Kiev-Ukraine was completed. Without the phase two flanking strategy of course, 'Typhoon' could have started in mid-August, after the Smolensk 'land bridge' had been secured, saving six weeks or more. The 4th Panzer Army from Army Group North and Guderian's 2nd Panzer Army in the Ukraine were now transferred back to Army Group Center. Along with its 3rd Panzer Army they formed the mobile striking force for 'Typhoon'. The reinforced Army Group Center seemed an impressive force with up to 1,929,000 men, 1,000 tanks and 1,390 combat aircraft.[27] There were three panzer armies (2nd, 3rd and 4th) and three all arms armies (2nd, 4th and 9th) with a total of 78 divisions including 14 panzer and 8 motorized. They were supported now by two air fleets, Luftflotten I and II, the former having been transferred from Army Group North. Just over half of the overall eastern front strength and 75% of the armor and air power was assigned to 'Typhoon'.

However, after the wear and tear of three and a half months on the offensive, long supply lines, and overall casualties of 551,000 by October 1st, the German combat power had declined. By November the combat power of the infantry divisions averaged only 60% of normal, and the panzer divisions were down to 45-50% of normal effectiveness. Opposing 'Typhoon' were three Russian Fronts, Western, Bryansk and Reserve. At the start of October these contained 1,250,000 men, 990 tanks, 7,600 guns and 667 aircraft, organized into 15 armies with 95 divisions, which now had smaller official establishments due to the previous massive losses.[28] This accounted for 40% of the Red Army's forces on the front between the Baltic and the Black Sea. On the face of it this modest overall German numerical superiority, should on past performance, have meant a decisive victory.

At first it was the same old story. The offensive opened on October 2nd and two more huge encirclement battles at Vyazma and Bryansk were completed by October 14th and 25th respectively. It was even worse than Kiev, with Russian losses of about 300,000 dead and 700,000 prisoners, along with 830 tanks and 6,000 guns. Seven of the 15 armies and 64 of 95 divisions were destroyed. As the disorganized 250,000 survivors straggled back, the road to Moscow seemed open. The Red Army combat strength along the entire eastern front fell to its lowest ebb of 2.3 million at the start of November 1941. With 2.7 million men at the front, down from 3.2 million on June 22nd, the Wehrmacht now had a slight, if temporary, superiority. It was also a low point of the entire war politically and psychologically for Soviet Russia. On October 15th the government, although not Stalin himself, was evacuated to Kuybyshev on the Volga, 500 miles to the east. There were also signs of civil disorder in Moscow for a few days. Stalin even briefly considered a separate peace, offering the Germans the Baltic States, Belarus and Ukraine.

However, with winter approaching the Germans were in a race against time, and time usually wins most of its contests. First came the autumn mud, which brought the offensive to a halt between October 20th and November 15th. The Russians had a vital respite to organize 11 more armies from over 50 newly mobilized divisions. The thrice destroyed Western Front had been reconstituted once more on October 10th and Zhukov, Russia's best general, was to command it. Moscow was declared under siege, with its militia drafted into the army, and its civilians mobilized to dig fortifications. The Russians also had one final military card to play. Russia and Japan had signed a non aggression treaty back in April 1941. In the event this served them both well until 1945, while they each concentrated on other fronts. Even so, Russia couldn't completely trust Japan prior to Pearl Harbor. In September 1941 they acquired reliable intelligence that Japan was preparing to attack the Western Allies in the Pacific, rather than joining Germany in the war against them. They had a 30 division sized, well trained and equipped Front, defending Siberia against a possible Japanese attack from Manchuria. In October and November 1941 they were able to accelerate the ongoing transfer of over 15 divisions, with an eventual 1,700 tanks and 1,500 aircraft from Siberia to the Moscow area by the end of 1941.[29] With these measures and the continuing mobilization, the combat strength of the Russian army on the German front increased from its 2.3 million low point at the start of November, to 4.2 million by early December 1941.

The freezing of the autumn mud allowed the temporary resumption of the German offensive from November 15th to December 4th, involving an attempted encirclement of Moscow from the Kalinin and Tula areas, 100 miles north and south of the capital respectively. However, the German army had made no winter preparations and its combat power was falling fast along with the temperature. They got to within 25 miles of Moscow before the offensive ground to a halt, less 66,000 more casualties. On December 5th 1941 the Russians Moscow winter counter offensive began.

'Barbarossa' had failed, narrowly. It was another decisive turning point of the war, only two days before Pearl Harbor.

German Mistakes and Alternative Strategies

Total German casualties on the eastern front from June 22nd to December 31st 1941 were 831,000, of which 174,000 were killed and 36.000 missing, along with the destruction of 2,850 tanks and assault guns.[30] Russian losses in 1941 were much greater, at about 4 million including 3.2 million 'irre-coverable' i.e. killed and prisoners. Over 17,500 tanks were destroyed, with proportionate losses in other types of equipment. An attacking force that was initially numerically equal in troops and vastly inferior in equip-ment, had achieved a favorable loss ratio of at least 5 or 6 to 1. It had also won almost every major battle in the five month long campaign. So why did the 'Barbarossa' campaign fail? Was it due to German strategic mis-takes? Could the outcome have been different?

A fundamental reason for the failure of 'Barbarossa' in 1941 was that the Germans underestimated the sheer scale of their opponent and of the task that they were attempting. It was probably impossible to reach the line Archangel-Volga-Astrakhan, which was the 'Barbarossa' final objective, and to do so in only five months. That would have required an advance of 900 miles on all sectors from the June 1941 position. This of course is dir-ect and assuming there would be no strategic detours. As it was the actual advance was between 500 and 600 miles, to just short of the line Lenin-grad-Moscow-Rostov. This alone was quite an achievement, capturing 600,000 square miles of territory, containing 77 million of the 1941 popu-lation of 194 million. Russia had lost 62% of its pre-war coal production, 67-71% of its iron and steel, 60% of its aluminum, 47% of its grain and 41% of its railway network. All these were essential sinews of the Russian war capacity.[31] On average, nearly half of Russia's war capacity had been eliminated. Yet it simply wasn't enough. The other half survived, and rein-forced by a massive factory evacuation program from the lost areas, was enough to materially continue the war.

Similarly the massive losses inflicted on the Russian army were an im-pressive military achievement. They amounted to almost the entire June 1941 strength of the army and air forces in both manpower and equipment. In that sense the aim of eliminating the Russian army and air force had been achieved, but only it's starting strength. The Germans massively un-derestimated Russian reserves and mobilization capacity. Halder, the OKH's Chief of Staff, famously noted in mid-August 1941: 'We have un-derestimated Russia: we reckoned with 200 divisions, but now we have already identified 360'.[32] By December they had identified 400 divisions. Russia could mobilize new troops and divisions faster than the Germans could kill, capture or destroy them. To be fair that wasn't true of equipment losses, at least not in 1941, although it would be later on. By the end of 1941 the Russian army was larger in terms of manpower and formations than in June 1941, despite losses of 4 million men. There were 4.2 million men at the front in December 1941 in 328 divisions, compared to 3 million in 170 divisions in June 1941.[33] The overall size of the armed forces would have increased from 5 million to about 9 million.[34] Russia did lose its previous massive superiority in equipment though, with only 1,984 tanks and 3,688 combat aircraft at the front by December 1941.[35] On the plus side for Russia, this equipment was mostly new and of a higher quality than at the start. Repeatedly during the 1941 campaign, the Germans would encircle and destroy the Russian armies at the front, only to face fresh armies from the Russian reserves. These in turn would be destroyed in new battles, until eventually the Germans ran out of time, facing the October mud and finally, by December, the Russian winter.

Russian resistance might seem to have been largely ineffectual. However, they managed to inflict higher absolute and proportionate losses on the German army than the Western Allies did in France in 1940. Nor were the Russians permanently on the defensive in 1941. Their military doctrine was, and remained, an offensive doctrine not a defensive one. The idea that the Russians withdrew into the interior, to exhaust the Germans and draw them into a trap, and then launch the winter counter offensive is pure propaganda. Strategically such a plan, sacrificing 4 million men and almost half the nation's economic capacity, is totally unsound and could easily have gone disastrously wrong, turning into a rout. Instead the Russians counter attacked whenever they could. Indeed for most of September they were on the offensive against Army Group Center near Smolensk, while the Germans diverted to the flanks, especially Kiev. However, until winter no Russian counter attack or offensive succeeded. The best they achieved were temporary stalemates, such as on the Luga front near Leningrad, and at Smolensk.

Underestimating their Russian opponent was thus a major German mistake. It was a major intelligence failure in the planning stage, and could only have been countered by not launching 'Barbarossa' in the first place. Indeed Hitler himself stated, with hindsight, that he wouldn't have attacked Russia if he had been aware of its numerical strength that was apparent by August, after the initial huge captures of men and machines.[36] They couldn't correct this intelligence failure once the campaign started, other than by not repeating it.

However, the Germans could have altered the major, indeed fatal, strategic operational errors that occurred. There is, partly with hindsight, a general consensus among analysts, historians and strategists, that by far the most important of these was the decision after the capture of Smolensk to divert the offensive towards Kiev and away from Moscow. Army Group Center which had advanced 440 miles in 7 weeks and was only 200 miles from Moscow was placed on the defensive for nearly two months between August 5th and October 2nd. By the time 'Typhoon' was launched, and despite the subsequent huge victories at the battles of Vyazma and Bryansk, time had run out for the capture of Moscow before autumn mud and winter snow. Even without hindsight, all the better German higher commanders, including Brauchitsch and Halder at OKH, and Bock, Guderian and Hoth at Army Group Center, wanted to advance towards Moscow and not Kiev at this time.

To be sure after the rapid advance since June 22nd and the major encirclement battles of Minsk and Smolensk, the 2nd and 3rd Panzer Armies of Army Group Center needed time to rest and resupply for the second phase of 'Barbarossa'. However, it didn't require a two month halt. Between 10 and 21 days seems to be the consensus for the preparation time needed for an early 'Typhoon' offensive against Moscow. August 5th to 25th i.e. 20 days, was the actual gap between the completion of the Smolensk encirclements and the start, by Guderian's 2nd Panzer Army supported by 2nd Army, of the Kiev offensive. Even part of this delay was due to arguments over strategy. The Kiev offensive then took them 275 miles to the south, to complete the encirclement at Kiev by September 16th and the destruction of the pocket by the 26th. They then had to retrace some of their route to redeploy for the start of 'Typhoon' on October 2nd, a total detour of almost 600 miles.[37] In other words there was ample time for Army Group Center to regroup, prepare, and then launch 'Typhoon' on say August 25th, or slightly earlier, instead of diverting to Kiev. The 2nd Panzer Army had also actually 'advanced' a greater distance in the four week Kiev operation, than they were from Moscow in August. They would have had 5 or 6 extra weeks to advance 200 miles to Moscow in summer weather. This is in addition to the time actually allocated to 'Typhoon', in October, when the Russians lost one million men in the battles of Vyazma and Bryansk, and Army Group Center advanced to within 25 miles of Moscow anyway.

A 'Typhoon' offensive launched in August would likely have used only two rather than three panzer armies. Hoppner's 4th Panzer Army was still with Army Group North, operating against Leningrad during August. Even so, two almost full strength panzer armies in August would have been at least equal to the three half strength armies that attacked in October. They would still have had the option of redeploying 4th Panzer Army to support 'Typhoon', but at the cost, depending on the timing of the switch, to operations around Leningrad. Russia would also have had less time to mobilize reserve armies to block the path to Moscow. Certainly Russia was no stronger on this central sector in August and September, than they were in

October. At best they were equal, and probably slightly weaker. With the extra 5 or 6 weeks of summer weather, and given what actually happened at Vyazma-Bryansk and all the previous encirclement battles, the outcome of an early 'Typhoon' is clear.

The German Army Group Center would have captured or isolated Moscow in September or early October 1941, in two or more huge encirclement battles. Indeed, an earlier start to the actual 'Typhoon' plan would probably have brought the front 50 to 100 miles beyond Moscow before winter. Moreover, since Stalin would have refused for political and military reasons to retreat, like his decision at Kiev, the Russians would have taken huge casualties in the largest battles of the campaign. It would very likely have been even worse than the actual one million losses at Vyazma-Bryansk in October 1941. Militarily and strategically it is difficult to see how Moscow, and the Western, Bryansk and Reserve Fronts could have survived, were 'Typhoon' launched in August instead of October.

There would have been one military glimmer of hope for Russia though. In the early 'Typhoon' scenario, the Battle of Kiev wouldn't have taken place, at least not in September, and the over 750,000 strong South West Front would have survived, for a while anyway. In theory, part of this force would have had the option of counter attacking against the right flank of German Army Group Center as it advanced on Moscow. Still, it is inconceivable that the very professional OKH wouldn't have taken precautions against this; such as by forming a flank guard with one of Army Group Center's three all arms armies. The German all arms armies were excellent at defense, outside of the Russian winter anyway. They had defeated all Russian counter attacks before December 5th 1941. More importantly the Russian Fronts in Ukraine had been weakened in the earlier stages of 'Barbarossa' and had already lost their initial armor and air superiority. They were being pushed back by Rundstedt's Army Group South across the lower Dnieper during August. There seems no reason why this wouldn't have continued, although probably without an annihilating encirclement battle. Rundstedt's forces on their own were about equal in size to their opponent, and superior in combat effectiveness and mobility. They were strong enough to 'pin' the Russian forces in Ukraine by a continuing advance from the west. As a result the Russian forces here would have found it near impossible to redeploy in any strength for a counter offensive to the north. The more likely outcome in the Ukraine would have been mere survival for the Russians, and a slower advance by the Germans towards the Donbass industrial area and Rostov.

There were other German operational strategic errors, such as the halt at the river Luga in mid-July. However, it would have been very risky to advance directly on Leningrad from there, with only one panzer corps immediately available, and only half its ammunition supply. The prize was great, but the outcome of the alternative option is very uncertain. A valuable panzer corps could have been trapped and lost. Ironically there was another chance to capture Leningrad, in September, by a reinforced conventional attack. The Germans cancelled that attack in favor of a siege, and more importantly to switch forces back to the Moscow axis for 'Typhoon'. They just didn't quite have the strength to do everything at once. 'Phase two' operations had to be sequential, which, if they had stuck to one plan instead of kept switching, would still have given them Leningrad or Moscow. Moscow was the more important objective politically, economically and militarily. The Germans could also have taken more risks in many of the other battles by striking deeper and attempting even larger encirclements.[38] Yet none of these were clear cut opportunities, or as crucial, or on the scale, as the two month diversion from Moscow.

What the Germans could have changed, indeed it was inexcusable not to have done so, was to anticipate and prepare for winter. The timing of the autumn mud season in the second half of October was fairly predictable. The effect was to almost halt all wheeled transport operations, and this was underestimated. There is not much they could have done about that, other than anticipate and plan for it by going over to the defensive. It would have been impossible to switch to the more expensive, heavier and difficult to produce tracked machines. There were about 3,500 tanks and 1,000 half track APCs initially deployed for 'Barbarossa', compared to up to 600,000 wheeled vehicles including those in supply units for all purpose use.

Winter preparations could have been made though, as was done in 1942 and in subsequent years. Indeed the Luftwaffe and the Waffen SS did so in 1941. It was the Heer that was negligent. Even without the miscalculation that the campaign would only last five months; it was known that there would have been forces in Russia during the winter, even if only on garrison duty. German army, but not Russian, lubricants failed at -20°C and below. This meant that machines of all types, not just tanks and artillery, but even basic items like rifles and machine guns would fail to work. It was this, along with the lack of winter clothing for the troops, which drastically reduced German combat effectiveness, rather than casualties per see.

When Zhukov's winter counter offensive began on December 5th 1941 on the central front, the Russians initially used 718,000 men, 720 tanks, 7,985 guns of all sizes and 361 aircraft, deployed with 3 tank, 5 motorized, 74 infantry and 22 cavalry divisions. This was a sizable force, but not unique for the frontage and by the standards of this campaign. The Germans, on the defensive, which normally would be an advantage, had 801,000 men, 1,000 tanks, 14,000 guns (all calibers and types) and 615 aircraft.[39] With an apparently slightly inferior force the Russians, under winter conditions, won their first major battle of the campaign. They were to follow this up with subsequent winter operations, resulting in an average advance of about 100 miles on the central sector by March 1942. The Moscow offensive was a complete reversal of what happened, with sometimes better odds for the Russians, in every big battle during the summer and autumn of 1941. The difference was that the Russians, some but not all of whom were the well trained Siberians, had fresh well clad troops. The Germans in contrast were exhausted, freezing, and ill fed and most of their equipment didn't work. Proper winter preparation by the Germans probably wouldn't have allowed them to advance. They could however, have achieved a defensive stalemate very close to Moscow; or beyond it, if they had opted for the early 'Typhoon' strategy and combined it with winter preparations.

The Germans also missed a rather obvious opportunity to exploit Soviet political and morale weakness in 1941. The massive number of about 3 million prisoners captured during 1941 should have alerted them to their opponent's situation. Stalin's dictatorship was more unpopular, among his own population, than Hitler's at this point of the war. This was especially so among the non-Russian Soviet republics and ethnic nations. The Baltic States, eastern Poland, Bessarabia and Bukovina; all seized only very recently under the terms of the August 1939 Nazi-Soviet Pact, had a largely non-Russian population of 22 million, and were mostly opposed to Stalin's regime. These territories, and even the Ukraine proper, which had suffered the brunt of up to 7 million deaths in an artificially communist created famine in the early 1930s, generally welcomed the Germans in 1941. Subtle propaganda at this point could have exploited a split between Stalin's communist ideology and the various nationalisms, even Russian nationalism, within the ethnically diverse Soviet Union. The huge number of ex-Soviet prisoners also provided a recruitment pool for the formation of anti-communist forces to help overthrow Stalin's regime.

The Germans, at least in 1941, failed to exploit this opportunity. Instead the Nazi's soon treated the occupied populations and prisoners as harshly, or more so, than Stalin's communists did. One might argue that this was inevitable, due to the Nazi ideology hating Slavs and communists alike. On the other hand, from 1942 and later, German attitudes did partly change, and ex-Soviet prisoners, of various nationalities including Russians, were recruited in large numbers. The Vlasov Army, named after a defecting Russian general captured in 1942, is the best known of the anti-communist forces. The total strength of all the pro-Axis and anti-communist forces by 1944-45 is estimated at about one million.[40] Including prior casualties the total recruited would have been more, and certainly would have been higher still had the Germans changed their policy, earlier and further than they actually did. How much difference this might have made in 1941 is difficult to tell. Its main material effect would have been cumulative, and into 1942, as the anti-communist forces and regimes would inevitably have taken time to organize, irrespective of Axis ideological attitudes. Even so, an earlier change of German political policy in this direction would have contributed to an Axis victory over Stalin's Russia. The margins, political and psychological, as well as military and strategic, were very tight for Stalin's Russia in late 1941. Stalin's own harsh measures against his own population during the war itself, and of returning Soviet prisoners previously captured by the Germans, shows that his regime considered the danger to be a mortal one.[41]

The final contributing factor to the failure of 'Barbarossa' was the indirect role of Britain. British intervention in Greece and the coup in Yugoslavia helped divert the Germans to the Balkans in April 1941, although Mussolini's failed invasion of Greece was the original cause. The effect on 'Barbarossa' was that 24 divisions, 670 combat aircraft and the airborne capability of two divisions and 500 transport aircraft were diverted for about a month. The airborne forces were never used again on a large scale after the losses in Crete. They would have been useful to support critical attacks, and help seal pockets in areas temporarily out of range of the all arms armies. The time delay from the originally planned May 15th start, to June 22nd might also have been significant, given the tight margins of 'Typhoon' by October. On the other hand the effect of the spring thaw, mud, and flooded rivers in western Russia lasting into June also militated against an earlier start to 'Barbarossa'. At any rate whatever the effect of the Balkan campaign, the Germans executed the conquest of Yugoslavia and Greece with speed and efficiency. They couldn't have completed it any earlier. The only change that could have been made was to make use of their airborne forces once the Crete losses had been replaced. General Student, the C-in-C of the airborne force, drew the opposite conclusion to Hitler, and certainly believed in the continued viability of this new type of warfare. The Western Allies and Russia agreed, and their own use of airborne forces in 1943-45 would prove this to be correct.

Whatever the combination of reasons for 'Barbarossa', embarking on a two front war, where none had existed before, is bad strategy. The Germans, from Hitler downwards, knew this. It was the reason that they entered into the 1939 Pact with Soviet Russia, and the concentration of force and victory over France was the result. They rationalized the decision on the grounds that Britain in 1941 was no threat, and thus 'Barbarossa' wasn't a two front war in the full sense of the term. What they meant was it wasn't a two front ground war, which was true since we cannot consider the minimalist deployment of 3 divisions with Rommel's Afrika Korps to compare with the 153 divisions for 'Barbarossa' in 1941. However, there were 45 inactive infantry divisions garrisoning Western Europe and Norway, guarding against a low level British amphibious invasion threat. About 750 Luftwaffe combat aircraft, one quarter of its strength, remained deployed and active against Britain in the Mediterranean and Western European theatres.

Some of these forces, less a minimum occupation force, would have been available had Britain been dealt with in 1941, and 'Barbarossa' postponed until 1942. The comprehensive Mediterranean strategy detailed previously, over the winter of 1940-41, followed by a renewed and better prepared 'Sealion' in the spring or summer of 1941, would have been the optimum 'Britain first' strategy. It would have entailed some risks in the east, especially as we now know that Stalin was preparing an offensive option. Yet we cannot be sure if or when he would have used it. The launching of a '1941 Sealion' would have been the optimum time, but as we have seen, Russia wasn't quite ready in the summer of 1941 to respond with an offensive of its own. Even with a 'Mediterranean-Sealion' strategy against Britain, Germany would still have had the bulk of its land forces, say 65% overall and 50% of the armor, or about 130 divisions including 10 panzer divisions, deployed defensively against Russia.

In conclusion the largest German mistake was at the level of grand strategy, which was to embark on 'Barbarossa' at all, and certainly before Britain had been defeated. With regard to the campaign itself, there was a major intelligence failure that led to the Germans heavily underestimating Soviet Russia during the planning stage. The extent of Russian military power was underestimated. The overall objectives were overambitious and the time scale insufficient. The intelligence failure was difficult to anticipate and correct. However, the objective could have been scaled back and winter preparations could definitely have been made, as a contingency against the time allocation overrunning. German forces, even with the very respectable 75% concentration obtained on one front, were barely adequate for the task. They lacked reserves and the necessary armament production levels behind the front. The latter was a major problem in its own right and affected other parts of the war as well, so we will leave that for now.

The tight margins in terms of forces though, meant that they couldn't quite do everything at once. That led to difficult operational choices and the one major mistake that could have been corrected. It was correct and an operational success in the first stage of 'Barbarossa' to target the known Russian forces within 200-300 miles of the frontier areas. In the second phase however, all the better military professionals agreed that the overriding and continuing territorial objective, should have been Moscow. Moscow could have been captured, and the cost of slower progress at Leningrad and in the Ukraine would have been modest. The Russians were in no state to seriously disrupt an early 'Typhoon' from the flanks. It is nearly always a mistake to keep switching strategies and objectives, as the Germans did with Moscow, Leningrad, Ukraine, and then back to Moscow again. In the event, 'Barbarossa' failed by a narrow margin. The 'Moscow first' strategy combined with winter preparation was achievable. It would have pushed Soviet Russia beyond that narrow margin, to the tipping point of collapse, and maybe over it.

Barbarossa: Consequences for the Wider War

Instead, for Germany and the rest of the European Axis powers, defeat meant the failure of their grand strategy to bring the war to a conclusion. We may recall that the strategic aim was to defeat Soviet Russia in a rapid campaign i.e. completing by mid-October and before winter at the very latest. Moreover 'Barbarossa' itself was an 'interim solution' within the overall war plan. The plan was to renew the offensive against Britain in 1942. With the Soviet threat removed in 1941, Britain's position would be worse than ever. With only Britain to defeat, and in control of the re-sources of all Europe and a conquered Russia, the Axis could even be con-fident of deterring or stalemating the anticipated American intervention in 1942.

With the failure before Moscow and Leningrad this sequence and timetable was in ruins. The rather dubious grand strategic logic for 'Bar-barossa' had backfired and placed the Axis in a worse position than before its start. Instead, the Axis now faced two undefeated great powers, Britain and Russia, with the USA presumed to be on the brink of intervention. Moreover, the operational strategy of 'blitzkrieg' had also failed to win a campaign for the first time. The strategy of 'annihilation' i.e. a rapid and total operational victory would now be supplemented by a slower 'attri-tional' type of warfare. Over time this would increasingly favor the Allies. The bulk of the German army and Luftwaffe would also be tied down in the east for the unforeseeable future. This would limit German strategic options in 1942, preventing any fundamental switch to other fronts. The Germans had therefore failed to create the necessary decisive precondition for concluding an overall victory in 1942. Still, that didn't yet mean that they would automatically lose the Russian campaign, or the war overall.

For Soviet Russia the failure of 'Barbarossa' was of decisive importance. It meant one thing: survival, for now. The failure of 'Typhoon' and then the successful Moscow counter offensives had given Soviet Russia a res-pite. They had pushed the Wehrmacht back about 100 miles on a 500 mile sector in the center of the front, as well as creating smaller incursions near Leningrad, Kharkov, and on the Kerch peninsular of the Crimea. However, the Axis armies were still 400-500 miles deep inside Soviet Russia. Russia had taken terrible punishment in 1941, losing almost all of its pre-war army and air force and over a third of its economy. That would have defeated any other nation. Yet help was slowly on the way, if they could just continue to hold on. The rest of the giant nation was still mobilizing new armies, and they would out produce Germany in most types of ground and air force equipment in 1942, just as they had done, marginally, in 1941. Moreover they now had allies, Britain and soon the USA. What they needed was practical help from their new allies, massive supplies, and above all a second front to take some of the burden of the land war off Russia. Russia had survived the cataclysm of 1941, just, yet there would still be no guarantees for 1942. The failure of 'Barbarossa' was thus a decisive change in the course of the war.

'Barbarossa' was also a major turning point for Britain, the USA and Japan. The British Commonwealth-Empire was henceforth no longer fighting alone, and would at the very least have a five month breathing space while the Germans concentrated on Soviet Russia. It didn't mean that the outcome of the war would be an inevitable Allied victory. Nor did it mean that Britain was in a position to threaten the German control of Western Europe, or even survive in the longer run. Instead, the pressure was off Britain, perhaps only temporarily, and they could resume their limited offensives in the Mediterranean, but no more than that. For Germany, Italy, Russia and Britain the course of the war had changed and the uncertainty of direction and of outcome had increased. In that sense, since prior to June 1941 the Axis powers were winning, and Britain was alone, 'Barbarossa' was a pro-Allied event.

Japan and the USA were indirectly affected. Both of these great powers had increased options, and decisions to make. Japan now had a more realistic option of advancing northward against the embattled Soviet Union. Instead they decided to await the outcome of 'Barbarossa', maintaining their April 1941 neutrality pact with Russia, and continued their plans to strike southward in the Pacific. The Americans, due to their 'Magic' intelligence intercepts, were broadly aware of the Japanese diplomatic policy. At the same time many Americans, the future President Truman among them, considered it to be a favorable development that the Nazi and Soviet dictatorships were at war with each other. For them each was equally objectionable, morally and ideologically, so one grand strategic option was to let them exhaust each other, and await developments. By the end of the war in 1945 this was broadly what happened. The German and Japanese dictatorships were destroyed, and the Soviet Russian dictatorship was exhausted and weakened. The USA emerged to take the prize as the most powerful nation and subsequently of world leadership.

That was for the future however, and there was no certainty in 1941 that such an outcome was inevitable. In 1941 the USA had to decide what the greater immediate threat to American interests was, Germany, Japan or Soviet Russia, and how to respond to the new, perhaps temporary, constellation of forces. They decided to continue with the 'Germany first' policy, accelerating the support 'short of war' for Britain and extended that aid to Soviet Russia as well. It was all very cautious though, because Roosevelt seemed certain, especially with Soviet Russia as a potential and awkward ally, that he couldn't get Congress or the American public to go to war, unless the USA was actually attacked. In the end both Japan and the USA broadly kept to their previous policies. It could have been different. 'Barbarossa' was important by opening up new options and potentially sending even the last two neutral great powers into a different course.

Finally, for anyone who still needs convincing that 'Barbarossa' was a decisive campaign of World War Two, let us consider the consequences of our alternative Axis strategy; the 'Moscow first' option combined with winter preparations. We have already concluded that it was realistic, indeed likely, that following this strategy; Moscow would have fallen before the autumn mud season and the Russian winter. Moscow was vitally important for Russia, Stalin and the survival of the Soviet regime. Stalin recognized this in October 1941 by his decision to stay in Moscow, even while the government bureaucracy was being evacuated to Kuybyshev. The Red Army would have been forced to stand and fight. If that had occurred in August or September, it would have been catastrophic in losses of manpower, material and territory. Moscow was an important industrial center with up to 10% of total production, and unique as a rail communications hub for all of European Russia. Its loss would have effectively cut the country in two, severely disrupting Russia's capacity to redeploy its armies, and even to some extent the ongoing mobilization and armaments production.

The largest damage of all would have been political, psychological, and the dramatic undermining of morale. Politically and psychologically, Stalin's regime was vulnerable, and they knew it. There had been mass surrenders totaling over 3 million troops during the 1941 campaign, and the population, especially in the Baltic States and Ukraine, had started to collaborate with the enemy. The Soviet regime had to resort to drastic fear based measures, such as NKVD blocking units, placed behind their own army units, to try and prevent them from deserting and retreating. Soviets had been shooting Russians and other nationalities well before the front neared Moscow. Stalin put out secret peace feelers in October 1941, using Beria's NKVD via Bulgaria as an intermediary. There were also the first signs of panic and crucially for the Soviet regime, the loss of fear by even Moscow's population. Up to one fifth of Moscow's civilian population i.e.

almost one million fled the city during the October crisis.[42] We cannot be completely conclusive with such psychological intangibles. However, it is clear that as it was, Soviet Russia briefly reached the edge of collapse in October 1941, directly after they had just lost one million men at Vyazma-Bryansk.

If Moscow had fallen in September 1941, or was even just encircled and therefore politically isolated as well, Russia would have been even closer to, or over, the tipping point of regime change. Stalin himself would have been forced to abandon Moscow if he wanted to survive, but at a severe risk of a coup, revolution or just a disintegration of the state and political system. If he had stayed, then Stalin's death would have meant the end of the Soviet regime in those circumstances. Foreign Minister Molotov has stated that if Stalin had left for Kuybyshev in October when most of the government was evacuated, that 'Moscow would have burned'. He went on to say that the city would have fallen and that the Soviet Union and the coalition against Hitler would have collapsed.[43] Had Moscow been encircled or fallen in September, as a result of a 6 or 7 week early operation 'Typhoon', then Molotov's predictions would have almost certainly occurred.

It is also highly probable that the fall of Moscow would have had military and psychological effects on other regions of Russia.[44] Most notably, Leningrad and Sevastopol, both isolated militarily and politically from a shaken or collapsing regime, would probably have fallen rapidly. There was already political tension between the central and local authorities, the former fearful of losing control over the isolated forces in Leningrad. Even had there been no overall surrender by Stalin's Russia, the prospects for 1942 with the central front back on the middle Volga and morale shattered, would have been dire. Regime survival was the most important objective for Stalin, and Moscow's fall, at the very least, would have forced him to negotiate a peace treaty. Lenin after all had signed the Treaty of Brest-Litovsk in 1918 in less drastic circumstances, and for the same reason, regime survival. The Germans would have had most of the cards in such a treaty and Russia, Soviet or post-Stalinist, would have been out of the war.

In that situation German grand strategy would have been back on track. The interim solution of 'Barbarossa' would have been completed in 1941. In 1942 most of the German ground and air forces, less a planned garrison of 56 divisions (out of 208), would have redeployed to the Western European and Mediterranean theatres. The prospects for the Western Allies, even if America had declared war immediately, and assuming the Axis didn't declare war on the USA, would have been much worse than the historical position. As it was Britain and the USA were largely on the defensive in both the Atlantic and Mediterranean theatres for most of

1942. The only major offensive campaign for most of the year was strategic bombing, which was largely an all British effort and not very effective in 1942. The Allies only gained the initiative in ground operations in the Mediterranean, with the Alamein and 'Torch' offensives, in late October and November 1942. At sea they lost 8 million tons of shipping in 1942, 6 million tons of it in the Atlantic, the worst year of the war there by a factor of two.

If Russia had been defeated at the end of 1941, Britain would have come under massive and indeed unsustainable pressure on several fronts during 1942, before the Americans could seriously intervene. The entire Mediterranean theatre, including Gibraltar, Malta, Egypt and the Middle East, along with large forces, would inevitably have been lost as previously analyzed. In Western Europe, the Axis would have had enough air power to neutralize the modest British strategic bombing offensive, and to launch an offensive themselves, at least as large as and probably larger than in 1940. With no serious threat on land, the Axis would have switched their production effort into more air and naval power. As a result they would have been even more successful in the Atlantic in 1942 than they were historically.

Most decisively, with the entire Luftwaffe force from Russia redeployed, extra air production, victories in the Mediterranean, an enhanced Atlantic submarine campaign, and a transfer of the Italian fleet via a captured Gibraltar; there would have been the best possible conditions for a renewed operation 'Sealion' in 1942. A larger, better prepared and renewed attempt at 'Sealion' in 1942 was certainly Hitler's intention, had he defeated Russia in late 1941. The Western Allies did the maximum they could in 1942, and other than attempt to increase the British home garrison with American troops; they wouldn't have had the forces or bases in 1942 for any counter strategies. The USAAF didn't bomb France until August 1942, or Germany until 1943. Britain could still have been defeated, even conquered in 1942 under these circumstances, or accepted a compromise peace. With Britain out of the war as well, the USA would have no bases in Europe, resulting in a global peace treaty with the Axis.

At the very least the war in Europe would have been stalemated indefinitely. Western Allied invasions facing an extra 100 German divisions from Russia in 1942 alone, which would have trebled their army in Europe and the Mediterranean, would have been impossible even in 1943-1945. Nor could strategic air power alone defeat such an Axis Europe, reinforced by the resources of a defeated Russia and a conquered Mediterranean, and oil from the Middle East. Finally, a neutralized or even pro-Axis non-communist regime in a post peace treaty Russia, would give the Axis control of most of Eurasia, linking German and Japanese conquests. Some limited aid, such as Russian oil, could even have been sent to help the Japanese economy for their war in the Pacific. Only the atomic bomb might, eventually, have won the war for the Allies under these disastrous circumstances. Even that assumes that they would continue the war, without Russia, through nearly four years of defeats and stalemate, and without the hindsight knowledge that the 'bomb' would work, or even win the war if it did. A defeat of Russia, in 1941 anyway, would therefore have created very favorable conditions for the European Axis to defeat Britain in 1942, and stalemate the Americans indefinitely.

Conversely, Russian survival was absolutely essential for the eventual Allied victory. Russia engaged in battle and contained, over the course of the entire war, between 60% and 75% of the German army, 40-75% of the Luftwaffe; and inflicted 90% of the total German killed and wounded casualties. If we include prisoners as well, but not the mass surrender at the very end of the war, when a majority of Germans for obvious reasons preferred to surrender to the Western Allies, then the Russians still inflicted 80% of the German casualties.[45] Even into the late war, after 'Overlord' in 1944-45, the Russians were engaging 60% of the German divisions and inflicting 62% of the irrecoverable losses. Even 1,700 of the Luftwaffe's 4,600 combat aircraft (38%) were still engaged in the east in June 1944.[46] 'Barbarossa 1941' was therefore the largest campaign of the war, and with the possible exception of an alternative conquest of Britain in 1940 or 1941, the most decisive as well.

Notes to Chapter 4

1. Both quotes. Joseph P. Nash, Roosevelt & Churchill, Andre Deutsch, London, 1977, p 348.
2. Heinz Magenheimer, Hitler's War: Germany's Key Strategic Decisions 1940-1945, Cassell Military Paperbacks, London, 1998, p 40.
3. ibid, p53.
4. Chris Bellamy, Absolute War: Soviet Russia in the Second World War, Macmillan, London, 2007, p 102.
5. ibid. p 114.
6. Magenheimer, Hitler's War, p 66 and 68.
7. Norman Davies, Europe at War 1939-1945, Macmillan, London, 2006, p 157.
8. Bellamy, Absolute War, p 124-125.
9. For this and what follows on German overall armed forces strength, tank and divisional strengths; see Cooper, The German Army 1933-45, op. cit. passim.
10. Ellis, World War II Databook, p 237. Magenheimer, Hitler's War, p 75-76.
11. Magenheimer, Hitler's War, p 75-76. Bellamy, Absolute War, p 170-71.

12. Ellis, Brute Force, p 41. Calculations and estimates of the Axis forces at the start of 'Barbarossa' do vary slightly, but not significantly. Bellamy, Absolute War, p172, gives a range of 3,206,000 to 3,513,000.

13. Dupuy, Understanding War, p 224-227.

14. Magenheimer, Hitler's War, p 302, fn 47.

15. Davies, Europe at War, p 216.

16. Magenheimer, Hitler's War, p 77-80.

17. Ellis, Brute Force, p 41.

18. Russian order of battle and what follows derived from: Magenheimer, Hitler's War, p 76-77, and Bauer, WW2 Vol 5, p 427.

19. Bellamy, Absolute War, p 206.

20. ibid. p 179. Magenheimer, Hitler's War, p 76.

21. Bellamy, Absolute War, p 182.

22. Here and elsewhere in this chapter, where it says 'estimated' strength or losses, is generally the author's calculation; derived from orders of battle and divisional totals, given in Bellamy, Magenheimer and Bauer. Usually it's a breakdown calculation for tank and air strengths for Russian 'Fronts', based on the known overall equipment holdings of the 1st Strategic Echelon in June 1941, and the distribution of the mechanized corps between the five Fronts in 1st Strategic Echelon. Ellis, WW2 Databook, is also invaluable throughout, including for Russian forces captured in specific pocket battles of 1941; see his table on p 41.

23. Bellamy, Absolute War, p 181; and for statistics to follow on the southern front during the frontier battle phase.

24. Bellamy, Absolute War, p 205-206.

25. Ellis, WW2 Databook, table 87 on p 277, table 92 on p 278.

26. John Erickson, The Road to Stalingrad, Phoenix Press, London, 2000, original 1975, p 210. Bellamy, Absolute War, p 262. Bauer, WW2 Vol 5, p 464. There is doubt about the number of Russians that escaped the Kiev pocket and forming the basis of the newly reformed South West Front. Bellamy says only 15,000. It is a very low figure, if not for the number of escapees, certainly for the later reconstructed Front, covering a huge area. It may, be a misprint, for the 150,000 given in the other two above accounts? Either way, Kiev was a total disaster for the Russians.

27. Bellamy, Absolute War, p 272. Bauer, WW2 Vol 5, p 467. Author's comment. The German manpower figure of 1.9 million, given in Bellamy, seems rather high for 78 divisions; it implies a divisional slice of 25,000, compared to 20,000 for all three army groups at the start of 'Barbarossa'. The 78 divisions of a reinforced AG Center account for half of the entire 'Barbarossa' German order of battle of 153 divisions, whose strength had fallen from the original 3.2 million to 2.7 million by this time. The author's estimate for AG Center manpower strength at the start of 'Typhoon' is therefore 1.4 million. Bellamy's tank and air strength is much more plausible, at least for machines immediately available, and compatible with panzer divisions being at only 45-50% of normal combat effectiveness by this stage of the campaign. Compare also the 1.9 (or 1.4) million figure for AG Center on October 1st, with Erickson's 0.8 million at the start of the Russian Moscow offensive on December 5th. German casualties were about 200,000 between these two dates, so something is amiss. Possibly Erickson's, Soviet sourced, figure only applies to a part of AG Center, those that took the brunt of the Moscow counter offensive; and he could be using a rather tighter definition of 'combat forces'; so perhaps it isn't strictly a like with like comparison.

28. Bellamy, Absolute War, p 277-279. For this and what follows on Russian casualties during the 'Typhoon' offensive and strength figures for both sides during November-December 1941.

29. Erickson, Road to Stalingrad, p 521.

30. Ellis, Brute Force, p 47. Bauer, WW2 Vol 6, p 489.

31. Erickson, Road to Stalingrad, p 223.

32. Hart, Hist of 2WW, p 176.

33. Bauer, WW2 Vol 7, p 658.

34. Ellis, Brute Force, p 77, says 3.2 million men inducted between June and December 1941. Davies, Europe at War, p 216, gives an initial mobilization of 5 million reserves in 10 days after June 22. Overall strength figures for Russia are difficult to come by. The author's approximate calculation for the end of 1941 is as follows. The June 1941 overall armed forces strength is widely given as just under 5 million. Additions during 1941 are the 5 million initial mobilization and an extra 3 million recruits up to December 1941; for a total of 13 million mobilized. The total number of pre-war trained men in June 1941, including reserves, is also widely given as 11-12 million. Casualties in 1941, mostly 'irrecoverable' is usually given as 4 million, possibly more; which when deducted from the 13 million above, gives an approximate size of 9 million for the total Russian armed forces at the turn of 1941-42.

35. Erickson, Road to Stalingrad, p 272.

36. Magenheimer, Hitler's War, p 63.

37. Heinz Guderian, Panzer Leader, Futura Macdonald & Co, London, 1974, p 200. Bauer, WW2 Vol 5, p 462.

38. Hart, Hist of 2WW, p 166-168, gives the argument for even deeper strikes and larger encirclements. These would of course, even if practical, been riskier. He also suggests that a switch to tracked vehicles from wheeled ones would have overcome the mud problem. The problem with that (see text), was the sheer scale and cost of switching. The numbers required made it impossible.

39. Erickson, Road to Stalingrad, p 272-273. Bauer, WW2 Vol 5, p 480. For this, and preceding Russian strength figures for the Moscow counter offensive. The author is slightly skeptical about these Soviet based sources, showing that the attacking Russian

forces, on their chosen sector of front, were slightly smaller than the defending Germans. Over the entire front there were 4.2 million Russians facing 2.7 million Germans (not the 5 million that Soviet based sources sometimes show). Still, there seems to be no alternative figures for the Moscow sector alone during the counter offensive, so we have used the Soviet ones, with caution attached.

40. Magenheimer, Hitler's War, p 97.

41. ibid. p 96-101; for Soviet political vulnerabilities and actions, such as the use of 'penal' battalions, NKVD blocking units, and oppressive fear based policies in general.

42. Ian Kershaw, Fateful Choices: Ten Decisions that Changed the World 1940-1941, Penguin Group, London, 2007, p 289-290.

43. ibid. p 290.

44. Magenheimer, Hitler's War, p 117-118.

45. Ellis, Brute Force, p 129-130. The total German killed and wounded figure is 4.9 million for the eastern front 1941-45, and 580,000 for the Western European, Italian and North African campaigns combined. Another 200,000 were killed and wounded in the Polish, French 1940 and Balkan campaigns combined, before Barbarossa began, which doesn't alter the overall imbalance much. Ellis, WW2 Databook, p 255, gives the German eastern front killed and wounded figure, counting prisoners and missing as killed: as 5.9 or 6.3 million up to December 31st 1944, and March 10th 1945 respectively.

46. Bellamy, Absolute War, p 635, Ellis WW2 Databook, p 165, 185, 231 and 233.

CHAPTER 5

GERMAN STRATEGY IN 1942

'The struggle for the hegemony in the world will be decided for Europe [i.e. Germany] by the possession of the Russian space'[1]

Adolf Hitler

American Intervention

The Russian winter offensive starting on December 5th 1941, followed by the Japanese attack on Pearl Harbor on December 7th 1941 transformed World War Two. The European War that had begun on September 3rd 1939 and the Sino-Japanese War of 1937-1941, were now linked and merged into a truly global conflict. Russia's survival of the 'Barbarossa' onslaught during 1941 and the entry of the USA and Japan into the war completed the Axis and Allied coalitions which would fight until the end in 1945. The line up was now complete with three Axis great powers, Germany, Japan and Italy facing three Allied great powers, Soviet Russia, the USA, the British Commonwealth-Empire, and also China which was of marginal great power status. Each side also had minor power allies. Romania, Hungary, Bulgaria and Finland, as well as the 'puppet' states of Croatia and Slovakia were allied to the European Axis, and 'puppet' regimes in China and Manchuria supported Japan. Communist China, Free France, which controlled a minority part of the French Empire and the exiled governments of the European countries occupied by the Axis in 1939-41, completed the Allied alliance. All members of each alliance were now at war with all members of the opposing alliance, with one significant exception. Russia and Japan remained neutral towards each other, maintaining their neutrality pact of April 1941 until the last weeks of the war in August 1945. The remainder of the diplomatic line up had been completed on December 11th 1941 when Germany and Italy declared war on the USA. This ranks second to the launching of 'Barbarossa' on June 22nd 1941, as the largest mistake of German and European Axis grand strategy of the entire war.

Historians have explanations for this apparently strange decision, but hardly sufficient or satisfactory ones. As we have seen the Germans expected the USA to be ready, militarily, to enter the war themselves in 1942. This was based on fairly accurate intelligence assessments of the rate of American preparations and rearmament. These had started from a low base after the fall of France in 1940 with the 'two ocean navy' shipbuilding plan. This along with the Selective Service Act in September 1940 and the material expansion of US forces before December 1941 could hardly be concealed. German intelligence miscalculated however, when it came to

American policy, strategy and war planning. They over emphasized the Pacific theatre, where as in reality, the Americans had decided on a policy of 'Germany first' in early 1941. German policy had been to try and keep the USA out of the war for as long as possible. They were well aware of the decisive American role that tipped the balance in 1918, leading to a German defeat. They didn't want a repeat of that, yet were aware that the Americans would likely enter the war at some point, probably 1942. German strategy towards the USA was therefore two fold. First, they would attempt to win the war before America was ready. This had contributed to the erroneous reasoning that they needed to attack and defeat Soviet Russia in 1941, in order to force Britain into a hopeless position and accept a peace treaty. The narrow failure of 'Barbarossa' had upset this timetable and sequence. The second track of Germany's grand strategy was the alliance with Japan, aimed at distracting and tying America down in the Pacific. With the launching and then the failure of 'Barbarossa', the attitude of Japan became more urgent.

Despite the Tripartite Pact of September 27th 1940 Germany remained uncertain about Japanese political and strategic plans. Japan had not joined the European Axis in their war against the Soviet Union in June 1941. Indeed Japan had a neutrality pact with Soviet Russia and resisted all German diplomatic efforts to involve them in the conflict. Japan however, like Italy, had not been consulted about the planning or decision for 'Barbarossa'. Germany and Italy were equally uninformed about Pearl Harbor or its timing. They had also attempted, and failed, to persuade Japan to attack Singapore and other British territories in Asia. Full political and grand strategic cooperation between the European Axis and Japan was therefore lacking during 1941. This led to misperceptions and uncertainty all round. Germany didn't know whether Japan would strike northwards against Russia; southwards against Britain and/or the USA; or, and this was the option they feared, conclude a diplomatic rapprochement with the USA.

It was November 1941 before Germany and Japan were negotiating a new enhanced alliance, the central objective and clause of which would be that there would be 'no separate peace' with the USA.[2] Japan already knew by then that its diplomatic negotiations with America were very likely to fail, leading to war very quickly. Each Axis power needed the other in any war with the USA, yet each also feared that its ally would renege, and leave them fighting the Americans on their own. No separate peace meant mutual support by all the Axis powers, were war to break out between any one of them and the USA. Crucially all would be committed to war, irrespective of who started the conflict. This was an important difference from the existing Tripartite Pact, which only committed all members to act if one of them was attacked by a neutral third party i.e. the USA, or prior to June 1941, Soviet Russia. Equally significant was that negotiations for the enhanced Axis alliance were still not completed before Pearl Harbor. Amazingly, even after Pearl Harbor the European Axis still feared a separate peace between the USA and Japan. Hitler considered that a failure to fully back Japan, by declaring war on the USA, would make this more likely. This was a diplomatic miscalculation by the European Axis powers, since after Pearl Harbor the Americans were even less inclined to offer a compromise peace to Japan.

The final factor in Hitler's decision was the situation in the Atlantic. America had steadily increased its support 'short of war' for Britain starting with the destroyer deal in September 1940. By late 1941, prior to Pearl Harbor, this had become a state of 'limited undeclared war'. The USA had extended its neutrality zone half way across the Atlantic and the USN was escorting British convoys as far as Iceland, which from July 1941 had been garrisoned by US marines. Finally in September 1941, Roosevelt ordered the USN to 'shoot on sight' against Axis submarines entering the, self declared, American neutrality zone. He was attempting to create incidents which might provoke the Axis into war or give America pretence for war. There were several clashes including the sinking of a US destroyer and the damaging of another. However, the Axis wouldn't be provoked into such a decision and Roosevelt still didn't have enough political or public support for all out war. In August 1941 after the Atlantic conference with Churchill at Placentia Bay, Roosevelt considered that Congress would take three months to debate a declaration of war on Germany, and then reject it by a two or three to one vote.[3] The German navy was under orders to avoid armed conflict with the Americans. Yet the Atlantic convoys were vulnerable to attack in the American protected zone, which included the assembly areas in Canadian waters. German restraint, as the doubling of sinkings to 8 million tons in the unrestricted conditions of 1942 would show, was thus to its disadvantage in the Atlantic during 1941, at least in a strictly military sense. Pearl Harbor gave them the option of unrestricted submarine warfare in the Atlantic, which they had dared not previously risk, for fear of provoking the Americans into war against the European Axis, while crucially, Japan was still neutral.

The reasoning for the European Axis declaration of war on the USA is therefore more logical than it first appears. It was an interaction between the primacy and then the failure of 'Barbarossa'; the need and uncertainty of Japanese support against America; and the operational advantages of unrestrained submarine warfare in the Atlantic. It seems that the European Axis powers were merely anticipating the presumed inevitable US declaration of war, expected in 1942. While logical up to a point, it was still not the optimum decision, especially after Pearl Harbor. An alternative was available that, while it couldn't ultimately prevent American entry into the European War, would have delayed it further and made the decision much more difficult for Roosevelt and the 'Germany first' strategists. It would also have achieved all other realistic German objectives.

An alternative German option after Pearl Harbor was to lift, perhaps secretly and quietly, all restrictions on the submarine war in the Atlantic, but make no formal declaration of war on the USA. They were under no obligation under the terms of the existing Tripartite Pact to declare war on the USA, since it had been Japan, not America that had initiated hostilities. A situation of official neutrality, but in practice of 'limited undeclared war' would have continued to exist for some time in the Atlantic after Pearl Harbor.[4] This would have been analogous to the actual neutrality between Japan and Soviet Russia after 'Barbarossa' had started, so Japan could have no complaints. The continuing situation of 'limited undeclared war' could, post-Pearl Harbor, have now involved unrestricted submarine warfare, which would have been to Germany's operational advantage in 1942; a contrast to the situation in 1941. It would have been a step up from the restricted submarine warfare of 1941, but still limited to naval warfare. Donitz and the Germans in general were caught by surprise by Pearl Harbor. Consequently there would be a month's delay before the actual submarine offensive, operation 'Drumbeat', was started in American waters in January 1942, but it wasn't dependent on a declaration of war.

Such a delay would have made it even more difficult politically for Roosevelt to get Congress to declare war on the European Axis directly after Pearl Harbor. It wouldn't have been easy, or even possible, for Roosevelt to do so and maintain the 'Germany first' policy under these circumstances anyway. He had the support of most diplomats at the State Department and the Army and Air Force strategists. The USN, most of the public, and given the two or three to one political odds in August 1941 against war, a majority of Congress would have favored a 'Japan first' or 'Japan only' grand strategy. To move beyond the 'undeclared war' in the Atlantic by deploying ground forces to Britain, initiating air operations over Europe, and then operation 'Torch' would have required a full Congressional declaration of war. The Axis was fully aware of the opposition to Roosevelt's policy and his caution during 1941; it was mostly democratic and open after all.

By holding back politically after Pearl Harbor, the Axis would have created major domestic problems for Roosevelt's policy in 1942. After all, Roosevelt didn't even attempt to get a full declaration of war on the European Axis powers, simultaneous with the declaration against Japan, immediately after Pearl Harbor. At the very least, full American entry into the European War, rather than 'limited undeclared war' in just its Atlantic theatre, would have been delayed many months. Even then the USA would have entered the European War less united and determined than was actually the case. The psychological component of war was perhaps America's only major weakness. The Axis could have exploited the relative unpopularity of the European War, compared to the war in the Pacific, by forcing Roosevelt to make the difficult decision for war himself, rather than do it for him.

Nor would there have been much change in the Pacific due to this European Axis option. Hitler had what he wanted for 1942 already; the Americans distracted by Japan. Pearl Harbor started the war in the Pacific, not any action by Germany or Italy. The Americans were focused on the Pacific historically, until the battles of Midway (June 1942) and Guadalcanal (August 1942-February 1943) halted the Japanese advance. This was despite the official 'Germany first' policy. Finally the Americans, barring naval disasters even worse than Pearl Harbor, were unlikely to offer a compromise peace with Japan.

The European Axis therefore missed an opportunity to delay further the American intervention in the European theatre. They couldn't prevent it altogether however, because it was America's decision to make. Roosevelt's America was more determined than Stalin's Russia to support Britain, at least using means 'short of war'. Soviet Russia, if left alone, might well have maintained the Nazi-Soviet Pact of 1939 and stayed neutral. 'Barbarossa' created an unnecessary enemy for the Axis, where as America was the leader of the Western democracies, even while neutral. For this reason we must rank 'Barbarossa' as Hitler's greatest mistake, and the declaration of war on America a close second. Even so, Pearl Harbor and subsequent events in the Pacific, as well as the enhanced Battle of the Atlantic delayed US offensives in Europe until operation 'Torch' in November 1942. The Axis still had most of 1942 to achieve a victory in Europe, before serious practical American military intervention.

At the turn of 1941-1942 however, the European Axis was on the defensive in both the primary theatre of operations, which was Russia, and in the secondary Mediterranean theatre. As we have seen, this situation was reversed rapidly in the Mediterranean in January 1942 and the Axis held the initiative there until the (third) Battle of Alamein in October 1942. To help achieve this they had to transfer the Fliegerkorps II with 390 combat aircraft[5] from Russia to the Sicily-Malta combat area at the start 1942. This was a significant redeployment of air power from the 2,465 combat aircraft on the eastern front in December 1941.[6] The Luftwaffe was becoming overstretched by an air war on three or four fronts: Russian, Western Europe including Germany, Mediterranean and Arctic. The German army still had only one main front in Russia, and they declined to transfer the very modest force of 3 or 4 divisions that would have doubled the size of Rommel's Afrika Korps in North Africa. That would have made all the difference in this theatre during the first eight months of 1942, rather than leaving the reinforcement until the Tunisian campaign, starting in November 1942.

On the eastern front it took longer for the Axis to regain the initiative. The Russian winter offensive on the Moscow front lasted from December 5th 1941 to January 7th 1942. This was followed immediately by a general offensive along the entire eastern front from January 8th to April 20th 1942. The Moscow offensive saved Russia and was the first major ground war defeat for Germany in World War Two. The follow up general offensive was premature, since Russia didn't have enough resources or sufficient overall superiority along the entire length of the front. In December 1941 the total Russian strength at the front was 4.2 million troops, 1,964 tanks and 3,688 combat aircraft. The comparative German strength at the front was 2.7 million troops, 1,453 tanks and 2,465 combat aircraft, which was less, especially in armor, than when 'Barbarossa' started on June 22nd 1941.[7] On January 1st 1942 a total of 328 Russian divisions faced 141 Axis divisions on the 1,000 mile front from Leningrad to Rostov. The general offensive failed in its objective of encircling the German Army Group Center, but nevertheless the Russians advanced an average of about 100 miles on a frontage of about 500 miles.

The front line by April 1942 was even longer, being unusually jagged with several salients and even isolated pockets on both sides. Hitler had ordered that there should be no retreat by the German army and that they should create fortified areas, commonly referred to as a 'hedgehog defense'. The military consensus is that this, at least initially, was the correct decision rather than a full retreat. It may even have prevented an Axis disaster of Napoleonic proportions, and certainly saved much heavy equipment that was difficult to replace at 1942 production rates. Other command decisions at this time however, had negative consequences for the future. Several key high commanders, including Brauchitsch the C-in-C at OKH, and all three army group commanders, Leeb, Bock and Rundstedt, as well as the talented Guderian, resigned around this time due to command disputes with Hitler. Even worse, Hitler assumed direct command of the army and the OKH as well as the OKW. From then on there would be hardly any professional checks and balances on Hitler's command decisions or the mistakes that he might make. Finally, during the course of these operations the Germans were able to use air supply to maintain 95,000 men cut off at the Demyansk pocket on the central front between February 8th and April 21st 1942. This was a forerunner of Stalingrad, or so they thought. In practice it contributed to the Luftwaffe overestimating their air supply capabilities at Stalingrad. Losses during this relatively unknown period from January to April 1942 were heavy on both sides: 240,000 German including 67,000 killed and missing and 776,000 Russian casualties including 272,000 irrecoverable losses i.e. killed and prisoners.[8]

As spring mud turned to summer and the resumption of mobile warfare, the initiative swung back to the Axis. Before the main German 1942 summer offensive however, there were three other major battles on the eastern front. On May 12th 1942 the rebuilt Russian South West and South Fronts with 640,000 men, 13,000 guns and mortars, 1,300 tanks and 926 aircraft in 6 armies commanded by Timoshenko, launched a major two pronged offensive against Kharkov in the eastern Ukraine.[9] Five days later the Germans counter attacked, isolating, encircling and then destroying the southern Russian pincer of 3 armies at Izyum by May 29th. It was another Russian disaster, 1941 style, with casualties of 277,000 men, 1,200 tanks, 2,000 guns and 540 aircraft.[10] German losses were only 20,000, and the battle showed that the Germans were still superior at offensive and counter offensive mobile operations. The Russians also suffered two other heavy defeats in the Crimea around this time. Between January and April 1942, starting with an amphibious operation the Russians had recaptured the Kerch peninsular in the east of the Crimea. Between May 8th and 21st the Germans recaptured it again, taking 170,000 prisoners, 258 tanks and 1,100 guns, for losses of less than 8,000. About 120,000 Russians escaped across the Kerch strait to the Taman peninsular on the other side. Then between June 2nd and July 9th 1942 the German 11th Army captured the fortress naval base of Sevastopol after an epic siege and battle, involving massive heavy and super heavy artillery exchanges, using some of the largest guns ever constructed. During the seven month siege from the start of 1942, Russian casualties at Sevastopol were 210,000 including 95,000 prisoners in the final battle. German casualties were 24,000 during the one month assault phase.[11] The Russians had therefore already been weakened by three major defeats before the primary Axis offensive of 1942, and all of them on the southern sector of the front.

Operation Blau: Stalingrad and the Caucasus

Operation 'Blau' (Blue) was the principal German strategic offensive on the eastern front during the second half of 1942. The planning basis for it was the 'Fuhrer Directive 41' which was completed on April 5th 1942. The overall objective was 'to finally destroy the remaining Soviet armed forces and as far as possible to deprive them of their most important sources of economic power'.[12] The main economic objectives were the Caucasus oilfields at Maikop, Grozny, and Baku, which accounted for 75-80% of the Soviet Union's production of 22 million tons in 1942. The Donbass coalfields and the grain producing regions of the lower Don and the North Caucasus steppe were the other economic targets. The oil production in particular was important for Russia's ability to continue the war, and to help fuel subsequent Axis operations. Yet at the time, Hitler and his economic advisers falsely considered that the Caucasus oil was essential for Germany. It would have more than doubled Axis oil production, assuming the oilfields were captured intact or otherwise repaired. In the event the campaign failed, yet Germany was able to continue the war. They only suffered an oil shortage from late 1944, due to a combination of both the Allied strategic bombing of the synthetic oil plants in Germany and the fall of Romania in September 1944. Axis conquest of the Caucasus would also cut the Western Allied supply route to Russia via Persia; put diplomatic pressure on neutral Turkey; and threaten a subsequent invasion of the British Middle East from the north.

Operation 'Blau' had two broad territorial objectives, which very importantly according to 'Directive 41', were to be achieved sequentially. The first and 'intermediate objective', was an advance down the 'Don-Donetz corridor' to secure the 'land bridge' between the rivers Don and Volga around Stalingrad. This would create a strong northern defensive flank on the river Don from Voronezh to Stalingrad, in order to protect the second stage of 'Blau'. The second and 'primary objective' was the Caucasus, a line from Batum on the Black Sea to Baku on the Caspian. The Don defensive flank would be extended along the lower Volga, from Stalingrad to Astrakhan on the Caspian Sea, as part of the advance on Baku. Finally, although not part of 'Blau', 'Directive 41' included a planned secondary offensive in the north to capture Leningrad and link up with the Finns.

The main German offensive in the summer of 1942 would therefore be by their Army Group South. Army Group's Center and North, except for the Leningrad operation, would remain on the defensive. Unlike 'Barbarossa' in 1941, the Germans were not strong enough to launch simultaneous offensives on all three sectors of the front. Even so on the southern front the distance to the objectives was immense. The direct distance from the start line at Kursk and Orel to Stalingrad, the 'intermediate objective', was 400 miles. That was less than the 1941 advance and assuming no diversions seemed achievable. To capture Baku, the most important of the oilfields, would require an advance from Rostov of 700 miles, which was further than the longest advance in 1941 and required the crossing of the Caucasus Mountains. Let us now consider the balance of forces in 1942 between Germany and Russia on the eastern front and on the southern sector.

By June 1942 the German armed forces contained 8,410,000 men, a moderate expansion of 1.2 million since the start of 'Barbarossa' one year earlier. Of these 5,750,000 were in the Army and 190,000 in the Waffen SS. The field army had 3,950,000 men of which 2,850,000 were on the eastern front and 1,100,000 on all other fronts combined.[13] The total ground combat force of the field army and the Waffen SS had therefore only expanded by a very modest 200,000 since June 1941 (From 3.8 million and 150,000 respectively). The number of divisions including the Waffen SS had expanded from 208 to 233, but not all of the latter were at full strength. The total number of tanks on all fronts and including reserves was 5,663 plus 780 assault guns. When compared with the 5,262 tanks and 390 assault guns of June 1941, we can see that the panzer forces reflected the overall modest numerical expansion. The same can be said of the Luftwaffe, whose operational combat aircraft strength was 3,725 compared to 3,451 a year earlier.[14] This much more modest expansion of the combat forces, and especially of the principal instruments of 'blitzkrieg', was also reflected in the forces actual deployed in the east.

Just before the start of 'Blau' 184 of the total of 233 German divisions were on the eastern front including the 5 divisions in northern Norway that were cooperating with the Finnish army. There were 49 divisions on all the other secondary fronts combined. The latter total was 9 less than in June 1941. The Army Group D in France was the largest of the secondary fronts, with 26 divisions including three panzer divisions, guarding against a possible, but unlikely, Western Allied invasion in 1942. The eastern army with 184 divisions, compared to 153 in June 1941, appeared to be stronger than before. However, the vital mobile striking force of 19 panzer and 16 motorized divisions was virtually unchanged. Most of the apparent increase was in the number of infantry divisions, however many of these were under strength. The eastern army overall was 308,000 troops or about 10% below establishment strength in May 1942.[15]

The German combat strength on the eastern front in June 1942 was 2,850,000 troops, 3,981 tanks and assault guns and 2,750 combat aircraft.[16] There was therefore no significant increase since the start of 'Barbarossa' in June 1941. However the quality, training, experience, unit leadership and combat effectiveness of the Wehrmacht, were still first rate and well ahead of the Russians, or even the Western Allies for that matter. Technology had also improved. The 1942 panzerwaffe for example, consisted mostly of the up gunned Pzkw III and IV medium tanks, while the production of light tanks had ended. Both sides now had rocket firing artillery; the Russian lead in 1941 with their 'Katyusha', was balanced in 1942 by the German 'Nebelwerfer'. Overall in armor and artillery technology, which were the most important heavy ground force weapons, the Russians still had a slight edge. The more professional German forces however, made better use of their weaponry.

One area of expansion for the Axis forces on the eastern front was in the contribution of Axis allied forces. In the far north the Finnish army maintained its strength of 18 high quality divisions and over 300,000 men. This was a notable achievement from a country with a population of only 3 million. Indeed, even in winter conditions, the Finns were more than a match for Russian forces of even two or three times their own size. However, Finnish cooperation with the Germans had been, and remained less than total. Finland's war aim was to recover the territory lost to Soviet Russia after the Winter War of 1939-40. They had recovered this during the 1941 advance. Thereafter they refrained from two operations that were probably within their capabilities and certainly would have contributed significantly to the Russian campaign overall. Firstly, the Finns failed to seriously attack Murmansk or its vulnerable rail link transporting Western Allied supplies to the rest of Russia. Secondly, although they recaptured the city of Vyborg (Viipuri) just north of Leningrad in 1941, they didn't assist in any full attack on Leningrad itself, or even to sever it from the Russians last supply route via the ice road over Lake Ladoga. The Finns knew that whatever the outcome of the war, they would have the Russian giant as a long term neighbor, and didn't want to make a permanent enemy.

More important for the 1942 campaign was the contribution of Romania, Hungary and Italy, all of whose forces were deployed in the sector of Army Group South. By July 1st 1942 there were 12 Romanian, 10 Hungarian and 6 Italian divisions deployed on this sector. By November 15th 1942 the Romanian contribution had increased to 25 divisions including one armored, and the Italian to 10 divisions including 3 Alpine. These were numerically significant forces forming four armies: 2nd Hungarian, 3rd and 4th Romanian and 8th Italian, with a total of 28 and later 45 divisions i.e. about 400-700,000 troops.[17] They would play a significant part in the 1942 campaign, but apart from the Italian Alpine Corps were of poor quality; only about half of the combat efficiency of German units according to the OKH.[18]

Russian military power continued to expand during 1942 despite heavy losses. By mid-1942 the overall size of the armed forces was over 10 million.[19] The combat force at the front and including the reserve armies in European Russia, was around 5.5 million with 6,190 tanks and 3,160 combat aircraft.[20] These were organized into 9 Fronts deployed from north to south as follows: Leningrad, Volkhov, North West, Kalinin, West, Bryansk, South West, South and Caucasus. There were 39 all arms armies at the front; with another 10 all arms armies and 2 tank armies, plus large numbers of independent divisions in the Stavka reserve. Finally there were 3 armies in the Trans Caucasus Front, guarding the southern border with Turkey and Iran between the Black Sea and the Caspian. The total number of divisions was passing 400 about this time.

It is true that all levels of formation had lower establishments than in June 1941; armies for example approximated to Axis and Western Allied corps in size and the new tank and mechanized 'corps' were now division sized.

Most of the larger pre-war mechanized corps had been destroyed in 1941. Armor losses had been so heavy that by the time of the Moscow counter offensive in December 1941, brigades and a few remaining divisions were the largest type of tank unit. That was the low point however. Tank and assault gun production increased massively from 6,590 in all of 1941, to 11,177 in the first 6 months of 1942 and 13,268 in the last 6 months.[21] The two Russian tank armies, there would be six of them by 1944, each consisting of two tank and one mechanized corps (i.e. division sized), were a new type of strategic attack formation, normally under Stavka rather than Front control, and showed the revival of the armored force. By this time a majority of the Russian armor consisted of the T34 medium and KV heavy tanks. These were still technically superior to the German Pzkw III and IV, but the German armored formations and troops remained better organized and trained. Germany was therefore outnumbered overall, at the front, in formations, and in most categories of equipment, except for air forces, where there was approximate equality. However, on the vital southern sector from Voronezh to Rostov and the Kerch straits it was different.

German intelligence was still mostly unaware of the Russian reserve armies and underestimated its manpower reserves and war production. Russian intelligence however, was equally faulty in its assessment of German operational plans for 1942. They considered, even feared, that Moscow would be the target of a renewed summer offensive, but were short on specifics. Their primary concern was to guard against a wide range of possible Axis breakthrough and exploitation encirclements that might threaten the capital. The forces in the south, where the blow actually came, were relatively weaker. There were two Fronts on the southern sector from Kursk to the Sea of Azov: South West with 4 armies and South with 5 armies. Before the disaster at Kharkov these had 640,000 men, 1,300 tanks and 926 aircraft. They were probably not completely back to full strength by the start of 'Blau' on June 28th. Guarding the Taman peninsular, opposite the Crimea, were 120,000 troops of the Caucasus Front, the survivors of the Russian defeat at Kerch in May. There were also three reserve armies behind the Don, and two further back behind the Volga at Saratov and Stalingrad. All these reserves along with the 5th Tank Army would eventually be committed to oppose the 'Blau' offensive i.e. about another 400,000 men and 1,000 tanks.

Of the aforementioned 184 German divisions in the east, 5 were on the north Norway-Finland front and 12 were security divisions guarding Axis supply lines behind the front.[22] The remaining 167 divisions including 19 panzer and 16 motorized divisions were deployed from north to south as follows in June 1942:

Army Group North:
16th and 18th Armies with 37 divisions including 2 panzer and 1 motorized.

Army Group Center:
2nd and 3rd Panzer Armies, 4th and 9th Armies with 61 divisions including 8 panzer and 8 motorized._

Army Group South:
1st and 4th Panzer Armies, 2nd, 6th and 17th Armies with 61 divisions including 9 panzer and 7 motorized.

3rd and 4th Romanian, 2nd Hungarian and 8th Italian Armies with 28 allied divisions. (36 divisions by August, 45 divisions by November)

Crimea: 11th Army with 8 divisions.

If we include the 28 allied divisions, then the Axis were able to concentrate 97 out of 195 divisions, including 16 of the 35 mobile divisions, on the southern sector of the eastern front for the 1942 offensive. The forces initially allocated to operation 'Blau' therefore amounted to about 1,200,000 German and 400,000 allied troops, with 1,850 tanks and assault guns, supported by 1,600 combat aircraft. The Russians therefore had an overall superiority, but on the southern sector, the Axis had the edge with a German superiority in mobile forces and air power. The attacking Axis concentrated about 50% of their entire force in the south, the defending Russians about 30%. On specific points of attack, and given superior German combat effectiveness, they were well capable of achieving breakthroughs and 'blitzkrieg' exploitation operations like those of 1941. An attacking force that was inferior overall, was thus using the classic strategic principle of concentration, to achieve equality in the chosen offensive theatre (the south), and superiority at specific points. The main Axis weakness was the high proportion of Romanian, Hungarian and Italian forces allocated to 'Blau'.

Operation 'Blau' started on June 28th 1942. It had been delayed at least 10 days due to the disruption to the timetable caused by the Russian Kharkov offensive in May. Army Group South was split into two groups, A and B, for 'Blau'. On the left (northern) flank was Army Group B commanded by Bock and then by Weichs. It consisted, from north to south, of the 2nd Army, 4th Panzer Army, 2nd Hungarian Army and the 6th Army, with 3rd and 4th Romanian Armies forming later. This left flank army group with 41 divisions including 5 panzer, 3 motorized and 10 Hungarian infantry divisions, attacked first between Orel and Kharkov across a 150 mile front between June 28th and 30th. The Russian South West Front, which had not fully recovered from its defeat at Kharkov-Izyum in May, suffered the brunt of this attack. Axis Army Group B quickly advanced the 100 miles to the river Don, capturing Voronezh on July 6th. They captured 88,000 prisoners by July 11th and destroyed 1,000 tanks and 1,700 guns. This was far less than expected and the Russians were able to avoid any major encirclements and retreat. Most of the Russians here survived to fight another day, but were disorganized and vulnerable during the rest of July and into August. Fearing that this attack was the southern pincer of a renewed offensive against Moscow, rather than the northern pincer of the first stage of 'Blau'; the Stavka committed the 5th Tank Army and five independent tank corps from reserve in a counter attack from the north towards Voronezh. The counter attack failed, but it did delay the 4th Panzer Army from executing encirclements to the south, thus facilitating the retreat of the nonetheless shattered South West Front to the east. By July 15th Hoth's 4th Panzer Army, leading Army Group B, had advanced 200 miles down the Don-Donetz corridor and was half way to Stalingrad in conformity with 'Directive 41'.

Meanwhile on the right flank, along the 200 mile front between Kharkov and the Sea of Azov, Army Group A started its offensive on July 9th, forming the southern pincer of a planned encirclement. List's Army Group A, deployed from north to south, consisted of Kleist's 1st Panzer Army, 8th Italian Army and 17th Army, with 24 German divisions including 4 panzer and 4 motorized along with 9 allied divisions. Their opponent was the Russian South Front. List's Army Group rapidly captured the Donbass industrial area and Rostov the 'gateway to the Caucasus' fell on July 23rd. However, the Russians were again able to retreat and avoid encirclement. This was despite a change of German plans, ordered by Hitler, against the advice of his generals. On July 13th Army Group B in the northern sector, instead of advancing in full force eastwards towards Stalingrad, diverted Hoth's 4th Panzer Army southward in a failed encirclement of the Russian South Front near Rostov. This left only Paulus's slower moving 6th Army to continue the advance towards Stalingrad, against what was at that time, disorganized opposition. Two other German strategic mistakes were also made around this time.

First, having achieved a superior concentration of force on the southern sector of the front, the Germans then started to disperse it after the offensive began. Two panzer and one motorized divisions were transferred to Army Group Center, a significant reduction from Army Group South's 9 panzer and 7 motorized division striking force. The German 11th Army after the capture of Sevastopol was also largely transferred along with its commander, Manstein, one of the best German generals of the war, to Army Group North for the planned attack on Leningrad. Only 2 of its 8 infantry divisions remained in the Crimea along with 6 Romanian divisions. As a general rule it is usually poor strategy to disperse or split your forces and deploy excessive strength in secondary theatres. The attack on Leningrad never took place as the forces were needed to help counter a Russian relieving offensive by their Volkhov Front in August and September 1942. The Russians paid a high price for this offensive however, with two armies largely destroyed and 114,000 casualties including 40,000 killed. German casualties were only 26,000.[23]

The second mistake was to replace the strategy of 'Directive 41' with the new 'Directive 45' on July 23rd. The essential features of 'Directive 41' were that both Army Groups A and B would coordinate their forces to achieve the intermediate objectives of the Stalingrad 'land bridge' and securing the Don defensive flank. Then once Army Group B was in place holding this defensive flank, a reinforced Army Group A would commence the Caucasus offensive. The two operations, Don-Stalingrad and Caucasus, were to be done sequentially, one at a time. 'Directive 45' changed this plan very early in the campaign, to a much riskier simultaneous offensive against Stalingrad and the Caucasus. Simultaneous offensives meant that they were committing the classic error of operational fragmentation, more commonly known as splitting your forces.

Under the new 'Directive 45', Army Group B in the northern sector would resume the advance from the Don bend to Stalingrad. Here Paulus's 6th Army was initially on its own. However on 30th-31st July Hoth's 4th Panzer Army, which we may recall had been diverted south towards Rostov and was temporarily part of Army Group A, was now diverted again, back towards Stalingrad and deployed supporting 6th Armies right flank. Behind these two German armies, and moving into defensive position behind the river Don on their left, were Axis allied armies; the Hungarian 2nd, Italian 8th, and later the Romanian 3rd. So in the end after delays, diversions and changes, two German armies would target Stalingrad and its environs, instead of the originally planned combined Army Groups A and B, with 4 German armies including both panzer armies.

Army Group A would now simultaneously advance from Rostov towards the Caucasus. Its German 17th Army on the right would move down the Black Sea coast with the Turkish frontier at Batum as the eventual objective. Army Group A's 1st Panzer Army in the center, would advance southeast from Rostov towards Grozny and then Baku, a huge distance of 700 miles. So under the new 'Directive 45' plan, the Caucasus offensive would also be only half as powerful as under the original 'Directive 41'. Its AG A would only have two German armies, 17th and 1st Panzer, instead of four, the 4th Panzer Army having been reallocated to the Stalingrad operation and the 11th Army redeployed from the Crimea to Leningrad. Two simultaneous instead of sequential offensives meant that each was only half as powerful as previously planned.

Moreover the two offensives were in divergent directions. Army Group B would move east towards Stalingrad, while Army Group A would advance south-east towards Baku, and south towards Batum. The risks were that each advance would be too weak to achieve its objective, and that vulnerable gaps would appear between them. The latter was particularly the case with Army Group A, which had huge distances to travel and the Caucasus Mountains to cross. As the advance proceeded with weakened and divided forces the frontage to be covered would increase. On June 28th when 'Blau' began it was 500 miles long. By July 25th when the line of the Don was reached it was 750 miles. The final objective line of: Voronezh, Stalingrad, Astrakhan, Baku, Batum, which was never reached; would have been 1,100 miles long excluding coastlines. The root of the problem was the failure to define the priority of either of the two main objectives; Stalingrad and the Caucasus. Hitler failed to adhere to the strategic principle of selecting and maintaining the main objective in 1942, just as he had failed in 1941.

Army Group A, targeting the Caucasus, had the furthest to go and initially made rapid progress. They crossed the Don east of Rostov on July 25th and Kleist's 1st Panzer Army advancing south initially, captured the first oilfield at Maikop on August 9th, a distance of 200 miles in two weeks. The Russians had destroyed the oilfield and the Germans got little use from it during their five months of control. The 17th Army advanced down the coast of the Sea of Azov a similar distance, but only managed to capture the port of Novorossiysk on the Black Sea on September 6th after a week long battle. Both German armies had reached the Caucasus Mountains, and Alpine troops even managed to scale the highest mountain in Europe, the 18,500 ft Mount Elbrus on August 21st 1942. However, that was as far as they reached. The Russians had been overrun in the steppes of the North Caucasus by the fast moving panzer units, but held the mountains. Nor did 17th Army make any more progress down the Black Sea coast; the front became static below Novorossiysk for a full year. From Maikop, 1st Panzer Army swung to the east and advanced another 200 miles with the Caucasus range to its right, reaching Mozdok and the river Terek in Chechnya on August 27th. Here they too came to a halt, 50 miles short of the second oilfield objective of Grozny.

After a rapid advance they were delayed by fuel shortages as well as by Russian opposition holding the mountains. The front stabilized here for four months until December 27th 1942, despite renewed and failed German attacks in September and up to early November. Army Group A with only about 20 divisions and operating at the end of long supply lines was simply too weak to breach the Caucasus barrier. Baku was still 300 miles away and they got no where near it. The Germans remained the masters of mobile warfare; however, static warfare in mountains or cities favored the defending Russians. The Axis were also becoming vulnerable on their left flank in the Kalmyk steppe, where there was a huge gap of 300 miles parallel to the Caspian coast, between 1st Panzer Army in Chechnya and the right flank of Army Group B holding the Volga south of Stalingrad. There was no continuous front here, only mobile patrols and on the Russian side, cavalry, which contrary to popular belief still had a role in certain circumstances and sectors of the eastern front. The Russians would later exploit this weakly held area as part of their Stalingrad counter offensive in November. It is to that decisive battle that we now turn.

From July 23rd to 31st the German 6th Army was on its own leading Army Group B's advance to the Don bend and Stalingrad. The Russians were at a low ebb of morale at this point and Stalin returned to the old policy of no retreats and executions of his own troops in order to enforce it. At the same time they were forming a new Stalingrad Front, out of the shattered and then disbanded South Front and reinforcements from the Stavka reserve. It was August 23rd before Army Group B, reinforced by now with the 4th Panzer Army, crossed the Don and then the 35 mile 'land bridge' reaching the Volga just north of Stalingrad. Two days later the Russians declared the city under a state of siege. Russian counter attacks failed to dislodge the Germans from the 'land bridge' at this time but these battles delayed the German attack on Stalingrad itself. The city had been under mass air attack since August 23rd when evacuation of 90% of its half million civilians had started. It was September 13th before the first serious ground attack against Stalingrad itself began. For just over two months, until November 19th, the front at Stalingrad and the 400 mile Axis defensive flank along the Don to the north-west was essentially static. The war of movement in this sector therefore ended around the end of August, roughly the same time as with Army Group A's over extended front in the Caucasus.

The balance of forces on the Stalingrad sector, not just in the city itself, i.e. German 6th Army and 4th Panzer Armies and the Russian Stalingrad and South East Fronts, was about even with 590,000 troops each on September 13th when the battle began. The Germans had 1,000 tanks against 600, and 1.000 combat aircraft against 389.[24] The urban fighting that characterized the first two months of the Battle of Stalingrad favored the defending Russians. Neither side committed all of the above forces to the city itself or all at once. Only two Russian armies, Chuikov's 62nd and 64th out of eleven in the Stalingrad and South East Fronts, fought this well known part of the battle. Although they were pushed back to the Volga the Russians were able to keep these two armies supplied, supported by artillery and maintained with replacements from the eastern bank. The normal German combat effectiveness superiority and edge in armor and air power was reduced under these conditions. The Germans committed a higher proportion of their forces; principally the 6th Army with an average strength of 250-275,000 and 300 tanks deployed in 20 divisions, including 3 temporarily attached panzer divisions. Again not all of these were in battle all at once on the 30 mile front of the city itself; however that was where their attack was focused. Epic and iconic as the battle inside the city itself was, the Russians, of choice, only reinforced Stalingrad enough to maintain a viable defense. More important, strategically and for the final outcome, was that they used their superior overall resources to increase their forces on both flanks of Stalingrad.

It is clear, especially in retrospect that 'Blau' had failed by about the start of September 1942. Army Group B had reached and was consolidating at the Volga at this time and was about to begin the battle for Stalingrad itself. At the same time, Army Group A's 1st Panzer Army in the Caucasus, was halted at the Terek, 50 miles short of Grozny. Stalingrad and the Terek were as far to the east as the Axis were going to advance in World War Two. The divided and thus weakened Axis 1942 offensive had come to a halt, with about 6-7 weeks of viable campaigning weather still to go. Middle to late October was the expected start of the autumn mud season this far south. Not only had 'Blau' failed, especially in the Caucasus, to achieve its territorial and economic objectives, it also failed to eliminate the remaining Soviet armed forces. The Axis had yet again under estimated the scale of Russian reserves, production levels and military capabilities. This along with strategy disputes caused further friction between Hitler and the OKH, contributing to the dismissal of C-of-S Halder, OKH's best planner on September 24th. Russian losses had been heavy, in the four month long Stalingrad defensive phase alone from July 17th to November 18th, there were 324,000 dead and prisoners and 320,000 wounded.[25] However, there were no massive encirclements and surrenders on the scale of 1941. Moreover, they were continuing to replace their losses of men and material and expand their forces as well. Without the change of strategy from 'Directive 41' to 'Directive 45' the Axis might have done more and made use of 6-7 more weeks of potentially mobile warfare. As it was, the 10 or so weeks of static warfare from the start of September to November 19th favored the Russians, and allowed them to prepare for new winter counter offensives.

Consequences for the Axis: Operations Uranus, Saturn and Mars

As the planetary codenames suggest, the Russian counter offensives, like most else on the eastern front would be massive. By November 1942 the total strength of the Russian field armies had expanded to 6,124,000 men, 77,734 guns and mortars, 6,956 tanks and 3,254 combat aircraft. There were 391 rifle divisions and 15 division sized tank and mechanized corps at the front, with another 25 rifle divisions and 13 tank and mechanized corps in the Stavka reserve.[26] Initial planning for operations 'Uranus' and 'Saturn' began in mid-September, ironically at the start of the urban phase of the Battle of Stalingrad. 'Uranus' was a planned envelopment from north and south of the German 6th Army attacking Stalingrad. 'Saturn' was its follow up, an even larger offensive from the river Don targeted on Rostov. If 'Saturn' succeeded it could trap the entire Axis Army Group A in the Caucasus, as well as smashing much of Army Group B on the Don during the breakthrough and exploitation advance. The Russians were thinking big as their resources grew.

For operation 'Uranus' the Russians had three Fronts or army groups. Vatutin's South West and Rokossovsky's Don Fronts would attack from the north of Stalingrad, using bridgeheads that they already held over the river Don. Eremenko's Stalingrad Front would attack from south of the city across the Volga bridgeheads and the open Kalmyk steppe. On November 19th 1942 when 'Uranus' began these three fronts contained 10 armies including 5th Tank Army, deploying 5 tank and one mechanized corps and 66 rifle divisions. The total manpower strength was 1.1 million with 15,000 guns and mortars of all calibers, 1,400 tanks and 1,100 combat aircraft, roughly double the strength of September 13th when the Battle of Stalingrad proper began.

At the maximum the Axis had 50 divisions on this sector of which 26 were German, including 5 panzer and 4 motorized divisions; and 18 Romanian and 6 Italian divisions.[27] The Axis establishment strength was 1 million men, 10,300 guns, 675 tanks and 1,134 aircraft. The actual strength would have been less, due to the two months attrition of the urban phase of the battle. Still, the balance of forces seemed to be only modestly in the attacking Russians favor. The offensive coincided with the onset of winter which helped the Russians, although this time unlike in 1941 the Axis had made preparations. Crucially the blow fell largely and intentionally on the Romanian 3rd Army to the northwest of Stalingrad and the Romanian 4th Army to the south of the city. The German 6th and 4th Panzer Armies, weakened by the urban phase of the battle, were largely unengaged at the start of the new offensive. Half of the defenders overall were the less combat effective Axis allies and only 15 Romanian and 7 German divisions took the initial brunt of the offensive.

The Russian 'Uranus' offensive which started on November 19th 1942 was a complete success. The two Romanian armies crumbled immediately, losing 5 divisions and 33,000 prisoners in only 4 days on the Don sector alone. The two Russian pincers met on November 23rd near Kalach on the Don, 50 miles west of Stalingrad. It was the first successful major Russian encirclement operation of the war. About 280,000 Axis troops, 150 tanks and 1,800 guns in 21 German and 2 Romanian divisions were trapped in the Stalingrad pocket, three times as many as the Russians originally estimated. Against the advice of his better generals, Hitler ordered that there would be no retreat and even refused the trapped 6th Army permission to attempt a breakout. Instead the Axis attempted to supply it by air and launch a relief attack under Manstein. Both strategies were unrealistic and both failed. The minimum supply requirement was 500 to 950 tons per day according to various authorities and calculations. Goering rashly promised that the Luftwaffe could manage the lower figure, while the actual average level achieved was only 90 tons per day. The trapped forces would thus inevitably have to surrender when they ran out of food, fuel and ammunition, or froze and starved to death, which is eventually what happened. The relief attack codenamed 'Winter Storm' lasted from December 12th to the 18th and got within 30 miles of the pocket. The improvised force from the battered 4th Panzer Army and various other reinforcements, called Army Group Don, was actually less than an army in strength, the minimum that even the brilliant Manstein required for success.

On December 16th the Russians began the follow up offensive, operation 'Saturn'. Its original target was Rostov, which would have threatened to cut off the two armies and 20 divisions of Axis Army Group A, which were still 200-300 miles to the south in the Caucasus. Manstein's 'Winter Storm' forced the Russians to modify this to a less ambitious plan, 'Little Saturn', aimed at countering Manstein's effort and clearing the Don-Donetz corridor. Even so 'Little Saturn' using the Voronezh Front, added another 425,000 men, 1,030 tanks, 5,000 guns and 36 divisions to the attack.[28] They struck across the Don to the north-west of the ongoing 'Uranus' offensive, and advanced south. Their main opponent was the Italian 8th Army with only 230,000 men, 1,320 guns and only 55 tanks in 10 divisions.[29] Facing these odds the Italian's were shattered. On January 13th the Voronezh Front extended its offensive against the 10 divisions of the Hungarian 2nd Army, holding the line to the north of the Italians. The entire defensive flank of Axis Army Group B on the Don from Stalingrad to Voronezh, manned from east to west, by the Romanian 3rd, Italian 8th, and Hungarian 2nd Armies, was thus attacked in successive offensives and demolished, along with the Romanian 4th Army to the south of Stalingrad.

Manstein's 'Winter Storm' counter attack delayed the process but couldn't prevent it.

We may recall that Army Group B's 400 mile long defensive flank from Voronezh to Stalingrad, was there to protect Army Group A's Caucasus offensive, which had been stalled since the start of September. On December 27th the 1st Panzer and 17th Armies of Army Group A, were finally ordered to retreat, to avoid being cut off in the Caucasus due to the collapse of Army Group B. The 1st Panzer Army narrowly won the 'race to Rostov', escaping through the city on February 1st 1943, just before the Russians recaptured it from the north five days later. The 17th Army retreated the shorter distance to the Taman peninsular, with an escape route to the Crimea to its west. Meanwhile the six armies of the Russian Don Front had been containing and then attacking the Stalingrad pocket. The Battle of Stalingrad itself finally ended on February 2nd 1943 with the surrender of the remaining 91,000 Germans in the pocket.[30] They had suffered losses of 147,000 killed since the trap closed on November 23rd 1942, giving a total German irrecoverable loss of 238,000 men, 150 tanks, 1,800 guns and 21 divisions destroyed. Only 25,000 wounded and 18,000 specialists were evacuated by air from the pocket.

'Uranus' was a total Russian victory. 'Saturn' was an important victory as well, however, the escape of Axis Army Group A, meant it fell just short of total annihilation of the enemy. That would have shortened the war rather than only turning the tide! Even so 'Saturn' and 'Uranus' together, almost destroyed Axis Army Group B. The Axis allied losses were massive. The Romanian's suffered 173,000 casualties in 6 weeks, from their strength of 268,000 in November 1942 when 'Uranus' began. Their 3rd and 4th Armies and 15 of their 18 divisions were largely destroyed.[31] The Italian 8th Army with 10 divisions was shattered, losing 85,000 men killed and missing and 30,000 wounded out of its strength of 230,000.[32] Finally the Hungarian 2nd Army of 10 divisions was virtually annihilated, losing 80,000 men killed, 63,000 wounded and 87,000 prisoners.[33] By the first week of February 1943 with the surrender at Stalingrad and the fall of Rostov the Russians had recaptured all of the territory lost to operation 'Blau' between June and September 1942. This was a much larger result for Russia than the Moscow counter offensive over the previous winter of 1941-42.

The Axis had 55 divisions, including 21 German, wiped out of their order of battle, out of 179 German and 45 allied divisions excluding the Finns, on the entire eastern front. Four Axis allied armies and the German 6th Army were destroyed. Only the German 2nd Army, retreating from Voronezh due to the collapse of the Hungarians on its right flank, and the remains of 4th Panzer Army survived the destruction of Army Group B. Thus around half of the Axis Army Group South committed to operation 'Blau' i.e. five of its ten armies and 55 of 105 divisions,[34] including Axis allied forces, had been destroyed by the start of February 1943. Russian losses in the counter offensive phase from November 19th 1942 to February 2nd 1943, had been heavy as well, with 155,000 killed or prisoners and 331,000 wounded.[35] However for the first time in the war, the Russians had achieved a major encirclement and destruction of a German army, and in the counter offensive phase inflicted more casualties on the Axis, albeit mostly Axis allies, than they suffered themselves. The Stalingrad campaign was therefore much more than a battle just for the city. We have to consider the entire scope of Axis operation 'Blau' and the Russian counter offensives of 'Uranus' and 'Saturn'. Stalingrad was the focus of events and an epic of endurance and of history. However, it was the campaign overall that was the decisive turning of the tide on the eastern front of World War Two.

The central sector of the eastern front was largely static while 'Blau' proceeded. Static doesn't mean unimportant or inactive however. The Germans were only about 100 miles from Moscow here. They held a large salient roughly 100 by 100 miles, jutting out from Smolensk in a north easterly direction to the city of Rzhev. Both sides were on the strategic defensive here during the summer of 1942. The Axis were concentrating on operation 'Blau' and the Russians were guarding Moscow against an expected offensive that never occurred. Once the 'Blau' offensive in the south came to a halt in September 1942, the Russians began planning for a counter offensive in the center as well. It was codenamed 'Mars', and the aim was to cut off and destroy the German 9th Army holding the Rzhev salient, thus reducing any threat to Moscow. The Moscow sector, as we saw during the 1941 campaign, was the most important one for the Russians, and it remained so in 1942 as well. This was despite 'Blau' and the threat to Stalingrad and the Caucasus. Russian forces here remained larger than those in the south throughout 1942. There were three Fronts or army groups guarding Moscow: North Western, Kalinin and Western. These contained 1.9 million men, 24,000 guns and mortars, 3,300 tanks and 1,100 combat aircraft. This was roughly half of the armor and 35% of overall Russian strength on the eastern front, deployed on only 17% of its extent. (200 miles as the crow flies, twice that due to the salients on this sector.)[36]

Originally timed for October 12th, bad weather delayed the start of 'Mars' until November 25th 1942. Therefore operation 'Mars' started within a week of 'Uranus'. However, until the collapse of Soviet communism in 1992, 'Mars' was rarely mentioned in the historical accounts. The reason is that it was another massive Russian disaster, coinciding with the victory at Stalingrad, and thus the Soviet's covered up the truth for propaganda reasons. Seven Russian armies with 667,000 men and 1,900 tanks, about half of each of the Kalinin and Western Fronts, attacked the Rzhev salient from both sides. On December 7th the Germans counter attacked against the Russian pincers which never met. The battle was over by December 23rd 1942 with Russian losses of 70,000 killed, 145,000 wounded and 1,600 out of 1,900 tanks destroyed.[37] The German salient held, but ironically in March 1943 they evacuated it voluntarily in order to shorten the front and economize on forces. With the failure of 'Mars', 'Jupiter', a planned follow up offensive against German Army Group Center as a whole, never took place.

The Axis 1942 campaign in the east was their last chance to win World War Two outright. They could only do so by concentrating on and defeating one of their opponents at a time, in this case Soviet Russia. The Moscow offensive in December 1941 saved Russia from immediate defeat, and gave it a breathing space up to the spring of 1942, but no more than that. The simultaneous entry of America into the war couldn't in itself save Russia during 1942. The USA and Britain were largely on the defensive during most of 1942, both in the Mediterranean and Atlantic theatres. They were slowly supplying Russia with lend lease materials as best they could, but it was only a small fraction, about 5% of Russia's own production in 1942.[38] Moreover a second front in Europe was impractical in 1942. The limited plan that they did have, codenamed 'Sledgehammer', was for implementation in the extreme emergency of a possible collapse of Soviet Russia. The only other Western Allied offensive campaign was the strategic bombing of Germany. In 1942 however, this was in its early stages; was largely a British rather than American or joint offensive; and had little impact on the Axis economies, being largely contained by the German home air defenses. In June 1942 for example when 'Blau' began the Luftwaffe had a total strength of 3,725 combat aircraft. Of these only 244 were night fighters containing the British bombing campaign, a total that rose to only 389 by December 1942.[39] The bulk of the Luftwaffe, about 2,750 combat aircraft, were on the eastern front in June at the start of 'Blau', and most of the balance, about 650, was in the Mediterranean. As for ground warfare, it would be October 23rd before the Alamein offensive started, followed by operation 'Torch' on November 8th 1942. The eastern front was thus by far the largest and most decisive theatre in 1942, and Russia could still lose or just collapse.

Axis operation 'Blau', and not just the Battle of Stalingrad, which was a component part of it, was therefore one of the decisive campaigns of World War Two. In retrospect 'Blau' had failed by mid-September 1942 when the relatively short two month period of mobile warfare ended on both the Stalingrad and Caucasus sectors. The following 7 week static period up to November 19th was a relative lull, and to the advantage of the Russians who were building their strength for the counter offensives of

'Uranus', 'Saturn', 'Mars' and potentially 'Jupiter'. The outcomes of these operations have already been detailed above.

The result in terms of casualties inflicted on the Axis, and the recapture of all the previously lost territory by the Russians, ranks this campaign as the most decisive that we have covered so far. First, 'Blau' and its planetary nemeses, was a turning point campaign for the European War; more so than Moscow, or the Battles of France or Britain, or any of the Mediterranean campaigns. Some of the others were major setbacks for the Axis, altering the course of the war; but they were able to recover, change their strategy and continue to advance. In contrast the situation in September and October 1942 marks the absolute maximum extent of the European Axis advance in World War Two. Secondly, after 'Uranus' and 'Saturn' were completed, it was probably impossible for the Axis to defeat Russia or to win the war outright. That wasn't the case with the outcomes of the previous campaigns. Finally, the campaign was a psychological turning point, increasing Russian and by default Western Allied morale, and reducing Axis confidence in final victory, especially in the Axis allied countries. We therefore have not only a change in the course of the war, but also a turning of the tide and the final closing off of a possible European Axis decisive and complete overall victory.

The Stalingrad and Caucasus campaigns were therefore as decisive as it gets. It could have been even worse for the Axis. 'Uranus' and 'Mars' each aimed at trapping and destroying a German army. 'Saturn' and 'Jupiter' aimed to destroy two entire Axis army groups; South and Center respectively. If the Russians had achieved all of these outcomes, the consequences would have been incalculable. Certainly the war would have been shortened, probably considerably. The Axis might even have offered immediate compromise peace terms, and the dictatorship regimes of Hitler and Mussolini would have been weakened or even seriously threatened from within by their own militaries. Soviet Russia's position as the 'leading victor' would have become much stronger relative to the Western Allies during and after the war. In the event the Russian plans were probably still overambitious for this stage of the war. They destroyed the German 6th Army and demolished mostly the non-German half of Army Group B. 'Blau' could also have been a decisive campaign in another sense as well. It might have gone better for the Axis than it did. In order to answer the question of whether the Axis could have won the war in 1942, we need to consider their options and the possible consequences.

Alternative Axis Strategic Options for 1942

There were two basic alternative Axis strategies available on the eastern front in 1942. First there is the avoidance of the modifications and mistakes associated with operation 'Blau'. Secondly there were alternative strategies to 'Blau' itself. We have already identified the changes made to the original 'Directive 41' for the 'Blau' offensive and need only a concise recap here, while concentrating on the outcomes and consequences of the alternative strategy. The most important error by far was the change from a two stage sequential offensive, to that of two simultaneous offensives. Despite the concentrating in June 1942, of about 50% of the Axis eastern army for the start of 'Blau', the margin of superiority over the Russians on the southern sector of the front was modest. The dispersion of about 9 divisions, including the 11th Army to the Leningrad sector, was a mistake. Splitting the operation however, into two simultaneous offensives, was even worse. The negative effect as we have detailed above, was to half the power of both the 'intermediate offensive' against the Don and Stalingrad, and of the 'primary offensive' against the Caucasus.

The only possible advantage of the historical change, to two simultaneous offensives against both Stalingrad and the Caucasus, would be in timing. In theory two simultaneous offensives would have been completed faster than two consecutive ones. In reality, the timing of the change was about as bad as it could have been, and unnecessary anyway. There was plenty of time for both offensives to be completed consecutively. The change occurs with 'Directive 45' on July 23rd and supplemented by the re-transfer of the 4th Panzer Army on July 30th, back from Army Group A targeting the Caucasus, to Army Group B targeting the Stalingrad area. The change of German strategy occurs when the Russians were at their weakest, especially on the Stalingrad sector. It is true that they had avoided huge encirclements like those of 1941 by retreating instead. In July 1942 however, the retreats of the battered Russian South West and South Fronts were hardly orderly, and there was a severe if temporary deterioration of morale at this time. So much so that Stalin issued his 'not a step back' order 227 on July 28th to counter the crisis.[40] As it was the Germans were able to reach the Volga just north of Stalingrad on August 23rd 1942. This was an advance of about 200 miles since the change to 'Directive 45' one month previously, and using only the 6th Army and later the re-diverted 4th Panzer Army.

Had they not deviated from the original 'Directive 41', they would have had twice this strength for this phase, the advance to Stalingrad, with Army Group A's 1st Panzer and 17th Armies advancing eastwards south of the Don as well. It cannot be claimed for certain that they could have captured Stalingrad itself in a 'surprise' attack, while the Russians were still in a state of poor morale and disorganization. Even so, with four armies instead of two, they certainly would have made faster progress to the Don-Volga 'land bridge', and even succeeded in encircling substantial Russian forces in this area before reaching Stalingrad proper. Stalin's renewed 'not a step back' strategy would only have facilitated this outcome, in circumstances where the Axis had twice the strength and were moving faster than they did historically. Even had they not captured Stalingrad quickly, they could still have formed a defensive flank outside the city, across the 35-50 miles of the Don-Volga 'land bridge', with the Axis allied armies defending their historical 400 mile front behind the Don back to Voronezh. This would have substantially achieved the 'intermediate objective' of 'Directive 41'. There was no need for the Germans to get involved in a lengthy urban battle of attrition for Stalingrad at all or to get distracted by the symbolism of it, as seemed to be the case historically. They had far better uses for their mobile forces and air power, namely 'Directive 41's' 'primary objective' of the Caucasus.

The question then arises as to whether there was time for the 'primary offensive' to the Caucasus, using the original sequential or consecutive plan of 'Directive 41'. Historically it took the Axis one month, starting on July 25th after the fall of Rostov, for the mobile 1st Panzer Army to advance 200 miles south to the Maikop oilfield and then 200 miles south-east to reach Chechnya on August 27th, their easternmost advance. Even the slower 17th Army advanced the 300 miles to capture Mt Elbrus in the Caucasus on August 21st. Under 'Directive 41' the Caucasus offensive would have started 3 or 4 weeks later than it did historically, i.e. around August 20th, after Army Group B had secured the Don and Stalingrad flank. There would have been two months of good conditions for mobile operations, until the autumn mud season in late October this far south. Then another month would elapse before the winter snows. Even if the central thrust had only achieved the historical pace across the steppes of the North Caucasus, taking one month to advance 400 miles to Chechnya, that still leaves one month to advance the extra 50 miles to the oilfields at Grozny and 300 miles to the ultimate prize of Baku.

On the Black Sea coast they would have had an extra 300 miles to advance from the historical limit of Novorossiysk to the Turkish frontier at Batum. Here one of the extra armies, the German 11th under the excellent Manstein would have been used. It would have had a head start, attacking across the Kerch strait from the Crimea only 60 miles from Novorossiysk; instead of using the 17th Army from Rostov 200 miles to the north. Not only would Manstein's 11th Army have already been closer to its objective, it could have started earlier as well, having completed the capture of Sevastopol on July 9th. Supplementary to this a more difficult attack across the mountains from Mt Elbrus was 100 miles from Batum. Finally, on the eastern flank of the Caucasus operation, there would have been the advance down the lower Volga, from around Stalingrad, to Astrakhan on the Caspian Sea, a distance of 200 miles across flat steppe terrain.

The total forces available under 'Directive 41', for the 'primary offensive' against the Caucasus, would have been twice as powerful as the historic ones, and even more so in armor and air strength. They would have consisted of 1st and 4th Panzer Armies and 11th and 17th Armies, about 40 divisions including 9 panzer and 7 motorized divisions. That comes to 700,000 men, 1,850 tanks, and most of the 1,600 combat aircraft committed to 'Blau'. The 6th Army would have remained behind, guarding the Stalingrad area and the Volga. Thus advance rates, especially when a battle was being fought in the open terrain, would likely have been faster than the historic ones. How far beyond the historical position would they have advanced?

Historically, the Russian defense consisted of the Trans-Caucasus Front with an eventual 8 armies, with 37 infantry and 9 cavalry divisions and 8 armored brigades; which at full strength comes to about 450,000 men, 500 tanks and 300 aircraft.[40] They managed to hold historically on the Caucasus mountain line, against the outnumbered Axis Army Group A's 1st Panzer and 17th Armies, with 22 divisions including 3 panzer and 3 motorized i.e. about 350,000 men and 500 tanks. However, even in the winter counter offensive, they couldn't hurt the Axis much on the steppe terrain to the north; only following them up as they retreated after December 27th 1942. Facing the original Axis 'Directive 41' plan, we can see from the above that the numerical balance would have been more than reversed in favor of the Axis. The Germans would also have had their combat effectiveness superiority as well. One final factor favorable to the Axis was that the population of the Caucasus and some of the Soviet forces deployed there consisted of various non-Russian ethnic nationalities. Stalin rightly feared these to be unreliable or hostile to Soviet rule. On previous performance, the Russians, outnumbered almost two to one, defending the 500 mile Caucasus front from the Black Sea to the Caspian in summer weather, stood little chance. Set against this, the defending Russians would have the advantage of the mountainous terrain, and the Axis advance would eventually become hampered by lengthening supply lines.

Astrakhan at the mouth of the Volga on the Caspian, only 200 miles distant across favorable flat terrain, would easily have been reached in two to three weeks on the immediately proceeding historical performance. That would have isolated the Trans-Caucasus and its oilfields by land from the rest of Russia and disrupted the main sea transport route along the Volga. This would then have caused supply problems for the defenders as well. In the center, the extra 50 miles to Grozny and then another 100 miles to the Caspian coast at Makhachkala across panzer friendly flat terrain, with twice the historical force and a month to achieve it, would have been another Axis victory. Beyond that the outcome of an advance the extra 200 miles to Baku down the 20-30 mile wide corridor between the Caucasus Mountains and the Caspian Sea is more uncertain. Unless Russian morale had collapsed by then due to previous defeats and isolation from the rest of the Soviet regime, which it could have done; then the military circumstances of geography and timing must eventually favor the defenders. Similar circumstances favoring the Russian defenders would have eventually applied on the Black Sea coastal sector.

There is no doubt that the Axis would have done better than historically and captured Astrakhan and Grozny, thus isolating the Caucasus. The outcome of the battles on the Caucasus line itself and the two coastal plains however, must be judged as uncertain but with the odds favoring the Axis. If the Axis had breached the Caucasus Mountain line, then the flat, wide Georgia valley terrain beyond, stretching from Batum on the Black Sea to Baku on the Caspian would have favored mobile warfare again, and the campaign would have been over. All that remained would have been to transfer most of the 1st and 4th Panzer Armies, and Luftwaffe air power, into reserve behind Army Group B on the Don, to counter the Russian winter offensive in November. That would have been necessary no matter what the outcome of the battle for the Caucasus line.

By keeping to the original 'Directive 41' strategy for operation 'Blau' it seems reasonable that the Axis would have reached at least the Caucasus Mountain line, and quite possibly the Turkish and Persian frontiers by about October 1942. They could also have avoided the urban phase of the Battle of Stalingrad and been in position to stalemate operations 'Uranus' and 'Saturn'. They were after all able to do the same historically against the slightly more powerful 'Mars' offensive in December 1942. The outcome of the 'Blau' campaign would have changed. The course of the war in the east, and by default the rest of it as well, would have changed. However, it might still not have led to an *immediate* overall Russian defeat.

The loss of the oilfields or even the isolation of Baku from the rest of Russia would have been a serious blow. However, Russia had considerable reserve stocks, and it is estimated that it would have been mid-1943 before the Soviet economy and military operations would become crippled by fuel shortages.[42] It would have been even later before the Axis could have fully benefited from control of the oilfields. They would need repairing and the oil transport facilities would need improving as well. To get the full benefit would have required sea transport via the Black Sea and the Turkish straits into an Axis controlled Mediterranean. Still, this was quite plausible. As we have seen, an Axis conquest of Malta and an advance to Suez was still possible in 1942, even concurrent with the Russian campaign. It would only have required a modest earlier commitment of about four extra mobile divisions to North Africa, of which two panzer divisions could have come from France rather than the eastern front. Axis forces at Suez and in the Caucasus could then have threatened or attempted to implement a variant of operation 'Orient', targeting the British Middle East in 1943.

With 40% of it population and over one third of its GNP under Axis control in 1941, the Soviet Union was at a low point economically in 1942.[43] In 1942 overall economic output fell, but mobilization meant that proportionally more of it went to war production. Therefore they managed to increase war production in 1942, especially in ground force armaments, but at a heavy cost to the civilian population's well being. There was even starvation due to the fall in food production, as well as draconian measures by the Soviet regime in order to prevent a production and morale collapse on the home front. Stalin's 'not a step back' order in July 1942, was as much about preventing the further loss of economic resources, as well as restoring army morale.[44] In overall economic terms then, they were at the limit in 1942. It wasn't true that the Russians could just continue to retreat indefinitely into Asia. The loss of the Caucasus into 1943 would have contributed to an increasing deterioration of the economy, instead of the recovery that actually started in that year. However, that might have taken six months or longer. There wouldn't have been an immediate victory over Russia that would have allowed the Axis to overly concentrate against the Western Allies, who were finally on the offensive in the Mediterranean in 1943. If Russia had collapsed due to the economic effects of a successful operation 'Blau' or Stalin decided that it was pragmatic to agree peace terms, then it would likely have been well into 1943 rather than the end of 1942.

Russia might not have immediately collapsed militarily either. Their actual overall casualties for 1942 of 3.2 million 'irrecoverable' i.e. killed, prisoners and missing, and 2.3 million wounded were bad enough.[45] This total of over 5 million Russian losses in 1942 was somewhat higher than for the six months of war in 1941, but spread over an entire year, so the rate of loss had almost halved. We may recall that apart from its economic aims, 'Directive 41's' objective was to 'destroy the remaining Soviet armed forces'.[46] A successful 'Directive 41 Blau' as outlined here would have inflicted heavier losses on the Russians than the historical outcome. The Russians were vulnerable to this in the operations in the Don-Donetz area in July and August, before they were able to fall back to Stalingrad. The Axis aimed for an encirclement here of 700,000 men of the South West and South Fronts, equal to Kiev or Vyazma-Bryansk, their two largest victories in 1941.[47] The other danger would have been a mass surrender and destruction of a trapped Trans-Caucasus Front at the end of the campaign.

Even so, it is difficult to see how the Axis could have maintained the rate of loss inflicted in 1941, by a more effective implementation of operation 'Blau'. The reason is that the largest Russian forces in 1942 remained on the central front guarding Moscow, rather than in the south. An Axis victory in operation 'Blau', using the original consecutive strategy of 'Directive 41' and no dispersion of forces to other fronts, was certainly possible, even probable. Such an outcome could even have crippled the Russian giant, economically and militarily, by mid-1943. However, it might not have brought about Russia's immediate and total collapse at the end of 1942.

A more optimum operational strategy for the Germans in 1942 might well have been an alternative to 'Blau' altogether. For Stalin, Moscow was more important than Stalingrad, the Caucasus or Leningrad. We have seen how close the Axis came in 1941 to capturing Moscow. How indeed they could have achieved it by an alternative strategy; and the deadly danger that such an outcome posed for the Soviet regime in political, morale and psychological terms, as well as for Moscow's importance as a transport hub and industrial center. Stalin expected the Axis to advance in the center again in 1942. He placed his main force here, and eventually launched operation 'Mars' to remove the Axis threat here. A renewed Axis offensive by a reinforced Army Group Center offered more decisive and immediate results than 'Blau'. If the aim was to destroy the Russian armed forces and thus win the war in the east in 1942, which it was, then Moscow rather than Stalingrad or the Caucasus was probably the better option.

In the summer of 1942 the Axis starting line was only 100 miles from Moscow, which was well within reach on the basis of the historical 1941 and 1942 campaigns. Unlike in the 'Blau' campaign, the Russians dared not retreat on the Moscow front. As we have noted with regard to operation 'Mars', the front line here was jagged with several salients that were suitable for a preliminary phase of encirclement battles. In particular immediately to the north-west of the Axis Rzhev salient, the Russian Kalinin Front defended an equally large and vulnerable salient. About 7 or 8 Russian armies in total were vulnerable on Army Group Center's sector alone to the classic Axis encirclement attacks, which would likely have inflicted more casualties than 'Blau' did.[48] The Axis might well have achieved a major victory, destroying an entire Front of over half a million men, just as a preliminary battle. This would have straightened and thus shortened the front allowing the Axis to accumulate reserves.

From there they could have launched a 1942 version of 'Typhoon', starting only 100 miles from Moscow and with about three months available to complete it. In other words a '1942 Typhoon' would be starting even closer to Moscow, and would have had more time to complete, than either the actual '1941 Typhoon' or the '1941 Moscow first' option that we have previously considered. The defending Russians would have been stronger than in 1941, consisting of the forces available for 'Mars' and 'Jupiter', less any, probably heavy, losses suffered in the preliminary 'salient battles'. They would have been facing Army Group Center, with about 50% of the entire Axis eastern front army; the same concentration achieved for 'Blau', but this time consisting of all German units, not the less combat effective Axis allied armies. The Wehrmacht would thus have achieved a roughly equal numerical balance of forces on this sector, and combat power superiority when you take German efficiency into account. Finally, the Russian defenders would have had no terrain or climatic advantages to help them. A '1942 Typhoon' targeting Moscow, and even the Volga industrial region beyond, would have had a good chance of success and even Stalin thought it very plausible. The likely outcome and consequences would be similar to the alternative 'early Typhoon' option we examined for the 1941 'Barbarossa' campaign. Moscow would have fallen and Russia could well have been defeated, resulting in the collapse of the Soviet regime and its alliance with the Western Allies. As for operation 'Blau', the concession of the Caucasus oilfields would have been an obvious clause in any peace treaty.

The Axis eastern campaigns in both 1941 and 1942 were 'close run things'. Contrary to popular belief the Soviet Union was fairly close to collapse. The operational strategy changes we have considered could have given the Axis victory in Russia in the autumns of either 1941 or 1942. Axis victory was possible rather than probable. The odds favored Russia and the historical outcome, but only marginally. The combat effectiveness superiority of the German army over Russia has been calculated at 3.1 to 1 in 1941, 2.58 to 1 in 1943 and still 2 to 1 in 1944.[49] This went a long way in countering the Russian numerical superiority and the advantages of defending, of space and climate, and sometimes of terrain. The strategic opportunities for the Axis were at least as good as for their unexpected victory over France in 1940. Instead in the Russian campaigns of 1941 and 1942, the Axis made too many operational strategic mistakes, and that made a decisive difference in a situation where either side could reasonably have won.[50] Finally we need to ask if Russia had been defeated in 1942, how it would have affected the war in the west?

The strategic situation in 1943 wouldn't have been quite as favorable to the Axis as that following a Russian collapse in 1941. Yet the balance of power would hardly have favored the Western Allies. The Axis would still have controlled most of Eurasia, linking the European Axis and Japanese Empires. In Europe, assuming the planned garrison of 56 divisions in Russia, an extra 130 or so German divisions and over 2,000 combat aircraft would have reinforced the Western and Mediterranean fronts. That would have more than doubled the Luftwaffe and trebled their army facing the Western Allies, backed of course by the entire economy of Axis Europe, unburdened of replacing losses in Russia. The transfer of resources would still have been easily enough to at least stalemate the war in the west. The Axis would even have had a good chance of holding Tunisia and reversing the verdict of Alamein and 'Torch'. It would depend on the timing of any Russian collapse in 1942 and how far the Western Allies had advanced in the Mediterranean by then. If the Axis had followed the alternative Mediterranean strategy sequence of 'Malta then Egypt', as well as the 'Moscow option' in 1942, then their strategic position following a Russian collapse would have been even better. The situation would then have favored the Axis in countering operation 'Torch'. In either case the Western Allies would have had to reinforce, redeploy and defend against an Axis invasion of the Middle East from the Caucasus in 1943.

The main difference from a 'Russian 1941 collapse' scenario would be that Britain would probably have been safe from invasion. The Battle of the Atlantic turned in the Allies favor in 1943, allowing a greater American reinforcement of Britain than in 1942. The Axis wouldn't have had the time or the resources, to both stabilize or conquer the Mediterranean and then invade Britain in 1943. The rest of the war however, would still have seen a stalemated strategic situation. No Allied invasions of Europe or in the Mediterranean theatre along historical lines in 1943-45 would have been possible. The Allied strategic bomber offensive would also likely have failed against enhanced Axis air power and a secure economic base. The logical conclusion is that unless the Allies waited until 1945 for the 'bomb', there would have been a compromise peace in 1943 following any Soviet Russian collapse in 1942. Roosevelt's 'unconditional surrender' declaration, made at the Casablanca conference in January 1943, was unenforceable unless the Allies were already winning the war. If Russia had been defeated in 1942, the Western Allies might not have lost outright, but they wouldn't have won either. A strategic stalemate would have been the outcome.

The final conclusions of our examination of the Russian campaigns in 1941 and 1942 are therefore as follows. First, because of their sheer scale, the outcomes of the Russian campaigns were decisive to the outcome of the war in Europe as a whole. Which ever side won the war in Russia, would win the war in Western Europe and the Mediterranean as well. By 'win', we mean in the Axis case, any compromise peace that left the Axis controlling most of Europe, Russia and the Mediterranean. Britain may or may not have survived, depending on the timing of any possible Russian collapse. A Russian collapse in 1941 would still have placed Britain in dire danger in 1942. By 1943, following any Russian collapse in 1942, Britain was probably safe. Secondly, either side could have won the Russian campaigns in both 1941 and 1942. The balance of probabilities favored the historical outcome of a Russian, rather than an Axis victory, but only marginally. It was a 'close run thing'. Thirdly, the Western Allies couldn't have won the war in Europe on their own, nor probably, given the close margins in the east, could Russia. This doesn't of course mean that anything the Western Allies did was unimportant. Western Allied aid to Russia and the minority of Axis forces deployed against them, indirectly benefited Russia and influenced the outcome of the war in the east, and thus overall. An Allied victory required all three of Britain, the USA and Russia to remain in the fight. Overall the Russian campaigns were not only by far the largest and most costly, but also the most decisive campaigns of World War Two in Europe.

Notes for Chapter 5

1. Heinz Magenheimer, Hitler's War: Germany's Key Strategic Decisions 1940-1945, Cassell Military Paperbacks, London, 1998, p 64.
2. Kershaw, Fateful Choices, p 414.
3. ibid, p 317.
4. ibid, p 385.
5. Magenheimer, Hitler's War, p 129.
6. Erickson, Road to Stalingrad, p 272.
7. ibid, p 272.
8. Bauer, WW2 Vol 7, p 668. Bellamy, Absolute War, p 349-350.
9. Bellamy, Absolute War, p 451. Erickson, Road to Stalingrad, p 344.
10. Bellamy, Absolute War, p 453.
11. ibid, p 464.
12. Magenheimer, Hitler's War, p 140.
13. Cooper, German Army, passim. Ian Dear et al. (Eds), Oxford Companion to the Second World War, Oxford 1995, New York 1996, p 468.
14. Ellis, WW2 Databook, p 237 and Cooper, German Army.
15. Bauer, WW2 Vol 9, p 795-797.
16. Cooper, German Army. Ellis, WW2 Databook, p 230.
17. Bauer, WW2 Vol 9, p 799.
18. Magenheimer, Hitler's War. p 302, fn 4.
19. Dear et al, The Oxford Companion.
20. Erickson, Road to Stalingrad, p 543. Ellis, WW2 Databook, p 230-231.
21. Erickson, Road to Stalingrad, p 558.
22. Bauer, WW2 Vol 9, p 795. Magenheimer, Hitler's War, p 142.
23. Bellamy, Absolute War, p 388.
24. Erickson, Road to Stalingrad, p 558.
25. Bellamy, Absolute War, p 550.
26. Erickson, Road to Stalingrad, p 453.

27. ibid, p 563. Bauer, <u>WW2 Vol 10</u>, p 887-888. For the strengths of both sides at the start of 'Uranus'.

28. John Erickson, <u>The Road to Berlin</u>, Weidenfeld and Nicolson, London, 1983, p17.

29. Bauer, <u>WW2 Vol 13</u>, p 1153.

30. Bauer, <u>WW2 Vol 12</u>, p 1115. For this and following Axis Stalingrad loss statistics. Calculations from different sources do vary slightly, but not significantly.

31. Andrew Mollo, <u>The Armed Forces of World War II</u>, Orbis, London, 1981, p 202-203.

32. Bauer, <u>WW2 Vol 13</u>, p 1153.

33. Erickson, <u>Road to Berlin</u>, p 34.

34. Magenheimer, <u>Hitler's War</u>, p 167. The author's calculation is as follows. There were 69 German divisions taking part at the start of the 'Blau' offensive, less nine transferred to other fronts, leaving 60 present throughout the campaign. The Axis allies eventually contributed 45 divisions by November, giving the total of 105 Axis divisions. The 55 destroyed divisions consisted of: 21 German, 10 Hungarian, 9 Italian and 15 Romanian. As Magenheimer says (p167), the Soviets, as in other battles, exaggerated Axis losses, in this case by a factor of two, claiming variously 100-113 German and Axis allied divisions destroyed and casualties of 1.5 to 1.7 million men. It was still a massive and decisive Axis defeat of course. One might ask why the post-Soviet Russians needed to exaggerate their military achievements in WW2. They were unparalleled and stand on their own merits. They don't need to be distorted or marred by propaganda, either before or after Communism's collapse in 1989-92.

35. Bellamy, <u>Absolute War</u>, p 550.

36. ibid, p 528-531.

37. ibid, p 543.

38. ibid, p 446.

39. Ellis, <u>WW2 Databook</u>, p 237.

40. Bellamy, <u>Absolute War</u>, p 504. Bauer, <u>WW2 Vol 9</u>, p 815-816.

41. Bauer, <u>WW2 Vol 10</u>, p 883, Erickson, <u>Road to Berlin</u>. p 28-32.

42. Alan J Levine, 'Was World War II a Near-run Thing?', in <u>Journal of Strategic Studies</u>, Vol 8, No 1, March 1985, p 56.

43. Bellamy, <u>Absolute War</u>, p 497.

44. Bauer, <u>WW2 Vol 9</u>, p 816.

45. Bellamy, <u>Absolute War</u>, p 9-10 and p 476. The author's calculation is from p 9-10, which gives total losses through 1941-45, and p 476, which gives a percentage breakdown for individual years.

46. Magenheimer, <u>Hitler's War</u>, p 140.

47. ibid, p 140.

48. ibid, p 146.

49. Dupuy, <u>Understanding War</u>, p 226-227.

50. Trevor N Dupuy, <u>Options of Command</u>, Hippocrene Books, New York, 1984, p 289. Bellamy, <u>Absolute War</u>, p 446-447. Dupuy concludes that the Germans had at least as good a chance of defeating Russia, especially in 1941, as they actual did of defeating France in 1940. Bellamy says that 'Blau' nearly succeeded, and that it was Hitler's best military and economic option in 1942. [Presumably better even than Moscow?] Moreover, he also says that the 5% Western Allied aid contribution to Russia's war effort in 1942, (and 10% in each of 1943-45), 'made the difference'. [Again, presumably between victory and defeat in 1942?]

CHAPTER 6

PEARL HARBOR

'Yesterday, December 7, 1941, a date which will live in infamy, the United States was suddenly and deliberately attacked by naval and air forces of the Empire of Japan'.[1]

F.D. Roosevelt

'I fear all we have done is awaken a sleeping dragon, who will exact a terrible revenge'[2]

Yamamoto

Countdown to Pearl Harbor: Strategies and Forces

The genesis of the Pacific War can be traced back as far as the turn of the 20th century, as both Japan and the USA simultaneously emerged as great powers and potential rivals in the Pacific. In 1898 victory in the Spanish-American War gave the USA control of the Philippines, Guam, and Wake, and they annexed Hawaii at the same time. Japan's great power emergence was signaled by its defeat of China in 1894-95, and especially of Russia in 1904-05. In 1910 Japan annexed Korea, and in 1919 as a result of World War One, acquired the Mariana, Marshall, Caroline and Palau island groups from a defeated Germany.

The more immediate causes were due to the clash over political and economic influence, and control of the underdeveloped, but potentially major resources and market of China. Between the collapse of the Manchu dynasty in 1911 and the creation of Communist China in 1949, China was a weak and divided power, which only managed to maintain its independence with difficulty. The USA wanted to incorporate China into an American led global free market liberal economic system, a policy that it called the 'open door'. Japan wanted exclusive influence and control of China, and to incorporate it into its own regional economic and political system, the 'new order' and later, from 1940, the 'Greater East Asia Co-Prosperity Sphere'. In 1931 Japan annexed the resource rich, strategically important, and previously semi independent province of Manchuria from China. A Japanese invasion initiated full scale war with the Chinese Nationalist central government under Chiang Kai-shek in July 1937. Initially this war went well for Japan, and it seized the rich north-east quarter of China including Peking (Beijing), Shanghai and Nanking. However, by the end of 1938 despite a Japanese army of 600,000 troops in China, their advance stalled and a stalemate developed. Chiang Kai-shek retreated to the interior of China, establishing a new capital at Chungking, and the Chinese received economic aid and military equipment from the USA, helping them to continue the war.

Japanese diplomatic relations with other great powers also deteriorated around this time. There were border clashes with the old enemy to the north, Soviet Russia. At Nomonhan on the border between Manchuria and Soviet controlled Mongolia, the Japanese came off worse, losing 17,000 men in August-September 1939. Amphibious attacks during 1938-39, against Chinese ports including Canton and the southern island of Hainan, also alarmed Britain, France and the Netherlands, all of which had important colonial territories in South East Asia. At this time, Japan wasn't yet fully allied with the European Axis powers of Germany and Italy. They were as surprised as everyone else by the Nazi-Soviet Pact in August 1939, which immediately preceded the invasion of Poland and the start of World War Two in Europe. Japan was now in an impasse, unable to secure a complete victory over China, unwilling to retreat, diplomatically isolated, and increasingly vulnerable to possible American economic sanctions.

Then, suddenly, there was a dramatic change in the strategic situation. The fall of France in June 1940 had major consequences in the Far East, as well as transforming the course of the European War. The oil rich Dutch East Indies (Indonesia), British controlled Malaysia, Singapore, Hong Kong and Burma, and French Indochina (Vietnam), were all now suddenly vulnerable to Japan. Japan decided in July 1940 to seize, what it termed the 'unique opportunity', to gain control of this 'southern resources area', by diplomatic means if possible, but by force if necessary. Control of these resources, especially oil, but also including tin, rubber, bauxite and rice production, would free Japan of its previous economic dependence and vulnerability to the USA. Moreover, control of Indochina and Burma would isolate China from Western supplies and help bring the China War to a victorious conclusion as well. The downside of this Japanese strategy would be an increased risk of war with the USA. Japan used diplomacy with other great powers to attempt to counter this danger.

On September 27th 1940 the Tripartite Pact allied Japan defensively with Germany and Italy. The essential clause was 'to assist one another with all political, economic, and military means, when one of the three contracting parties is attacked by a power at present not involved in the European War or the Sino-Japanese conflict.'[3] This was designed as a deterrent to the USA attacking Japan, following any Japanese attack on the South East Asian resources area. In April 1941 Japan concluded a non-aggression pact with Soviet Russia, to secure the Manchurian-Siberian border, while plan-

166

ning to strike southward against South East Asia. The pact with Russia was successful to that extent. However, Japanese hopes of expanding these treaties into a global quadruple alliance, of the three Axis powers and Russia, directed against Anglo-American intervention, failed. Operation 'Barbarossa', of which Japan wasn't informed, thwarted this grand strategy. It was a grand strategy that could have brought the Axis ultimate victory, although its dependence on the continued cooperation of Stalin's Russia was a major uncertainty.

Japan briefly considered an alternative, 'northern strategy' at this time. 'Barbarossa' meant that there might never be a better opportunity to strike at Soviet Russia while it was tied down with the war against Germany, a war that Russia seemed to be losing in 1941. However, this strategy was rejected for several reasons. There was no certainty that Germany was going to win in Russia, and the more prudent course for Japan was to wait and see. The Russian Far Eastern Front was also a formidable opponent, as the border clashes of 1939 had shown. Japan would face a technically superior opponent, especially in armor and artillery, backed by fortified positions, difficult forest and mountain terrain, and the harsh Siberian climate. Finally, although Siberia had huge natural resources, they were located far from the border and difficult for Japan to exploit. Moreover it didn't have the most important resource of all, oil, at least not in the 1940s. In short, the costs and risks of a 'northern strategy' outweighed the benefits.

On its own the Tripartite Pact also failed in its objective of deterring the USA. Instead the USA was provoked and took countermeasures to what it saw as continued Axis aggression. In September 1940 Japan had occupied northern Indochina from a helpless Vichy France. The USA responded in October 1940 with an embargo on the export of iron and scrap metal to Japan, and with increased loans to China. The pattern repeated itself at a more dangerous level in 1941. In July 1941 Japan seized the rest of French Indochina and was thus in position to attack the Dutch East Indies for its oil, and to cut the Burma road, the last land supply link to China. The American response, backed by the Dutch and British, was an oil embargo on Japan and the freezing of its economic and financial assets in the USA. They hoped this would pressure Japan to withdraw from Indochina, China and Manchuria. This time it was the Americans who miscalculated. Japan's oil stocks, if not replenished, would last between 18 months and two years. Japan wouldn't retreat. Instead, with the oil clock ticking and diplomacy deadlocked, their only option was to attack. The final countdown had begun; the Pacific War was now inevitable.

Japan can be described as a 'hybrid maritime and land power'. Like Britain it was a medium sized, relatively resource poor, island industrial state, dependent on seaborne trade for its economic survival. Unlike Britain, it had direct imperial ambitions against its immediate continental neighbors. Japan's wars against Russia in 1904-5 and China in 1937-45, were both major ground wars. The role of the Imperial Japanese Navy (IJN) was to protect the transport and supply of the army to the theatre of operations. The Army was also generally more influential than the Navy in Japanese politics and policy making. However, when the opponent was a naval power as well, such as with tsarist Russia, America or Britain, then Japanese naval strategy obviously assumed at least equal importance. Control of the sea was an irreducible pre-requisite for land operations by an island based great power. Indeed in the Pacific War, naval power was the single most important component of victory. Japan emerged as a great naval power with the war against Russia in 1904-05, culminating in the victory at Tsushima. By the end of the First World War in 1918 it had the world's third largest fleet, after Britain and the USA. Inter-war naval treaties at Washington in 1922 and London in 1930 confirmed this position. However, they restricted the size of Japan's fleet to 60% of either Britain or the USA in battleships, and 70% in the other categories of warships. This inferiority was yet another issue of conflict between Japan and the West.

In the inter-war period Japanese naval operational strategy for any war against the USA, and with a smaller fleet, was thus defensive. The plan was to weaken the larger American fleet as it advanced, by air and submarine attacks from the Japanese controlled Pacific island bases. Only then would the weakened American fleet be engaged in a decisive naval battle, in the western Pacific, far from Americas own logistic bases. In August 1939 Yamamoto became the new C-in-C of the Japanese Combined Fleet and updated this operational strategy. The previous strategy was seen as too defensive and conceded the initiative and timing of operations to the Americans. The fleet would be needed to protect and support army amphibious operations against South East Asia. Striking southward from Japan, part of the fleet might be out of position, divided in its tasks and be vulnerable to an American counterstroke from Hawaii. Alternatively, the Americans might wait until they had an even greater superiority, due to the transfer of their Atlantic Fleet to the Pacific, or from new shipbuilding before starting an offensive.

The new Japanese operational plan was therefore for a pre-emptive attack, forcing a decisive naval battle at the outset of war. With command of the sea secured by an immediate decisive battle, success in subsequent combined operations in South East Asia and the Pacific would follow. There were historical precedents for a pre-emptive naval attack against larger opponents. Japan had started its war against Russia in 1904 by a surprise attack against their fleet at Port Arthur. If the planned attack against Pearl Harbor was to have the benefit of surprise, which was virtually essential for success, it would have to be carried out from the air. Yamamoto was a keen advocate of aircraft carrier warfare and it was a category of weaponry where Japan had a relative advantage in 1941.

The balance of naval power in the Pacific, and the overall balance between Japan and the USA at the outbreak of war in December 1941, is shown in table 2.[4]

Table 2: Naval Forces in the Pacific: December 1941

	BB	CV-CVL	CA	CL	DD	SS
Japan	11	10	18	17	113	63
British Empire	2	-	1	7	13	-
Netherlands		-	-	3	7	13
USA Pacific	9	3	13	11	80	56
Allied Total	11	3	14	21	100	69
USA Atlantic	8	4	5	8	93	56
USA Total	17	7	18	19	173	112

Careful examination of table 2 reveals the pertinent facts. Firstly, the balance of naval power between Japan and the Allied total in the Pacific is almost even in all categories of combat ships, with the very important exception of aircraft carriers. Secondly, the Americans constituted the vast majority of Allied naval strength in the Pacific, with most of their force based at Pearl Harbor in the Hawaiian Islands. Of their Pacific strength, the American Asiatic Fleet based in the Philippines, consisted of only 3 cruisers, 13 destroyers and 29 submarines. Thirdly, the American fleet as a whole was divided about evenly between the Pacific (including the Asiatic fleet) and the Atlantic. If the Americans were able, depending on their global strategic priorities and the circumstances, to concentrate their entire naval power in the Pacific, then they would have an overall superiority of around 3 to 2 over Japan. In the event a partial transfer from the Atlantic to the Pacific did largely take place, but spread over a period of months, after Pearl Harbor and up to about September 1942.[5]

The balance in aircraft carriers and naval air power was different. Even including the US Atlantic Fleet, Japan would have a slight edge. Of Japan's 10 aircraft carriers, 6 were the more powerful fleet carriers (CV), 3 were light fleet carriers (CVL), and one was an escort carrier (CVE) used for training air crews. The American force consisted of 7 CVs (3 in the Pacific, 4 in the Atlantic), and one small CVE in the Atlantic. The total aircraft capacity of the two carrier fleets was almost equal: 619 aircraft for Japan, and 618 for the Americans (Pacific 261, Atlantic 357). The Pacific War, unlike the Battle of the Atlantic, was largely a contest for naval supremacy and command of the sea. Which ever side had command of the sea, or at least control of parts of it, would be free to use it for amphibious invasions, transport and supply of ground and air forces, and for mercantile purposes. The fast fleet and light carriers (CV, CVL), organized into 'task forces' would soon become the new basis for naval power, rather than the traditional fleets of battleships. Surface combat forces i.e. battleships, cruisers and destroyers, were still required to protect the fast carrier task forces, and for multiple general purpose use. Very importantly, this changeover from battleships to fast carriers would only become fully apparent to both sides with the actual clash of battle, at Pearl Harbor, Coral Sea and Midway.

As ever the basic numerical balance of forces has to be qualified by circumstantial and quality factors. Japan's surface ships tended to be larger and more powerful than their Allied counterparts. Most of the capital ships of both sides dated from before the 1922 Washington Treaty. However, all 10 of Japan's battleships from this era had been virtually reconstructed during the 1930s. This made them superior to all but three of the Allied capital ships, two of which were new American battleships in the Atlantic. The British *Prince of Wales* was the other, and it would be sunk right at the outbreak of the war. Moreover, the new Japanese battleships *Yamato* and *Musashi,* completed in December 1941 and August 1942 respectively, were the largest and most powerfully armed and armored ever constructed. At 73.000 tons fully loaded, they were almost twice the size of all but four US battleships of the *Iowa* class, which wouldn't be completed until 1943-44. Japan's heavy cruiser force was the most powerful in the world, and secretly exceeded treaty limitations that applied to their Allied counterparts. These and the Japanese destroyer force outmatched their individual opponents. All Japanese surface combatants were armed with the vastly superior Type 92 'long lance' torpedoes; and their firepower effectively doubled with a unique reload capacity.

Japanese aircraft were also generally superior during 1941-42, much to the surprise of the Allied air forces and intelligence services. Their famous 'Zero' fighter was superior to the standard and contemporary American navy F4F Wildcats, army P40s, and British Hurricanes. In the air war though, it was the superior quality of the Japanese pre-war carrier pilots and air crew that was their greatest advantage. These had an average of 700-800 flying hours of experience, much of it in combat in the China War. This was over twice that of their Allied equivalents, or even of their own land based contemporaries. The Japanese aircraft carrier aircrew were the best trained in the world in 1941-42 for a force of equivalent size, about 600 crews. The weakness of this elite force was that they were almost irreplaceable. The pre-war training system produced only 100 pilots per year, and it took up to five years training and experience to reach this elite level.[6] Another Japanese weakness was that they didn't have radar and remained behind in this technology, even after acquiring it in 1943-44. This didn't seem to matter much in the night surface battles of 1941-42, where Japanese training and tactics proved superior. However, it might, have given them some warning of American air attacks at Coral Sea and Midway! Maybe?

The balance of forces in land based air power also favored Japan. Japan, like the USA had separate army and navy air forces. The army air force had around 1,375 combat aircraft overall and about half of these were allocated to the southern offensive. The Malayan campaign was supported by 550 army aircraft, operating from the newly acquired bases in French Indochina. About 175 army aircraft were in Formosa for operations against the Philippines. The rest of the army's air power, 600 combat aircraft, was held back in China and Manchuria, with 50 more in reserve in Japan. The Imperial Japanese Navy (IJN) committed almost its entire combat air strength of about 725 land based and 600 carrier planes to the Pacific offensive. Of the land based aircraft, 150 were for the Malayan and 300 for the Philippine campaigns. There were 275 naval aircraft in Japan and the Pacific island groups. The total air strength for the Pacific offensives, from both services and including the aircraft carrier elite, was therefore about 2,100 combat aircraft, over 75% of Japan's total of 2,750.[7]

In contrast the total initial Allied combat air strength, spread across the vast theatre of operations, was only about 1,000; half of Japan's attacking force. America had the strongest Allied forces with 280 army, navy and marine land based combat aircraft in Hawaii, 180 in the Philippines, and 12 at each of Wake and Midway islands. There were 216 navy combat planes on the Pacific Fleet's three aircraft carriers. Britain had only 158 first line aircraft in Malaya and 37 in Burma, and the Dutch 144 combat aircraft in the East Indies.[8]

Japan's total ground forces in December 1941 consisted of about 1,250,000 regulars, backed by 2 million trained reserves. They were organized in 51 divisions, 59 independent brigades and 10 depot or training divisions. Unlike the offensive allocation of the entire Combined Fleet, and 75% of Japan's air power, the bulk of these ground forces were tied down with the Chinese War or guarding the Manchurian border against Russia. Only 11 of the 51 divisions were available for the Pacific offensive. There were 25 divisions in China, 13 in Manchuria and 2 in Korea. The attacking force had about 250,000 combat troops with another 150,000 men in administrative, follow up garrison and independent units. Allied ground forces in the targeted territories were almost as large. The British Empire had 12,000 men in Hong Kong, 89,000 in Malaya and Singapore and 35,000 in Burma. In the Philippines, the Americans had 31,000 regulars including 12,000 Philippine Scout troops, and a partly trained Philippine army of 100,000 men. The Dutch had 25,000 regular troops and an Indonesian militia of about 40-60,000 men.[9] Almost half the Allied defenders were therefore poorly trained local troops. More importantly, the strong Japanese commitment of most of their naval and air power, meant they had a much better balanced force, that could choose the timing and location of its attacks and invasions.

Therefore Japan seemed to have most of the military advantages, in the short term at least, and especially in the quality, training, experience and combat effectiveness of its armed forces. Much however, would depend on the coming great naval battles that would determine control of the sea. In the longer term, if the war lasted more than a year, then certain deep weaknesses such as inferior economic, industrial and shipbuilding capacity and an insufficiently large merchant fleet would affect outcomes. In the meantime the Americans had one immediate advantage, in intelligence gathering. Their 'Magic' organization could read both Japanese diplomatic and from April 1942, naval encrypted communications, and maintained this capability for most of the Pacific War. These still had to be interpreted correctly of course, and that could vary greatly, from disastrous at Pearl Harbor to brilliance at Midway.

With the Japanese superiority in qualitative factors, along with high discipline and morale, and their initial advantage in the balance of naval air power, we can see why at the operational level they favored the new preemptive naval strategy. If Japan could eliminate the threat of the US Pacific Fleet at the outset, it would gain command of the sea over most of the western Pacific. It could then conquer the various Allied territories in South East Asia. The southern offensive would initially involve simultaneous attacks against Malaya, Hong Kong, British North Borneo, and the American controlled Philippines. When these and the British fortress of Singapore had been taken, the conquest of Burma and the Dutch East Indies would follow. They allocated 50 days for the conquest of the Philippines, 100 days for Malaya and 150 for the Dutch East Indies. In the Pacific the capture of the American islands of Guam and Wake, and the British Commonwealth controlled Solomon and Gilbert Islands, as well as northern New Guinea, would complete the Japanese defense perimeter. There would then be no Allied base within air attack range of Japan. An examination of any map will reveal the vast geographical extent of these offensives, and also the primacy of the maritime environment. With the 'southern resources area' secured, and a vast chain of island bases in the Pacific, backed by the Combined Fleet, Japan would then go on to the defensive. They were confident that the war would be a short one, and that the Americans, with their Pacific Fleet lost, would be incapable of redressing the balance, even with their Atlantic Fleet, and would soon tire of the effort. A peace treaty would follow, leaving Japan in control of its 'Greater

East Asia Co-Prosperity Sphere'. The plan was breathtaking in its speed and scope.

Pearl Harbor and its Consequences: December 1941-April 1942

The story of the 'day of infamy', as President Roosevelt called the attack on the US Pacific Fleet at Pearl Harbor on December 7th 1941, is well known. The outcome and strategic consequences are what concerns us here. Admiral Nagumo's 'Kido Butai', the First Carrier Air Fleet, with 6 fleet carriers, 433 combat aircraft, 2 fast battleships, 3 cruisers and 9 destroyers, was the most powerful and best trained naval force in the world at this time. It took Nagumo's fleet, accompanied by 8 tankers for refueling at sea, 11 days to traverse the 3,500 miles from a secret anchorage in the Kurile Islands, just north of Japan, across the emptiest ocean on the planet to their attack position, 230 miles north of Oahu. The Americans 96 ships and 394 aircraft of all types, and 50,000 armed service personnel, operating on peacetime routines, were caught completely by surprise.

Due to their cryptography efforts the Americans knew that war was close, but not the precise timing or exact operational targets. They didn't expect a simultaneous attack against Hawaii and South East Asia. Of the 8 Pacific Fleet battleships present at Pearl Harbor, 4 were sunk, 1 beached and 3 damaged. Three of the 8 cruisers were damaged. Of the 29 destroyers, 2 were sunk and 2 damaged. A total of 188 aircraft of all types were destroyed and 159 damaged and put out of action. Most were caught on the ground. American casualties were 2,403 killed and 1,178 wounded.[10] Japanese losses were only 29 aircraft. It was an overwhelming Japanese victory, eliminating the American Pacific battleship fleet and their Hawaiian based air force. The Japanese had achieved their objective of preventing serious intervention, or a counter offensive by the US Pacific Fleet, against their simultaneous offensives in South East Asia.

It could have been even worse for the Americans. Nagumo, against the advice of Genda, his air commander and a brilliant strategist, refused to launch a second attack against the crippled American forces. Pearl Harbor's oil tanks and dockyards, along with the undamaged 5 cruisers, 25 destroyers, 5 submarines and other auxiliary ships, were virtually without air cover and very vulnerable. Genda also wanted 'Kido Butai' to remain in the area and seek out the three American Pacific Fleet carriers, that crucially were absent from their base when the attack occurred. One of these, *Enterprise* leading a small task force of 3 cruisers and 9 destroyers, was returning to Pearl Harbor from Wake, and only 200 miles west of Pearl Harbor, i.e. within immediate air search and attack range. The carrier *Lexington* with 3 cruisers and 5 destroyers was delivering aircraft to Midway.

This force was 700 miles west of Pearl Harbor, but could still have become involved later in any post attack operations.

Nagumo was cautious, anxious to keep his fleet intact and feared an American ambush from their unlocated carrier forces. Japan had taken a risk with the Pearl Harbor strike and achieved a major victory, so why gamble further? No one said that command decisions in war were easy. A bolder Japanese commander, or even Yamamoto himself, would have prolonged the battle, and with six carriers against one or two (404 remaining aircraft against 144 on the two American carriers) and superior combat experience, the Americans would very likely have lost more valuable ships. Since Pearl Harbor was by far America's major base in the Pacific, the destruction of the oil reserve and dockyards would have further crippled American recovery and delayed operations in 1942. As it was, the survival of the US carriers would be crucial. It was of necessity that they replaced the battleship as the main weapon in the US Navy (USN). The USN had little choice, with only one battleship and three carriers left operational in the Pacific. The third carrier, *Saratoga* and the battleship *Colorado* were refitting on the Pacific coast at the time of Pearl Harbor.

One final and unanticipated outcome of Pearl Harbor was the political and psychological impact. Because of incompetence at the Japanese embassy in Washington, their declaration of war had been delayed until after the attack began. The surprise attack was widely regarded as treacherous by the Americans, 'unprovoked and dastardly' as Roosevelt termed it, and it united their previously divided and isolationist public. Even more than with the European Axis four days later, the Japanese decision to open hostilities, and the way that they did so, eased Roosevelt's domestic political task of bringing America into the war, and in a united and determined manner. In the immediate term however, Pearl Harbor had secured command of the sea for Japan from the mid-Pacific to Ceylon. They made full use of it over the next five months.

The American islands of Wake and Guam had only small Marine garrisons of about 500 men each and formed the line of communication across the central Pacific, between the Hawaiian Islands and the Philippines. Guam was captured easily on December 10th. The defenders at Wake repulsed an invasion on December 11th, sinking two Japanese destroyers, before succumbing to a renewed invasion on December 23rd 1941. In the Philippines, American General MacArthur's forces were caught in the middle of a process of expansion and a change of strategy. He had only 19,000 American and 12,000 Philippine Scout regular personnel, and one regular division on the main island of Luzon. The newly raised 100,000 men and 10 divisions of the Philippine Army were only half trained and equipped. The US Army Air Force had 277 aircraft in total, of which 180 were combat types, including 35 B17 heavy bombers, to which Japan had no equivalent, and 107 P40 fighters. War plan 'Orange', of which WPO-3 was the latest version, was the traditional Navy-Army compromise strategy for war against Japan. For over 30 years, with only small regular forces available, American strategy had been to withdraw to the defensible Bataan peninsular, adjacent to Manila Bay, and await reinforcements as the USN advanced across the central Pacific route from Hawaii. The rest of the Philippines, deemed indefensible, would be temporarily abandoned. In August 1941, anticipating the ongoing expansion of his forces, MacArthur switched to a new strategy of defending the entire territory of the Philippines. It proved to be a premature change, for the ground and air force expansion wasn't planned to be completed until at least April 1942. The Americans had hoped to avoid war until then.

The 475 Japanese combat aircraft on Formosa achieved air superiority over Luzon from the start, destroying half of the American B17s and P40s on the ground on December 8th 1941.[11] Preliminary landings on Luzon, to secure advanced fighter bases, followed from December 10th. Two American weapon systems, the heavy bombers and the large submarine fleet of 29 vessels, performed unexpectedly badly and failed even to delay the invasion. On December 22nd 43,000 troops of the Japanese 14th Army's 57,000 total, began their main invasion at Lingayen Gulf, about 100 miles north of Manila. Two divisions of Philippine troops (20,000 men), defending long coastline sectors, were unable to hold the line. MacArthur's revised strategy had failed, and on December 24th he changed back to the previous WPO-3 instead, and retreated to Bataan. Manila fell on January 2nd 1942.

At Bataan the besieged defenders had 80,000 men, moderately outnumbering the Japanese attackers. However, they were poorly supplied and equipped and most were the less well trained Philippine army forces. Even so and weakened by starvation and disease, they held out for over four months until April 9th 1942, long enough for the campaign to enter American military legend. On May 5-6th Corregidor and its satellite Manila Bay fortress islands fell, effectively ending the Philippine campaign. The Americans entire ground and air force in the Philippines was lost and became casualties or prisoners. Japanese casualties were about 12,000. Nevertheless the Philippine campaign lasted five months, far longer than the 50 days that Japan had planned for, it was the only South East Asian campaign to do so. In the end the real problem for the Allies, here and elsewhere at this time, was that Japan had complete sea and air superiority. Thus the defenders were isolated from outside supply and reinforcements and at best could only postpone the inevitable.

Hong Kong was the most isolated and vulnerable British colony in the Far East. Attacked immediately by 20,000 troops from Japanese controlled China, its garrison of 12,000 capitulated on December 25th 1941. Japanese casualties were only 3,000. Fortress Singapore however, was the lynchpin of British power in the Far East. As with the American 'Orange' war plans, Singapore's defense was ultimately premised on a relief offensive by a superior fleet. British pre-war strategy had allocated their Mediterranean Fleet for this purpose. Unfortunately events in Europe in 1940-41 seemed to make this strategy virtually impossible. The fall of France meant that its fleet was unable to take responsibility for the Mediterranean, while the British attempted to relieve Singapore; yet another consequence of that decisive campaign. Britain's navy was overstretched in all theatres. Instead, Churchill managed to send a 'deterrent squadron' of two capital ships, the new battleship *Prince of Wales* and the battlecruiser *Repulse*, to reinforce the Singapore fleet just before the outbreak of the Pacific War. It failed to deter Japan and turned into a disaster, when both were sunk by Japanese land based aircraft on December 10th 1941. They were attempting to intercept an amphibious invasion of Malaya.

Even so Malaya and Singapore should have been able to hold out longer than they did. The British Empire had 89,000 men in three, and later four divisions here. The air force with only 158 combat aircraft, against 700 Japanese in Indochina, was weak though, and Japan had air and sea superiority. Despite this and unlike the Americans in the Philippines, Britain was able to reinforce Singapore and Malaya from the west. They brought in 50,000 extra men and over 150 aircraft before Japan sealed its blockade. General Yamashita's attacking Japanese 25th Army had 70,000 men in 3 divisions, adding another later, giving a total strength including support forces of about 110,000. The two armies seemed well matched and the only obvious Japanese material advantage was their 211 tanks. The British were initially poorly deployed, spread across Malaya defending airfields and beaches. They expected a seaborne invasion in the south and at Singapore, against which its fortress defenses and heavy guns were prepared.

Instead the Japanese attacked northern Malaya, deploying 26,000 men by sea from December 8th, and the rest moving by land via Thailand, a nominal Japanese ally. Advancing southward through jungle and mountain terrain, they outmaneuvered and outfought the British Empire army at every stage. Reaching Singapore from the north, they attacked its vulnerable 'landward' side from Malaya on February 8th 1942. Singapore fell and the considerable remaining army of 85,000 men surrendered on February 15th 1942. Total British Empire casualties, mostly prisoners, in the 70 day long Malayan campaign were 139,000. It was the largest single disaster in British military history and defeat by an Asian great power was terminal for the Empire's power and prestige in the region. Japanese casualties were under 10,000 and the campaign was completed one month ahead of schedule.

The great prize for Japan in South East Asia was the Dutch East Indies (Indonesia), with its oil production of 7 million tons p.a. This would be sufficient for Japan's needs, if the facilities could be captured undamaged or otherwise repaired and if the oil could be transported to Japan. Multiple small invasions began here on January 10th 1942, well before the Malayan and Philippine campaigns were complete. Japan used three combined service task forces, each about a division strong, protected by heavy cruisers and destroyers and supported by land based aircraft deploying to newly captured bases as the advance proceeded. The Eastern Force proceeded via Celebes, the Moluccas and Timor. The Central Force advanced down the Macassar Strait, between Borneo and Celebes, capturing the Borneo oil centers of Tarakan and Balikpapan. The Western Force, supported by a small airborne landing, seized the oil center of Palembang in Sumatra on February 16th 1942, almost simultaneous with the fall of Singapore. The Dutch ground forces with 25,000 regulars and up to 60,000 poorly trained and equipped local militia, scattered across this huge countries many islands, were outmatched in quality rather than numerically.[12] Again Japanese sea and air superiority, which gave them the strategic flexibility to concentrate superior power successively against their isolated opponents, was the key to victory.

The Japanese offensives finally converged on Java, the political center of the islands, with two separate division sized invasions on February 28th 1942. A multinational Allied surface fleet, of 4 cruisers and 9 destroyers, had attempted to intercept the eastern invasion, resulting in the Battle of the Java Sea on February 27th. They were opposed by 4 cruisers and 16 destroyers, protecting a large invasion convoy. The Allies lost 2 cruisers and 4 destroyers sunk in this apparently evenly matched battle. Superior Japanese ships, night tactics and their devastating 'long lance' torpedoes, the most powerful and longest ranged in the world, decided the outcome. The double invasion of Java defeated the remaining Allied, mainly Dutch ground forces by March 9th 1942, completing the conquest of the East Indies two months earlier than planned. In the final stages of the campaign, Japan deployed its carrier striking force, the 'Kido Butai', devastating the Australian base at Darwin on February 19th and destroying the remnants of the Allied surface fleets that were fleeing Java between March 1st and 3rd 1942. The Japanese were on their way to the Indian Ocean, to conduct a major raid. The British feared it would be much more than that.

The successful attack at Pearl Harbor had changed the balance of naval power in the Pacific from rough equality to clear Japanese superiority. For this reason alone Pearl Harbor was a decisive battle of World War Two. Its outcome determined the strategic circumstances and course of the war in the Pacific for the next five months. From December 7th 1941 to the end of April 1942, the Allies had lost 7 battleships sunk and 3 damaged and put out of action. One carrier (Britain's **Hermes**) 10 Allied cruisers and 15 destroyers were also sunk, compared to only 5 Japanese destroyers.[13] This Japanese command of the sea and air was the decisive factor for success in the subsequent Philippine, Malayan and East Indies campaigns. A huge territory of over one million square miles had been captured in five months, primarily due to the flexibility and mobility of seaborne invasions. Japan gained control of the economic resources it needed and established a vast Pacific island defensive perimeter, from Wake in the central Pacific, via the Marshall, Gilbert and Solomon Islands, to New Britain and New Guinea, just north of Australia. Their strategic objectives had been achieved ahead of schedule, except in the Philippines, and at a far lower cost than expected. They feared they might lose 25% of the fleet instead of a mere 5 destroyers. However, the Pearl Harbor attack also created unforeseen long term difficulties for Japan.

Alternative 1941 Japanese Strategy: 'No Pearl Harbor'

The ultimate problem for Japan was the combination of America's massive industrial and potential military power, combined with its united determination following Pearl Harbor. In the long run the creation of this unity and determination outweighed the short term advantages of the Pearl Harbor attack. The Americans were down, but not out after Pearl Harbor. The USN's pre-war battleline was largely destroyed but the carriers survived. Clear Japanese command of the sea only lasted six months until their defeat at Midway. Even the damage that was inflicted was eventually mostly repairable. The 188 destroyed and 159 damaged aircraft were less than one week's production, although it did take longer to redeploy replacements to Hawaii. The three damaged battleships were repaired by March 1942. Even three of those sunk in the shallow Harbor, would be raised and repaired by 1943-44. Only the **Arizona** and **Oklahoma** were permanent losses. Japan underestimated both American power and its perseverance. Avoiding the Pearl Harbor attack and not declaring war on the USA at all might well have been a better strategy for Japan. This was essentially the traditional defensive naval strategy, existent before Yamamoto became C-in-C of the Combined Fleet in August 1939. We will call it the 'No Pearl Harbor' strategy.

All of Japan's economic objectives, especially the oilfields, were located in the colonial territories of Britain and the Netherlands. The Philippines were important for their strategic location flanking Japan's supply lines, but only if America was at war. If Japan had attacked the European colonial territories alone, without declaring war against the USA, it is uncertain

178

if or when the US would have responded. The immediate consideration was political. In the months prior to Pearl Harbor, American leaders had declined to make any definite military commitment to the British and Dutch. They feared an adverse public reaction, should such an understanding leak out. America was anti-colonial and it would have been difficult to morally justify such a war to the public. In December 1941 Roosevelt finally told the British ambassador Lord Halifax, that if Japan attacked them or the Dutch, then 'we should obviously all be together' and that this meant 'armed support'. Even so opinion is divided on whether Roosevelt had the necessary Congressional support, required by the US Constitution, for a declaration of war.[14] Even if Congress did declare war in these circumstances, without America being attacked directly, the nation would have been divided and less determined than after Pearl Harbor.

War plans 'Orange', version WPO-3 (1938), and 'Rainbow 5' (1939), would determine US strategy in this situation. 'Rainbow 5' covered the contingency of simultaneous war against Germany and Japan, while WPO-3 had governed strategy against Japan alone. These plans became incorporated into 'Plan D' in November 1940, commonly known as the 'Germany first' strategy. Germany was considered the greater threat due to its larger industrial potential, existing control of most of Europe, and proximity to America's main and potential allies, Britain and Russia. The primary American offensive would thus be in Europe. America would initially be on the defensive against Japan. 'Defensive' against Japan, was however, undefined in terms of its details and left ambiguous. It wasn't interpreted by the USN to mean falling back to the line Alaska, Hawaii, and Panama. The Philippines were after all under American control and needed defending. Therefore there would still be a secondary offensive, led by the USN, against Japan. As we have seen under WPO-3, MacArthur's army was to hold the Philippines, or at least Bataan and Manila Bay, while the USN advanced across the central Pacific to reinforce them. The USN supported by marine and army amphibious forces, planned to seize Japanese bases in the Marshall and Caroline Islands en-route, as well as relieving or retaking American Guam and Wake.

The uncertainties were in the timing and the fact that America wasn't fully ready for war in December 1941. MacArthur planned to be ready in April 1942, doubling the size of his ground forces to 200,000 men, combined with an offensive bomber force of 180 B17s, compared to the actual 35 available in December 1941. It was estimated that the US Pacific Fleet, reinforced from the Atlantic, would take six to nine months to fight its way through.[15] The USN would be stretched in aircraft carriers, destroyers and amphibious auxiliaries. With no Pearl Harbor however, the American battleline would be intact, and including the redeployed Atlantic Fleet, numerically superior. Given this, if they had gotten a declaration of war, they would almost certainly have put the offensive provisions and interpretation, of 'Rainbow 5' and WPO-3 into operation. Neither side though, prior to the clash of battle, would be fully aware of the full power of the aircraft carriers. Militarily, it would have been better for the Americans to delay their declaration of war a few months until they were fully prepared. That might have been more difficult politically. Congressional and public support for war, uncertain anyway without Pearl Harbor, might have declined over time, once the immediate effect of Japan's new aggression receded.

If Roosevelt had been unable to secure a Congressional declaration of war at all, in response to Japanese aggression against the British and Dutch alone, then the 'No Pearl Harbor' strategy would have quickly achieved almost all of Japan's objectives. Without American intervention, South East Asia and the western Pacific, except for the Philippines, Guam and Wake, would have fallen even faster than historically. Australia and New Zealand, unless they were able to secure future American guarantees or support, would have been so vulnerable that their only option would be a separate and early peace. Britain's remaining position in the Indian Ocean would be equally vulnerable, Japan having no front in the Pacific to worry about. It too would be forced into an early settlement. Finally, Chiang Kai-shek's China would have been completely isolated. China's collapse also, would be inevitable, if a little delayed.

There would have been dire consequences in Europe for the Allies as well. With no Japanese attack on the USA, there would have been no declaration of war by Germany and Italy either.[16] American entry into the European War would be prevented, delayed, or become less decisive than was historically the case. In circumstances where political and public support for war against Japan was insufficient, it is even less plausible that a declaration of war against the European Axis was achievable. In the end, American entry at some stage, into both wars, was absolutely essential to Allied victory in both. Even delayed US entry could have been fatal for the Allied cause, given the precarious situation in 1942. Without the USA, the Axis would likely have won in both theatres, and probably even against Russia as well in the end. Britain and Russia would have had to accept peace terms as soon as possible before they lost too much. Political failure to get Congress to declare war, following a Japanese 'No Pearl Harbor' option, is the worse case scenario for the Allies.

Assuming that the political hurdles were surmountable however, then outcomes in the Pacific would depend on the implementation of WPO-3 and 'Rainbow 5'. It was the operational doctrine of both the USN and the IJN, to seek a decisive naval battle, in the tradition of Mahan, the leading proponent of the theory of sea power. In the circumstances outlined here, and with both battlelines intact, that is exactly what they would have got. A

'Mahanite' decisive battle, would involve the main battle fleets of both sides, with command of the sea at stake. Command of the sea would give the victor freedom of action to conduct amphibious invasions, and deny that capability to the loser. One or more decisive naval battles, on the central Pacific axis between Hawaii and the Philippines, would have decided the war. That's what happened anyway ultimately, with Pearl Harbor, Midway, Philippine Sea and Leyte Gulf. Pearl Harbor gave Japan command of the sea between Hawaii and Ceylon for six months. The Japanese carrier fleet was then surprised and shattered at Midway. Midway created a situation of balance. The weakened IJN was then defeated in the last two 'Mahanite' battles, Philippine Sea and Leyte Gulf, by a largely newly constructed US Pacific Fleet in 1944. In early 1942 however, following a Japanese 'No Pearl Harbor' strategy, the circumstances would be much more evenly balanced.

A best case scenario for the Americans assumes no Pearl Harbor losses, reverses transfers to the Atlantic made in 1941 prior to war, and accelerates their actual wartime transfers from the Atlantic up to September 1942, to occur prior to an optimally timed US declaration of war. The naval balance in the Pacific in March 1942 would then be roughly as shown in table 3.

Table 3: Pacific Naval Strength: March 1942 if 'No Pearl Harbor'[17]

	CV	CVL	BB	CA	CL	DD	SS	Aircraft Capacity
Japan	6	4	11	18	17	113	63	591
USA Pacific: Dec 1941	3		9	13	11	80	56	261
Transfers	3		5	2	4	21	8	250
Pacific Total	6		14	15	15	101	64	511
USA Atlantic	1		3	3	4	72	48	86
USA Global	7		17	18	19	173	112	597

The Japanese fleet is its strength in December 1941, plus the CVL *Shoho,* completed in January 1942. The American destroyer and submarine strength is the actual strength in the Pacific in March 1942 and adjusted, i.e. increased slightly for the actual losses, that with 'No Pearl Harbor' wouldn't have occurred since December 7th 1941. Historically even after Pearl Harbor, and the redeployments to the Pacific, the Americans left forces in the Atlantic. These were the last reserves, predominantly light forces for the Atlantic convoy war. The carrier *Ranger* remained in the Atlantic, used for training the future naval air arm, and the last three Atlantic Fleet battleships were the oldest and least powerful in the USN. They could thus perhaps have increased their light forces in the Pacific a little more, to give themselves a modest edge in these categories. However, we need to remind ourselves that under 'Plan D' and 'Rainbow 5', Europe and the Atlantic was the overall priority, even if within this most USN forces would deploy to the Pacific.

The 'No Pearl Harbor' scenario assumes that Japan has quickly conquered all British and Dutch territories in South East Asia, with few naval and air losses, as it did historically by March 1942. The Americans, even with complete political and military freedom of action, would probably not have been ready in time to save them. If they had been able to delay their declaration of war, MacArthur's strengthened forces would be just about ready by March-April 1942, to hold the Philippines until relieved.

Virtually all the carriers and battleships, most cruisers, and perhaps half the destroyers would constitute both main fleets for the decisive battle. Many destroyers, on both sides, would be required for convoy and invasion escort, patrol, and other tasks throughout the Pacific. The two main battleship-carrier fleets would have been evenly matched. The Americans had more battleships, but only two of them, *Washington* and *North Carolina*, were fast and modern. The slightly smaller, but faster Japanese battleline, consisted of reconstructed and modernized pre-1922 vessels, led by the new and peerless *Yamato*. In carrier air power however, Japan would have had a numerical and qualitative advantage. The numbers of lighter vessels was fairly evenly balanced, with an American option of stripping the Atlantic Fleet of all its cruisers, and more destroyers, to achieve a slight edge. However, the superior Japanese 'long lance' torpedo, and night fighting tactics, would have given them a quality advantage. It was also pre-Pearl Harbor Japanese doctrine, to use submarines and land based air power, to attrition American naval strength as they advanced. American submarines were divided in their task, being used for commerce attack, as well as against warships. Yet neither side's submarines were a decisive factor historically in 1942. The Americans still lacked a proficient torpedo, and the noisier Japanese submarines were more vulnerable to ASW.

Japanese land based naval air power, of the type that sank the *Prince of Wales* and *Repulse*, would however have been important. The Americans would be advancing through the Japanese controlled Marshall, Caroline and Mariana Islands, en-route to the Philippines. Unless and until they seized intermediate bases in this area, they would be exposed to superior Japanese land based air power. Japan had up to 275 uncommitted naval combat aircraft in December 1941, available for Pacific operations. There were 300 naval and 175 army aircraft on Formosa, to deal with MacArthur's air force in the Philippines, which would have been an even battle by April 1942. The 150 naval aircraft in Indochina might also have been available as reinforcements following the collapse of the British and Dutch. An extra 275-425 naval aircraft, about half of them specialized anti-shipping medium bombers, combined with Japan's larger and elite carrier fleet would have been a major advantage for Japan. The only clear advantage the Americans would have, as they did historically by April 1942, was their 'Magic' cryptography intercepts of Japanese plans.

The numerical balance of naval forces would therefore be fairly even. However, the circumstances of the campaign, and qualitative factors, would mostly have favored Japan. There would have been unpredictable surprises for both sides as well. Before Pearl Harbor the Pacific Fleet was commanded by Kimmel, who was a battleship traditionalist, but also favored an offensive strategy. Instead of being surprised at Pearl Harbor by Japanese naval air power, he would have met this, and the enemy's superior night fighting and torpedo tactics, at sea, in the much more exposed circumstances of a central Pacific offensive campaign. On the other hand the American cryptography advantage, if properly acted upon, might have given them the benefit of operational surprise, and even the favor of chance, as it did at Midway. In conclusion the balance of probabilities, in a 1942 'Mahanite' decisive battle due to a 'No Pearl Harbor' strategy, ranges from even to favorable to Japan. Still, there are enough uncertainties that the Americans might just have fought through to Manila Bay, against the odds. On the other hand if uncertainty, surprise, and chance, had favored Japan, given that the known circumstances favored it as well; then the Americans risked near annihilation, Tsushima style. A disaster of that magnitude, far from their bases, would have been more decisive than Pearl Harbor itself.

Either way, the outcome of such a battle would likely have been pivotal for the Pacific War, shortening its duration. If the American Pacific Fleet had been near annihilated at sea in the spring of 1942, then even a stronger Philippine garrison would have eventually fallen, with greater American ground and air losses than historically. Guam, Wake, and even Midway would have been lost. Even Pearl Harbor and Hawaii, without a viable fleet, would be in serious danger. The situation would have been worse than the historical one for the Americans. Given the changed political circumstances of the outbreak of such a war, an America forced back to Hawaii or even California, and not previously angered by the 'day of infamy', might have accepted a compromise peace. Questions about the wars purpose, and American, as against perceived Allied interests, in both theatres, might have resurfaced. Some of the blame for defeat might indeed have been directed against Roosevelt and other American politicians. The traditional defensive 'No Pearl Harbor' strategy could therefore have worked better for Japan, avoiding the wrath brought by the 'day of infamy'. Any compromise peace treaty would have secured Japan's historical April 1942 defensive perimeter. The US would have lost the Philippines, Guam and Wake, but by diplomacy if nothing else, probably held Hawaii and still secured the eastern Pacific.

However, there are no certainties. At the other end of the spectrum of outcomes, the Americans could still have won, and shortened the war as well. A decisive Japanese naval defeat, by a maximum reinforced American Pacific Fleet in 1942, would have advanced the historic course of the war by nearly two years. With the central Pacific route secured, the Philippines would have been relieved in 1942. Historically it was October 1944, after the decisive battles of the Philippine Sea and Leyte Gulf, that this position was reached. Any American losses would have been replaced by 1943 shipbuilding. With the Philippines secured, Japan would have been cut off from its newly conquered oil supplies in the Dutch East Indies, blockaded, and eventually bombed by B17s. There would be no atomic bomb this early, and an invasion of Japan would likely have been required. That would have been traumatic in casualties, for both sides, but the Pacific War would have finished near the turn of 1943-44. Alternatively, in this last stage, an invasion of Japan might just have been avoided. With no Pearl Harbor, a compromise peace near the end might still have been possible. This time though, the terms would have favored the Americans, probably not dissimilar to the historical ones.

Notes to Chapter 6

1. Ronald H. Spector, Eagle Against the Sun: The American War with Japan, Penguin Books, London, 1987, p 7.
2. Bellamy, Absolute War, p 754, fn 39.
3. Kershaw, Fateful Choices, p 123.
4. Dupuy, Encyclopedia of Military History, p 1233. Hart, Hist of 2WW, p 217.
5. Paul H Silverstone, US Warships of World War II, Ian Allen, London, 1965, 1971, p 12. Between December 1941 and September 1942, 3 carriers, 5 battleships and 2 heavy cruisers were transferred from the Atlantic to the Pacific.
6. Antony Preston, Aircraft Carriers, Hamlyn, London, New York, Sydney, Toronto, 1979, p 132.
7. Encyclopedia of Air Warfare, Spring/Salamander Books, London, 1975, 1977, p 135.
8. ibid, p 135. Also, Hart, Hist of 2WW, p 218.
9. Hart, Hist of 2WW, p 217. These and preceding air power figures for both sides are widely quoted. The figure for the Dutch ground forces, especially the Indonesian militia, does vary more, from a total of 40,000 to as high as 100,000.

10. A J Barker, <u>Pearl Harbor</u>, <u>Purnell's History of the Second World War</u>, Macdonald, London, 1970, p 158-159.

11. The International Date Line separated Pearl Harbor from all of the other Japanese offensives. The offensives occurred simultaneously, December 7th 1941, the 'Day of Infamy' at Pearl Harbor, and in the USA, was December 8th in the Philippines, Wake, Guam, Malaya and the rest of South East Asia.

12. Dupuy, <u>Encyclopedia of Military History</u>, p 1244. Hart, <u>Hist of 2WW</u>, p 217. Again, Dutch figure uncertain.

13. Ellis, <u>Brute Force</u>, p 447. Total includes three US battleships 'sunk' at Pearl Harbor, and not raised and repaired until 1943-44.

14. Spector, <u>Eagle Against the Sun</u>, pp 86-87. Kershaw, <u>Fateful Choices</u>, p 375.

15. Spector, <u>Eagle Against the Sun</u>, p 85. The Authors tables 2 and 3 show the naval balance of power in the Pacific in December 1941, pre-Pearl Harbor, and the US Atlantic Fleet, potentially available as reinforcements.

16. See Chapter 6, <u>German Strategy in 1942</u>; section 1:<u> American Intervention</u>

17. Derived from table 2.

CHAPTER 7

JAPANESE STRATEGY IN 1942

'If war should come, I will run wild for the first six months or a year, but I have no confidence for the second or third years'[1]

Yamamoto

The Battles of Coral Sea and Midway

By April 1942, except for the isolated and soon to fall American-Philippine garrisons at Bataan and Corregidor, Japan had achieved all its territorial and economic objectives. The original plan was now for Japan to move to the defensive, repulsing any Allied counter attacks and force them to negotiate a peace treaty. However, two factors seemed to favor a reconsideration of this strategy. First, the apparent ease and speed of their victories meant they could consider further offensive operations. Secondly, while Japan still had naval superiority, Yamamoto wanted to complete the destruction of the US Pacific Fleet, especially its carrier forces. There were three broad offensive strategic possibilities. Japan could either advance westward into the Indian Ocean: or southward towards Australia: or eastward towards Hawaii. They didn't have the resources to strike at all three of these widely separated objectives, at least not simultaneously.

An offensive to the west would end the 150 years of British sea control in the Indian Ocean, and threaten the South African supply route to its armies in the Middle East and India. An amphibious invasion of Ceylon would be the initial objective. Larger strategic possibilities would be the collapse of Britain's Indian Empire, and a link up with European Axis forces advancing towards the Middle East, via Egypt and the Caucasus. This however, was far too grandiose for Japan's Army high command. The army, and its air force, were thinly spread after the conquest of South East Asia, and as we have seen, the majority of their ground forces were still deployed against China and Russia. They were not even prepared to allocate the one division needed to invade Ceylon, and in practice it might have required more. There were no where near enough ground forces or logistic capabilities to conquer the sub-continent of India. The Indian army had nearly one million men, of which 600,000 were in India itself.[2] Nor could there be any practical cooperation with the European Axis until the land fronts were much closer.

Instead the IJN conducted a major, but temporary, raid into the Indian Ocean. Ironically, by drawing reinforcements from around the world, Britain had managed to form a powerful Eastern Fleet of its own. By April 1942, Admiral Somerville's fleet comprised 3 aircraft carriers with 100 aircraft, 5 battleships, 8 cruisers and 15 destroyers. Unfortunately this was too late to save Singapore, and no match for Nagumo's 'Kido Butai', which had 5 aircraft carriers with 360 superior naval aircraft, 4 fast battleships, 3 cruisers and 9 destroyers for this operation. It was fortunate for Somerville that his fleet failed to intercept Nagumo's raid against Ceylon between April 2nd and 8th, which sank the British carrier **Hermes**, 2 heavy cruisers and 1 destroyer, before they could join the main force. A separate Japanese task force commanded by Ozawa consisting of 1 light carrier, 6 cruisers, and 8 destroyers, destroyed 112,000 tons of merchant shipping in the Bay of Bengal, and covered by Nagumo's larger operation against Ceylon. Japan's main loss was about 90 of its elite carrier planes, in exchange for 300 RAF aircraft during these operations.

In the end however, the Indian Ocean operations led nowhere. Britain would likely have suffered the most disastrous naval defeat in its history had the two fleets met. However Japan, except for deeper naval raids and the possible capture of Ceylon, didn't have spare ground forces to follow up against India, let alone the Middle East. Britain wisely withdrew its Eastern Fleet to East Africa, and later gradually dispersed its ships back to the more urgent Mediterranean and Atlantic theatres. More importantly, the Indian Ocean was a secondary theatre. America rather than Britain was Japan's main enemy. The 'Kido Butai' was redeployed back to the Pacific, for it was only there that Japan's war could be won, or lost.

The 'Mahanite' concept of the decisive battle was central to Japanese, and American, naval doctrine. Decisive victory over an opponent's main fleet would result in command of the sea. From this, in any maritime based conflict, all else followed. At Pearl Harbor Japan appeared to have achieved this result, with the destruction of the American battleships. However, the American carriers survived, along with a considerable cruiser and destroyer force, and these formed the nucleus of a new fleet. Whilst inferior for the moment, the Americans reinforced their Pacific Fleet from the Atlantic, the most important transfers being three of their four fleet carriers (CVs): **Yorktown** in January 1942, **Hornet** in April, and **Wasp** in July. In 1943, the Americans could expect massive reinforcements, as the first major vessels of their 'two ocean navy' shipbuilding plan started to commission.

In the meantime they had not been idle, even while Japan conquered South East Asia. The irreducible defensive requirements of holding Hawaii, Australia, and the Pacific island line of communication between the two, was the primary American strategy in early 1942. However, they were keen to launch counter attacks, even early offensives, when and where they could. Small carrier raids were made against Japanese Pacific bases from January to April 1942. These culminated in the 'Doolittle raid' on Japan itself on

April 18th. It inflicted insignificant material damage, but was important psychologically. The American raid had used the north Pacific route, between Midway and the Aleutians, and had revealed a vulnerability in Japan's defensive perimeter. It helped tip the Japanese strategic debate in favor of a renewed offensive, on the central Midway-Hawaii axis.

This wasn't the only new offensive that Japan, primarily the IJN, was planning. Australia was a major Allied base directly adjacent to Japan's newly won defensive perimeter. From here American forces, commanded by MacArthur after his dramatic escape from the Philippines in March 1942, were beginning a ground and air build up, and given time could launch a major counter offensive. The Japanese Army however, objected to a direct attack on Australia. It would have required 10 divisions that it couldn't spare from other fronts. It was also at the limit, indeed probably beyond, Japanese seaborne logistic capacity, given the distance and continental size of the objective. Instead the strategy, supported by both armed services, was to cut the island line of communication between Australia and the USA. New Guinea and the Solomon Islands, where Japan already had footholds from its initial expansion, would be the first targets. New Caledonia, Fiji and Samoa would then be seized. This would isolate Australia and New Zealand from American supply and reinforcements. It was probably impossible for Japan to conquer Australia directly, but neither could Australia on its own threaten Japan's new empire.

Fatally however, Japan had underestimated its opponents, and split its forces and objectives, breaking cardinal strategic principles. They began two major strategic offensives at the same time. Moreover, they were in divergent directions. The 'Australia' offensive targeted the south Pacific, widely separated from the 'Midway-Hawaii' offensive in the central Pacific, aiming eastward. The first stage of the southern offensive, operation 'MO', began on May 1st 1942, with planned amphibious invasions against Port Moresby, the main Allied base in New Guinea, and the island of Tulagi, adjacent to Guadalcanal in the southern Solomon Islands. They detached two of the First Air Fleets six fleet carriers (*Shokaku* and *Zuikaku*) to reinforce the local forces for operation 'MO'. Total Japanese strength was 2 fleet carriers and 1 light carrier with 174 combat aircraft, 9 cruisers and 15 destroyers. These were deployed operationally into Admiral Takagi's carrier striking force of the 2 fleet carriers, 2 heavy cruisers and 6 destroyers, with the rest divided into four separate invasion, support and covering groups. It was a typical rather complex Japanese operation. They expected only outclassed local naval opposition, from the 3 cruisers and 3 destroyers in MacArthur's South West Pacific Area.

They were in for a surprise, for the Americans with their cryptography advantage knew the Japanese objectives and roughly the timing of 'MO', but not their precise order of battle. Nimitz, C-in-C of the Pacific Fleet (CIN-PAC) in Hawaii, was able to send half his combat strength in Fletcher's Task Force 17 the 3,500 miles to intercept operation 'MO'. This resulted in the Battle of the Coral Sea between May 6th and 8th 1942. Nimitz's other main force, TF16 with two carriers *Hornet* and *Enterprise,* was only just returning from the Doolittle raid, and couldn't reach the battle in time. Such was the vast size of the Pacific War theatre. With 2 fleet carriers, *Lexington* and *Yorktown*, and 143 combat aircraft, 8 cruisers and 14 destroyers in total, the two sides were evenly balanced. Both sides had land based aircraft available, but scattered over a wide area they played little part in the battle.

Coral Sea was the first all out carrier battle ever, no battleships took part and there was no surface action between cruisers and destroyers. All the damage was inflicted by the specialized carrier aircraft: dive bombers and torpedo planes. Both sides made tactical mistakes, misidentifying and attacking secondary targets. It was after all a new type of warfare and strategy and tactics were evolving under the test of battle. The result was a tactical victory for Japan, but a strategic victory for America. The USA lost the fleet carrier *Lexington* and a destroyer sunk, and the *Yorktown* damaged. Japan lost only the light carrier *Shoho* and a destroyer sunk. The *Shokaku* however, was damaged and put out of action for two months and the *Zuikaku* lost half its aircraft. Both sides took heavy naval air losses: 74 American and 80 Japanese.[3] Strategically, with insufficient air cover remaining; Japan aborted the Port Moresby invasion. The Battle of the Coral Sea was the first check on Japan's expansion, and as it turned out the limit of its advance in this sub-theatre of the south west Pacific. For these reasons Coral Sea was the most important battle in the Pacific since Pearl Harbor. But it wasn't decisive for the Pacific War overall, because neither side committed its main fleet. At Midway they would do so, and crucially two of Japan's six most powerful carriers would be missing, because of the damage suffered at Coral Sea.

Even so Japan still had overall naval superiority for the planned decisive battle. Midway was chosen as the target because of its strategic location. A mere spec of an island at the western edge of the Hawaiian chain, it was 1,100 miles north west of Pearl Harbor and out of attack range for most of the land based aircraft in Hawaii. Yet it was important enough in Japan's control to threaten Hawaii and it would likely force the American fleet to fight. If not, then strategic logic meant a subsequent invasion of the Hawaiian Islands would trigger the decisive battle. Pearl Harbor and Hawaii were essential for American power in the Pacific. There was nothing except 2,400 miles of ocean between Hawaii and the USA itself, and Midway was Hawaii's advanced sentry.

Table 4: Japanese Forces for the Midway Campaign

	CV	CVL	BB	CA	CL	DD	SS	Carrier Aircraft
2nd Carrier Fleet	1	1			2	3		82
Aleutian Invasion Forces				3	2	10		
1st Carrier Fleet	4		2	2	1	12		272+60 reserve
1st Fleet Main		1	3		1	8		17
1st Fleet Guard			4		2	12		
2nd Fleet Main		1	2	4	1	8		24
2nd Fleet Support				4		2		
Midway Invasion Force					1	10		
Submarine Screen							21	
Total	5	3	11	13	10	65	21	395+60 reserve

Table 5: American Forces for the Midway Campaign

	CV	CA	CL	DD	SS	Aircraft
TF 8 / Aleutians		2	3	13	6	136 Combat + 20 Patrol (all Land Based)
Midway						83 Combat + 32 Patrol
TF 16	Enterprise Hornet	5	1	9		158 Carrier Aircraft
TF 17	Yorktown	2		5		75 Carrier Aircraft
Submarines					19	
Total	3	9	4	27	25	233 Carrier, 219 L.B. Combat 52 Patrol

Japan had a considerable material superiority for the Midway campaign as a comparison of tables 4 and 5 shows. However, some very important clarifications to the basic balance need to be made. Firstly, the massive Japanese fleet of 165 vessels of all types, was split into a total of 16 separate task forces, of which the principal combat groups are listed in table 4, the remainder being various auxiliary, minesweeping, fuelling and seaplane tender groups. The dispersion of forces was over a frontage of 1,300 miles from the Aleutians to Midway, and to a depth of 300 miles. This was in accordance with Yamamoto's very complex strategic plan. The objective of the strategy was to bring the American fleet to battle and trap them between the various Japanese forces. The Aleutian Islands would be attacked first as a diversion, in order to draw the American fleet northward from Pearl Harbor, and out of position. The advanced submarine screen, deployed off Pearl Harbor, would give them warning of American movements. Midway would then be invaded and its air force eliminated by Nagumo's First Carrier Fleet. Finally, as the Americans redeployed southward to defend Midway, they would be brought to battle, first by either or both Japanese carrier forces and then ultimately by the First Battle Fleet under Yamamoto's direct command.

The Japanese would sail dispersed, trap their opponent between separate forces, and then converge for the decisive battle. Without using hindsight it seemed a plausible plan at the time. Its weaknesses were that it depended on surprise and on the Americans reacting in the way expected. Moreover, in the initial stages with their task forces dispersed and not mutually supporting, the IJN would be vulnerable. This can be seen by comparing any of the individual task forces from tables 4 and 5, rather than the total balance. In fact, the actual battle would be largely between the Japanese First Carrier Fleet and the American TF16 and TF17, which were deployed close together, a more even balance, nullifying Yamamoto's overall superiority.

Secondly in air power, even the overall balance, was much less to Japan's advantage than with surface naval forces. The Americans would have land based air support in the Aleutians and at Midway. At Midway itself, the land based air power, along with Task Forces 16 and 17's carriers would actually give the Americans a slight numerical edge of 316 combat aircraft over the Japanese First Carrier Fleet's 272 machines. The 60 Japanese aircraft in reserve were to replace losses and to transfer to Midway, after its presumed capture. Set against this the American Midway based air forces were a mixture of army, navy and marine aircraft, and mostly not specialized anti-ship types. Japan still had the quality advantage of superior carrier aircraft and air crew training. The American PBY patrol flying boats however, gave them an important search advantage in both range and numbers. Japan largely used surface ship seaplanes for reconnaissance, rather than carrier planes at this time, which was an inferior system to the American one.

As at Coral Sea, the Americans retained their cryptography advantage and were aware of the Japanese plans, codenamed AL and MI. Before the battle they were able to reinforce the Midway garrison to 3,600 troops and 115 aircraft, the islands maximum capacity. Japan underestimated the scale and speed of the USN's response as well. They thought that both US carriers at Coral Sea had been sunk and that only two would be available for Midway. The damaged *Yorktown* however, had been repaired in three days by herculean efforts at the Pearl Harbor dockyards. The Americans, forewarned of Japanese plans, sortied their TF16 from Pearl Harbor on May 26th followed by TF17 led by the repaired *Yorktown* on the 28th, before the Japanese submarine screen was in position to monitor their moves. By June 2nd 1942 the two US task forces rendezvoused 325 miles north east of Midway, at the appropriately named 'point luck', two days ahead of the expected attack and ready to spring a trap of their own. The Americans did make one modest strategic error in the deployment phase. They could have left the defense of the Aleutians, a known diversionary target, to ground and air forces, instead of diverting a scarce surface task force there.

The sequence of events and decisions is the key to understanding the battle itself and its outcome. On June 3rd 1942, Japan's Second Carrier Fleet launched its diversionary air attacks against Dutch Harbor, the main American base in the Aleutians. The American northern TF8 was at sea, but neither side's naval forces were able to locate the other due to rain and fog, which were standard weather conditions for the region. On the same day, far to the south-west of Midway itself, PBYs located part of Japan's Second Fleet. This was a secondary target, and Fletcher commanding the combined American fleet of TF16 and TF17, held back to await Nagumo's First Carrier Fleet, which the intelligence reports indicated would approach from the north-west. Instead, Midway based B17s attacked the Second Fleet at long range, inflicting little damage.

June 4th 1942 was the decisive day. At dawn both sides began air searches, and Nagumo launched an air strike against Midway with 108 aircraft, half his attack force, holding the rest back to await developments. Before Nagumo's first wave reached Midway the Americans located his fleet. They immediately launched their maximum air attack strength, both from the carriers and from Midway. The Japanese first wave then struck Midway, defeating its obsolescent fighter defense. They failed however, to knock the base out of action or catch any American aircraft on the ground. A second attack against Midway would be required and accordingly Nagumo ordered his reserve second wave to be armed for attacking the island base. Meanwhile the American Midway based planes, a mixture of different types, executed an uncoordinated attack against the Japanese fleet. They lost half their force and inflicted no damage. Then to his surprise, Nagumo's search planes located the American TF17. He ordered his second wave to be rearmed again, this time for attacking ships. However, this all took time and he wouldn't be able to launch the second wave's full attack before recovering his first wave, returning from Midway and low on fuel. Before this process was complete, disaster struck his fleet.

The American carrier planes reached the Japanese fleet and attacked, but in an apparently uncoordinated manner, the different squadrons having become separated en-route. The American torpedo planes without fighter escort attacked first, and were almost wiped out losing 41 out of 47 aircraft and inflicted no damage. They had however, drawn the Japanese fighter defense (combat air patrol or CAP) down to a low altitude and out of position. By chance, 54 American dive bombers arrived almost immediately and were able to execute a virtually unopposed surprise attack. Moreover the Japanese carriers were hit at a vulnerable time, recovering, rearming and refueling aircraft, thus multiplying the damage caused. Three of Nagumo's four fleet carriers, *Akagi*, *Kaga* and *Soryu*, were immediately put out of action and would later sink. This was the decisive moment of the battle, and probably of the entire Pacific War itself. Nagumo was able to counter attack from his last carrier the *Hiryu*, and with the assistance of a submarine, sank the *Yorktown* and a destroyer. The *Hiryu*, and the next day a heavy cruiser, were then sunk by the carrier aircraft of TF16. Without air cover and with his First Battle Fleet still 300 miles away, Yamamoto abandoned the invasion and the attempt to trap the American fleet. The Americans also prudently withdrew, to avoid the still massive IJN surface superiority.

Midway was the most decisive battle of the Pacific War. Japan lost 4 fleet carriers and one heavy cruiser, 332 carrier aircraft and 3,500 men. The Americans lost one fleet carrier and a destroyer, 150 aircraft and 307 men.[4] They held Midway and the only Japanese gains were the occupation of two remote islands, Attu and Kiska, at the western end of the Aleutians. It was an unexpected American victory against the odds. Three factors, Japanese mistakes and overconfidence, American intelligence gathering and operational brilliance, and chance, account for the outcome.

Yamamoto's dispersion of his huge fleet nullified his greatest advantage. His complex battle plan relied on the Americans reacting as expected, which they didn't. Dividing their forces into so many different task forces, and not taking the initiative and imposing superior force at the decisive point on their opponent, were Japanese strategic errors. However, without the American 'Magic' intelligence system, giving advanced knowledge of Yamamoto's plans, his mistakes wouldn't have been fatal. Nimitz was able to use this knowledge to correctly deploy his fleet and surprise his opponent. Had Yamamoto concentrated his fleet however, especially all 8 carriers, it is unlikely, even with foreknowledge that the Americans could have won. Nimitz himself has admitted as much, stating:

'had the Japanese fleet been properly concentrated...it is inconceivable... even with the most complete warning...that the three US carriers could by any combination of luck and skill still have defeated and turned back the seven [actually eight] carriers, eleven battleships, and the immense number of supporting vessels which the Japanese committed to this action'[5]

The Americans were simply not strong enough, even with luck, to knock out eight carriers at once. Assuming they had surviving carriers, then the longer the battle lasted, the more the Japanese numerical and elite pilot advantage would have come into play, to at least even the losses. It only took their one surviving carrier, **Hiryu**, to sink the **Yorktown**. Five surviving Japanese carriers, out of a concentrated force of eight, would likely have inflicted greater damage, even sinking all three American carriers. The losses would then have been three fleet carriers each.

Admiral Spruance, commanding TF16, took the bold and correct decision, which worked, to launch an all out maximum first strike as soon as the enemy was located. This became the norm of the new carrier tactics from then on. It still required luck however, by arriving coordinated at the target, and at the most vulnerable time for Nagumo's carriers, to bring about the outcome it did. The American strike wave had become separated enroute, and the **Hornet's** dive bomber squadrons for example, never reacquired their target at all. Chance can thus play a role, especially in the short term. Over the longer run, such as in most of the other campaigns we have examined, it tends to even out over a myriad of small actions and decisions. Naval battles are different. They tend to be shorter in duration, rather than the more typical drawn out attrition of land and air warfare. In those circumstances, especially when the main fleets meet for a decisive battle, chance can be more important, as it was at Midway. Even so it took all three factors in combination, Japanese mistakes, proper American use of their intelligence advantage, and luck, to account for the outcome. If any one of the three had been absent, the outcome would almost certainly have been different, resulting in either a drawn battle, or a Japanese victory.

Table 6: Pacific Naval Strength after Midway: July 1942[6]

	CV	CVL	BB	CA	CL	DD	SS	Carrier Aircraft
Japan	4	2	11	17	17	107	63	352
USA	4		8	14	11	92	61	340

The decisive strategic consequence of the Battle of Midway was that it changed the balance of sea power in the Pacific from Japanese superiority to near parity. In other words it neutralized the strategic advantages of command of the sea that Japan had gained at Pearl Harbor. It changed the naval balance back to parity, but not to immediate American superiority.

As we can see from table 6 the Japanese advantage after Midway is only modest in all categories.

They had lost their previous large superiority in aircraft carriers, and over half of their pre-war elite carrier air crews had been lost by this time, mostly at Midway. The Americans had also been restoring their battleship strength, by transferring four ships from the Atlantic, and repairing three of those damaged at Pearl Harbor. The defeat at Midway also marks the maximum extent of Japanese territorial expansion, and a change in the strategic initiative in the Pacific. Japan reverted to its previous plan, to go onto the defensive and to fortify and consolidate its perimeter. For the Americans, it meant that the previous threat to Hawaii and Australia and their sea lines of communication (SLOC) was ended.

From the post-Midway point of balance, the Americans took the initiative in two ways. In the south-west Pacific, they began a limited offensive at Guadalcanal in August 1942. This was a hard fought and close run campaign, on land, sea and air. The naval balance remained roughly even for the remainder of 1942 and it wasn't until February 1943, that Guadalcanal was finally secured by the Americans.

Midway also gave the Americans the strategic flexibility to start re-focusing on their 'Germany first' global grand strategy. 'Germany first' had been the preferred pre-Pearl Harbor strategy, codenamed 'Plan D' and 'Rainbow 5'. These envisaged a strategic offensive against Germany, combined with a defensive or limited offensive, against Japan. Between Pearl Harbor and Midway however, while 'Germany first' was still official doctrine, the practical strategic priority had been to counter Japanese expansion. For example by June 1942 there were 400,000 armed forces personnel in the Pacific theatre compared to only 60,000 deployed in Europe.[7] The Pacific theatre was of course an overwhelming USN and USMC priority throughout the war, and it required unexpectedly large army air force reinforcements as well. Even with the Midway victory, it would be November 1942 before America began operation 'Torch', its first offensive in the European theatre, three months after the Guadalcanal offensive in the Pacific. Indeed, even as late as the end of 1943, 18 months after Midway, the Americans still had roughly equal sized armed forces deployed against both Germany and Japan.[8] In the Pacific, 1943 was a year of slow American progress in MacArthur's Southwest Pacific Area, combined with a massive naval build up at Hawaii, as the 'two ocean fleet' started to commission. It was November 1943 however, before the really decisive American strategic counter offensive began, commanded by Nimitz, in the central Pacific at Tarawa.

Midway was therefore the decisive turning point in the Pacific War. However, it didn't determine the outcome of the war all at once. Rather its importance lies in the fact that it broke Japan's naval supremacy and restored the balance. The period of balance lasted at least six months, and in terms of the capacity for regaining command of the sea and thus the more rapid re-conquest of territory, even 17 months. Midway allowed time for the massive American economic mobilization, especially the 'two ocean fleet', to come into play. It was this that was America's greatest advantage and which would ultimately win the war.

It is also worth recalling at this point the longer term consequences of Pearl Harbor. For American economic and hence military material superiority, to have its full decisive effect, it needed to be combined with other important components. These were a determined and united national will, to carry on to victory, which the perceived unprovoked and treacherous nature of the Pearl Harbor attack provided. The other factors were time, and the necessary geographic bases, to begin the fight back once resources were available. The victory at Midway gave the Americans time to regroup their existing fleet and make use of their economic mobilization. It also protected the vital base at Hawaii, and indirectly due to the blunting of Japan's main offensive weapon, the 'Kido Butai', Australia as well.

Hawaii and Australia, secured by sea control, were the vital bases from which the strategic counter offensives of 1943 and especially of 1944 were possible. If the American Pacific Fleet had been largely lost at Midway, Hawaii would have been in major danger, and Australia indirectly isolated. The front line might have been pushed back to the American Pacific coast, along with a devastating blow to morale at all levels. Even with the massive resources of 1943-1944, it would have been a very long way back from there. Midway, June 4th 1942, was the decisive day of a decisive battle of history, but its course and outcome could easily have been very different.

Japanese Options: The Alternative Battle Scenario of Midway-Hawaii

Despite the decisive defeat at Midway, the strategy of seeking a decisive battle was largely correct. The problems were at the operational level rather than with the higher strategy. Given the situation in April 1942, after the completion of Japan's initial expansion and the establishment of its defensive perimeter, several strategic options were available. As we have seen four of them were rejected. The 'northern option' against Russia had been rejected in July 1941. Despite the Army's concern that war might resume on this front in the spring of 1942, the reasons against it were more valid than ever, reinforced by the fact that Japan was now at war with America and Britain. Nor did the failure at Midway invalidate the reasons previously given against moving the strategic focus against India or Australia. Both would remain secondary fronts and full scale invasions were impractical. Continuing the original offensive-defensive strategy, and fortifying the new perimeter against American counter offensives was a fourth option, indeed it was the default strategy after the Midway defeat. However, pre-Midway it would have given away the initiative, and since the Americans hadn't offered to negotiate a peace treaty at that point, it didn't seem to offer decisive results. Instead, Japan had to try and inflict a further decisive naval defeat on America and push it to a position from which it couldn't recover.

We therefore return to the Midway-Hawaii and the isolation of Australia strategies. Australia's isolation would be a default result of any decisive Japanese naval victory at Midway or Hawaii, but the reverse wasn't the case. Isolating Australia by an advance into the south Pacific wouldn't, on its own, offer decisive results. The central Pacific axis directly confronting the main enemy, America and its Pacific Fleet, was the vital strategic fulcrum in mid-1942. Japan's mistakes were operational ones, specifically the failure to concentrate its ironically named main offensive weapon system, the Combined Fleet. They fatally split their naval forces between the Coral Sea and Midway operations, and then further divided the Midway forces as well. If they had concentrated their fleet and executed sequential operations, they could have achieved enough superiority at both battles in turn, to literally leave nothing to chance. As we have seen, not even the 'chance' that heavily favored the Americans at Midway, would have been enough, on its own, to win. Alternatively Japan could simply have postponed or scrapped the Coral Sea offensive and concentrated everything against Midway-Hawaii.

Table 7: Pacific Carrier Strength mid-1942[9]

	Japan			America	
	CV	CVL	Aircraft Capacity	CV	Aircraft Capacity
April 1942	6	4	622	4	337
Reinforcements					
May	Junyo		53		
June				Saratoga	90
July	Hiyo		53	Wasp	84
Max by August	8	4	728	6	521

The crucial balance of power in carriers, excluding for the moment any losses, is shown in table 7. The Japanese fleet includes the CVL *Hosho,* which was normally used for training, but was exceptionally deployed

197

with Yamamoto's 1st Battle Fleet at Midway. The *Junyo* and *Hiyo* were new ships. *Saratoga* was completing repairs from torpedo damage in January 1942, and sailed from San Diego on June 1st 1942, only days late for Midway. *Wasp* was the last pre-war US carrier to be transferred from the Atlantic, although the CV *Ranger* (86 aircraft), normally used for training would have been available in an extreme emergency. In late 1942 Japan would commission only one more CVL, the *Ryuho* (30 aircraft) in November, and the first of the wartime US *Essex* class CVs (100 aircraft each), was completed on the very last day of 1942. In the critical year of 1942 therefore, Japan had the prospect of maintaining a clear carrier superiority of up to two to one. In carrier aircraft it would be rather less than that, but Japan still had its elite air crew advantage. They also maintained a moderate numerical and quality edge in surface combatants in 1942, even taking into account American transfers from the Atlantic.[10]

By concentrating the entire carrier and most of the surface fleet at Coral Sea and then Midway in sequence, even assuming that this would cause a delay for the Midway operation, and thus the presence of the *Saratoga* and a few extra US surface escorts, Japan would have had a superiority of 6-7 CVs and 4 CVLs against 4-5 US CVs at either or both battles. This analysis assumes that the Americans are able to make maximum operational use of their cryptography advantage, and deploy their full available strength against both Japanese offensives in turn. The outnumbered Americans would have had to inflict 2:1 losses, at each battle, just to maintain their relative strength for subsequent operations.

Even historically at Midway, by concentrating their actual force, Japan would have had 5 CVs and 3 CVLs against the Americans 3 CVs. The lucky American first strike at Midway eliminated 3 Japanese CVs. That would have left a Japanese advantage of 2 CVs and 3 CVLs against 3 US CVs with depleted aircraft complements for the second strike phase of the battle. As it was, the temporarily surviving CV *Hiryu* was able to sink the *Yorktown*. An extra four untouched Japanese carriers, at full strength having landed aircraft from the lost carriers, would surely have inflicted equivalent damage and probably sunk the *Enterprise* and *Hornet* as well. Without air cover, any damaged American carriers or escort ships would easily have been sunk, as Yamamoto's vast surface forces followed up and swept the battlefield. Equal losses of 3 CVs each at Midway, would have meant a Japanese victory, due to its greater overall carrier strength. By assuming that the Americans would have made maximum operational use of their intelligence advantage, and the bias of 'Midway luck' in their favor, our analysis here is a best case for America and worst case for Japan.

The only change from the historical course, is that we assume Japan concentrates its carrier fleet, both strategically at each operation in sequence, and then tactically within each operation. In other words we have only changed operational and strategic command decisions, which were entirely under Japan's control. All they needed to do was take no risks; they didn't even have to suspect that the Americans were reading their codes. Concentrating a fleet was standard strategy in all navies, in both the preceding battleship and emerging carrier task force eras. The Japanese had become complacent after their easy victories following Pearl Harbor. They later termed it 'victory disease' and it led to them neglecting the cardinal strategic principle of concentration of force. The conclusion, even with assumptions favoring the Americans, is therefore that by concentrating its fleet, Japan would have won, or at the very least drawn with even losses, decisive naval battles at either or both of Coral Sea and Midway.

It could easily have been worse for the Americans. The extent and importance of chance was never repeated in any other Pacific War battle for either side. Nor were the Americans always able to make maximum operational use of their cryptography advantage. Pacific distances and timing meant that the Americans, on the defensive and reacting to Japan's moves, wouldn't always, as at Coral Sea and with the *Saratoga* after Midway, be able to achieve maximum concentration. The Americans could very likely have lost four or even five of their precious fleet carriers; *Lexington* as historically at Coral Sea, all three of the Midway CVs and even *Saratoga* as well had the battle been delayed. In exchange, at most Japan would take equal losses; CVL *Shoho* at Coral Sea and the presumed still surprised CVs *Akagi, Kaga* and *Soryu* at Midway.

Maximum Japanese carrier concentration at each of Coral Sea and Midway in sequence would have slightly delayed both battles. However, it would have given them a two to one balance or more at each, and because there would have been two battles, reduced the importance of chance. In this case the *Yorktown,* which was damaged at Coral Sea, would almost certainly have been lost there against a larger Japanese force. Consequently the presence of *Saratoga* wouldn't have improved the odds or American chances at Midway. Overall Japanese losses would likely have been rather less in this variant. Midway was a case like France 1940, where actual history was stranger than fiction. Analyzing the alternative Japanese strategy, and it is only a modest change of operational technique, merely reinforces the decisive importance of these naval battles, and especially of Midway.

Just as important would be the new strategic situation following such an American defeat at Midway. Most importantly, the balance of naval power and especially naval air power would have moved even more in Japan's favor. It would have remained so for the remaining half of 1942 and even well into 1943. The Americans would have at best, only 3 fleet carriers, *Saratoga, Wasp* and *Ranger* for the rest of 1942. All of them, along with the four new battleships of the *South Dakota* class, completed between August and December 1942, and most of the Atlantic Fleet's remaining cruisers and more destroyers, would have to be deployed to the Pacific to try and stem the tide. There would have been a cost to naval air training and expansion. In contrast Japan's 'Kido Butai' with at least 5 CVs and 3-4 CVLs, along with the Combined Fleet's 12 battleships and other surface forces would be largely intact. They would have retained the strategic initiative in the Pacific well into 1943. Only at the very end of 1943, after the completion of 7 *Essex* class CVs and 9 *Independence* class CVLs, could America perhaps achieve modest naval air superiority. A lot could have happened in the intervening 18 months, especially the remaining six months of 1942 after Midway.

Meanwhile the US Atlantic Fleet would have become even weaker than historically, relying on a few escort carriers and destroyers to protect convoys. In the Atlantic theatre in 1942, shipping losses reached a peak of 6 million tons, plus 2 million tons elsewhere. It would have become an overwhelmingly British responsibility. With less American commitment, these losses which were predominantly off the US eastern seaboard and in the Caribbean, i.e. in the American defense zone, would have been even higher. The result would have been increased and continuing pressure on the American 'Germany first' strategy. Offensive operations starting with the invasion of North Africa, operation 'Torch' in November 1942, would likely have been delayed or cancelled due to the enhanced Allied global naval and shipping transport crisis. The American ground-air build up in Britain and lend lease aid to Britain and Russia would also have been reduced. These indirect effects on the European War would have come at the worst possible time for Britain and Russia. Britain was fully mobilized, at maximum production already, and overstretched globally in 1942. Russia was also at its weakest point, with German expansion towards the Caucasus reaching its greatest extent.

With command of the Pacific retained and enhanced after a victory at Midway, Japan would have had the same options as before. They could return to the defensive or strike at India, Australia and the south-west Pacific, Hawaii or even the Aleutians. Even more than before Midway and for the reasons previously stated, Hawaii would have been the only option that offered decisive results. In addition, holding and supplying an outpost at Midway, vulnerable to a counter offensive from an intact American base at Pearl Harbor, would be strategically pointless. Midway was a vital stepping stone, Hawaii the ultimate strategic prize in the Pacific. The 'Eastern Operation' as the Japanese termed the invasion of Hawaii, was already in an advanced stage of planning at the time of Midway. It is almost certain that this would have been the next operation, and even more than Midway itself, the decisive battle of the Pacific War.

Japanese victory would have been no certainty however. The Americans would have been reduced to two or three carriers after a Midway defeat. Available surface forces for each side, prior to new battleship completions, would have been similar to the historical situation in July 1942, shown in table 6. The Americans would likely have lost a few extra cruisers and destroyers in a Midway and/or Coral Sea debacle, balanced by their last and emergency transfers from the Atlantic. Japan, deploying and concentrating the entire Combined Fleet, would have had a moderate surface superiority. Moreover they still had a quality advantage in ships and tactics, as the actual surface battles in the Guadalcanal campaign showed. With 5 or more CVs and 3-4 CVLs with 500 carrier aircraft however, there would have been a clear Japanese advantage in the crucial arm of naval air power. Even so Hawaii, and specifically Oahu with its Pearl Harbor base, would have been a formidable bastion. At the time of Pearl Harbor it had an army garrison of 40,000 men in two divisions and 394 army and navy aircraft, 280 of them combat types. By June 1942 the land based air forces, almost wiped out at Pearl Harbor, had been replaced and the ground forces increased to three divisions, about 65,000 men including garrison and service troops.

The USN, although depleted in carriers is certain to have fought for Oahu, hopefully backed by land based air power to somewhat even the odds. It would have had to, because without naval support, the ground and air forces would have been at a severe disadvantage. The political cost alone of abandoning this future American state would have been catastrophic. Hawaii's isolated position, 2,400 miles from the Californian coast, was beyond the combat radius of all American aircraft until the B29 bomber entered service in 1944. The island's third of a million civilian population and its military garrisons were not self sufficient. Everything, including fuel, ammunition, replacement aircraft and weapons, and even most of the food, had to be supplied by ship from the US mainland. Only unloaded heavy bombers and the largest transport planes, not much use without bombs or cargo, could manage a one way trip. The convoy route, which included a large land based aircraft gap, would be very vulnerable to Japanese carrier and surface strikes. For the side with the initiative and naval superiority, these rather than submarines, were by far the most devastating anti-shipping weapon systems in World War Two. Submarine attacks would simply supplement this, further stretching American naval defenses and transport routes throughout the eastern Pacific. The USN, Hawaii's air forces and US morale, would likely have been reduced further in these preliminary convoy battles.

Oahu couldn't be seriously attacked by land based aircraft from Midway alone, due to its small capacity of around 100 planes. The distance was

1,100 miles, which was at the extreme radius of action for Japanese medium bombers, but well beyond that for fighter escorts. An invasion would require preliminary landings, along the Hawaiian chain between Midway and Oahu, and/or against Johnson and Palmyra Islands, far to the south. The latter would disrupt the American air and sea communication, transport and supply route towards Australia. This would have been followed by major invasions against one or more of the main islands, other than Oahu, probably Hawaii. Eventually Japanese land based air power, deploying via sea transport to the newly captured advanced bases, would have come into range of Oahu. The air battles would have been furious and both sides would have been operating at the end of long supply lines. With a superior fleet however, Japan would have the edge in the battle of supply and replacements.

Finally, if they had gained air superiority, Japan could have invaded Oahu itself. It would have entailed serious ground operations by Japan, about 5 divisions and 100,000 troops in total. This would have stretched Japanese amphibious invasion and sea transport capabilities to their maximum limit. The 'Eastern Operation' would therefore have been a naval, air and amphibious invasion campaign, lasting several weeks, rather than a single battle. Time wouldn't have been a problem though, because after a victorious Midway, Japan had six months or more of clear naval air superiority. At each stage and especially before land based air power could be brought into range, most of Japan's Combined Fleet would be required to cover the operations. At some point, taking advantage of its 'Magic' intelligence intercepts, the USN would have committed its outnumbered Pacific Fleet to battle. When that happened, it would have been the decisive moment and battle of the entire Pacific War.

As before, if Japan had concentrated its large carrier and surface fleet superiority, it would have had the overall advantage. The Americans would have been relying on their superior cryptography, timing of operational surprise and any remaining land based air power to even the odds. The combined balance of forces and circumstances would have favored Japan, but not by much. A Japanese victory at Hawaii would have been no certainty. Operational and tactical decisions, mistakes, as well as chance, could all have affected the outcome. The result would have been decisive for the rest of the Pacific War, just as Midway was historically.

If the Americans had won a naval battle at Hawaii, against the odds, the consequences would have been similar to Midway. Any ongoing Japanese invasions of the Hawaiian Islands would have been aborted. The naval balance in the Pacific would be restored, first to rough parity and gradually in 1943 to American superiority. Within a few months, a captured Midway and any lost Hawaiian islands would have been retaken. Japan couldn't have sustained relatively isolated garrisons, this far forward and relatively close to an intact American base at Pearl Harbor, without a clear naval superiority. In the end, with the crucial Pearl Harbor base held and intact, and the naval balance restored, there is no strategic reason why the rest of the Pacific War would alter much from its historic course. America, its morale restored as well by a Hawaii victory, just as it was at Midway, would probably have persevered and won in the end. Depending on the precise balance of carriers and naval air power, future events would merely have been delayed by a few months at most. Nimitz's decisive central Pacific campaign, premised on carrier superiority, might even have proceeded almost on schedule in November 1943. The rest would be history as we know it.

If Japan had won the decisive naval battle off Hawaii however, history would likely have been very different. Consider the immediate consequences first. Once the Americans had lost their 2 or 3 carriers, the naval battle itself could easily have been catastrophic for them. Their outclassed surface forces would be harried on a 1,500 mile or more retreat, towards the safety of land based air cover in California. Japan's Combined Fleet, seeking a Tsushima like annihilation, would have been superior in all categories of weapon system; naval air power, battleship and cruiser gunnery, the 'long lance' torpedo, and if the Americans had committed their remaining pre-war battleline, faster as well. A defeat of this magnitude, which is a reasonable possibility for an outnumbered and outclassed 1942 surface fleet stripped of its air cover, would be decisive. Even American recovery, using the new shipbuilding of 1943 and 1944 would have been in doubt.

Next, the Americans would have lost their considerable garrison of 65,000 troops in three divisions and any remaining land based air forces in the Hawaiian Islands. The medium sized land battles, especially for Oahu, would have been prolonged, perhaps a month or more, and agonizing for America. Yet without naval and air support the result cannot be in doubt. Oahu would have fallen after a severe battle; just as every Japanese garrison at Tarawa, Kwajalein, Saipan, Guam, Iwo Jima, Okinawa and elsewhere fell, once they were isolated by air and sea. A blocked, sabotaged and then repaired Pearl Harbor, would later become a secure base for Japan's fleet, well beyond the range of American air power on the Pacific coast.

The morale and psychological effects on the American political leadership, public and even within the armed forces and their bureaucracy, would likely have been catastrophic. Near annihilation of the fleet and the total loss of an American, not a Philippine or Allied, but an American garrison of 65,000 men, would be by far the most disastrous in the nation's history. Although, strictly speaking Hawaii doesn't become a US state until 1959, such a defeat would have occurred on what was widely considered American territory proper. A huge disaster at Hawaii would also have been the final culmination of a year of defeats, at Pearl Harbor, the Philippines, and Midway. Japan's political aim was to gain a peace treaty. Yamamoto, who had more knowledge of America than most Japanese leaders, knew that they needed to inflict continuous, massive and decisive defeats to achieve this objective. Japanese strategies and victories at Midway and Hawaii, as analyzed here were viable and reasonable probabilities, although not certainties. They were about the maximum that Japanese strategy could do to achieve a peace treaty. Would it have been enough?

Consequences: Could Japan Have Won the Pacific War?

We are dealing with intangible factors of morale, psychology and their effect on politics and diplomacy, so it is impossible to be certain. On the one hand, America was provoked and determined after Pearl Harbor and success in any 'turn of the tide' battle, at Midway or Hawaii, would likely have restored the war to its historical course and outcome, eventually. On the other hand, no nation is undefeatable. America itself could never have been actually invaded or conquered by Japan or Germany. However, as it's only ever defeat, Vietnam, later showed, it was vulnerable in morale, psychologically and when its political system was divided and in turmoil. The alternative course of events outlined here, would certainly have highlighted these weaknesses and produced those circumstances by late 1942.

Even if a Hawaii defeat or catastrophe didn't result in a near term peace treaty, it would still have secured a strategic position for Japan that was as impregnable as it was possible to be. With near total naval superiority by this time, Japan could have completed the expansion of its defense perimeter in the secondary sub-theatres. This could have been safely accomplished without risking superiority at Hawaii. Capture of Hawaii, would already have indirectly isolated Australia and New Zealand from the USA. The resumption of operations in the south-west Pacific, supported by land based air power, would have completed that process. Japan would certainly have captured Port Moresby in New Guinea and retained Guadalcanal and the Solomons. Without a viable fleet, the USA couldn't have launched its historical counter offensive in this area, or even seriously contested Japanese operations. Instead, Allied loss of New Caledonia, Fiji and Samoa would complete Australia's isolation. In the north Pacific, further gains in the Aleutian Islands, might even extend as far as Dutch Harbor, the main American base in the region. That would have blocked any alternative American counter offensive strategy, via the Alaska, Aleutian, and Kurile Island route in 1943-44. Not that this route, rejected by the Americans historically because of its poor climate, difficult terrain and logistical limitations, was a realistic option anyway.

With the superior Combined Fleet based at Pearl Harbor, Australia isolated, and all avenues of counter attack blocked by strong garrisons, backed by land based air power, it is difficult to see how and when the USA could have overthrown Japan's position. Most of the Japanese bastions would have been beyond the deployment range of sizable and properly supplied US land based air power. It would have been 1944, before any newly built American carrier based fleet, could even achieve equality. Even the historic submarine offensive, based on Pearl Harbor, Australia and later the Marianas as Nimitz advanced, would be set back. Bases, range and patrol duration, were the crucial considerations here, and submarines couldn't win the war on their own. Nor, without naval and carrier superiority to secure command of the sea, could the other essential components of victory; the USMC-Army amphibious forces and an in range SAC offensive, play their historic role. Even the atomic bomb couldn't win the war by itself. That is assuming the Americans, under extra strategic and industrial planning pressure, continued the finance and development of this speculative and untested weapon, after a series of catastrophic defeats in 1942. Would they then have waited for it, not knowing if it would work, through two or more years of conventional war stalemate? Historically, the 'bomb' was the culminating blow, building on three years of conventional warfare advance and success. Japan was close to defeat anyway by the time of Hiroshima and Nagasaki and of course the 'bomb' needed secure SAC bases, in the Mariana Islands, within B29 range of Japan.

In the meantime, Japan would have all of 1943 and more to consolidate its perimeter. Moreover they could also have further disrupted any American recovery during 1943. The Americans would have considered their Pacific coast to be vulnerable if Hawaii had fallen. In circumstances of near panic, worse than Pearl Harbor itself, the defense of American territory proper, would automatically take priority over all other global strategic considerations. In practice, Japan's naval air fleets were not the ideal instrument for attacking the economic targets, such as oilfields, shipyards and aircraft factories located there. Even so America, without a viable fleet in 1943, would have to warp its historical mobilization and force deployment, to create a solid air and ground defense, along the very long 1,200 mile front between Seattle and San Diego. This would further strain and probably break the 'Germany first' strategy, with incalculable but dire consequences, for Allied diplomatic cohesion and the survival chances of Britain and Russia.

The American Pacific defense would be most vulnerable to raids, but not invasions, on the flanks. In particular the Panama Canal was potentially vulnerable to naval air and surface attack. It was vital for any new naval build up in the Pacific, and the global movement of the Allied merchant fleet. New naval construction, especially carriers and battleships, was concentrated on the Atlantic coast, but needed to be deployed to the Pacific. Conversely merchant fleet production was split about 50-50, but more of it needed to deploy to the Atlantic. The alternative route around South America was much longer, although rather distant from Japan's perimeter. Even so its protection against carrier, surface and submarine raids would place a heavy burden on stretched naval resources. Although Japan couldn't advance beyond the Aleutian-Hawaii line, the Pacific War would still be effectively stalemated. A 1943 stalemate that persisted into 1944, even as far as the presidential election in November of that year, again suggests the outcome of diplomatic negotiations and a peace treaty.

Nothing in military or naval history is inevitable or certain. Instead, there are balances of probabilities. Japan faced very difficult odds and circumstances against America, probably more adverse than for the European Axis. The longer the war lasted without a decisive Japanese naval victory, then the more likely it would be that the Americans would win in the end. Shortly before the outbreak of the Pacific War the IJN made its own, from Japan's point of view gloomy, assessment of the situation. It calculated that at the end of 1941 Japan's naval strength was 70% that of the American global total. They estimated that if current trends continued, without war and any losses, this would decline to 65% by the end of 1942, 50% by the end of 1943, and to 30% by the end of 1944.[11] If Japan was going to risk war with the USA, which seemed inevitable once the oil embargo clock was ticking in July 1941, then sooner was better than later. The IJN's assessment was largely correct, as the actual naval strengths in December 1941 and production for the years 1942-1944, in table 8 shows.[12]

As we have seen the Americans had a larger fleet to begin with, except for the vital category of aircraft carriers. In 1942 American production increases the disparity in surface forces somewhat, but the situation is still manageable from Japan's point of view. It is noteworthy however, that Japan actually increases its lead in aircraft carriers, or would have done, if it wasn't for the war losses, especially at Midway. Here lies the truth in Yamamoto's remarks about having a year to win the war. They had to do so in 1942, and do so by forcing and winning a decisive naval battle. The 'Mahanite' concept of the decisive battle wasn't just doctrine for the IJN; it was rational strategic calculation as well. In 1943 as we can see from table 8, American production increases massively and finally starts to focus on the vital fast aircraft carriers. To keep pace in 1943 and thereafter, Japan would have to have wiped out the pre-war US carrier fleet and most of the surface forces as well. They would have to have done so in 1942 and taken very few losses themselves, especially in carriers. In fact they actually sank 4 US CVs in 1942, but only at the unacceptable cost of 4 CVs and 2 CVLs of their own.

Table 8: Naval Strength and Production 1941-1944

Japan	BB	CV	CVL	CVE	CA	CL	DD	DE	SS
Dec. 1941	11	6	3	1	18	17	113	4	63
1942 Pr	1	2	2	2		4	10		61
1943 Pr			1	3		3	12	15	37
1944 Pr		5	1			2	24	99	39
Japan Total	12	13	7	6	18	26	159	118	200
USA									
Dec. 1941	17	7		1	18	19	171		112
1942 Pr	4	1		18		9	82		34
1943 Pr	2	6	9	50	4	7	128	298	55
1944 Pr	4	7		37	1	11	74	194	81
USA Total	27	21	9	106	23	46	455	492	282

Even if Japan had achieved an annihilating victory over the US carriers in 1942, American carrier production in 1943 would replace their losses and restore parity (but not yet clear superiority) at the start of 1944. In surface forces the odds were only slightly less daunting for Japan. There were far more American surface forces than carriers however, and the cruisers and especially destroyers were more dispersed as well, some even remaining in the Atlantic. It would therefore have been more difficult to annihilate all of them in a decisive battle or battles, again with few Japanese losses. Actual losses in 1942, most of which occurred during the Guadalcanal campaign from August onwards, were about even. Japan lost 2 battleships, 6 cruisers and 19 destroyers, compared to 7 cruisers and 21 destroyers for the US.[13] Equal and heavy attritional losses such as these, but without a decisive annihilating battle, were bound to favor the Americans due to their greater shipbuilding. If there had been a more decisive battle or battles, some American surface vessels would still have survived even a worse case scenario, to be reinforced by shipbuilding in 1943, so as to achieve parity by the end of that year.

A decisive and annihilating naval victory, giving Japan superiority through 1942 and most of 1943, with the USN reaching parity only by the turn of 1943-44 was Japan's best case scenario. It might have been enough, just. In reality the Americans, with a comfortable lead by then, were able to start their critical central Pacific offensive. Within a year, from November 1943 to October 1944, this offensive brought them over 3,000 miles forward from Tarawa in the mid-Pacific to the Philippines. With the 'Mahanite' battles of Philippine Sea and Leyte Gulf along the way, this is what essentially won the Pacific War for the Americans. If Japan had won decisively in 1942 however, thus leading to parity only at the end of 1943, the Americans would be over a year behind schedule. That probably means no serious US naval counter offensive until the end of 1944. It would be presidential election time by then, and the war would still be in stalemate, no further forward, and maybe worse than the historical 1942 position.

The chances for an overall Japanese victory therefore hinged on a decisive and annihilating naval victory. It would have to occur in 1942, and preferably on the decisive central Pacific axis. All the alternative Japanese options outlined for 1941 and 1942 were plausible, but none were certain. Indeed the odds were against the near annihilation of the USN that would have been required in 1942. The traditional pre-Yamamoto 'No Pearl Harbor' strategy could have resulted in favorable circumstances for Japan, ambushing the Americans as they advanced to relieve the Philippines. Indeed, it might have resulted in no American declaration of war at all, and a Japanese victory by default. A stroke of political policy rather than military strategy could have won the war for Japan. On the other hand, the Americans could still have won against the circumstantial odds in such a battle, and thus shortened the war as well. Even worse for Japan, depending on the political situation, would have been the Americans holding back until their new 1943 fleet was ready. Japan's operational strategy at Pearl Harbor itself could also certainly have been improved. On balance, once he had achieved the initial surprise and success, Nagumo was far too cautious with the odds in his favor.

Pearl Harbor was unlikely to win the war on its own for Japan however. The Americans still had half their fleet in the Atlantic and a second decisive battle would still have been needed. Midway-Hawaii was the logical place to force such an encounter, due to the decisive importance of the real estate. Hawaii was essential geographically and logistically for any American comeback within a plausible timeframe. Midway was Hawaii's sentry and tripwire. Japan was lax, even incompetent in the implementation of their Midway operation; they later called it 'victory disease'. They certainly could have won that battle, with a few plausible and rational changes that were theirs to make, especially concentrating their superior carrier fleet. Victory wouldn't have been dependent on American mistakes, as the actual US victory partly was on Japanese ones. Concentrating the Japanese carriers would have cancelled out the American code breaking advantage and sheer luck. Yet even a Japanese Midway victory wouldn't have won the war there and then. They would still need to have attempted the more difficult, and evenly balanced, 'Eastern Operation'; a full naval, air and amphibious campaign against Hawaii. That could have gone either way, but Hawaii and Pearl Harbor would have to be taken, and by default the USN near destroyed in the process, if Japan were to gain a plausible chance of a compromise peace at the end of 1942. We don't adhere to the view that Japan's task was totally impossible. Japan might, just, have won the Pacific War, but the odds were definitely against it.

1. B.C. Nalty, (Ed), <u>War in the Pacific</u>, BCA, London, 1991, p 20.

2. <u>Times Atlas</u>, p 67.

3. Hart, <u>Hist of 2WW</u>, p 363.

4. A Preston (Ed), <u>Decisive Battles of the Pacific War</u>, Hamlyn, London, 1979, p 59.

5. Ellis, <u>Brute Force</u>, p 456, see fn 10, p 595. CW Nimitz & EB Potter (eds), <u>The United States and World Sea Power</u>, Prentice-Hall, Englewood Cliffs, NJ, 1955, p 685.

6. Table 5, is derived from the authors Table 2 and; Ellis, <u>Brute Force</u>, p 452, which gives the size of the US Pacific Fleet in March 1942; and then subtracting the Coral Sea and Midway losses, and adjusting for other known changes and transfers.

7. Overy, <u>Why the Allies Won</u>, p 34.

8. P. Paret, (Ed), <u>Makers of Modern Strategy</u>, Clarenden Press, Oxford, 1986, p 720. On December 31st 1943, there were 1.8 million personnel (all services), 17 divisions, 8,800 combat aircraft, and 515 combat vessels deployed against Germany; compared to 1.9 million personnel, 16.5 divisions, 7,900 combat aircraft and 713 warships, deployed against Japan. The American war effort, two years after Pearl Harbor, and less than two years from the end of the war, was still evenly divided, not weighted towards the official 'Germany first' strategy. –

9. Derived from: Silverstone, <u>US Warships of World War Two</u>, and AJ Watts and BG Gordon, <u>The Imperial Japanese Navy</u>, Macdonald, London, 1971.

10. See tables 2 and 6.

11. G.W. Baer, <u>One Hundred Years of Sea Power</u>, Stanford University Press, Stanford, California, 1994, p 169.

12. Ellis, <u>WW2 Databook</u>, p 280. Carrier breakdown into CV, CVL, CVE and cruiser breakdown into CA and CL, is the author's calculations, using Silverstone, <u>US Warships</u> and Watts and Gordon, <u>IJN</u>.

13. Ellis, <u>WW2 Databook</u>, p 262, table 66.

CHAPTER 8

OVERWHELMING FORCE

'So we had won after all! …Hitler's fate was sealed, Mussolini's fate was sealed. As for the Japanese they would be ground to powder. The rest was merely the proper application of overwhelming force.'

Churchill

War Potential: Manpower, Money and Steel

Churchill made the above remarks commenting on Pearl Harbor.[1] Although the desired result came in an unexpected way, it had been his primary diplomatic and grand strategic objective since becoming Prime Minister, to get America into the war. He went on to estimate that together the 'British Empire, Soviet Russia and now the United States, ultimately had twice or even thrice the force of the Axis states'.[2] In this view victory for the Allies was inevitable, at least with hindsight. Many economic determinists also believe in the iron laws of GNP. In modern interstate wars the countries with the largest gross national production (GNP) tend to win in the end; assuming that is, that they survive in the first place.[3] Is this view correct? Let us start with Churchill's own rule of thumb calculation, and consider the ultimate resources available to each great power and the two coalitions at the start of the war in 1939. Table 9 shows the peacetime production and resources before the outbreak of war, 1940 for the USA and Japan and 1938-39 for the other powers. Population, GNP and steel production, which approximates a states industrial resources in this era, represent the eventual war potential of the combatants.[4]

Table 9: Great Power War Potential 1938-40

	Pop M	GNP $ B	Steel M tons
British Comm	70	24	17
France	42	10	8
USA	130	100	60
Russia	170	31	18
Germany	80	33	24
Italy	45	7	2
Japan	70	9	7
Allies Total	412	165	103
Axis Total	195	49	33

Churchill's calculation seems largely correct. In overall power the Allies have twice the potential manpower and three times the economic and industrial production of the Axis. However, these totals include France and it is only after Pearl Harbor that both coalitions are complete. We need to address the question of timing.

From September 1939 to June 1940 when Germany faced Britain and France, the balance of potential resources for war was very even. The GNPs and industrial production were about equal and Germany's population of 80 million was rather less than the 112 million of France, Britain and the independent Commonwealth, but still not a decisive difference.[5] The Allies hoped to exhaust Germany economically with a long war, while staying on the defensive on the western front. Given at best, a very slight potential economic edge, even that strategy might never have worked. Yet economics doesn't suggest a German victory either, and totally fails to explain the rapid German conquest of France and the rest of continental Western Europe in 1940. Even the military forces were of roughly equal size, as the analysis of the French campaign showed.

In June 1940 France leaves the war and Italy enters it on the side of the Axis. For a year until June 1941, Britain and its Commonwealth-Empire are alone, facing the European Axis. By adding France's resources, except for an unwilling population, to the European Axis we can approximate their control of conquered Europe as well. The British Empire is outmatched about two to one in overall resources. The European Axis has a GNP of $50 billion compared to $24 billion for the British Empire; and potential Axis steel production is 34 million tons against 17 million tons. The Axis powers have a loyal population of 125 million, against 70 million for Britain and its Commonwealth. Yet the Axis makes remarkably little progress in this period, failing to win the Battle of Britain or exploit their opportunities in the Mediterranean. Economic determinism doesn't seem to explain this year of the war either, nor indeed the next period.

From June to December 1941 Russia and the British Empire are at war with the Axis controlled Europe. Potential economic and industrial resources are about even again. Allied GNP is $55 billion compared to $50 billion for the Axis; and the potential steel production is: Allies 35 million tons, Axis 34 million tons. Russia's larger population however, gives the Allies a potential two to one manpower superiority during this six month period dominated by 'Barbarossa'. On this basis, Russia and Britain should have had a slight edge, or at least be able to hold the Axis. Instead the first five months of 'Barbarossa' were a disaster for Russia. Russia does hold on eventually, just, but only after losing up to 40% of its resources in the territories occupied by 'Barbarossa', and being almost knocked out of the war in the process. Economic potential alone is thus a

211

poor guide to the course and outcome of the first two years of the war. Still, we are talking about potential, so perhaps we are not allowing enough time for it to have an effect.

The final change in the balance covers the stage of the war from Pearl Harbor to the end. The two coalitions are finally complete, and remain so for nearly four years. America adds massively more potential power to the Allies than does Japan for the Axis. America alone had about 40% of global economic and industrial production during the World War Two period, almost thrice that of each of its nearest rivals, Germany and Russia. For 1942-1945 by again adding captured French resources, except for population, to the Axis total we can confirm Churchill's two or three to one approximation. The Allies have a willing population of 370 million compared to the Axis 195 million. The Allies GNP superiority is $155 billion against $59 billion. Their potential steel production advantage is 95 million tons against 41 million tons. Yet even against these apparent odds the Axis continued to advance during 1942. In the end however, from 1943 to 1945 inclusive, the course and outcome of the war are at last compatible with the predictions of economic determinism. The economists it seems were correct, eventually, for about half of the wars duration. Is that all there is to it? If you want to predict the outcome of wars, all that is needed is to calculate the relative size of the combatants economies and industry, even if you have to wait for a while; the iron law of GNP?

In fact, even within the sphere of economics, we have made some major assumptions, that we are not really entitled to do. GNP, industrial production and population, are the resource base of a nation. To have an impact on war, they need to be mobilized and converted to its purpose. Manpower has to be trained, organized and equipped to become armed force, or indeed to produce for the economy as well. GNP represents all production, civilian as well as military, and no nation, even at 'total mobilization', has ever been able to get above about a 60% allocation to war, and 40-50% is a more typical sustainable maximum. Steel production is the best single indicator of industrial power for war in the pre-electronic age. Even so steel and the rest of industrial output, is not much good until it is converted into tanks, artillery, ships, aircraft and other usable equipment. Most important of all, we have assumed equal efficiency, in the timing, speed, and rate of industrial and economic mobilization of all the great powers involved. In fact, the production of armaments only approximates to economic and industrial potential, after full mobilization. It was as late as 1944 before that position was reached, when all of the great powers (except defeated France and Italy) were simultaneously at maximum armaments production. The timing and speed of economic mobilization varied between the different great power combatants. That timing could have been changed, and there were of course strategies and campaigns, by both sides, to disrupt enemy economies and production.

Before examining armament production itself it is useful to identify any changes in the overall size of the economies as the war progressed. GNP measures everything but can be problematical due to different exchange rate and inflation calculations, so we will use steel production instead.

Table 10: Steel Production 1939-1945 (millions of tons)

	1939	1940	1941	1942	1943	1944	1945
France	7.9	4.3	4.2	4.4	5.1	3.0	1.6
Britain	13.4	13.0	12.3	12.9	13.0	12.1	11.8
Canada	1.4	1.7	2.5	2.8	2.7	2.7	2.6
Russia	17.6	18.0	14.8	8.0	9.8	11.8	12.3
USA	47.1	59.8	74.0	76.8	79.3	80.0	71.1
Allies at war	22.7	14.7	29.6	100.5	104.8	106.6	99.4
Germany	24.5	20.3	22.0	21.9	22.4	20.0	1.7
Axis Europe	2.4	10.8	12.5	12.9	15.0	9.5	1.0
Ger. Total	24.9	31.1	34.5	34.8	37.4	29.5	2.7
Italy	2.3	2.3	2.1	1.9	1.7	1.0	.4
Japan	5.7	6.7	7.9	8.0	8.8	6.5	.8
Axis at war	24.9	33.4	36.5	44.7	47.9	37.0	3.9
World total (inc neutrals)	133.6	138.9	152.0	149.7	157.7	149.9	111.0

The collapse of French production between 1939 and 1940 clearly shows the effect of conquest. During the occupation its industrial economy seems to have operated at about half its maximum production. It remained however, the most important of Germany's European conquests in economic and industrial terms. French production is also included in the 'Axis Europe' totals from 1940 to 1944 inclusive in table 10.

Britain's industry was operating at maximum capacity already in 1939 and more or less sustained that throughout the war years, despite the effects of the German U-boat campaign against its Atlantic supply lines. It was more a matter of how quickly Britain could shift production to wartime uses. Commonwealth and Empire production, of which Canada was the most important, clearly expands during the war. Australia, India and South Africa had a combined steel production of 2.3 million tons in 1937 expanding to 3.5 million tons in 1944, adding somewhat to the British totals shown. Even so over two thirds of the Commonwealth-Empire's industrial economy was located in Britain itself.

Russia had the third largest economy and industry in 1939-1940, almost equal in size to that of Germany. What is significant however, is the damage that the loss of territory due to 'Barbarossa' does to Russia's economic and industrial capacity. The decline starts in 1941, and in 1942 and 1943, despite the evacuation of industry to the east, Russian economic resources are reduced to barely half the pre-war levels. Analysis of other indicators such as GNP, oil or coal production and so forth which we needn't detail here, would confirm that general trend. For much of the war it seems, Russia had an economy only about the size of Britain. It makes the Russian armaments production performance the most difficult, indeed heroic and sacrificial, to sustain of all the combatants on either side.

Even so, Russia's heavy economic, industrial and resource losses due to 'Barbarossa' in 1941-1942, probably put their combination with Britain at a long term disadvantage, compared to a fully mobilized, conquest enhanced, European Axis. The Allies needed the largest economy of all, the USA, in order to finally move the resource potential overwhelmingly in their favor. The USA was the only economy that wasn't operating at full capacity when the war began in 1939. It alone had not fully recovered from the great depression of the 1930s, and had suffered a secondary depression in 1938. All of the other powers, boosted by peacetime rearmament in the later 1930s, were at full, but still largely civilian orientated capacity by 1939. America, unlike the others, used her underutilized economy, boosted by rearmament, to grow rapidly between 1939 and 1941. US steel production increases by more than half, from 47 to 74 million tons, from 1939 to 1941. From 1942 to 1944 with production fairly stable at 77-80 million tons, the US economy is at maximum capacity. Clearly and even when it was underutilized, the American industrial economy dominates the Allied alliance and the world.

German production which includes an incorporated Austria is fairly static until the end of 1944. There is a slight drop in 1940, perhaps reflecting some dislocation due to the wars outbreak. Bombing also seems to have reduced German steel production in 1944, by a modest 10%. The massive collapse in 1945 was due to Allied invasion and the end of the war. Germany already had the world's second largest economy and industry in 1939. What really enhances its resources is the military conquest of Europe. The 'Axis Europe' production in table 10, adds only Czechoslovakia for 1939, captured in March of that year, after Hitler broke the Munich agreement of September 1938. From 1940 to 1944 it also includes the considerable German controlled steel and other industrial resources, of

France and the Low Countries, and the lesser ones of Poland and the Balkans. Just as America dominates the Allied alliance economically, so does the expanded German 'Empire' the Axis alliance. The combined potential resources at Germany's disposal after mid-1940 were twice that of either the British Empire or Russia alone and, given the Russian military and economic calamity in 1941-42, probably greater than the two combined. German resources alone, and especially when enhanced by the conquest of the developed and industrial economies of Europe, were much larger than those of its Japanese ally.

Japan's conquests, while equal in size of territory and larger in population than those of Germany, were largely underdeveloped economically. Japan's empire solved its shortage in most raw materials, but didn't add much industrial strength. Based on the post-war growth record, it would have taken two or three decades of peaceful economic development for Japan's East Asian empire, to rival either America or a German Europe. Here is a major explanation for the American 'Germany first' strategy embodied in war plans 'D' and 'Rainbow 5'. The combined German Europe had a war potential of about half that of the USA, but was clearly the most dangerous of the Axis powers. The threat to even the Americans would be if Germany had been able to defeat either Britain or Russia, or both, in 1940-42, and then add their resources to its own. Even with a conquered Britain and/or Russia at a reduced output, as France's experience shows they would have been; economics as well as geography would have made such a Germany immune to American counter offensives. Given peaceful development as well, it would also have become a serious post-war rival 'superpower' to the Americans well before Japan did.

There were therefore significant changes to the size of some of the industrial economies during the course of the war itself. Russia suffers the most and its resource base was reduced. The USA in contrast, grew to its full industrial capacity in 1941 and slightly expanded thereafter. Germany's conquests in Europe added to its power, and this potentially enhanced its advantage over Russia and Britain, but still left it only half the size of America. Britain's economy didn't change in size much throughout the war. Japan did expand, but remained far less powerful than Germany. Overall this more detailed analysis of steel production, roughly confirms the potential power changes between the two coalitions previously identified. Expanded American production for example, more than compensated for Russia's economic difficulties. At the start of the war Germany and the Anglo-French coalition were evenly balanced. The fall of France leaves Britain and its Commonwealth-Empire outmatched two to one, until 'Barbarossa' brings Russia into the war. This should have restored equality between the two coalitions, but Russia's disastrous losses put that in doubt. Only

American entry into the war in December 1941, finally gives the Allies a two to one power potential advantage, which is retained until the end.

Economic determinism is important then, but only over the longer run, as an explanation of the course and outcome of World War Two. The theory correlates with events from 1943 to 1945 inclusive, when the Allies with much superior resources came back to eventually win. As we have shown however, it fails to explain the course of the war from 1939 to 1942, when greater resources didn't always win. Most importantly, we have so far only been examining potential resources. The situation with regards to actual mobilization for war and armaments production was rather different.

Mobilization and Armaments Production

Not only did the Allies eventually have more than twice the economic resources of the Axis, they mobilized this war potential faster, and in Russia's case, more fully than their opponents as well. In other words, the Allied advantage in actual armaments production was even greater than in their overall economic resource base. Moreover, this superior Allied armaments production occurs almost from the start of the war. It is not confined just to the period after the USA enters the war.

This is illustrated best of all in the very important area of aircraft production. Russia and Germany were predominantly land powers, while Britain, Japan and the USA were predominantly maritime powers. However, all of them were also air powers. Tactical air power was indispensable for both army and navy. Half of Japanese and one quarter of American combat aircraft production went to their respective naval air forces. Britain and the USA with their heavy bomber fleets were also strategic air powers as well. Aircraft production therefore more accurately reflects the relative size of armaments production between all the combatants, unencumbered by a land or maritime power bias. At maximum production in 1944, it equates more closely to the war potential of each power that has just been analyzed.

The total aircraft production for the major combatants, which was predominantly combat types but includes transports and training planes, is shown in table 11.[6] The USA has a clear lead, producing just over 40% of the world's military aircraft in 1944, roughly the same proportion as its overall economy and war potential. Russia and Germany are equal second, each producing just under half as many aircraft as the USA; just as they were in GNP and steel production in 1939. Finally air production is representative of the different rates at which the powers mobilized their economies for war; the details of which are shown in table 12.

The first thing that is apparent when examining aircraft production is the enormous number of machines produced.

Table 11: Aircraft Production (all types)

	1939	1940	1941	1942	1943	1944	1945
France	3,163	2,441					
Britain	7,940	15,049	20,094	23,672	26,296	26,461	12,070
Comm	250	1,100	2,600	4,575	4,700	4,575	2,175
Russia	10,382	10,565	15,735	25,436	34,845	40,246	20,052
USA	5,856	12,804	26,277	47,836	85,898	96,318	49,761
Allies at war	11,353	18,590	38,429	101,519	151,739	167,600	84,058
Germany	8,295	10.826	11,776	15,556	25,527	39,807	7,544
Italy	1,692	2,943	3,503	2,818	967		
Japan	4,467	4,768	5,088	8,861	16,693	28,180	11,066
Axis At war	8,295	13,769	15,279	27,235	43,187	67,987	18,610
Ratio per 1 Axis	1.35	1.35	2.5	3.7	3.5	2.5	4.5

The actual size of air forces at any point in time was no where near these massive production levels. There was an enormous rate and ratio of 'wastage' of aircraft during the war and it wasn't just losses due to enemy action. This wastage rate was far higher than for ground forces heavy equipment or warships. The average lifespan of a WW2 aircraft was about one year. Warships in contrast would typically last 20-25 years and tanks and artillery only moderately less. Compared to modern aircraft, WW2 air-craft were rather fragile machines. Aircraft had a limited lifespan, before it was impossible to maintain them indefinitely and they would be scrapped or cannibalized for spares. Many were also lost in training, ferrying to bases, or in other accidents. Damaged aircraft, given the more exacting re-quirements of flying and combat, were also far more likely to be written off, than say ships, tanks or artillery. Aircraft production was therefore vi-tal just to maintain an air force, even if combat activity was relatively low, which wasn't very often. The effect of all this is that vast numbers needed to be produced, just to maintain much smaller sized actual air forces. Un-der wartime conditions in this era, it was impossible to maintain air force strength equal to even a year's production, and six months or less was more typical. Unfortunately, there is no precise or easy rule of thumb to equate production to actual air force size; it varied between combatants, over time and by circumstance.

What is clear is that the Allied advantage in aircraft production was greater than the balance of economic resources or war potential. In 1939 and 1940 it was a moderate 1.35 to 1. This was reflected in the relative sizes of the German and Franco-British air forces up to the French campaign. They were evenly balanced overall, inclusive of the RAF home forces. There is little change in the aircraft production ratio however, during the year that Britain stood alone against Germany and Italy. Britain actually slightly out produces the European Axis in both 1940 and 1941, despite the Axis having an economic war potential that was twice that of the British Commonwealth-Empire. Britain's greater aircraft production as we have seen was a major factor in the Battle of Britain. When 'Barbarossa' adds Russian production in 1941, the Allied-Axis ratio increases to 2.5 to 1, where as overall war potential was about even. Finally, after Pearl Harbor, instead of a two or three to one steel or GNP advantage only! The aircraft production ratio is higher still, at over 3.5 to 1 during 1942 and 1943. Only in 1944, as Germany and Japan convert their economies fully for war, does aircraft production roughly equate with potential resources. The ratio of both by then was about 2.5 to 1 in the Allies favor.

The Allied production advantage, in aircraft at least, wasn't just potential, it was real. By mobilizing for war faster and earlier than the Axis, the Allies were able to out produce them even before America enters the war. The effect of this is to undermine further the theory of economic determinism. The Axis secured their spectacular military victories in 1939-1941, against the odds. The Anglo-French ground and air forces were about equal to the Germans in 1940, but had a higher armaments production. Russia vastly outnumbered the Germans in 1941 in all types of army and air force equipment, and both it and Britain, individually, out produced them as well. The Axis was even able to make progress in 1942, after US entry and against even heavier production ratios. German military efficiency and operational strategy went a long way to offset Allied numerical advantages.

Table 12: Aircraft Production as % of Maximum

	1939	1940	1941	1942	1943	1944
Britain	30	57	76	90	99	100
Russia	25	26	39	63	86	100
USA	6	13	27	50	89	100
Germany	21	27	30	39	64	100
Japan	16	17	18	31	59	100

Teutonic efficiency wasn't repeated in the area of economic mobilization for armaments production however, at least not at first. Table 12 shows the speed and rate of expansion of the main combatant's aircraft industries. For example the 30% figure for Britain in 1939, means that the 7,940 military aircraft produced in that year, was 30% of Britain's maximum ever output of 26,461 machines, which occurred in 1944. All of the major powers reach their absolute maximum aircraft production in 1944. The Allies mobilize faster however, and were very close to maximum by 1943, or even, in Britain's case, 1942. Most instructive is to compare Britain and Germany, who both enter the war at the start. Even in 1939, completely contrary to the popular belief, Britain, in aircraft production at least, is already more highly mobilized for war than Germany. Britain then expands its aircraft production at maximum speed, until in 1942 it is at 90%, almost full capacity. There is only a slight 10% increase after that and production is at a maximum plateau for the rest of the war. Britain was fairly certain that war was coming following Hitler's seizure of all of Czechoslovakia in March 1939, followed by his territorial demands on Poland. From table 12 it seems that maximum capacity was reached by mid-1942. It therefore takes Britain three years, from the start of mobilization, to reach more or less maximum aircraft production.

This mobilization timeframe is typical of all the other powers as well, except for Germany. The USA starts mobilizing for its own defense, or a possible entry into the war, after the shock of the fall of France in mid-1940. It doesn't just wait for Pearl Harbor. American aircraft production then approximately doubles each year, until full capacity is reached in mid-1943 at the latest. Like Britain, America takes nearly three years to mobilize its aircraft industry, from decision to maximum production. Russia was already operating at 25% capacity in peacetime, and had the largest air force in the world when 'Barbarossa' began in June 1941. It reaches maximum production by the start of 1944, and maintained it thereafter. Russia's mobilization timeframe is therefore also about two and a half years, under difficult wartime conditions, but starting from a peacetime situation of permanent partial mobilization. Even Japan takes only two to three years to reach full production once it is fully at war. Before Pearl Harbor Japan had been at war with China, which wasn't a first rate air power. Japan's aircraft production was almost static at a partially mobilized level of 16-18% from 1939 to 1941. Rapid expansion, almost doubling each year, then occurs during both 1942 and 1943, before reaching maximum in 1944.

The trajectory of German aircraft production is in sharp contrast to the other major air powers. Its production in 1939 is only 21% of capacity, which while equal to Britain in absolute numbers, was less proportionate to the size of their industries. Moreover, German production then increases only very slowly up to 1942. By that time, when Britain is at 90% of maximum capacity, the German industry is still operating rather leisurely at only 39% of its eventual maximum. Germany it seems, took 5 years from 1939 to 1944 to reach maximum aircraft production, compared to 2 to 3 years

219

for all the other major air powers. Or does it? Once production does start to accelerate, its growth rate is in fact equal to the others. In the three years from 1941 to 1944 it increases from 30% capacity to maximum production; almost exactly the same performance as Britain's three year expansion from a 30% level in 1939 to 90% in 1942. In fact, Germany's mobilization of aircraft production occurs mostly over just two years, increasing by 61% of maximum capacity from 1942 to 1944, i.e. 39% in 1942 to 100% in 1944. Only the USA between 1941 and 1943 (+62%), and Japan between 1942 and 1944 (+69%), mobilized their aircraft production at that rate over a two year period. In the early war, Germany performed poorly in the area of aircraft production, relative to its potential resources and industrial capacity. Its performance after 1942 however, shows it to be a late decision to mobilize its considerable potential, rather than any inherent problem of resources, economics or industry. Germany's maximum production of 39,807 aircraft in 1944 was almost in line with overall resources, greater than Britain, equal to Russia, and just under half of American aircraft production. It might have been even higher, given the effect of the Allied strategic bombing campaign, but that is a story for later.

Table 13: Tank, Assault Gun and SPG Production[7]

	1939	1940	1941	1942	1943	1944	1945
France	c 700	c 700					
Britain	969	1,399	4,841	8,611	7,476	4,600	2,100
Russia	2,950	2,794	6,590	24,446	24,089	28,963	25,450
USA	?	331	4,052	24,997	29,497	17,565	11,968
Allies at war	1,669	2,099	11,431	58,054	61,062	51,128	39,518
Germany	740	1,643	3,790	6,180	12,063	19,002	3,932
Italy	40	250	595	1,252	336		
Japan	c 200	1,023	1,024	1,165	876	342	94
Axis at war	780	1,893	4,385	8,597	13,275	19,344	4,026

The Allied superiority in ground forces armaments, typified by tank and armored self propelled gun (SPG) production, was if anything even greater. The trend is similar to that for aircraft production, with some notable differences. Unlike with aircraft, because of their greater inherent lifespan, most of the tank production shown in table 13 would remain 'on strength', unless and until it was destroyed in action. In the Western Allies case, much of their vaster production would be in reserve, ready to quickly replace losses, rather than being in the front line strength of divisions all at once. The Germans and Russians had a higher proportion of their armor deployed with their armored divisions at any one time, but continuous combat activity would strain their replacement systems, more than that of the Western Allies.

In the early war France, which had built 3,500 tanks from 1935 to 1940, was roughly equal to Germany in both production and the size of its armored force by the 1940 campaign. Between 1939 and 1942 Germany didn't have any numerical, or indeed technological, superiority in the weapon system that was at the heart of the 'blitzkrieg'. Its victories were achieved by operational techniques and strategy rather than by numbers or technology. The expansion of Britain's armored forces was behind that of both France and Germany in the years just before the war, and its 1939 production represents almost its entire strength at this stage. Amazingly however, Britain which was predominantly a maritime and air power, then slightly out produces Germany up to 1942 in tanks, and for a while even in artillery as well! This is because the German production schedule was at the same leisurely pace in the first half of the war, followed by spectacular growth from 1942 to 1944, as it was with its aircraft industry. The other Axis powers contributed little. Tanks were not the decision making arm of ground warfare in the jungles and mountains of Asia and the Pacific that they were in Europe. Consequently they were a low priority for Japan. Italy simply didn't have the industrial capacity to build a large armored force.

The really big story in tank production and armored forces is that of the two future superpowers, and especially of Russia. In the 1930s Russia's five year economic plans had concentrated on expanding its heavy industry. Industry was already designed and geared for a rapid shift from peacetime to wartime production. For example, state owned and controlled tractor plants could quickly become tank factories. Not that the peacetime armaments industry, especially for the army, was negligible either. Russia's 30 tank plants had been producing at the 1939-40 rates for several years before the war. By the start of 'Barbarossa' in June 1941, as we have seen, it had built up a massive force of 24,000 tanks, which was being reorganized into 61 armored divisions. Most of this force, about 17,500 machines, was destroyed in the debacle of the 'Barbarossa' campaign up to the end of 1941. At the same time, factories in danger of being overrun had to be evacuated to the Urals and Siberia. Thereafter however, the speed and scale of the mobilization of production for ground warfare was spectacular. Between 1941 and 1942 Russian tank production quadruples. This maximum war production is then maintained at a level almost ten times greater than in peacetime. Over half of the new production from 1941 onwards was the T34 medium and KV heavy tanks. These gave the Russians a vital technological edge as well up to mid-1943. Even when better German tanks then appeared, both basic mass produced Russian types were progressively modified to keep pace. From 1942, despite still suffering greater losses than the Germans, the Russian armored force gradually recovered. The combination of vast numbers, equal or superior technology, and eventually improved operational techniques, turned the tide in the tank war on the eastern front in 1942-43.

Table 14: Artillery Production (all calibers inc A.T and A.A.)[8]

	1939	1940	1941	1942	1943	1944	1945
Britain	538	4,700	16,700	43,000	38,000	16,000	5,939
Russia	17,348	15,300	42,300	127,000	130,000	122,400	62,000
USA	?	1,800	29,615	72,658	67,544	33,558	19,699
Allies at war	538	4,700	59,000	242,658	235,544	171,558	87,639
Germany	1,214	6,730	11,200	23,200	46,100	70,700	12,650
Japan	?	?	2,250	2,550	3,600	3,300	1,650
Axis at war	1,214	6,730	13,450	25,750	49,700	74,000	14,300

This huge and rapid increase in production between 1941 and 1942 was duplicated in other ground force weapon systems. Most notably in artillery production, including anti-tank and anti-aircraft guns, which increased from a typical pre-war level of 15,300 in 1940, to 42,300 in 1941 and 127,000 in 1942, and then roughly maintained at that level thereafter. Needless to say that even more than with armor, the Russian artillery force started and remained the largest in the world, by a considerable margin. Apart from the normal complement of artillery with its tank, mechanized and infantry divisions, the Russian army had a special strategic reserve. By 1944 there were 94 artillery divisions, which were normally under Stavka or Front level of control. No other army had anything remotely comparable. In contrast US artillery production peaked at 72,658 in 1942 and declined after 1943. Maximum German artillery production was 70,700, which again wasn't reached until 1944, when it was far too late.

What is most impressive and unique, is that this rapid and massive mobilization of armaments production was achieved on an overall Russian economic and industrial base that decreased in size between 1941 and 1942. Russia mobilized proportionately more of its resources for war production than any other combatant, friend or foe. Its civilian population and already low living standards paid the price. It was a case, not that they had much choice, of working like a slave for Stalin's regime, or risking extermination by Hitler's. Survival, fear of both dictatorships, and patriotism, were the primary motivators for the Russians, both at the front and behind it. In the end the Russian army and its tactical air forces, backed by their massive production effort, was the single most important component of Allied victory over the European Axis.

American armor production, but not artillery or other ground force weaponry, matched that of Russia and exceeded that of Germany. However, the Americans had an unequalled economic and industrial advantage over all the other powers. America had about 40% of global economic and industrial capacity before the war began. It had the highest per capita productivity and standard of living as well. Its steel production, albeit partly due to wartime damage suffered by the other powers, would reach 50% of the world total and its oil production was 60% of global output. The US was also almost self sufficient in raw material supplies. International trade amounted to less than 10% of its GNP, and the very few deficiencies that there were, could be imported from Canada or Latin America. Industrial substitutes, the most important of which was probably synthetic rubber to replace South East Asian production conquered by Japan, dealt with any remaining vulnerabilities. Most important of all, unlike all of the other combatants, America itself was totally safe from enemy attack. This enabled it to plan its economic mobilization much more deliberately than all the other powers. In contrast to Russia's desperate situation, America took WW2 in its stride.

The six fold expansion of US tank production in one year from 1941 to 1942 was even slightly greater than that of Russia. It was possible because the USA already had by far the world's largest car and vehicle industry. In 1939 there were already 35 million civilian cars and vehicles in the USA, compared to only 3 million in each of Britain, France and Germany, and the US was producing over 4 million cars per year. The American economy was fully mechanized and uniquely its society was fully motorized as well. America matched Russia for a while and out produced Germany in tanks. Like Russia's T34, they concentrated on one mass produced type. Of 88,000 US tanks produced, about 50,000 were M4 Sherman medium tanks. The M4 wasn't as good as the T34 or most German tanks after 1942, but numbers, reliability and serviceability, like with most US equipment, were more than enough compensation.

The Americans also produced a total of 200,000 smaller armored vehicles other than tanks, such as half track APCs, 'Amtracs', and many others, a total unmatched by any other power. Finally, the vast US vehicle industry produced 2.4 million trucks at the rate of 600,000 per year from 1942 to 1945. All the other powers, Allied and Axis combined, only managed to build 1.3 million trucks in total. The American army of 90 divisions was the only one that was totally motorized, and almost half a million of their trucks were sent to Russia. These, along with Russia's own much smaller total production of two hundred thousand trucks, were enough to motorize the 40 division sized Russian tank and mechanized corps from 1943 onwards. It was only a small proportion of the Russian army, which from 1943 maintained about 500 infantry divisions and by 1944, 94 artillery divisions as well. It turned out to be enough however, and was about equal in size to the total German motorized force. The overstretched Russians built the largest tank force of the war, but they needed considerable American help to motorize it as well, and thus from 1943 make it fully mobile, and therefore operationally more effective.

The balance of production between the two coalitions in ground weaponry, especially tanks and artillery, therefore increases sharply in 1942. In tank production it becomes almost 7 to 1 in the Allies favor. Very few of the Western Allied ground forces are in action at this time of course. Even so, the Russians alone produce 4 tanks to each German for the vital eastern front in 1942, some of them at Stalingrad and Leningrad going symbolically, and literally, directly from factory to battlefront. The Russian to German artillery production ratio peaked at 5 to 1 in 1942. Eventually a persistent production ratio, in new and effective heavy weapons, of four or five to one, month after month becoming operational on the eastern front was going to have its effect. The Germans considered that they had a year to defeat Russia after Pearl Harbor before American power made itself felt. It seems that Russia's own, rapid, effective and gigantic mobilization, in its own right, imposed a similar time limitation. Superior combat effectiveness, strategy and operational techniques, enabled the Axis to offset Allied numbers well into 1942, but there are limits.

The logic of economic determinism, eventually, worked its way onto the battlefields. In October 1942 the British launch their offensive at Alamein, with force ratios in troops, tanks, artillery and aircraft varying between two and four to one. In November the Americans finally take the offensive with operation 'Torch'. Then in the same month, the Russians began the series of vastly larger offensives, operations 'Uranus', 'Mars' and 'Saturn'. The economic determinists may have been right eventually, but they underestimated the scale and ratio of the imbalance, that was ultimately required to halt the Axis and turn the tide in the Allies favor. It seems that a production ratio of around four to one had to become operational on the eastern front and even in the global air war in 1942, for the tide to turn. That's what the ratio of production that could be deployed in 1942 was. In the air war globally in 1942, the Allies produced 3.7 aircraft to each one of the Axis, or 3.2 to 1 in combat aircraft alone. On the eastern front in 1942, the Russian to German production ratio was 4 to 1 in tanks and 5 to 1 in artillery.

Was there anything the Axis powers could do to counter, delay or avoid the huge tide of Allied production, which was inexorably turning the balance of power and the war in their favor? In fact both sides had strategies to damage their opponents economic and production capacity. In addition, the Axis and especially Germany could have made better use of the resources they did have, by mobilizing their economy earlier. Would or could any of these strategies make a decisive difference to the course or outcome of the war?

The Battle of the Atlantic

Churchill was relatively sanguine about the Battle of Britain. He knew that Britain had hidden advantages that evened the balance, and that the English Channel and the Royal Navy were formidable obstacles to invasion. The Battle of the Atlantic which lasted the entire war and on the face of it didn't permanently turn in the Allies favor until May 1943, had him worried. Churchill stated 'The only thing that ever really frightened me during the war was the U-boat peril'.[9] What was at stake and could the Germans have won?

For Britain, the maintenance of what today are termed sea lines of communication (SLOC) was absolutely vital. Even for normal economic survival Britain depended on seaborne trade. It imported half of its food and two thirds of its raw materials, including almost all of its oil.[10] All of these supplies past through the Atlantic, mostly from or via North America. Britain's oil supplies in this era, both peacetime and wartime, came from the USA (60%) and Latin America (40%), and not from the Middle East. After the fall of France, Britain's prosecution of the war was also totally dependent on its SLOCs. The Cape route around South Africa maintained the Empire's considerable forces in the Middle East, India and the Far East. Once America joined the war, the Atlantic route was the only means to transfer both ground and air forces to reinforce Britain, and then to take the offensive against Axis controlled Europe. Two of the three aid routes to Russia: the Arctic convoys to Murmansk and Archangel, and the Persian route via the South African Cape, were also dependent on secure Allied SLOCs, especially in the Atlantic. Finally, we have already analyzed the role of sea power in the Mediterranean and its interdependence with the North African campaigns, as well as its dominant place in the Pacific War. In short, Britain probably couldn't survive if the Atlantic SLOC was cut, and the Americans, no matter what their production and force levels, couldn't seriously attack the European Axis if they were confined to North America.

For all these tasks, in 1939 the British Commonwealth-Empire had by far the world's largest merchant fleet, consisting of about 4,000 ocean going vessels totaling 21 million tons. The Americans had a 9 million ton merchant fleet, and these were available as part of the normal trading routine, and especially as American involvement such as 'Lend Lease' aid increased, even before Pearl Harbor. The combined Allied global merchant fleet was therefore about 30 million tons or 33 million tons if we include France in 1939. In peacetime about 50% of this Allied fleet operated on the North Atlantic route, with the rest scattered between all the other oceans of the world.

Our purpose here is not to give a detailed account of events; the reader can find that in many other specific works focused on the one subject. Rather it is to consider the Battle of the Atlantic as a continuous war of attrition. It is the effect on the Allied merchant fleet, Britain's economy and all the other Allied purposes identified above that are important. The Axis tonnage war against Allied shipping should be considered as a seamless global continuum. Within this, the North Atlantic was the fulcrum of the campaign, accounting for 80% of Allied global losses over the war as a whole.

One important factor within the overall picture is often overlooked, even by many specific accounts of the Battle of the Atlantic. Apart from changes due to losses and shipbuilding, the basic Allied fleet of 30 million tons, was augmented by ex-neutral shipping from the countries conquered by the Axis in 1940-41. France, Norway, Netherlands, Belgium, Denmark and Greece had a considerable combined merchant fleet of 14 million tons, of which 4 million tons was captured by the Axis in port, and 10 million tons became available for the Allies.[11] Churchill for all his concern over the shipping situation, was certainly aware of this often overlooked bonus for the Allied cause.[12] Taking all gains and losses into account, the overall situation developed as shown in table 15.[13]

Table 15: Allied Merchant Fleet (millions of gross tons)

| | Shipbuilding | | | | | | | |
	British Empire	USA	Allied Neutrals	Total Gains	Losses	Net Change	Fleet Size	British Imports
1938 Str	21	9	3 (Fr)				33	92
1939 4m	0.2	0.1		0.3	0.8	- 0.5	32.5	12
1940	0.8	0.4	5.7	6.9	4.4	2.5	35.0	42
1941	1.2	0.8	1.6	3.6	4.4	- 0.8	34.2	25
1942	1.8	5.3		7.1	8.2	- 1.1	33.1	24
1943	2.2	12.4		14.6	3.6	11.0	44.1	31
1944	1.7	11.6		12.3	1.4	10.9	54.0	57
1945 6m	0.6	6.3		6.9	0.5	6.4	61.4	19(5m)

The traditional view of the Battle of the Atlantic is that Britain came close to defeat on two occasions, the so called 'happy times' of the German U-boats, and that the battle finally turned in May 1943. The U-boat 'happy times' were periods when Allied losses rose. The first was between June 1940 and June 1941, and the second occurred from January 1942 to March 1943. As we can see from table 15, 1942 was the worst year for the Allies with very heavy losses of over 8 million tons, twice those of each of 1940 and 1941. Allied shipping losses then fell dramatically between April and May 1943, with most of the 1943 losses occurring before the so called decisive phase. At the same time U-boat losses became so severe that they exceeded production for the first time, and Donitz even had to temporarily withdraw them from operations in late May 1943.

When we survey the overall situation using table 15 however, a rather different picture emerges. Allied shipping losses have to be placed within the context of additions to the fleet and set against the overall size of the fleet. Otherwise there is no way of assessing whether or not the Allies, and specifically Britain, came close to defeat. You cannot assess the health of a company by examining only one side of its balance sheet, and ignoring its cash reserves! The same principle applies to analyzing the Battle of the Atlantic. Even the heavy losses in the years up to and inclusive of 1942, are balanced by new construction, and by ex-neutral shipping joining the Allies. The size of the Allied fleet is remarkably stable during this period. The net losses of around one million tons in each of 1941 and 1942 only reduce the fleet by 3% per year and put it back to the same size as 1939. It might not have seemed like this to the sailors and submariners, who suffered some of the heaviest proportionate losses in any campaign. Over the entire war 30,000 British merchant seamen died, which was half of the crews of the ships that were sunk. U-boat crews lost 28,000 men killed out of 39,000 who served, and 785 out of 1,171 U-boats built were sunk.[14]

The battle itself was therefore hard fought, with changes in tactics, the increasing use of aircraft by the Allies, as well as technological and code breaking advances playing a central role. However, it was an attritional battle, a seamless global continuum, not a single event. Churchill observed that there were; 'no flaming battles and glittering achievements'. Instead the results were judged by, 'statistics, diagrams, and curves unknown to the nation, incomprehensible to the public'.[15] These show that the efforts of both sides cancelled each other out between 1939 and 1942. The net effect was that the Axis only managed a mere dint in the Allies 33 million ton global merchant fleet. Even the role of the 'Ultra' code breaking efforts wasn't decisive. 'Ultra' enabled Allied convoys to re-route and avoid the enemy, but only in the early years, when there were insufficient U-boats to form a continuous patrol line. In 1941 when it had most impact, 'Ultra' may have prevented losses of 1.6 million tons, which again, doesn't alter the overall situation much.[16] During 1942 the Germans had a temporary advantage in the code breaking war, and by 1943 their U-boat fleet was so large that the Allies were unable to avoid attacks, even if forewarned by 'Ultra'.

What did alter the situation, as in other areas of the war, was the entry of the USA and its massive shipbuilding effort. In 1942 Allied losses increased, primarily in the US defense zone off their Atlantic coast and in the Caribbean. The USN was unprepared operationally and even slow to introduce convoys in 1942. Even so, the USA's dramatic increase in shipbuilding meant that the Allies cancelled out 7 million of the 8 million tons lost in 1942. In 1943 American shipbuilding dwarfs the Axis efforts, even before the turning point on the actual Atlantic battlefield in April and May. In fact the 'curve' of production exceeds that of losses in late 1942. From then on the size of the fleet changes, from stability, to a dramatic increase of almost one million tons per month for the rest of the war. By 1945 the Allied shipping fleet had doubled in size from that of 1939-1942. From this perspective we can see that the Axis didn't even come close to winning the Battle of the Atlantic.

Or can we? The final column of table 15 shows the tonnage of British imports. Even though the size of the shipping fleet is stable, British imports drop substantially from the peacetime level of 1938. Even in 1939-1940 they drop by half. Much of this can be accounted for by the introduction of convoys themselves. As the experience of 1917-18 had shown, convoys were absolutely essential and unavoidable defensive measures for the Allies. The downside was that they were a relatively inefficient method of moving cargo, due to delays in assembling ships and the constraint of moving at the speed of the slowest. British imports were bound to fall automatically, no matter what happened on the battlefield. In 1941 and 1942 they fall further, too barely a quarter of peacetime levels. Even this reduction in imports however, failed to defeat Britain by blockade. Civilian living standards, rather than production or the prosecution of the war, took the hit. We have seen previously that British armament production increased each year up to 1942, and in all sectors. The economy overall, as typified by steel production, also maintained its maximum output. Britain's maximum armaments production capacity, as typified by tanks and aircraft, was about one quarter of the USA's. This was about the same as the relative sizes of their overall economies and industry. There is thus little evidence that the shipping losses, or even the reduction in imports, seriously impaired Britain's economy or armaments production.

It isn't clear exactly how much extra damage the Axis needed to inflict on the Allied shipping fleet in order to bring Britain down. As a means of comparison, the much more successful US campaign in the Pacific reduced Japan's merchant fleet from 6 million tons in 1941 to 1.5 million tons in 1945. Japanese imports fell by over 90% between 1942 and 1945.

Japan was on the brink of defeat before the atomic bombs were dropped, but even then it definitely wasn't all down to the US submarine campaign. Japan's navy had to be destroyed, some of its island conquests recaptured to secure bases, and the conventional SAC offensive launched in order to finish the job. All these were major operations. Indeed, they were most of what the Pacific War was all about!

Britain proved, like Japan, to be more resilient against blockade than even Churchill feared. Admiral Donitz estimated that monthly sinkings of 700,000 tons would win the war and that he needed a fleet of 300 U-boats to achieve it.[17] The Germans just about managed to reach both these levels in 1942, but it proved insufficient. To reduce the Allied merchant fleet from its stable size of 33-35 million tons by 75%, the equivalent to Japan's experience, would have required the Germans to sink an extra 25 million tons before the end of 1942. This is in addition to the actual 17 million tons that were sunk during 1939-1942, for a total requirement of over 40 million tons; two and a half times their actual sinkings! The task was enormous, indeed nearly impossible and well above Donitz's calculations. In 1943-1944 of course, once American shipbuilding was fully mobilized as shown in table 15, the Axis task in the Atlantic was impossible. Once again the Axis had underestimated their enemy and especially the scale of the task required; the latter by a wide margin.

The Battle of the Atlantic was a decisive battle of World War Two, but specifically because of the severe consequences for the Western Allies had they lost it. Britain would have been isolated and its economy and production would have eventually collapsed. America would have found itself unable to take the offensive in Europe without Britain as a viable base. In short, the Western Allies would have been neutralized, and the war stalemated, forcing a compromise peace. However, it was a slow attritional battle and these results would have taken time. More importantly, it doesn't seem that the Allies came close to losing, or even anywhere near it.

At best the U-boat campaign delayed the American build up in Britain and the Allied counter offensive. Even that isn't certain however, there were other factors involved. American decisions on the global deployment allocations for its merchant shipping, as well as for ground and air forces were the first of these. The strategic debate, indeed controversy, between America and Britain, about global strategy priorities were the others. The Allies chose to start their counter offensives in the Mediterranean, (Operation 'Torch') and the south-west Pacific theatres, (Guadalcanal and New Guinea). They could have made a different choice, specifically delaying or scrapping 'Torch', and the early Pacific offensives until Nimitz's new fleet was ready at Hawaii in November 1943. That would have saved enough shipping and ground and air forces, to build for an invasion of Europe from Britain in 1943, instead of 1944, operations 'Bolero' and 'Roundup'. Whether it was wise or a sound plan is another matter. The point is these were the Allies decisions to make; the U-boats probably couldn't sink enough ships to prevent them.

The only way the Germans might have won the Battle of the Atlantic was to inflict the 1942 level of losses, or more, much earlier in the war, before American shipbuilding increases came on line. One million tons of losses per month, every month between September 1939 and the end of 1942, would have amounted to the 40 million ton requirement that would have pushed Britain into an equivalent state of economic collapse to that of Japan in 1945. For that the Axis needed a larger U-boat fleet much earlier in the war. In 1939 there were only 57 U-boats instead of the required 300. However, the need for greater Axis forces is an argument that could be made in every other campaign we have analyzed as well. All of the alternative Axis strategies that have been considered so far are based on the balance of forces as it actually was. Any commander or strategist can make their task easier simply by adding extra resources. It has to be plausible however, that extra production could have been created in the first place. That is an important scenario all of its own, which will be turned to later. Meanwhile, the opponent in war is attempting to achieve exactly the opposite, to reduce the enemy's economy. Blockade was only one method of achieving this.

The Impact of Strategic Bombing

Without the availability of a superior surface fleet, submarines, supplemented by mines and aircraft were the practical instruments of blockade. It proved to be a much more difficult method of defeating even an apparently vulnerable maritime island economy than it first appears. As for Germany, once it had conquered France and most of Europe, it was immune to the Allied naval blockade. Strategic bombing was a more direct method of attacking an opponent's economy and production. The German 'blitz' against Britain in 1940-41, was the first serious bombing campaign against a civilian economy. From the attackers point of view the results were meagre. Only 37,000 tons of bombs were dropped in 1940 and 22,000 tons in 1941. There was no noticeable reduction on British war production, which as noted previously was undergoing a rapid expansion at this time. The pre-war predictions about bombing destroying a nation's civilian morale, and thus indirectly weakening an economy, due to say, absenteeism or unrest, also proved fallacious.

The British and American bombing campaigns against Germany eventually reached a far vaster scale. They both started slowly however, and in the earlier years of the war were no more effective than the German 'blitz' had been. Daylight attacks by Britain's Bomber Command in 1940 were quickly abandoned due to unsustainable losses. No Allied fighter had the range to reach even western Germany until 1943. Without fighter escort the daylight bombers were almost helpless. That the 'bomber will always get through' was another pre-war myth that was quickly dispelled. The British switched to a night bomber offensive, which lasted until the end of the war in 1945. The problem was that in 1940-41, there was no techno-logy that enabled aircraft crews to see very well in the dark. The British civil service Butt report in mid-1941 noted that only one aircraft in three even got within 5 miles of its target, never mind about hitting or damaging anything useful.

The German air defense system called the Kammhuber Line, stretching from Paris to Denmark, had radars, night fighters and masses of anti-air-craft guns or 'flak'. It was as effective as the British system during the Battle of Britain, and had the upper hand over Bomber Command in 1940-41 and even through 1942 as well. Britain took heavy losses of 492 bombers in 1940 and 1.034 in 1941.[18] The bomb tonnage dropped by the RAF was only 13,000 in 1940 and 32,000 in 1941.[19] It wasn't until 1942 that with increasing numbers of four engined heavy bombers replacing the earlier medium types, and the first of a series of electronic navigation aids that matters improved. Even so the 45,000 tons of bombs dropped in 1942, although hitting area targets i.e. cities, more often by then, was only just exceeding the German efforts during the 'blitz' of 1940-41. The American daylight bombing campaign had only just started in August 1942 and de-livered only 1,400 tons in that year, mostly in warm up raids against France rather than Germany itself. The effect on German war production before 1943 was almost zero. The very slow rate of build up of German armaments production from 1939 to 1942 inclusive was definitely not due to the Allied bombing efforts.

It was only after the Casablanca conference in January 1943 and the Allied decision to launch a 'combined bomber offensive' that there were notice-able and increasing effects. In 1943 the campaign intensified. In July, Hamburg was destroyed by a firestorm after German radar defenses were blinded by aluminum strips called 'window'. For a time German leaders, including armaments minister Speer, feared that civilian morale would col-lapse and even armaments production come 'to a total halt' if such Allied successes were repeated.[20] They weren't repeated, because the Allied ad-vantage in the electronic war was only temporary. The combined bomb tonnage delivered by the two Allies in 1943 was 215,000 tons. Allied losses rose as well however, to 2,314 RAF and 1,100 USAAF bombers in 1943. German production takes off in 1943, at the very time that the bombing campaign sharply increases. However, the mobilization of the

German economy was probably less efficient than it might have been from this point onwards. As well as suffering direct damage, factories had to be dispersed, sometimes to new underground sites. The German effort was divided between protection from the bombing, and purely managerial considerations of economies of scale and production efficiency. In 1944 the Allied bombing campaign reaches its peak, but so does German armaments production. The total combined bomb tonnage dropped was 1,157,000 tons in 1944. This was a five fold increase over 1943 and it was more accurate than before and therefore more damaging to German production as well.

How much effect the bombing campaign had on German production in the peak year of 1944, remains an uncertain and controversial issue. At the lower end of the scale, the immediate post-war US strategic bombing survey, estimated that Germany lost 10% of its production in 1944.[21] On the other hand in January 1945, Speer and his officials calculated that due to bombing, Germany produced 35% fewer tanks, 31% fewer aircraft and 42% less trucks than planned in 1944.[22] These higher estimates along with the diversion of effort into air defenses, one third of artillery production was allocated to A.A. guns for example, might even have made a decisive difference on the battlefield in 1944. On Speer's calculations, Germany would have produced 30,000 tanks and assault guns instead of 19,000; and 58,000 aircraft instead of 40,000. That would have given Germany a tank production equal to the maximum output of either America (in 1943) or Russia (in 1944). Aircraft production would have been higher than Russia's 40,000, but still second to the USA's massive 96,000. Speer's calculations are compared against 'planned' production however, which might have been overambitious irrespective of bombing of course.

Even so, the full range of estimates from 10% to over 30% are plausible, and well within what is known about the overall and relative size of German economic and industrial resources in 1944. We may recall that Germany, including their European conquests, which were mostly intact until the last quarter of 1944, had an economic and industrial base about twice the size of Russia, and half the size of the USA. Maximum potential German armament production figures, prior to bombing, that fall between those of the two future superpowers, and taking into account a land power bias for Russia and Germany, are all very plausible. In terms of German mobilization, the reduction due to the bombing campaign shows that the potential, even in the early war and certainly after the fall of France, was even higher than the actual 1944 peak production levels. How much higher? The answer is at least 10% overall and possibly up to 30-35% in the crucial categories of tanks and aircraft.

German Armament Production Strategies

Historians have no easy explanations as to why Germany failed to immediately mobilize its economy for war from 1939, and at a rate similar to all the other industrial powers. It certainly could have been done, as Germany's own experience from 1942 to 1944 shows, even under the impact of strategic bombing. Nor was it due to a lack of overall economic and industrial resources, or of advanced preparation.[23] As has been seen, even in the inter-war period prior to 1939, Germany had the world's second largest GNP and industrial output. In the First World War the Hindenburg-Ludendorff programme had pioneered the concept of 'total war', including the full mobilization of the economy and industry for military production. There had already been massive investment in the 1930s geared to the military economy. They built the world's largest aluminum industry, essential for aircraft production. With the construction from 1938 of the huge new Volkswagen complex, the German car industry was on the verge of a massive expansion, from about 300,000 per year, to a 1939 capacity of 0.5 million and a planned 1.5 million, making it a clear second only to the USA. The chemical industry, which Germany had invented prior to 1914 and still led the world in, was constructing synthetic production plants to make them self sufficient in oil and rubber, vital for the new mechanized warfare. In short, by 1939 Germany already had the first 'military-industrial complex'.

In 1938-39 it assimilated extra resources in central Europe. German speaking Austria added oilfields, iron ore and machine building. Czechoslovakia added a strong armaments industry, including the Skoda works, and brown coal (lignite) for synthetic oil production. Along with Poland, it added extra iron, steel and coal production. The conquest of France and the Low Countries in June 1940 gave Germany control of almost all of continental Europe's large coal, iron ore and steel industry, a massive bonus analyzed above. France had continental Europe's second largest GNP, and also provided labor and large amounts of looted stocks, such as industrial machines, metals and oil. With 17% of the total, it was the largest producer of bauxite, the basic raw material for Aluminum and hence aircraft production. French agriculture alone, made the German Europe impervious to a blockade such as that of 1914-18. Finally in 1941 the Balkans added yet more raw materials, including yet more bauxite from Hungary, Yugoslavia and Italy. All the remaining neutral states of Europe either became Axis allies (Finland, Romania, Hungary, Bulgaria), or were dominated economically by Germany (Spain, Sweden, Switzerland, and even Turkey).

In 1939 instead of an immediate full mobilization though, the economy remained geared to a short war only. It mirrored the operational concept of 'blitzkrieg', which was designed to defeat Germany's opponents quickly, and one at a time. After each military success, it was presumed that there would be time to replenish military stocks, at the semi-mobilized peacetime rates. The low losses of the early campaigns further contributed to this complacent attitude. The Germans also kept changing their strategic and armament production priorities at this time.[24] In June 1940 as France was collapsing; it was temporarily decided to reduce the overall size of the army from 165 to 120 divisions, while increasing the number of panzer divisions from 10 to 20. Britain was the only remaining opponent, and the plan was to switch manpower from the army, to air and naval armaments production. They had been taken by surprise by the speed of the French collapse. There was no amphibious force ready to invade Britain. Instead one had to be built from scratch, and quickly. With the failure in the Battle of Britain however, the planning for 'Barbarossa' became more important. As a result armaments policy, or what passed for it, changed again.

The three armed services competed for the partially mobilized resources of the economy. Even worse, Goering was nominally in charge of the economy, as well as the Luftwaffe. He was both incompetent in management and administration and biased in favor of 'his' Luftwaffe. The Luftwaffe had a high 40% of the still un-mobilized armament production resources at this time, compared to 50% for the army, and 10% for the navy. Still, this didn't do much for aircraft production in 1941. It was assumed that 'Barbarossa' would be over in five months, again allowing time to replenish afterwards. In fact even in June and July of 1941, when 'Barbarossa' was just beginning, armaments plans were switched again, in favor of the Luftwaffe and Kriegsmarine. It seems that they kept anticipating victory, and were planning production for the next campaign, instead of the one that they were actually fighting.[25] Finally, it was a mistake giving the armed forces rather than industry the predominant role in weapons production. The armed forces tended to prefer too wide a range of specialized types, rather than standardized mass production. German weapons were of a high production quality, and often but not always technically superior to those of the Allies. Unfortunately that made them expensive and difficult to produce.

Germany didn't make the decision to fully mobilize the economy for war until the turn of 1941-42. In December 1941, Hitler issued a Fuhrer Decree on 'Simplification and Increased Efficiency in Armaments Production'. This ordered industry to embark on 'mass production on modern principles'.[26] In February 1942 Speer, who in complete contrast to Goering was a brilliant organizer, was appointed Minister of Armaments, and industrialists were finally given a predominant role. From the start of 1942 compromise and improvisation was progressively replaced by central planning. Latent resources and underused factories were brought into production. Even so it took time, perhaps a year to sort out the mess, and it was 1943 before production really accelerates and maximum output is reached in 1944. The overall armaments production index starting from a base of 100 in January-February 1942 reached a peak of 322 in July 1944.[27] Aircraft, tanks and artillery all show this tripling of production from 1942 to 1944.[28] From mobilization decision to maximum production therefore took between two and two and a half years. Germany was therefore capable after all, of economic and armament production mobilization at the same rate as the other powers. The problem was a late decision not lack of capability.

The failure of Germany to mobilize its economy for war earlier and even just at a rate similar to Britain or the other powers, was a major mistake of Axis grand strategy.[29] The very slow increase in production up to 1942 inclusive is clearly shown in table 16. It occurs in all air and ground heavy weapons categories. In 1942 after three years of war, which as we have seen was ample time for economic mobilization by all the other powers, the production of combat aircraft, tanks and SPG, and artillery is only about 33% of their 1944 maximum. It is slightly higher, but still only a leisurely 39% for overall aircraft production. U-boat construction is the only partial exception, reaching almost 90% of maximum in 1942, instead of 1944. Even here Donitz considered that U-boat construction could have been faster and should have had a higher priority. The U-boat exception to the general trend, only confirms what could have been done in ground and air armaments, arguably more important categories for a predominantly land power.

Table 16: German Armaments Production[30]

	Aircraft (all types)	Combat Aircraft	Tanks & SPG	Artillery inc A.T. & A.A.	U-Boats
1939	8,295	4,733	740	1,214	7
1940	10,826	6,201	1,643	6,730	48
1941	11,776	7,624	3,790	11,200	198
1942	15,556	11,266	6,180	23,200	243
1943	25,527	18,953	12,063	46,100	277
1944	39,807	33,804	19,002	70,700	237
1945	7,544	6,987	3,932	12,650	79

A German decision to fully mobilize the economy at the outbreak of war in September 1939, would have brought forward its armament production levels by two years. Leaving aside submarine construction, which reaches close to maximum in 1942 anyway, the 1944 maximums shown in table 16 in the ground and air armaments would have been reached in 1942 as well. The intermediate 1942 and 1943 production levels could have been reached in 1940 and 1941 respectively. A rapid expansion from 1940 to maximum production in 1942 and its maintenance at that level thereafter, is what happened in Britain, entering the war at the same time in 1939. Even if we were to assume that resource constraints in 1939, might, have limited immediate German expansion, they could still have made the mobilization decision in mid-1940, after the fall of France gave them control of the resources of all continental Europe. Even this is to make a fairly conservative assumption. It has already been shown how considerable were overall German economic resources, even in 1939. In addition, they were receiving large economic supplies of all kinds from Russia at this time, under the terms of the Nazi-Soviet Pact.

Using the 1940 mobilization variant, the German armament production schedule would still have advanced by at least one year, or even up to 18 months, reaching maximum production in 1943. Finally, we must remind ourselves that these are rather minimalist assumptions of what could have happened. The effect of strategic bombing means that maximum German capacity was at least 10% higher than its actual 1944 peak production, maybe more. Before 1943 Allied bombing was ineffectual, but they were already doing everything they could. The Allies therefore had no alternative strategic options, bombing or otherwise, that could have even slowed, never mind prevented a rapid German mobilization of war production from 1939 to 1942.

The effect of increasing production, even by just one year, would have been considerable. In air power, because of the rapid attrition rates and short lifespan of aircraft, it is better to make a proportionate analysis, rather than simply adding absolute numbers of extra aircraft produced. For example the combat aircraft production of 7,624 in 1941, occurring in 1940 instead of the actual 6,201, means a capability to maintain the Luftwaffe 20-25% larger than its actual average size (3,300) in 1940. Even this modest assumption might have made a difference in the delicately balanced Battle of Britain, and even changed the outcome. It would have meant that, in combat aircraft at least, German production would have matched that of Britain in 1940. Britain would have lost possibly its most important advantage, and at the very least the Luftwaffe would have avoided the gradual decline in its strength during the battle. Continuing the same 'one year production level advance' for Luftwaffe combat aircraft; gives it a further increase in size of 45% in 1941 and 70% in 1942; again compared to its actual fairly static average size of 3,000-3,500. In other words, the Luftwaffe instead of just maintaining its strength in the crucial early war, would have expanded, and with increasing margins from 1940 onwards. An early mobilization of production by only one year would have enabled the Luftwaffe to maintain total combat aircraft strength of at least 3,500-4,000 in 1940, 4,500-5,000 in 1941, and 5-6,000 in 1942. These are conservative estimates; they are based on a proportionate rather than absolute increase in production numbers. The assumption is that a proportion of the extra aircraft production would be lost from non-combat causes and unserviceability. If that didn't happen, then the one year production level advance, mobilizing in mid-1940, would have increased the size of the Luftwaffe even more.

A two year advance of aircraft production levels, which is by no means unreasonable, would almost certainly have been decisive, and disastrous for Britain and Russia. Readers may do their own maths for themselves if they wish. It would have almost doubled the size of the Luftwaffe combat force by the end of 1940, increased it to two and a half times its actual in 1941, and triple in 1942. The increase in total aircraft strength, including non-combat types, would have been slightly less; an increase of 50% in 1940, double in 1941, and two and a half times actual size in 1942. Considering the tight margins of the Battle of Britain, 'Barbarossa' and the Mediterranean campaigns, and the entire Axis strategy options that have been examined, it seems fairly conclusive. One shudders to think how an extra 50% overall production, and over 11,000 combat aircraft produced in 1940, instead of the actual 6,201, would have changed the Battle of Britain. It would have given the Germans equality, at about 15,000 each in overall production, and a 3:2 advantage over Britain's 7,771 combat aircraft produced in 1940. Britain's historical advantage in 1940 wouldn't just be cancelled, it would be reversed. Extra production of this magnitude would almost certainly have given the Germans victory in the Battle of Britain in 1940.

In addition the increasing overstretch of the Luftwaffe and the need to carefully re-sequence various subsequent operations and campaigns would also have been solved. It would have been much easier, for example, for the Axis powers to have carried out a comprehensive Mediterranean strategy against Gibraltar, Malta, and Egypt in 1940-41. These were all air power intensive operations. This could have been done without compromising the 'blitz' bombing campaign, which otherwise would have to have been scaled back by half if these Mediterranean options had been adopted. Furthermore, the extra air power would have enabled Mediterranean operations to continue or be extended, such as by operation 'Orient', simultaneous with a full historical strength 'Barbarossa' from June 1941. Britain, even if it survived 1940, would have had no respite, at home or in the Mediterranean. Historically, such respites occurred due to the Axis need to keep redeploying their overstretched air power; such as between Malta and Libya, and between Western Europe, the Mediterranean and Russia. Extra margins of this magnitude for the Luftwaffe in 1940-1942, would have given it comfortable air superiority in many extra situations, and contributed massively to a defeat of Britain or Russia, or both, before US entry.

Expanding the Luftwaffe would also require more pilots, but here again it's largely a matter of earlier increased production for training. Historically, the main bottleneck was in operational conversion using combat types rather than basic training. The higher increase of combat, and especially of fighter production from 1943, brought forward by earlier mobilisation, would dove tail with this requirement. The main problem for the bomber arm was the overstretched Ju52 force, torn between the competing demands of bomber training and air transport operations. Ju52 production rose slowly from 388 in 1940 to 573 in 1942, before doubling to 1,028 in 1943. Again, early mobilisation, bringing forward this doubling to 1941 or 1942 would be timely.

With ground weaponry, absolute amounts of extra production would largely accumulate campaign by campaign, year on year. Tanks and artillery, unlike aircraft, didn't tend to wear out or become permanently unserviceable after short timescales, unless they were destroyed in battle! Even mobilizing after the fall of France and bringing production levels forward by a modest one year, would have given Germany an extra 1,000 tanks and SPGs in the second half of 1940, plus over 2,000 more during 1941, and another 6,000 during 1942. By the start of 'Barbarossa' in June 1941, instead of the actual 3,500 tanks in 19 panzer divisions, Germany could have deployed an extra 2,000 tanks giving 5,500 in total. With these they could have formed an extra 10 panzer divisions at the 1941 establishment levels. Or alternatively, they could have maintained the actual divisions, plus Rommel's 2 panzer division strong Afrika Korps, at the higher 1940 establishment of 250-300 tanks each, instead of having to reduce to the 1941 level of about 180. With either an extra 10 panzer divisions or a 50% greater armored punch for the actual ones, it is difficult to conceive that the extra margin wouldn't have been decisive, considering how close run 'Barbarossa' was anyway in 1941. This is not all. An extra production of over 1,000 tanks during the second half of 1941, as 'Barbarossa' proceeded, would have gone a long way towards preventing the attritioning of the panzer force. By the time of operation 'Typhoon' at the start of October 1941, the crucial final phase, the panzer divisions temporarily averaged only about 45-50% of their original combat strength i.e. about 1,500 tanks instead of 3,500 for 19 panzer divisions. Instead of this, the cumulative extra production of over 3,000 in 1940 and 1941, would give a 'Barbarossa' panzer force of around 4,500 tanks by the time of 'Typhoon', in either 19 or 29, still almost full strength divisions.

The conclusion is becoming clear already. Even the modest option of full armaments mobilization after the fall of France, bringing production levels forward by only one year, would have given decisive extra margins for the panzer force in 1941. 'Barbarossa' would have been 50% stronger in armor than was historically the case and attrition reduced as well. It would also have been even easier to reinforce Rommel's Afrika Korps, to over double its actual size, and successfully invade Egypt and the Middle East, even simultaneous with 'Barbarossa'. Tanks were the arm of decision for the 'blitzkrieg' between 1939 and 1942 inclusive. The extra production would also have consisted of the more powerful of the types used in 1941, the Panzer III and IV mediums, further increasing the firepower of the panzer divisions.

Making similar calculations for artillery is not really necessary. Early mobilization, even by one year, is bound to result in extra resources for the German artillery arm, infantry divisions and all arms armies. These formations and their weaponry were far more numerous anyway than the panzers or aircraft, and the 1939-42 historical resource margins not as critical. Manpower limitations would mean there wouldn't be extra infantry divisions. Rather, that the existing ones would have more firepower and be brought and maintained up to strength more easily. It gives the more conventional bulk of the German army, as well as the panzers, greater and increasing margins in every operation, battle, campaign, and alternative option from 1939 to 1942 inclusive. Since they won most of them, and when they lost it tended to be marginal, then any extra resources on the scale just identified, are going to convert lost battles into victories.

The 'one year early production level mobilization' alone, is clearly enough to have changed the eventual narrow defeat of 'Barbarossa' by December 1941 into a German victory. They would still have had to make the necessary operational strategy changes of course, in particular maintaining the focus on Moscow throughout. We concluded that such changes would have resulted in the fall of Moscow in 1941, and probably of the internal collapse of Stalin's Soviet system. Extra German production levels of one year, especially in tanks and aircraft, simply reinforce that outcome to a near certainty. Even if Russia had survived the almost inevitable fall of Moscow in 1941, the Axis still had 1942 to win the war. The 'Blau' campaign targeting the Caucasus was also close, and the Axis could have advanced further as it was, by a more careful and plausible re-sequencing of operational strategy. If we add extra production here, in the form of a 70% stronger Luftwaffe, 3,000 extra panzers from 1940-41, and 1942 tank/SPG production of 12,000 instead of the historical 6,000, plus more artillery as well, then the balance shifts decisively to the Axis. Moreover, such a campaign would have had an advanced starting front, with Moscow and probably more besides already under Axis control from 1941.

239

A 1939 mobilization bringing ground forces production levels forward by two years, results in huge extra margins. It would have given Germany over 4,000 extra tanks in 1939-40, up to one third of them ready for the French campaign, which was a decisive, course of the war changing victory anyway. Add to this an extra production of 8,000 in 1941 i.e. the 1943 level of over 12,000 instead of the actual 3,790, nearly half of it ready for 'Barbarossa'; and maximum production of 19,000 in 1942 instead of the actual 6,000. If this seems too rapid a build up, it is only the same as what occurred with actual German production from 1942 to 1944 and under the impact of bombing. It also seems, examining the American and Russian experience from 1941 to 1942, that it was inherently easier to expand ground forces production faster than for aircraft or ships. Remember the new Volkswagen factories. They only ever operated at one-fifth of capacity and the car industry overall at 50% for war production. That's just for armor production. Don't forget the doubling and tripling of the Luftwaffe in 1941-1942 and extra artillery and infantry firepower.

There is no need to proceed much further with such an argument. Immediate armaments production mobilization from the start of the war in 1939 would have meant, given what happened anyway, that Germany would have won every land battle, campaign and operation, either actual or alternative, from 1939 to 1942. There would have been ample margin as well to conduct more than one operation at a time, and many of their historical operational strategy mistakes, wouldn't have mattered as much either. Combine this with optimum strategy changes as well, then it is certainly clear that Russia could, indeed would, have been defeated in 1941 or 1942, and the entire Mediterranean zone from Gibraltar to Persia captured. The Western Allies would have been stalemated by that, with no chance of returning to the continent even in 1943-44. Britain would be isolated, or even conquered, given an early doubling and trebling of German aircraft production, and depending on Axis strategic choices and the timing of any Russian collapse. Alternatively, with this much earlier aircraft production mobilization, an enhanced Luftwaffe makes Britain very vulnerable to attack and invasion in 1940 or 1941, before any decision for 'Barbarossa'.

In other words an early German production mobilization, especially starting in 1939, gives them all sorts of extra options and margins. The Axis could have won the war in Europe in more ways than one, and before any effective American intervention in 1943. What is worse for the Allies, the mobilization decision was Germany's to make. There was no Allied counter strategy, with bombing being ineffective before 1943. The Allies were relying on a major Axis grand strategy error, which fortunately they got. Immediate German total economic mobilization, no different to the other industrial powers, would have been a dangerous and terrifying scenario for the Allies.

Having frightened ourselves, with this powerful and all too plausible German alternative mobilization option, it is necessary to delineate its limits. Despite Donitz's complaints, the scope for earlier expansion of the U-boat fleet was very limited. When war broke out in 1939, the Kriegsmarine abandoned the pre-war 'Z Plan', for a massive surface fleet that wouldn't be ready until 1944. Instead they planned merely to complete the major vessels already under construction, such as the giant battleships **Bismarck** and **Tirpitz**, the carrier **Graf Zeppelin** and a few cruisers and destroyers. They would concentrate on U-boats, with a target production of 29 per month, reduced in March 1940 to 25 p.m. after one year i.e. by late 1940.[31] It never quite reached that rate, even from 1942 to 1945. The actual monthly production rate was only 2 during the first half of 1940, and 6 during the second half, for a total of 48 over the year. In 1941 it grew from 13 to 20 p.m. by the middle of the year, for a total of 198. Production remained at about that level for the rest of the war as shown in table 16.[32] The build up therefore actually does starts after the fall of France, and is very rapid in 1941, to reach a peak production of 20 p.m., ten times its initial level. U-boat production therefore increases much earlier and faster than for air and ground weapons.

Maybe they could have increased production even earlier, but only by about 6 months at the most, from a September 1939 decision for U-boats to have priority. That would give them a production of 114 U-boats in 1940 instead of 48, and 240 in 1941 instead of 198, and no change thereafter. It isn't very plausible though, because ground and air forces for the French campaign, not U-boats, would have had first call on any extra industrial resources before mid-1940. It assumes that Donitz's plan for maximum production after one year was achievable, but at the actual 20 p.m. maximum, not his planned 25 or 29 p.m. An extra 100 or so U-boats produced over 1940 and 1941 would obviously make some difference. The actual fleet was small during this period, 57 at the start of the war and only 81 at the end of 1940, but increasing rapidly in 1941 to 249 by the start of 1942. During the first 'happy time' from July 1940 to June 1941, U-boat efficiency is also at a peak in terms of tonnage sunk per U-boat. An extra production of 100 or so U-boats in 1940-1941, would have increased the size of the fleet by about one quarter by the end of 1941; i.e. over and above the 57 starting strength and the actual production of 8 in late 1939, 48 in 1940, and 198 in 1941; for an actual cumulative total of 311. U-boat losses in this period were very low. Assuming all else was equal, the larger fleet, inflicting 25% higher losses, might have added one million tons to the toll of Allied shipping in each of 1940 and 1941, and two million in 1942, for a total of 4 million tons extra during the critical first half of the war. Given our previous analysis of what was required for the Axis to win the Battle of the Atlantic, and strangle Britain's economy to the same degree that eventually collapsed Japan's production; an extra 25 million ton requirement, it probably wouldn't have been enough.

Moreover, there was always a long delay for crew training between completing a vessel and its first operation. Not all, of the few extra boats, would have been available for the 'happy time' after the fall of France. Of the actual 249 U-boats at the start of 1942, only 91 were operational, with the rest, mostly from the surge of production in 1941, still working up in the Baltic. Most important of all, from the previous discussion of the Battle of the Atlantic, the task of depleting the 33 million ton Allied merchant fleet was enormous. This couldn't be achieved quickly, even with at best, a modestly increased U-boat force. The conclusion has to be that the limited extra production, which might have been possible, probably still wouldn't have been enough to win the Battle of the Atlantic, certainly not as early as 1940 or 1941. It would have contributed to a possible Axis victory certainly, but only in combination with the other strategies that have been analyzed.

The contribution of German aircraft and surface raiders to the Battle of the Atlantic might also have been increased, but only marginally. Aircraft accounted for only 13% of Allied global merchant shipping losses and surface raiders only 7%. The carrier *Graf Zeppelin* had been launched and was 85% complete at the outbreak of war in September 1939.[33] It could have been completed in December 1940, followed by a sister ship in December 1941. Instead carriers were erroneously ranked lowest in construction priority after U-boats and surface combatants. Work on the *Graf Zeppelin* was halted in July 1940 and on its sister ship in September 1939. Carrier support for the surface raider campaign in 1940-41 would have added to Britain's naval problems at a critical stage, perhaps partially offsetting the critical role of Britain's own aircraft and carriers, on general convoy escort duty, and most notably in the *Bismarck* operation in May 1941. Even so the surface raiders were heavily outnumbered and Germany couldn't have completed any more carriers until 1943-44, far too late to have a serious impact.

Cooperation with the Luftwaffe was also poor. Goering opposed the creation of a naval air arm. Long range aircraft, the critical variable for Atlantic operations, were also few in numbers and a low Luftwaffe priority. There were never more than a couple of squadrons of the four engined Fw200 'Condors' available, a type converted from civilian airliners. Suitable pre-war heavy bomber designs existed such as the Do19 and Ju89, but these were never put into series production. The wartime He177 was technically over complex, delaying and limiting production. A long range heavy bomber program might have been possible, but only as part of an early armaments production mobilization as outlined previously. Otherwise such a program would have been at the expense of easier to produce fighters, ground attack, and medium bombers. These were essential for the Luftwaffe's priority mission which was tactical air support for the army, not the Battle of the Atlantic or strategic bombing. The possibilities for increased production in the categories of U-boats, aircraft carriers, surface combatants and long range bombers were therefore limited, and probably insufficient to give Germany victory in the Atlantic.

Next, although early German economic mobilization starting in 1939 or 1940, would give it large margins and extra strategic flexibility up to and including 1942, they still wouldn't have out produced the Allies in the end. Even with maximum German production by 1942, instead of 1944, the Allies would still be surpassing the Axis by then. This assumes of course that Britain and Russia survived that long, and that America is in the war by then. A fully mobilized Germany at its actual 1944 level, compared with the Allies actual production in 1942, is shown in table 17.

Table 17: Allied 1942 and German Maximum Production[34]

	Aircraft (all types)	Combat Aircraft	Tanks & SPGs	Artillery inc AT & AA
Britain	23,672	16,102	8,611	43,000
Russia	25,436	21,480	24,446	127,000
USA	47,836	23,396	24,997	72,658
Allied Total 1942	96,944	60,978	58,054	242,658
Germany (1944)	39,807	33,804	19,002	70,700
Italy (1942)	2,818	2,054	1,252	+1,800
Japan (1942)	8,861	5,368	1,165	+2,550
Axis Max 1942	51,486	41,226	21,419	+75,050

The Italian and Japanese artillery production in table 17 is understated because it only includes field artillery. Their totals of all types and calibers, may, have been two or three times greater. It doesn't alter the overall situation much. Germany's overall production capacity may also have been 10% higher or even 30%, taking into account the effect of Allied bombing on the actual 1944 levels. That might have made a difference at the higher, 30% end, of the estimate. However, since the bombing effect was uncertain and controversial it is safer to ignore it, yet bear in mind that our conclusions will be somewhat bias towards the Allies.

Even with early and maximum German economic mobilization, the Axis cannot ultimately match the Allied armaments production. As long as Britain, and especially Russia, survived, and America entered the war, the Allies would be producing more armaments than the Axis by 1942. The margins and ratios however, wouldn't have been as bad for the Axis as the actual ones. Allied aircraft production would have been double that of the Axis, although somewhat less in combat aircraft alone, where the Allies would have produced only 1.5 aircraft for each Axis machine. This is only half the actual 1942 production ratios. The Germans at least, would probably have retained air superiority with those ratios throughout most of 1942, and on most fronts. They retained air superiority on the eastern front in 1942 anyway, up to the Russian counter offensive at Stalingrad in November 1942. This was due to superior quality, especially in air crew training; combat experience, and technology, rather than numbers. Early production mobilization would therefore have enhanced and extended the period of Axis air superiority into 1943. Over Western Europe and the Mediterranean it would have still taken time for the Americans to deploy and get into action. Britain, if still in combination with Russia, could probably only have achieved equality at best in 1942, against an enhanced Luftwaffe. If Russia had been knocked out in 1941, Britain alone, with America not yet deployed, would have been in mortal danger in 1942 against the extra Axis air power.

In ground weaponry including the crucial armor category, however, the Axis would still be out produced in 1942 by 3 to 1; or 2 to 1 if Speer was correct that Germany had a tank production capacity of 30,000, reduced by bombing to the actual 19,000 in 1944. That's still much better than the actual 7 to 1 or more in 1942. On the crucial eastern front the Russian-German production ratio would be reduced to only 1.3 tanks and 1.8 artillery pieces to each German. That would have been a substantial change from the actual four and five to one ratios. We may recall that the German 'Blau' offensive, got as far as Stalingrad and the Caucasus, backed by an actual 1942 tank and SPG production of only 6,000, compared to over 24,000 for Russia! What this means is that maximum German tank production of 19,000 or more in 1942, combined with their continuing combat effectiveness advantage, which was over 2.5 to 1, the Germans would still have the advantage over Russia in 1942. The clock would still be ticking for the Axis, but much slower than before. Greater Russian production would still come into play, eventually. Moreover, it would also still have been the turn of 1942-1943 at the earliest, before the Western Allies could have diverted even modest German forces away from Russia.

Early German mobilization would therefore have given them a greatly increased chance of winning the war in 1940-42, by knocking Britain or Russia or both out, before the USA could have effectively intervened.

1942 would still have been the crucial year. It would probably still have been the last chance for an outright Axis victory. Allied overwhelming force would still be inevitable, but only if the war lasted long enough. Early German mobilization could have delayed it considerably, and limited it to the overall Allied-Axis economic balance, and the actual production ratio of 1944, which were both about 2.5 to 1. It wouldn't ultimately have changed that imbalance had the war lasted into 1943 and later. In 1943 both America, and Russia if it survived, would reach maximum production and increase the 1942 margins. If the Axis had not won the war outright in 1942 or earlier, the maximum they might have achieved after that would still be a stalemate. This was the historical situation as well, and even early German mobilization would only have extended the Axis window of opportunity a few months, beyond the end of 1942.

Early German production mobilization therefore, would have greatly increased their chances of winning the war outright between 1940 and the end of 1942. This is especially so when combined with the other Axis alternative strategies that we have already analyzed for this period. Germany's failure to fully mobilize its economy for war from the start, or 1940 at the latest, which it could have done, was one of, if not *the*, greatest mistake it made of the entire war.

Notes to Chapter 8

1. Churchill, Vol 3, p 539.
2. ibid, p 540.
3. Bellamy, Absolute War, p 468.
4. Purnell's History of the 20ᵗʰ Century, Vol 17, p 1663. Ken Waltz, 'The Emerging Structure in International Politics', in International Security, Vol 18, No2, Fall 1993, p 62.
5. The British population figures include the independent white Commonwealth, i.e. Canada, Australia, New Zealand and white South Africa, with a combined population of 22 million, plus Britain's 48 million. India and the colonial territories of the British, and French, empires are excluded. The white Commonwealth countries were both economically developed, and independently supported the war, at a mobilization level equivalent to Britain itself. For example, Britain mobilized 5.9 million men from first to last: 12% of its population. The white Commonwealth mobilized 2.4 million; 11% of their population. India and the colonial empires in contrast, were both underdeveloped economically, and despite the former having a volunteer army, relatively unwilling. They were in effect subject or conquered countries, more comparable with the unwilling conquered states of Nazi Europe and Imperial Japan. Their war efforts reflect these factors. India mobilized a considerable 2.6 million men, yet this was less than 1% of its population of 375 million. To equate the vast, unwilling, populations

of the underdeveloped colonial empires, with the industrial great power combatants, wouldn't be a like with like comparison. Economic, GNP, and steel production figures, here and elsewhere, do include the British Empire, and where noted, the German conquests in Europe. These do, inherently, reflect aspects such as underdevelopment or, as later discussed, reduced production.

6. Ellis, WW2 Databook, p 278. Paul Kennedy, The Rise and Fall of the Great Powers, Unwin Hyman, London, 1988, p 354.

7. Ellis, WW2 Databook, p 277, Overy, Why the Allies Won, p 331-332. Note, our table 13 production figures are for tanks and assault and self propelled guns. The latter categories are essentially turret less tanks, in many cases based on the same chassis as their tank counterparts; they were slightly easier to produce, by a 5:4 ratio. Our armor production and strength figures, throughout, do not include armored personnel carriers or other types of armored vehicles, unless specifically noted. Some sources do, and don't always specify. Overy, above, for example, gives slightly higher figures for Germany only (not the other powers), which we believe, from the actual numbers, must include other categories of armor, possibly some half track APCs. Some other sources give even higher figures for Germany, typically 27,000 for 1944; which definitely must include half track APCs.

8. Ellis, WW2 Databook, p 277, Overy, Why the Allies Won, p 332. The US figures exclude light calibers. It doesn't distort the comparison much however. Total US artillery production 1940-45, including lights, was 257,390; compared to 224,874 medium and heavy only. The Japanese and Italian totals are for field guns only, excluding light calibers and AA and AT guns. They are not a like with like comparison; see text. Italy's total field gun production was 7,200; the yearly breakdown is the author's assumption, of even production. Still the Italian and Japanese totals are relatively low compared to the larger industrial powers, so they hardly distort the comparison between the two alliances.

9. Churchill, Vol 2, p 529.

10. Overy, Why the Allies Won, p 28.

11. Author's calculation, from Ellis, WW2 Databook, p 249, which gives the tonnage of the pre-war merchant fleets; and Times Atlas, p 203, which gives the tonnage of losses, captured in port, when Germany overran the relevant countries in 1939-42.

12. Churchill, Vol 4, p 782.

13. Churchill, Vol 5, table on p 5. Ellis, WW2 Databook, p 249. Times Atlas, p 203. Again, table 15 is the author's calculation, constructed from all three above sources (see also fn 11, above). Import figure from Ellis, Brute Force, p 160.

14. Ellis, WW2 Databook, p 269. Overy, Why the Allies Won, p 61.

15. Churchill, Vol 2, p 524.

16. Ellis, Brute Force, p 147.

17. Overy, <u>Why the Allies Won</u>, p 45.

18. ibid, p 112.

19. Ellis, <u>WW2 Databook</u>, p 233-35. For this and what follows on bomb tonnages.

20. Overy, <u>Why the Allies Won</u>, p 120.

21. ibid, p 128.

22. ibid, p 131.

23. For this and what follows see; Overy, <u>Why the Allies Won</u>, pp 198-207; and Magenheimer, <u>Hitler's War</u>, pp 64-70.

24. ibid, Magenheimer, pp 64-70.

25. ibid, pp 89-90.

26. Overy, <u>Why the Allies Won</u>, p 203.

27. Magenheimer, <u>Hitler's War</u>, p 182.

28. See table 16.

29. Magenheimer, <u>Hitler's War</u>, p 68, says from autumn 1940 at the latest.

30. Ellis, <u>Brute Force</u>, tables 37 and 41. <u>WW2 Databook</u>, pp 277-278.

31. Bauer, <u>WW2 Vol 4</u>, p 306.

32. ibid, p 306-307. Ellis, <u>Brute Force</u>, table 37.

33. German aircraft carrier construction schedule from, Siegfried Breyer, <u>Graf Zeppelin</u>, Schiffer Publishing, Pennsylvania, 1989, p 11 and p 34.

34. Author's construction, derived from previous tables.

CHAPTER 9

TRIUMPH OF THE DICTATORS ?

The Decisive Campaigns and Strategies of World War Two

So how could the Axis powers have won the war? What would have happened had they done so? We will start by summarizing their chances of winning the decisive battles and campaigns of WW2, and then combine this into overall scenarios. All of the decisive campaigns and battles of WW2 that have been examined were, historically, either Allied victories, or incomplete Axis victories. These latter cases need a little recap. Dunkirk itself was an Allied victory because the BEF was successfully evacuated, and was therefore able to fight another day, and become a trained cadre for the future expansion of the British army. This is despite the fact that it formed a sub-battle of the much larger French campaign, which was a decisive and consequential German victory in its own right, and despite also Churchill's accurate observation that wars are not won by evacuations. 'Barbarossa' was an incomplete Axis victory, despite the fact that the Russians suffered at least five times the casualties and heavy equipment losses as the Germans, not to mention huge amounts of territory and economic capacity. The final stage of 'Barbarossa', operation 'Typhoon', narrowly failed to capture Moscow, thus making the previous five months of German victories incomplete. At Pearl Harbor the Japanese achieved a major, but still incomplete, operational victory. Moreover, as previously discussed, in the longer run it was probably a strategic mistake.

Each of the campaigns have now been analyzed for three main purposes. Firstly, the reasons for the historical outcome and the consequences of that outcome have been identified. Second, the closeness, or otherwise, of the campaign has been considered. Alternative Axis strategies have been examined for each, so as to determine the likelihood of an Axis victory, or greater Axis victory in the cases where their historical victory was incomplete. Thirdly, the extent of the consequences on the war as a whole, resulting from both the historical and alternative outcome, has been considered.

In this way it has been possible to assess actually how decisive these often presumed, decisive campaigns, really were. Table 18 summarizes the general conclusions for each campaign, and in some cases of sub-campaign variants or strategies. It is of course only a summary, and no substitute for the individual chapter discussions, and nuances, on each campaign. Moreover each campaign, and its alternative strategies, outcomes, and consequences, has so far been primarily considered in isolation. What table 18 does now provide is an overall and comparative summary of all the campaigns. The 'yes' and 'no' conclusions summarized here are not absolute certainties. We are after all summarizing judgments, albeit based on evidence, circumstances and the balance of forces, but also as we have seen, dealing in some cases with intangible variables such as politics, morale, or even chance. 'Yes' and 'no' in table 18 therefore really range from: 'more likely Y/N than evens or uncertain', too 'probably, almost certainly Y/N'.

Table 18: Decisive Campaign and Strategy Summary

	Alternative Axis Strategy Successful			Course of War Changed		Outcome of War Changed		
	N	Evens	Y	N	Y	N	?	Y
Dunkirk 1940			X		X	X		
Britain 1940-41								
Air phase		X			X	X		
Naval phase		X			X			X
Ground phase			X		X			X
Mediterranean								
Gibraltar		X			X	X		
Malta		X			X	X		
Egypt		X			X	X		
Middle East		X			X		X	
Barbarossa 1941								
Moscow option			X		X			X
Germany 1942								
No DoW on US		X			X		X	
Blau original		X			X		X	
Moscow option		X			X			X
German Mobilization		X			X			X
Atlantic 1939-43	X			X		X		
Anti-bombing		X		X		X		
Pearl Harbor			X		X		X	
No Pearl Harbor		X			X			X
Midway			X		X		X	
Hawaii		X			X			X

Moreover, by summarizing the various campaigns together it is now possible to draw some general conclusions about WW2 as a whole. Firstly, the outcomes of most of the campaigns and battles that we have chosen to examine were not sure things. The possibility of a changed outcome, due to a different Axis strategy or decision, is evens or higher in most of the cases listed.

Only in the Atlantic campaign do we think that Axis chances of success were much closer to zero than even or uncertain. In the Battle of the Atlantic the Axis task, given the size of the Allied merchant fleet and American shipbuilding capacity, was probably too great, even with the possibility of a modest and earlier increase of U-boat production. The only way that Germany might have won this campaign was if America had not entered the war at all, and hadn't increased its shipbuilding above peacetime levels; say the one million tons p.a. of 1941. With respect to the other campaigns not covered, our aim has been to focus upon campaigns and battles whose outcomes, actual and potentially alternative, determined the course and outcome of the war as a whole.

Secondly, it is clear that there are biases within the list of campaigns and battles where the Axis had a reasonable or good chance of winning. All of them occurred before the end of 1942 and the start of 1943. The Stalingrad-Caucasus campaign and the Battle of Midway were *the* two most important actual turning points of the war. They mark the respective Axis high points, in the greatest land war ever fought, and the greatest naval war ever fought. After this point, Axis options and chances of winning rapidly diminish.

There is also a bias towards Germany rather than Japan. Germany had a better chance of winning the European part of WW2, than did Japan the war in the Pacific. The reasons should be generally obvious from reading the Japanese chapters, and 'Overwhelming Force'. Russia was a formidable opponent for Germany. However, it was geographically vulnerable to Germany's main strength, which was a superb operational strategic technique and combat effectiveness in land warfare. America was an even more formidable opponent for the Axis, and especially for Japan. America had, by a good margin, the largest economy and armaments production spread across all categories, land, sea, and air. This averaged about 40% of the global total at the 1944 level of maximum output. Only in armor and artillery was it moderately out produced, and then not by the Axis, but by Russia. Moreover, and maybe even more important, the USA alone of all the WW2 combatants on either side, was geographically invulnerable to serious attack.

The third conclusion is that almost all of the campaigns significantly altered the course of WW2. This is true of most of the actual historical outcomes, and would have been, had the alternative outcomes occurred. Our summarized judgment of 'no change' in the case of the Atlantic derives from the low chances that the Axis could have won. Had they done so, no matter how unlikely this outcome, then the consequence would have been a drastic change in the course of the war. In the unlikely event of an Axis

250

victory in the Battle of the Atlantic, Britain would, eventually, have been forced into a compromise peace. Probably all of the alternative outcomes, had they occurred, would have altered the immediate course of the war, in some cases drastically. From the Axis point of view, one might say at this point, so far so good. With the relevant changes of strategy, they had an even or better chance of winning most of the campaigns and battles examined. Next, had they won, it would have changed the immediate course of the war in most cases.

Our fourth conclusion, however, is that very few of these changes of the wars course, on their own, would have led to an Axis victory in the war overall. There are some cases, primarily the Axis Mediterranean options, that were relatively easy for the Axis to have won, and would have noticeably altered the course of the war by conquering these territories; but wouldn't, on their own, have won the war for Germany. There are other cases where the consequences of an Axis victory are uncertain to the result of the war, mainly involving Japan, where an overall stalemate was the best that could have been achieved. Finally, we arrive at the right hand column of table 18, those few cases where Axis victory had a high probability of winning the war for them. Unfortunately for the Axis, in some of these, their chances of winning the required campaigns or battles themselves were only evens or lower.

There were in fact no sure things for the Axis. The closest are those cases where the Axis had a high chance of winning the campaign, **and** altering the course of the war, **and** winning the war outright. This, three 'yes' result, occurs only four times. These cases are: the ground phase of operation 'Sealion'; the early Moscow strategy in 1941; Moscow again in 1942, instead of operation 'Blau'; and finally, and possibly their best chance of all, the often overlooked earlier i.e. 1939 or 1940, German mobilization of armaments production strategy. The 'Sealion' case of course presupposes that the Axis were successful in the more difficult, air and naval phases, of any alternative Battle of Britain. Axis victory in those two phases using alternative strategies was possible, but uncertain at best. All of these better Axis chances, confirming our earlier surmise, occur in the first half of the war, and all fall to Germany rather than Japan.

How the Axis Powers Could Have Won the War

Germany could have won WW2, but it would have been difficult, and the odds were against it. To do so they needed to knock Britain and Russia, or both, out of the war before American intervention could become effective. The best Japan could achieve was a stalemate rather than outright victory. In both European and Pacific theatres the Axis needed to avoid their historical mistakes. Moreover, drawing upon our conclusions from table 18, one extra single campaign success was generally not enough to win the war. To win the Axis needed to combine more than one alternative strategy and campaign victory. From this it is possible to construct plausible scenarios of how the Axis could have won WW2.

There is a rough consensus on the list of well known historical strategy mistakes that the Axis made. Some might argue of course that the first mistake was starting WW2 in the first place. The causes of the war are largely outside the framework of reference for this book. We simply assume that the pre-war state, territorial, power, military, economic and ideological rivalries, are a given. The main argument is that the Axis was doomed to defeat from the start due to the imbalance of resources. This was examined in depth, concluding that economic determinism only becomes decisive in 1943 and thereafter. Moreover, earlier German mobilization would have altered the imbalance of armaments production in 1940-42, and both delayed and reduced the impact of Allied overwhelming force.

The failure of Germany to mobilize the economic resources that it did have, from the start of the war in 1939, was its first major mistake of grand strategy. Every other combatant mobilized its economy as quickly as it could after entering the war, and it took two to three years between decision and maximum armaments production. Instead, Germany waged the battle of production leisurely for over two years, until Speer became Minister for Armaments at the start of 1942. This is the one mistake that is, very erroneously, ignored or skimped in many lists and accounts. Erroneous, because the mistake was major, and had consequences in virtually every battle and campaign that was fought. Greater resources, especially in the campaigns where the numerical odds were even, or the Axis was outnumbered, which was most of them, are always of benefit. Moreover, given that most of the few campaigns and battles lost by the Axis in 1940-42 were close run things, then it is almost certain that even modest extra resources would have changed outcomes. The required margins were well within what could have been achieved in German armaments production by mobilizing in 1939, or even after the conquest of France in 1940, instead of 1942. We would even go as far as saying this mistake was possibly Germany's greatest, ranking at least alongside 'Barbarossa', and the declaration of war on the USA. The production margins, certainly of the two year earlier mobilization, combined with the Moscow strategy option, would have been enough to defeat Russia. In contrast, no German or Axis strategy could have conquered America; but it could have been stalemated by a German defeat of Britain or Russia, or both.

The more conventional list of Axis strategy mistakes starts with Dunkirk. Given the situation after the German panzers reached the Channel at Abbeville and cut the Allied armies in two, it should have been relatively easy for them to continue on apace, and prevent the evacuation of the BEF. The reasons for the famous, but temporary, halt order have been discussed, and none of them were militarily valid. The Germans quickly, but not quickly enough, realized this, as the reversal of the halt order after two days showed. Since the Allies had no viable counter strategy at that point, then the outcome at Dunkirk was clearly due to an easily avoidable German mistake. However contrary to popular opinion, unless there had been a psychological collapse of British political-military leadership and morale, which was possible but unlikely, a complete Axis victory at Dunkirk wouldn't on its own have forced Britain to make peace.

The Battle of Britain, especially if it had followed an Axis victory and capture of the BEF at Dunkirk, is another matter entirely. German victory here, resulting in an invasion of Britain, would have ended the war, period. Without Britain as a base, America would probably not have entered the war in Europe. Even if it had, restarting the war in 1942 after a gap of over a year, the geographic barrier of the Atlantic would have been insurmountable, for either side, resulting in stalemate and a compromise peace. So why and politically how, in this situation, would America have restarted the war in the first place? Britain's remaining Commonwealth-Empire, fighting on alone, would have been totally incapable of liberating Britain or Europe. The only way the war would have continued after a German conquest of Britain, would have been by Hitler, or Stalin, breaking their 1939 Pact. Without an unconquered Britain, and later the USA, in Germany's rear, the odds on the eastern front given the actual narrow outcome of 'Barbarossa', would then have favored Germany.

The problem for the Axis was actually winning the air, and potential naval phases, of the Battle of Britain in 1940, or 1941. Their failure to do so was only partly due to the main German strategy mistake, of diverting from the 'counter air' strategy against the RAF, to the bombing of cities. As showed, there were deeper reasons for the outcome, such as greater British aircraft production, and the circumstances of the battle. Moreover Britain had alternative options as well, principally withdrawing the RAF out of range, and relying more on its strongest card, the Royal Navy. The Axis had their own alternative options, especially when combined with other campaigns. The most dangerous for Britain, would have been for the Axis to have waited until 1941. They could have used the delay to weaken Britain, by combining the historical air campaign with the conquest of the Mediterranean, especially Gibraltar. Both the German and Italian fleets could then have combined, backed by the entire Luftwaffe, to improve the Axis chances in the crucial air and naval phases of a 1941 'Sealion'. The build up from an early Axis mobilization of armament production, would also have had a larger impact by 1941 than in 1940.

The third Axis mistake was therefore the failure to exploit their, relatively easy, opportunities in the Mediterranean between the fall of France in June 1940, and whichever would be their chosen strategy for mid-1941. Had the Axis chosen a Mediterranean strategy and diverted greater resources to it, principally about half of the Luftwaffe and a few of the many panzer and motorized divisions available, they could have conquered Malta, Gibraltar, Egypt and the Middle Eastern oilfields. This would have secured Italy from attack, and set the Axis up for a decisive strategy in 1941. In 1941 they would then have the choice of either invading Britain, or the historical 'Barbarossa' campaign. Prior conquest of the Mediterranean would have improved their chances in either. Due to the relatively modest force requirements, the Axis could still have conquered the Mediterranean, from Gibraltar to Suez at least, even as late as 1942 and simultaneous with the Russian campaign.

In 1941 Hitler commits what is widely viewed as his greatest mistake, invading Russia. On balance we largely agree with this conclusion, but with some important caveats. Certainly it was a major and avoidable error. Germany and Russia had a non-aggression pact at this time, while Britain was still fighting alone. Neither Hitler nor Stalin really trusted each other. Instead, like most treaties, the pact was based on the perceived national interests of both sides in 1939. Either side could have broken the pact. Due to the unexpected fall of France in 1940, and despite German failure in the Battle of Britain, the strategic balance by 1941 had moved towards Germany. Stalin had military contingency plans to attack Germany, at least as early as 1940. However, we cannot be certain of his political intent, and especially of the timing. He may have been planning to attack as early as July 1941. Still, with hindsight anyway, we know, given what happened in the first five months of 'Barbarossa', that Russia wasn't ready for war at this early date. The caveat here of course is that at the time, neither side had a full intelligence picture of the others intentions or capabilities.

There are other caveats as well. It is not accurate to assume that a Russian victory was obvious, or inevitable from the outset, even with hindsight. Germany came very close, not to conquering all of Russia's territory, but of defeating Stalin's regime in October-November 1941, and briefly again in July-August 1942. The failure to do so, after a remarkable run of victories in 1941, was due primarily to German operational strategy errors. The failure to concentrate on Moscow in August 1941, immediately after regrouping from the frontier battle phase of 'Barbarossa', was the greatest of these. The Germans wasted almost two months diverting to Leningrad and especially to Kiev. Given how close operation 'Typhoon', begun as late as October 1st 1941, came anyway, Moscow could certainly have been captured. We may recall that even Molotov, hardly biased against his own regime or country, considered that coming on top of all the previous disasters, that the fall of Moscow would have destroyed the Soviet regime. Nor did Stalin have any counter strategy available. He at least, knew the priority importance of Moscow, and had already concentrated the maximum defensive force there in both 1941 and 1942. Remember the relatively unknown operation 'Mars' offensive on the Moscow sector in November 1942; it was larger than the better known and simultaneous 'Uranus' offensive at Stalingrad.

Finally, the Germans made more operational errors during the 'Blau' offensive against the Caucasus in 1942. The Caucasus oilfields could have been captured, had they stuck to the original Directive 41, the *sequential* plan for the campaign. Changing to Directive 45, *simultaneous* offensives against Stalingrad and the Caucasus reduced their chances in both. Moreover, although it isn't absolutely certain that they could have captured Stalingrad, the Axis could definitely have avoided getting tied down in an unnecessary urban battle there. Stalingrad was a part, albeit an important part, of the Don-Volga defensive flank to protect the offensive against the Caucasus. The Caucasus oilfields were more important than Stalingrad. Stalingrad's loss wouldn't have defeated Russia. In contrast, loss of the oilfields would have gradually crippled the giant's economy and military operations into 1943. Alternatively operation 'Blau' itself, on balance, was possibly the wrong strategy for 1942. Moscow was still more important in 1942, and far closer to the German starting position than in 1941. An Axis offensive here in 1942, would also have forced too battle, and probably encircled, the main Russian armies, rather than just pushing the southern Fronts back as operation 'Blau' did.

The next major German mistake was to declare war on the USA in December 1941. If Roosevelt had been unable to get Congress to declare war on the European Axis, or Japan, then this was a potential, indeed almost a certain war winner for the Axis. Britain and Russia on their own could probably not have defeated the European Axis, without full American participation in the war. Without the USA, a British only invasion of France, and even the defeat of Italy, was impossible. The German-Russian war was a very close run thing, probably close enough that a modest transfer of Axis resources from the western fronts to the east, combined with lesser American aid, could have made the difference. A more likely scenario is that American entry into the war would have been delayed, rather than prevented altogether. Even so, American unity and moral determination, important for democracies, would have been reduced. Even delayed American entry in the crucial year of 1942, could have been critical for Russia, and thus consequently for the Western Allies as well. Combined with alternative Axis operational strategies against Russia, even a delayed US intervention, would likely have been fatal for the Allies.

There were therefore four really decisive European Axis strategic mistakes: the failure to fully mobilize the economy for war from the start; the failure to concentrate on Britain in 1940-41; the decision to invade Russia, and having done so the failure to maintain the operational focus on Moscow; and finally the declaration of war on the USA. Avoidance of any one of these strategic mistakes would have gone a long way to winning the war for Germany. In combination, avoiding two or more of them would have made a German victory more likely than not. Avoiding all four mistakes, a European Axis victory in WW2 becomes a near certainty.

Japan's greatest mistake was undoubtedly declaring war on the United States. The strike against Pearl Harbor and the diplomatic bungling over the timing and coordination of their declaration of war merely compounded the error. Japan should simply have seized the Dutch Indonesian oilfields and attacked Britain in the Far East, but left the Americans well alone. Like Germany and Italy, it couldn't prevent the Americans declaring war, but all three Axis powers, by restraint, could have delayed it, and at least made Roosevelt's political and diplomatic task as difficult as possible. Despite the, incomplete, operational success, Pearl Harbor was outweighed by the long term consequence of American wrath. The traditional 'No Pearl Harbor' strategy of awaiting an American counter offensive, probably along the central Pacific axis of war plan 'Orange', would have had at least an equal chance of success in 1942.

Having roused America with the mistake of Pearl Harbor there was probably no going back for Japan. Given this, the strategy to finish off the American Pacific Fleet at Midway was reasonable. However, the plan itself, and the execution of operational strategy at Midway was rather abysmal by the Japanese side. Good American strategy at Midway, and luck, played their part, but without the Japanese mistake of dispersing their carriers, including those deployed to the Coral Sea operation, America couldn't have won. A Japanese victory at Midway would have given them an even shot at Hawaii. Success there would have been Japan's best chance of creating a permanent stalemate in the Pacific and a compromise peace.

By avoiding their major errors and using the alternative strategies we have identified, in a plausible **combination** of campaigns, it is possible to see how the Axis could have won WW2. In all cases, the Germans needed to fully mobilize their economy for war from the start, preferably from 1939, or in 1940 after the conquest of France at the latest. That would have brought forward their actual ground and air armament production levels by one or two years. This would have prepared them for the possibility of a long war, and would have increased their margins, options, and chances of success, in every campaign and battle that they fought from 1939 to 1942, and even into 1943. Given Germany's actual mobilization, starting in 1942, and what happened in every other industrial combatant; it was certainly within Germany's power, and its decision to make.

Next, given that the eventual Allied alliance would still, eventually, command greater economic and thus military resources than the Axis; the Axis aimed to take on their opponent's one at a time. They knew this, and indeed successfully used this strategy in 1939-1940. The 1939 Nazi-Soviet Pact shocked the world, and this diplomacy created the necessary strategic conditions that avoided a two front war, contributing along with Manstein's brilliant stratagem to the fall of France in June 1940. At that point the European Axis had two immediate great power rivals left, Britain and Russia. They accurately estimated that America wouldn't be ready to enter the war until 1942, and do anything effective until 1943. In July 1940 Hitler could have continued the 'one at a time' strategy, while mobilizing for a possible long war. He had two choices, Britain first or Russia first? Since Britain was already at war, and he had the non-aggression pact with Stalin, the strategic choice should have been Britain.

With maximum economic mobilization, starting in 1939-40, bringing production levels forward by one or two years, an alternative Axis grand strategy, targeting Britain, could very plausibly have had the following sequence. From July 1940 to spring 1941 an enhanced Battle of Britain, is followed, or better still combined, with a comprehensive Mediterranean strategy, with Gibraltar the priority target. The fall of Malta, Egypt and the Middle East with its oil, is a given. In the spring or summer of 1941 instead of 'Barbarossa', Germany, supported by the Italian fleet redeployed via a captured Gibraltar, and a Luftwaffe up to twice its historical size invades Britain. The 1941 'Sealion', given up to two years early Axis production, would have had a better than even chance of success, but still not a certainty due to the Royal Navy. If they had defeated the RN, with the extra air and naval power, Britain would have fallen.

From there the Axis could either have kept the Nazi-Soviet Pact indefinitely; or attacked an isolated Russia in 1942, with a second front in the Caucasus and backed by all of Europe mobilized at its 1944 production level. The Axis would have run the risk that Stalin might have broken the Nazi-Soviet Pact, and attacked Germany in 1941, while it was launching an invasion of Britain. That would have been the optimum timing for Stalin, but still very risky, given that Russia wasn't ready for war in 1941. Even with an extra year of Russian peacetime preparation, the balance of power would still have favored the Axis in 1942. Either way, with Britain out of the war in 1941, Russia is either still allied to the Axis, or Stalin is attacked and defeated, and an anti-communist Russian regime becomes an Axis ally.

The European Axis, an allied Russia, and Japan, control most of Eurasia and into North Africa. Finally, the Axis avoids a declaration of war on the US, so as to make Roosevelt's political and diplomatic task as difficult as possible. Japan follows suit with the 'No Pearl Harbor' strategy, attacking only Britain and the Dutch, and if America didn't respond, even assisting a 1942 'Barbarossa'. If a less united America did declare war, then Japan would have had an even chance, or better, of defeating any war plan 'Orange' type offensive in 1942. By 1942-43 such a combined Axis coalition, would have been as powerful as even a mobilized United States. Without Britain as a base, and no Pearl Harbor, America, still safe from attack itself, would likely have accepted the global stalemate. The Axis would have won the war.

The alternative Axis grand strategy following the fall of France would have been to target Russia first. This was the grand strategy that Hitler actually chose, and his failure to defeat Russia was the main reason that Germany lost the war. However, given that 'Barbarossa' was a much closer run campaign than is commonly believed; then a very plausible combination of German strategy changes could definitely have made the difference. Again German production mobilization from 1939-1940, would almost on its own have been a war winner. Next, and in any event, Germany had almost a year before 'Barbarossa' to exploit missed opportunities in the Mediterranean. The European Axis had enough time and resources to capture Gibraltar, Malta, Egypt and the Middle East as far as Persia during this interlude. Britain's historical Mediterranean campaigns in 1940-42, would have been impossible. Britain would therefore have been further weakened and strategically neutralized until 1943, giving the Axis a free hand against Stalin's Russia for up to two years.

With Axis economic mobilization from 1939-40, combined with the Moscow strategy, they might not have needed even that long.[1] Even a one year advance of ground and air production levels, mobilizing in 1940, would have increased Luftwaffe strength by 20-25% and produced at least an extra 1,800 combat aircraft by June 1941. Moreover as we have seen, there would also have been 2,000 extra tanks, an increase of over 50% in this critical arm of the blitzkrieg for 'Barbarossa'. They would still have had to change their strategy to target Moscow in August 1941, immediately after the completion of the frontier battle phase. Otherwise, even with the extra forces, 'Typhoon', starting in October, would still have run out of time before the autumn mud and Russian winter.

The combination of early production mobilization, and the Moscow option in August 1941, would have been unstoppable. The Moscow option alone would have given the Axis the edge. Combined with the 1939 two year early production, it becomes a near certainty. Moscow would have fallen in September or October 1941. We may also recall that the Russians would have been in no position in 1941, to seriously counter an early Axis Moscow option from the other sectors of the front, principally from the Ukraine. Moreover, there would likely have been early knock on effects, such as the surrender of an isolated Leningrad, and a massive psychological and morale impact, capable of shattering Stalin's weakened Soviet regime there and then. The margins from extra Axis production and forces further reinforce these conclusions. Finally, prior Axis conquest of the Middle East as far as Persia would have opened a second front against Russia in the Caucasus in 1941, threatening 75% of its oil supply. The combination of three Axis strategies: immediate mobilization; Mediterranean; and the Moscow option; would in all probability have defeated Stalin's Russia by the end of 1941.

Even if it hadn't, Germany would still have had 1942 to finish the job, against a Russia that would have been far weaker than historically. By not declaring war on the USA in December 1941, and conquering the Mediterranean prior to 'Barbarossa', plus full production at 1944 levels by 1942; the Axis would have extended this time window into 1943. Western aid which was 5% of Russia's war effort in 1942, and 10% in 1943, and which some historians consider critical, would also be reduced. Moscow and probably Leningrad would already have fallen in fall 1941, giving the enhanced Axis an advanced starting position for the 1942 campaign. Extra production and less pressure from the Western Allies would mean they needn't have limited their 1942 offensive to the southern part of the front. The Axis could have advanced to the middle Volga, Gorky, and the reserve capital of Kuybyshev, as well as capturing the Caucasus oilfields from two directions. Finally, as Stalin's political control faltered, it would be sensible for the Axis to capitalize, by creating non-communist regimes and forces, from the inevitably fragmented and alienated subject nationalities of a collapsing Soviet Union. They did this historically, but not until 1943-45, far too late. It could have been done in 1941-42, taking advantage of the initial goodwill towards the Axis and the great mass of up to 4 million prisoners who deserted Stalin's armies at this time. At low ebb anyway by 1942, the probability of Stalin's Russia surviving in this scenario is virtually zero. As Molotov said, the Soviet Union would have disintegrated and the alliance with the West dissolved.

The collapse of Stalin's Soviet regime would most likely have occurred at the end of 1941, after the inevitable fall of Moscow, and certainly in 1942. Non-communist and pro-Axis regimes could have been created among the non-Russian nations, including the Baltic States, Ukraine and the Caucasus republics. A post-Stalin, non-communist Russia itself, almost certainly a military regime appealing to nationalism, would have no choice but a separate peace. A truncated, initially chaotic, but still considerable independent Russian power would still have survived beyond the Volga, but only at the price of becoming an Axis ally. It would likely have been a larger version of Vichy France or Franco's Spain, supplying the Axis with economic resources and linking them geographically with the Japanese Empire. Let us also assume again, that Japan follows the optimum, 'No Pearl Harbor' strategy in December 1941, avoiding war with the USA for as long as possible.

Where would that have left the Western Allies? In a very bad position is the answer. It's almost as bad as the Axis 'Britain first' strategy and scenario. The European Axis, fully mobilized by 1942, a pro-Axis Russia and Japan, control all of Eurasia and North Africa, except for a partially isolated Britain, and perhaps an equally isolated British-India. With the Battle of the Atlantic still in its worst year of 1942, the Mediterranean lost, Russia out and allied to the Axis, and America entering the war late and uncertain, or worse not at all, Britain would still be in dire danger in 1942. The German Europe, at full 1944 production levels, no active eastern front to worry about, a Luftwaffe twice or thrice its historical size, and the Italian and German fleets combined; would be in a strong position to launch a 1942 version of 'Sealion'. The odds and circumstances would again favor the Axis much more than in 1940. Britain would likely have fallen, or made peace to avoid defeat. At any rate, even if a much weakened Britain survived as a base for America, such an Axis Europe, indeed Eurasia, would still be invulnerable to Western Allied invasions. Once more there would have been a global stalemate between America, perhaps a neutralized independent Britain; and an enhanced Axis controlled Eurasia. The Axis would have won World War Two.

The Post War World: Dark Age or Cold War?

What difference would an Axis victory have made? This might seem a strange question. Of course it would be different, very different for the conquered countries, but globally there are considerable nuances. Between the fall of France and the Battle of Britain, Churchill claimed that if Britain lost, then the whole world, including the United States, would fall into a new Dark Age. Of course his speech was aimed at America as well as Britain. One purpose was to support his diplomatic aim of gaining increased American support and entry into the war, rather than being an accurate statement of fact. The great man was after all, a politician.

Few in the West today, doubt that the Axis powers, with regard to their dictatorship ideologies, were dark forces. Yet so for that matter was Stalin's Russia, and they, eventually, were on the side of the Allies. The plausible estimates for the number of civilians killed by Stalin's Soviet regime, is about 22-25 million. This excludes secondary economic and demographic effects such as lost births. The comparable total for Hitler's Nazi's, aggregating all the civilian losses in the European theatre, and excluding deaths due to Allied bombing and those caused by the Russian advance into Germany in 1945, is about 23 million. Estimates of civilian losses in the Japanese occupied area, primarily China, are more uncertain, perhaps 10-15 million. That the Axis powers and Soviet Russia were dictatorships that killed millions is well known. They could of course, as we have seen, ended up on the same side if the course of WW2 had gone differently. A new Dark Age? Yes, but it wouldn't have covered the entire world. Our point and subject of enquiry, much less explored, is that an Axis victory in WW2 would have impacted some countries far more, or less, than others.

Central is to consider, in global terms, what an Axis victory in WW2 would have looked like. It is not simply the opposite of the Allied victory in 1945. The Allies conquered their enemy in 1945. The Axis regimes of Germany, Italy, and Japan, along with their various vassal states, ceased to exist. Moreover Germany, Italy and Japan, ceased to exist as great powers, at the top rank of international politics. Nor in the post-war world were they able, even over decades, to restore that rank. The post-war 'economic miracles' in Germany and Japan didn't make them anywhere near as powerful, or of the same 'superpower' rank, as the USA or USSR. To claim, as some do, decades after 1945, that Germany and Japan, even Italy, somehow won WW2 because they were, much later, able to overtake Britain in economic size or living standards, is inaccurate. For one thing these economic changes occurred post-war, not during the war itself. Moreover, the trends were in that direction anyway. If the Axis had won, Germany and Japan would have overtaken Britain earlier, and even been ahead of Russia, and closed the gap on the USA. Nor did the heavy price paid by the Allies mean that they somehow lost the war, or that it might have been better not to fight it. Clearly the Allies, especially Russia and Britain, suffered heavily during WW2 as well. Soviet Russia lost 26 million people, far more than any other state. Britain was further weakened economically by the war, and quickly lost its empire and great power status after 1945. Only the USA suffered relatively lightly, and greatly expanded its power by 1945, and into the post-war world. None of this alters the fact that the Allies won, and the Axis lost.

Yet an Axis victory was certainly possible, and plausible. However, the circumstances and odds were against it. Just as the balance of power, resources, circumstances and likely outcomes, favored the Allies during the war; so it is with the completeness of any victory. Even the largest Axis victory, in contrast to the Allied one, wouldn't have meant complete conquest of the enemy. Axis grand strategic objectives in WW2, and their maximum strategic reach, were regional, not global. It is a crucial and substantial difference to Allied and especially American objectives and capabilities. An Axis victory, no matter how dictatorial their regimes, would have meant regional hegemony, not world domination.

The European Axis was exactly that, European. Hitler's new order view rarely extended beyond the continent of Europe. It was mostly focused, strategically, economically, and ideologically, on Soviet Russia. Even there, we may recall that the ultimate objective for 'Barbarossa' was the line Archangel-Volga-Astrakhan; vast, but still continental. The rest of the Nazi strategic objectives were about overthrowing the Versailles Treaty, defeating the old WW1 enemy, France, and controlling Western Europe. They wanted Britain neutralized and America kept out of Europe, but showed little interest outside of Germany's traditional, pre-Nazi, continental view of the world. Their view of the British Empire, as a source of stability, and a possible future ally, was strangely ambiguous. The Mediterranean was largely left to Mussolini's Italy, helping to explain missed German opportunities there. Only the German Navy and the Foreign Ministry, predictably, had a more global view. Yet resource constraints meant that any serious Axis power projection beyond Europe, Russia, and the Mediterranean and Middle Eastern littoral, was strategically unrealistic.

The Nazi occupied area was also far from a homogenous empire. This was true during the war itself and would likely have continued post-war had they won. The harshest part of the dictatorship was in Eastern Europe, especially Poland and the occupied part of the Soviet Union. This is where most of the civilian losses under Nazi rule occurred: 6 million Poles, and possibly 13 million for the Soviet Union. The estimates for Soviet deaths in WW2, military and civilian, has changed many times over the decades since and some, a minority, were caused by Stalin's regime rather than Hitler's.[2] Western Europe suffered relatively less. Denmark for example even retained its parliament until 1943. Other parts of the Axis Europe consisted of allied states; Mussolini's Italy, Hungary, Romania, Bulgaria, Slovakia, Finland, and Croatia. Finally there were pro-Axis neutrals; Vichy France, Franco's Spain; to which, had the Axis won, Sweden, Switzerland, Eire, Portugal and Turkey would inevitably have been added. Economically, the European Axis would have been an autarkic capitalist empire, about half the economic size of the USA. A victorious Axis Europe, adding Britain, European Russia, and Middle Eastern oil, would have been self sufficient and potentially equal in economic size to the Americans.

Similarly with Japan's 'Greater East Asian Co-Prosperity Sphere'; the name delineates its vast, but still regional limits. Japanese strategic war plans didn't extend to objectives beyond Hawaii. Even then, Midway, Hawaii, and the various South Pacific operations and objectives were 1942 revisions, driven by 'victory disease', to the original 1941 expansion. In addition, Japan aimed to overthrow both Nationalist and Communist China, and establish a pro-Japanese regime there. It isn't clear whether Japan had the capability, to control the British-Indian Empire. Certainly Japan had no ambitions, and knew it was incapable, of overthrowing the USA, or even of having any influence whatsoever in the American hemisphere. Regional hegemony and economic autarky, or self sufficiency, were the aims. In the 1940s Japan's East Asian empire would have been economically largely self sufficient, but in industrial terms, much weaker than either the USA or a German Europe.[3] Given two or three decades of economic development, as occurred historically, culminating later still in the emergence of China as a state capitalist economic power, the gap would have closed. China was so large, that even a pro-Japanese regime, would likely have become, over decades, more independent and co-equal with Japan.

The third continental dictatorship resulting from an Axis victory would have been Russia. Indeed as we have seen, for the Axis to have won the war, they needed to retain Russia as an ally, or else defeat it and establish a pro-Axis regime there. Stalin's Soviet regime could have been defeated, overthrown, or replaced; but Russia's total territory was too vast to be militarily conquered and occupied. A Russian state of some kind would have survived an Axis victory and been an important component of any Axis post-war order. There were two possibilities for Russia. First, following a successful 'Britain first' Axis strategy in 1940 or 1941, Stalin's Russia could still have survived. With all Europe mobilized and under German control, a peace settlement with a conquered Britain, and a still neutral America, Germany would have options. They needn't fear Russia in that situation, and didn't have to attack it. Stalin's Russia could have maintained the 1939 Nazi-Soviet non-aggression pact, and the 1941 neutrality pact with Japan. Nazi Germany, Soviet Russia and Imperial Japan would have been an uneasy triumvirate, but nonetheless an alliance of dictators controlling all of Eurasia.

The second possibility is that Germany would still have attacked Russia, either 'Russia first' in 1941, or in 1942 following a 'Britain first' strategy. Combining the immediate mobilization, Britain first and Moscow strategies, the Axis would still have had the advantage in 1942. A defeated Soviet Union would certainly have split apart on ethnic national lines, just as it did historically in 1991-92. In this scenario, the western republics:

263

Ukraine, Baltic States, the Caucasus republics, and possibly Russia proper, up to the 'Barbarossa' objective line of Archangel-Volga-Astrakhan, would be either occupied or become Axis client states. A truncated, non-communist, pro-Axis, Russian state would still remain. It would control most of the ex-Soviet territory, from the Volga to Vladivostok, including Siberia, and probably all of Central Asia. A conciliatory peace treaty by the Axis, in return for a Russian alliance, might even have returned territory, giving it the borders of the post-Cold-War Russian Federation. Either way, such a state would only have half the population, economy and industry of the ex-Soviet Union. Immediately following defeat it would have been relatively weak. Yet over time, a decade or two, it too would have become a potential great power, more a partner rather than vassal to the German and Japanese empires to its west and east. Alas for the Russian people, and unlike in 1991, there seems no plausible scenario with the possibility for Russia to have emerged from WW2 as a democracy. Soviet communist or pro-Axis militarist, Russia would still have been a dictatorship, but at least one with some independence.

Of all the powers, the one that would be least affected by even the largest plausible Axis victory, is the USA. They had easily the greatest freedom of action and safety margins of any of the WW2 combatants, friend or foe. There is no plausible scenario where the Axis powers of WW2, could even seriously attack the continental USA, never mind conquer it. We have seen how the Atlantic and Pacific oceans were protection enough, even after a possible German conquest of Britain and a Japanese advance as far as Hawaii. American sea power was almost equal to the combined Axis fleets even in 1939-42. That is without including any residual British fleet and taking into account inevitable Axis naval losses in Europe prior to US entry into the war. In any case the Axis, if they were to win the war, would be focused on the defeat of Britain and Russia in those early years. With the massive combat shipbuilding production of 1943-45, the USN would become larger than the combined Axis fleets. It would, under any circumstances, be impossible for the Axis to gain command of the sea, even of part of it, or temporarily, in order to invade North America. In any case the Americans, defending near their own bases would have complete land based air superiority as well. Even in the air age of the 1940s, the Atlantic and Pacific were proof against trans-oceanic air operations. The USA and the rest of North America, and indeed even South America, were safe from invasion.

No matter what the course and outcome of WW2, America was bound to emerge from the war as one of the most powerful nations. The issue is the extent of that power, 'great power' or 'superpower'. With the Allied victory in 1945, the Americans emerged as the stronger of only two superpowers. If the Axis had won, probably ending the war in 1942, America would still have been one of three or four great powers in a multi-polar post-war world. The other great powers would definitely have included Germany and Japan, probably Russia, and much less plausibly a weakened British Commonwealth-Empire. Indeed even after an Axis victory, America would still have emerged as the single greatest power. The difference from its actual superpower emergence would be that, like Germany, Japan and Russia, its power would be largely continental and regional, rather than truly global.

Following an Axis victory, Canada and any surviving exiled British forces would inevitably become allied and come under US protection, adding about 10% to America's economic and military resources. The rest of the Americas, certainly as far south as the US controlled Panama Canal, and probably all of South America, would remain a US sphere of influence. Just as was historically the case, US control would be informal and indirect. Even so most, probably all, of the Latin American states, a mixture of democracies and military dictatorships, would likely become US allies and be tied to North America economically. Fears about German or Fascist influence or expansion in South America were exaggerated.

There would also still be American allies further a field, among the remnants of the British Commonwealth-Empire. Australia and New Zealand, although isolated by any Japanese victory in the Pacific, were probably still beyond Japan's ability to conquer. With a defeated Britain unable to protect them, they too, as historically, would come into the American orbit. South Africa and even much of British colonial Africa south of the Sahara, would also be beyond Axis strategic reach, although not under solid Allied control either. Most of the French Empire in Africa however, would have been under Vichy control. Had the Axis won, then Vichy France would have become an even closer and more permanent Axis ally. India would be the most vulnerable part of the ex-British Empire, although still difficult for either Japan or the European Axis to formally conquer.

Economically, the USA was very secure. Apart from Russia, it was the most self sufficient of the great powers anyway, only about 10% of its GNP was dependent on international trade in the 1940s. Most of this trade was within its still considerable sphere of influence. Even post-war, the US trade dependency ratio only ever reached 20% at the most. From the 1950s America did become an increasing importer of oil. Again however, contrary to popular belief, most of this was still from the Americas, not an unstable Middle East, that would be under Axis control had they won WW2. The big difference would have been that the industrial economies of Western Europe and Japan would be Axis, and largely unavailable to US trade. Yet Axis control of most of Europe and East Asia during WW2 itself didn't seem to hurt the US economy. Overall, considering the USA's high level of internal self sufficiency and still considerable sphere of influence, the American economy and standard of living would only have been marginally affected by an Axis victory. During WW2 the already developed US economy had about 40% of global production. Historically this gradually declined during the post-war decades to about 20% by 2010. The American economy still grew of course. It was a relative decline, as the various less developed regions expanded faster. An Axis victory, bringing an era of regional autarky instead of a global economy, certainly wouldn't have accelerated this trend to America's detriment. The Axis empires, especially Japanese East Asia would have closed the gap over time. Even so, America would probably still have remained the largest economy, with the highest living standard, for decades into the post-war world.

Yet man, especially liberal-democratic man, doesn't live on bread alone. An Axis victory would have considerably reduced the post-war expansion of democratic government. Again Western Europe, Japan and East Asia, and probably India, would have come under dictator control instead. Nor would the collapse of Communism in 1989-92 have likely converted the ex-Soviet empire into democracies, or versions thereof. Only the British Commonwealth countries, Canada, Australia, New Zealand, and later perhaps South Africa, would for certain have remained democratic. South America of course, as it was, oscillated between democracy and dictatorship in the post-war era. Yet, since the USA had both military and economic security, there is no reason why American democratic government itself would have changed. It is a myth that the world couldn't exist, to paraphrase Presidents Lincoln and Reagan, 'half free and half slave'. In reality it has always been the case, prior to WW2, during the Cold War and even today, that the world has a variety of political systems, democratic, non-democratic, and partial versions of both. An Axis victory would certainly have been a major setback for democratic government globally, more so even than the advance of Communism after 1945. However, it definitely wouldn't have distinguished it. To return to Churchill, the Dark Age of dictatorship wouldn't have encompassed the whole world, and the United States would have remained free, and because of geography, economics, and later of nuclear weapons, indefinitely so.

That very likely wouldn't have been true for Britain though. Given Churchill's implacable defiance in 1940, any Axis victory in WW2 would have meant Britain's eclipse. It would merely be a matter of degree. A successful operation 'Sealion' in 1940-42, however it was sequenced with other Axis strategies, would have led to Britain being conquered and occupied. A British version of Vichy France would have been the result, combined with an Axis occupation. A less harsh fate, a neutralized Britain with a measure of independence, would be the other end of the scale of outcomes. This would most likely have occurred as the result of a separate peace, secured by diplomacy to escape from a hopeless military situation, say an isolated Britain following an Axis defeat of Russia. Either way, any serious Axis victory would have brought forward the end of the British Empire as a global great power. Its various components would either fall to the Axis, such as in the Mediterranean, Middle East and Far East; or else sought American protection, such as with the independent Commonwealth.

India is the main uncertainty. It was difficult, because of its size and location, for Japan and the European Axis to conquer. On the other hand an Axis victory, giving them and an allied Russia control of Eurasia, would surround India on three sides. A British remnant, backed by America, would find it nearly impossible to maintain control at the end of long SLOCs via South Africa or Australia. Finally, the Indian's themselves were about to achieve independence from British rule anyway in 1947. Axis victory in 1942 would have brought that forward a few years. A weak India, nominally independent, but aligned by power realities to the Axis is the most plausible outcome.

An Axis victory in WW2 would certainly have led to an alternative Cold War in the decades that followed. America and its various allies, identified above, would have been on one side. On the other would have been the alliance of dictators, led by the great power triumvirate of Germany, Japan and Russia. With America being the single strongest power, this wouldn't have been a simple three to one unbalanced contest that a first glance might suggest. Geography and the limitations of 1940s conventional military technology, and logistics; would have brought a global stalemate and a natural end to WW2 following any Axis victory in Europe, Russia and the Pacific. However, the nuclear age couldn't be denied, or delayed for long. Historically the USA became an atomic power in 1945, Russia in 1949, and Britain in 1953. Germany was behind the USA during WW2, but ahead of Russia. We can reasonably surmise that a victorious German-Europe would have acquired the 'bomb' in 1946-48. Japan had no atomic programme during WW2. However, it equaled Britain in its economic and armament production by the peak year of 1944. With a post-war East Asian empire, Japan would have the economic, technological and industrial capacity to become an atomic power, at least as early as Britain did historically.

A USA-Axis Cold War would likely have been similar, in its broad parameters, as the real Cold War. Both sides would soon have acquired atomic weapons, and later the various associated technological developments, such as the Hydrogen bomb, SAC, ICBM and SLBM delivery systems, and multiple warheads. As in the actual Cold War, by the 1950s both sides could reach and hurt each other, by the 1960s and thereafter, they could devastate each other. Inevitably though, even for dictator empires like Nazi Germany and Imperial Japan, just as was the case with the communist dictatorships of Russia and China, nuclear weapons endanger an attitude of extreme caution. An Axis-American Cold War would be likely that, a Cold War, not a nuclear WW3. Very dangerous and frightening, yes, but so was the real Cold War. Instead, in cold wars, open power competition occurs in non-nuclear areas, such as conventional proxy wars, economics, and ideology. The conflict zones for these would have been in those areas of uncertain control: Sub-Saharan Africa, India, maybe Latin America.

There would have been some major differences as well. An Axis coalition of a German Europe, Russia and a Japanese East Asia, after a period of economic, industrial and technological development, could in combination, eventually out produce America and its allies. This is the reverse of what actually happened in the real Cold War. The USA allied to Western Europe, the British Commonwealth, Japan, and controlling most of the non-Eurasian world, outmatched the resources of the Soviet bloc, even when combined with China. The result, although taking nearly half a century, was the collapse of the Soviet bloc in 1989-92. The Europe-Russia-Asia combination however, would have given the Axis the advantage over time. It was also a massive reason why, for the Allies, WW2 had to be fought, and was so important. They had to stop the Axis from achieving, over the long term, this potentially stronger geo-strategic position.

It doesn't mean on its own however, that the Axis coalition would inevitably have won an ensuing Cold War against America. There are two other major factors of grand strategy to consider. First, a multi-polar system behaves differently, in its power interactions, to a bi-polar one. An Axis coalition of three great powers wouldn't have been as cohesive as the actual Soviet bloc, dominated by one superpower, Russia. Over time there could be opportunities for American diplomacy to divide such an Axis coalition. In the real Cold War, the Nixon-Kissinger diplomacy in the 1970's, exploited and enlarged the existing Soviet-Chinese tensions into a split. It was the single largest movement of power during the Cold War, further increasing the American advantage over Soviet Russia. Multi-polarity could therefore have potentially helped the Americans.

Unfortunately the other major difference favors the Axis. Communism also collapsed because, long term, its economic system was relatively inefficient. Like the shambles of German mobilization from 1939 to 1941, it didn't make the maximum use of the resources it did have. The Axis powers in contrast, had a state capitalist economic system, more akin to post-Cold War Russia and China. As it was, capitalist Germany and Japan also achieved well known 'economic miracles' after 1945. The 'state-capitalist' economic system, long term, is certainly more efficient than the communist one, although perhaps, the verdict is still out, not quite as efficient as all out Western capitalism. What this means is that Cold War Axis powers would have lasted longer than the Soviet bloc did. Either side in an Axis-American Cold War could have won. Most likely it would still be continuing into the 21st century. Multi-polar worlds can be quite stable, even if competitive, the last European version lasted a century, from 1815 to 1914.

We have almost come full circle. Clearly the strategic decisions, course and outcome of WW2 were massively important. The Allies had the advantage but their victory wasn't inevitable. Different decisions could have changed the course of the war, and there was a minority probability that the Axis could have won. That would have brought a multi-polar world of four continental based superpowers. Three of the four, Germany, Russia and Japan, would have been dictatorships of one type or another. The single most powerful would still have been a democratic USA. Ironically after the long USA-USSR bi-polar Cold War, a multi-polar world is emerging in the 21st century. As of 2010, America is still the world leader, but China is rising fast, Russia recovering, Islam emerging, and India, perhaps a united Europe, even Brazil, are potential superpowers as well. The struggle for world power it seems, never really ends. The big difference, that made World War Two and the Cold War worthwhile, for the West anyway, is that there are fewer great dictatorships, and more democracies, or at least what passes for democracies, among them.

Finally, there are also broader and general lessons for today resulting from our little excursion into an 'alternative WW2'. At the diplomatic level of grand strategy, it is clear that difficult and uncomfortable choices often confront democracies. Alliances with dictators are sometimes necessary for the purpose of national security. Without the alliance with Stalin's Russia, the Axis powers of WW2 wouldn't have been defeated. The key variables in alliance behavior are power and security, not ideology. This is a major problem for democracies, often putting them at a disadvantage compared to the dictators. Hitler and Stalin were able to negotiate their world shaking pact in 1939, while the British and French held back, partly due to their moral objections to Stalin's regime.

Similarly, domestic politics are often a constraint on democracies. This is not always of benefit for the national security. Pre-war American pacifism and isolationism constrained Roosevelt's intervention policy, be it support for the Allies short of war, or direct involvement. Concepts of power and strategy are often far removed from a democratic public that prefers the simpler idea of the moral cause. Sometimes even democratic politicians have to manipulate the international circumstances. A common requirement is the need, if possible, to get the enemy to declare war and fire the first shot. War then becomes a matter of clear self defense, easily explained to an otherwise reluctant democratic public.

Roosevelt's policy in the Atlantic in 1941, placing USN ships in harms way while America was still neutral, clearly had this objective in mind. On this occasion it didn't quite work. Despite several armed clashes with German U-boats, the American Congress and public were not persuaded. Even Hitler and Mussolini restrained themselves from responding, until Pearl Harbor that is. Pearl Harbor itself was a much more controversial case in this regard. Presenting an opponent with unacceptable terms, which they then reject and go to war instead, is another age old diplomatic strategy. Demanding Japan's withdrawal from China and then activating the oil embargo clearly pushed it on the road to war, but not necessarily directly against the US, or to the Pearl Harbor attack. Only partisan political opponents of Roosevelt adhere to the extreme case that he knew about and allowed the Pearl Harbor attack to occur. Complacency is a more likely explanation than conspiracy here. Most would say that in the context of WW2, using hindsight, that these moves by a neutral America were justified and in their national interest as well. Since then other similar cases of 'manipulation of the circumstances', such as the interventions in Vietnam in 1965, Serbia in 1999 and Iraq in 2003, are more controversial.

The broadest lesson of military strategy for the Allies from WW2 is the sheer scale of the effort and the odds that were required to win. In 1942 it took production and sometimes force ratios, of up to 4:1 on the eastern front and globally in the air war to stem and then turn the Axis tide. By 1944 when all sides were fully mobilized, the Allies out produced the Axis economically and in armaments by an average of about 2.5 to 1. Yet Allied victory wasn't inevitable or pre-ordained, even by their superior overall economic size, and thus eventual military power. This did give them inbuilt underlying advantages however. Greater resources, while no guarantee of victory, was the Allies greatest advantage. Technology is also, largely, dependent upon economics. More resources include more for the research and development of new weapons. Even so victory still had to be fought for on the battlefields, often as in Russia's case, at a terrible cost. The Allied forces needed to increase their military effectiveness as well. The Russians, especially after 1942 were able to do this, although neither they nor the Western Allies became quite as professional at war as the Germans.

Casualties per se, don't always give a clear guide to victory or defeat either. Overall Russian casualties of at least 11 million military and over 13 million civilians were by far the largest of any combatant. They sustained this, just, and came out on the winning side. But they could have lost, the margins were slight, and as we have seen there were many factors deciding the outcome on the eastern front. The Japanese suffered over 90% killed in most of the later Pacific island ground battles. In contrast the ratio of wounded to killed in the Western Allied and German armies was typically about three or four to one, and in the Russian army, one to one in aggregate. The Japanese army was the only one that repeatedly fought almost to the last man. Yet they still lost, overwhelmed by American production, firepower, and in the later war, at least equality in military efficiency.

Finally, as we hope we have shown as the heart of our analysis, strategy, both operational strategy and grand strategy, was the central cause of victory and defeat for both sides, in battles, campaigns, and for the war overall. The Western Allies, especially Britain, were generally more cautious in their operational strategy than the Axis. They could afford to be, due to the extra security margin of the maritime environment and greater production. The democracies were also more conscious of the need to keep casualties down and avoid risks. In contrast the Russians were wasteful, taking huge losses of men and material, even when they had the initiative and were winning in 1943 and later. The Axis with narrower margins also took risks, and as we have seen, made more strategic mistakes. Some of these were decisive to the outcomes of battles, campaigns and the war.

The broad factors therefore that determined the outcome of the battles, campaigns and the war were: the grand and operational strategic decisions of both sides; economic size transformed into arms production, military resources and technology; and military efficiency, morale and combat effectiveness. Clausewitz was correct, war is interested in us, and it matters. Good doesn't triumph over evil just because it is good. Decisions and choices about war, diplomacy, power and strategy, matter, as do the outcomes of those choices. In World War Two, power and resources rather than history per se, was on the side of the Allies, but the Axis could still have won. History and the future, for better or worse, are neither automatic nor inevitable.

Notes to Chapter 9

1. For this and what follows, see chapter 8, especially the discussion of potential ground armaments production for 1940-42 and its impact on Barbarossa.
2. For a concise overview of Soviet Russian war losses, see, Magenheimer, Hitler's War, p 271-274, and Bellamy, Absolute War, p 1-15.
3. Again, see chapter 8, for GNP and steel production comparisons.

Bibliography and Further Reading

Alexander, Bevin, How Hitler Could Have Won World War II: The Fatal Errors That Led to Nazi Defeat, Three Rivers, New York, 2000.

Allen, Thomas B. and Polmar, Norman, Codename Downfall: The Secret Plan to Invade Japan, Headline Book Publishing, London, 1995.

Baer, George W. One Hundred Years of Sea Power: The U.S. Navy, 1890-1990, Stanford University Press, Stanford, California, 1994.

Bauer, Eddy, The History of World War II, 30 Volumes, Orbis Publishing Ltd, London, 1983 edition. Originally 1966, 1972, 1978.

Bellamy, Chris, Absolute War: Soviet Russia in the Second World War, Macmillan, London, 2007.

Breyer, Siegfried, Graf Zeppelin, Schiffer Publishing, Pennsylvania, 1989.

Churchill, Winston S. The Second World War, Volumes 1-6. Penguin, London, 1988 reprint. Original, Cassell, 1950.

Cooper M. The German Army 1933-1945: Its Political and Military Failure, Macdonald and Jane's, London, 1978.

Cowley, Robert, Ed. What If ? Macmillan, London, 2000. Penguin Putman, New York, 1999.

Cowley, Robert, Ed. More What If ? Macmillan, London, 2002, Penguin Putman, 2001.

Cutler, Thomas J. The Battle of Leyte Gulf: 23-26 October 1944, Harper Collins, New York, 1994.

Davies, Norman, Europe at War 1939-1945: No Simple Victory, Macmillan, London, 2006.

Downing David, The Moscow Option: An Alternative Second World War, New English Library, Times Mirror, London, 1979, 1980.

Dunnigan, James F. Ed. The Russian Front: Germany's War in the East 1941-1945, Arms and Armor, London, 1978.

Dupuy, Trevor N. Options of Command, Hippocrene Books, New York, 1984.

Dupuy, R. Ernest and Dupuy, Trevor N. The Collins Encyclopedia of Military History: From 3500 BC to the Present, 4th Edition, BCA, Harper Collins, London, 1993, second reprint 1995.

Dupuy, Trevor N. Understanding War: History and Theory of Combat, Leo Cooper, London, 1992. Originally New York 1987.

Ellis, John, Brute Force: Allied Strategy and Tactics in the Second World War, Andre Deutsch Ltd. London, 1990.

Ellis, John, The World War II Databook, BCA, Aurum Press, London, 1993.

Erickson, John, The Road to Stalingrad: Stalin's War with Germany, Volume I, Phoenix Press, London, 2000. Original, Weidenfeld & Nicholson, London, 1975.

Erickson, John, The Road to Berlin: Stalin's War with Germany, Volume II, Weidenfeld & Nicholson, London, 1983.

Grove, Eric, World War II Tanks, Orbis, London, 1976.

Guderian, Heinz, General. Panzer Leader, Futura Macdonald & Co. London, Sydney, 1982. Original, Michael Joseph Ltd. London, 1952.

Harper, Stephen, Miracle of Deliverance: The Case for the Bombing of Hiroshima and Nagasaki, BCA, Sidgwick and Jackson, London, 1985.

Hart, B.H. Liddell, History of the Second World War, Pan Books, London, 1973. Original, Cassell, London, 1970.

Keegan, John, Ed. et al. The Times Atlas of The Second World War, Guild Publishing, Times Books Ltd. London, 1989.

Kennedy, Paul, The Rise and Fall of the Great Powers: Economic Change and Military Conflict from 1500 to 2000, Unwin Hyman, London, Sydney, 1988.

Kershaw, Ian, Fateful Choices: Ten Decisions That Changed the World 1940-1941, Allen Lane, Penguin, London, 2007.

Krivosheyev, G.F., Soviet Casualties and Combat Losses in the Twentieth Century, trans, Lionel Leventhal Ltd, Greenhill Books, London, 1997.

Lenton H.T. American Battleships, Carriers and Cruisers, Macdonald, London, 1970.

Macintyre, Donald, The Naval War Against Hitler, B.T. Batsford, London, 1971.

Macksey, Kenneth, Ed. The Hitler Options: Alternate Decisions of World War II, Greenhill Books, London, 1995.

Macksey, Kenneth, Invasion: The German Invasion of England July 1940, Greenhill Books, London, 1990. Original, Arms and Armor, 1980.

Macksey, Kenneth, Military Errors of World War Two, Arms and Armor, London, 1994, original 1987.

Magenheimer, Heinz, Hitler's War: Germany's Key Strategic Decisions 1940-1945. Cassell, London, 2002 edition. Original, Arms and Armor, 1998.

Mollo, Andrew, The Armed Forces of World War II, Orbis, London, 1982.

Nalty, Bernard C. Ed. War in the Pacific: Pearl Harbor to Tokyo Bay, BCA, Salamander, London, 1991.

Overy, Richard, Why the Allies Won, Jonathan Cape, London, 1995.

Paret, Peter, Ed. Makers of Modern Strategy: From Machiavelli to the Nuclear Age, Clarenden Press, Oxford, 1986.

Preston, Antony, Ed. Decisive Battles of the Pacific War, Hamlyn, Bison Books, London, 1979.

Quarrie, Bruce, Hitler: The Victory That Nearly Was, David and Charles, 1988.

Shulman, Milton, Defeat in the West, Pan Books and Martin Secker & Warburg Ltd. London 1988, Original 1947.

Silverstone, Paul H. U.S. Warships of World War II, Ian Allen, London, 1965,1971.

Spector, Ronald H. Eagle Against the Sun: The American War with Japan, Penguin, London, 1987. Original, Macmillan, USA, 1984.

Spick, Mike, <u>Luftwaffe Victorious: An Alternative History</u>, Greenhill Books, London, 2005.

Terraine, John, <u>The Smoke and the Fire: Myths and Ant-Myths of War 1861-1945</u>. BCA, Sidgwick and Jackson, London, 1981.

Tsouras Peter G. <u>Hitler Triumphant: Alternate Decisions of World War II</u>, Greenhill Books, London, 2006.

Tsouras Peter G. Ed. <u>Rising Sun Victorious: The Alternative History of How the Japanese Won the Pacific War</u>, Greenhill Books, London, 2001.

Tsouras Peter G. Ed. <u>Third Reich Victorious: Alternate Decisions of World War II</u>, Greenhill Books, London, 2002.

Watts A.J. and Gordon B.G. <u>The Imperial Japanese Navy</u>, Macdonald, London, 1971.

Miscellaneous Articles

Levine, Alan J. Was World War II a Near-run Thing? in <u>Journal of Strategic Studies</u>, vol 8, no 1, March 1985.

Harper, Bruce, <u>Alternative Wars</u>, in <u>ULTRA</u>, Winter 2008, ULTRA Publications and AWAW, at www.AWAW.org

Appendix 1: Military Codenames

German
Barbarossa – Invasion of Russia, June 22nd 1941.

Blau or Case Blue – Offensive against Stalingrad and the Caucasus, June 1942.

Case Red – Offensive against France, second stage June 1940.

Case Yellow (Fall Gelb) – Invasion of France and the Low Countries, May 1940.

Drumbeat – U-boat offensive against the USA, January 1942.

Eagle Day or Adlertag – Start of the air offensive against Britain, August 13th 1940.

Felix – Planned invasion against Gibraltar, January 1941.

Hercules – Planned invasion of Malta, April-September 1942.

Orient – Planned invasion of the Middle East, July 1941.

Sea Lion or Seelowe – Planned invasion of Britain, September 1940.

Typhoon – Offensive against Moscow, October 1941.

Winter Storm – Counter Offensive to relieve Stalingrad, December 1942.

Z Plan – Naval construction program.

Japanese
Eastern Operation – Planned invasion of the Hawaiian Islands.

MI – Invasion of Midway, June 1942.

MO – Invasion of Port Moresby, May 1942.

Russian
Jupiter – Planned offensive against German AG Center, follow up to Mars.

Little Saturn – Modification to Saturn, counter to German Winter Storm.

Mars – Offensive against German 9th Army and the Rzhev salient, November 1942.

Saturn – Planned offensive against German AG B, follow up to Uranus.

Uranus – Offensive against German 6th Army and Stalingrad, November 1942.

Western Allied Operations (US-British unless specified)
ABC or ABC-1 – American, British conferences, January to March 1941.

Ariel – Evacuation of the BEF from France, second stage, after Dunkirk, June 1940.

Battleaxe – British offensive against Libya, June 1941.

Crusader – British offensive against Libya, November-December 1941.

Dyle or Plan D – Franco-British movement into Belgium, May 1940.

Dynamo – Evacuation of the BEF from Dunkirk, May 26th to June 4th 1940.

Husky – Invasion of Sicily, July 1943.

Overlord – Invasion of Normandy, France, June 6th 1944.

Orange – Series of pre-war US plans for war against Japan.

Pedestal – Malta convoy, from Gibraltar, August 1942.

Plan D or Dog – US memorandum for the Germany first strategy, November 1940.

Rainbow 5 – US plan for simultaneous war against Germany and Japan, 1939.

Torch – Invasion of Vichy French North Africa, November 1942.

WPO-3 – War Plan Orange, version 3, 1938.

Appendix 2: List of Abbreviations and Terms

AG – Assault Gun, essentially tanks with fixed turrets.

AG – Army Group, when followed by a name or number.

ANZAC – Australian and New Zealand Army Corps.

APC – Armored Personnel Carrier, usually half-tracks in WW2.

ASW – Anti-Submarine Warfare.

BEF – British Expeditionary Force.

Blitzkrieg – Lightning War, German mobile warfare strategy.

CAP – Combat Air Patrol.

CIGS – Chief of the Imperial General Staff, British.

C-in-C – Commander in Chief.

CINPAC – Commander in Chief Pacific Fleet, American.

CoS – Chief of Staff.

Counter Air – Air offensive strategy, focused on the enemy air force.

DCR – Division Cuirassiers Reserves, French armored divisions.

DLM – French Light Mechanized (armored) division.

Front – Russian army group.

GHQ – General headquarters.

GNP – Gross National Production.

Heer – German Army, as a whole, not specific formations.

IJN – Imperial Japanese Navy.

Kriegsmarine – German Navy.

KMG – Cavalry Mechanized Group, Russian.

Lebensraum – Living space, Nazi expansionist policy.

Luftflotte, Luftflotten – German air fleet.

Luftwaffe – German Air Force.

MD – Military District, Russian.

NKVD – Soviet internal and border security forces, WW2 equivalent of the KGB.

OKH – Oberkommando des Heeres, High Command of the German Army.

OKL – Oberkommando der Luftwaffe, High Command of the German Air Force.

OKM – Oberkommando der Marine, High Command of the German Navy.

OKW – Oberkommando der Wehrmacht, High Command of the German armed forces.

RN – Royal Navy, British.

SAC – Strategic Air (i.e. bombing) Campaign.

SLOC – Sea Line of Communications.

SPG – Self Propelled Gun.

Stavka – Russian supreme military council or command.

Wehrmacht – German armed forces.

Appendix 3: United States Navy Abbreviations.

BB – Battleship.

BC – Battlecruiser. (they use CB, we've used the easier to recall BC)

CA – Heavy Cruiser.

CL – Light Cruiser.

CV – Aircraft Carrier. Specifically, fast fleet aircraft carrier, the most powerful type.

CVE – Escort Aircraft Carrier.

CVL – Light (fast fleet) Aircraft Carrier.

DD – Destroyer.

DE – Escort Destroyer.

SS – Submarine.

USMC – United States Marine Corps.

USN – United States Navy.

Index

Made in the USA
Middletown, DE
04 August 2015